# BEHAVIORAL FORENSICS

# BEHAVIORAL FORENSICS

## Using Applied Behavior Analysis in Psychological Court Evaluations

DOUGLAS H. RUBEN, Ph.D.
*Okemos Road, Okemos, MI, United States*

ELSEVIER

ACADEMIC PRESS
An imprint of Elsevier

Academic Press is an imprint of Elsevier
125 London Wall, London EC2Y 5AS, United Kingdom
525 B Street, Suite 1650, San Diego, CA 92101, United States
50 Hampshire Street, 5th Floor, Cambridge, MA 02139, United States
The Boulevard, Langford Lane, Kidlington, Oxford OX5 1GB, United Kingdom



**Library of Congress Cataloging-in-Publication Data**
A catalog record for this book is available from the Library of Congress

**British Library Cataloguing-in-Publication Data**
A catalogue record for this book is available from the British Library

ISBN: 978-0-12-819805-6

For information on all Academic Press publications visit our website at https://www.elsevier.com/books-and-journals

*Publisher:* Stacy Masucci
*Acquisition Editor:* Elizabeth Brown
*Editorial Project Manager:* Thomas Van Der Ploeg
*Production Project Manager:* Paul Prasad Chandramohan
*Cover Designer:* Matthew Limbert

Typeset by TNQ Technologies

*In warmest memory of,*
*And the inspiration for my writing,*
*To my sister,*
*Ellyce R. Field*

# Contents

## 5. Intracontingency variables in criminal responsibility evaluations



## 6. Risk of alcohol recidivism in evaluating reinstatement of a Driver's license



## 7. Behavioral forensic analysis of competency-to-stand trial in the evaluation of an offender accused of car jacking and breaking and entering



## 8. Social contingencies potentiating vandalism and violence



## 9. Insularity effects of self-reinforcement under concurrent variable interval punishment schedules in the assessment of repeated embezzlement



## 10. Cultural contingencies of survival intermingled with domestic violence: A case of evocative effects of metaphorical extension



## 11. Contingencies of vicarious conditioning resembling Munchausen by proxy in the assessment of parental competence



## 12. Intrafamily contingencies exposing contradictory testimony and parental incompetence in two parents vying for child custody



## 13. Avoidance/escape (operant) conditioning and respondent biophysical arousal in the behavioral forensic assessment of an adolescent arsonist

# About the Author

**Dr. Douglas Ruben** is a forensic and licensed psychologist and national consultant in Applied Behavior Analysis, Personality Theory, Addictions, Rehabilitation, and Parenting. Locally, he conducts forensic evaluations and conducts a family and individual behavior therapy practice. He has conducted over 4000 forensic evaluations. His seminars on forensics, parent empowerment, schools, Personality Disorders, and Adult Children of Alcoholics appear nationwide through different seminar organizations. He literally has given over 3000 workshops across the United Stated from Portland, Oregon to Portland, Maine. Dr. Ruben is author and co-author of over 73 scholarly and self-help books and over 100 professional articles. Among his practitioner-books include *Behavioral Guide to Personality Disorders (DSM 5), Tantrum Survival Kit: The Definitive Guide to Tantrum Management; Effects of Bad Parenting and What to do About It; Treating Adult Children of Alcoholics-A Behavioral Approach; Assessing and Treating Addictive Disorder; Avoidance Syndrome; Handbook of Childhood Impulse Disorders and ADHD; Reassessment in Psychology; New Ideas in Therapy; Current Advances in Psychiatric Care; Transitions: Handbook of Managed Care; Family Addiction;* and *Aging and Drug Abuse* He co-edited four books with Dr. Turner including *Readings in Aphasia; Readings in Muscular Dystrophy; Readings in Cerebral Palsy, Homebound Teaching,* and *Behavioral Management in Public Schools: an Urban Approach.* His self-help books recently include *Evil Inside Use: Dangers of No Impulse Control, Parent Guide to Children of Alcoholics, 25 Secrets to Emotional Self-Healing; Forever Sober, No More Guilt-10 steps to a shame-free life, Bratbusters: say goodbye to tantrums and disobedience, and Family Recovery Companion.* He has been in private practice for 35 years.

# Preface

In the last known published paper by Kantor (1987), prominent psychologist and father of interbehavioral psychology, he stated unequviocally that, "…to be effective in any sort of professional practice it is necessary to base one's efforts upon authentic scientific foundations" (p. 3). Kantor, unlike his famous contemporary B.F. Skinner, wrote about how his scientific model applied to other natural science disciplines with the same revered integrity as biology, chemistry, mathematics, and physics. He literally laid out the blueprint for integration of his interbehavioral model in *The Science of Psychology: An Interbehavioral Survey* (Kantor & Smith, 1975). Kantor's message, and one shared by many professionals worried about the echo-chamber effects of speaking to only one's endemic audience, is that real advancement of science must go beyond the boundaries of one's discipline. In the scientific psychology of Applied Behavior Analysis (ABA), this need for proliferation of its philosophies, principles, and technology outside of its indigenous boundaries faces a similar predicament. The majority of books, articles, monographs, workshops, and other scholarly products promoting elementary and advanced research, ideas, and methods of ABA largely are for behaviorally-minded readers or in forums (conferences, publishers, conferences, etc.) attracting behaviorally-trained students and professionals. In this respect, insularity precludes new developments in research and theory from reaching wider interdisciplinary practitioners for whom the ABA science is fundamentally imperative to improve its naturalistic origins and contributions.

This book, like many previous books by the author (e.g., Ruben, 2001, 2015; Smith, Mountjoy & Ruben, 1983), invites other disciplines within and outside of ABA and traditional psychology to consider the role of evidence-based research. *Behavioral Forensics: Using applied behavior analysis in psychological court evaluations* speaks to the plethora of struggling mental health evaluators in court cases assigned the task of making sense of ominous behaviors in a suspect or victim early in the adjudicative process. Psychologists, psychiatrists, social workers, or other specialists working for the State or independently who evaluate risk behaviors, competency to stand trial, criminal responsibility, or advise attorneys regarding these cases are a unique class of diagnosticians. They must investigate an array of data–from documents (educationally, medically, police) and the clinical interviews to results from psychometric tests–to determine the state of mind (or behavior) of the examinee for the court process to properly proceed. Inherent in this investigative assignment is to uncover authentic behavior probabilities likely causal in the commission of a crime, much like sorting out pieces of a jigsaw puzzle to accurately assemble the completed puzzle. The investigator's hypotheses to assemble the pieces of the puzzle may engender complex psychic, transcendental or abstract concepts such as personality, mindset, inherited genes, or behavior typologies. These concepts reify a state of action, belonging to the personality or behavior typology, but do not explain *the naturalistic or functional events responsible for the action.* To say, for example, Sam shot his wife out of revenge for his wife having an affair lays a general "psychological theory" absent of the controlling or functional variables likely responsible for Sam's commission of the crime. What was the frequency of Sam's homicidal threats even before his wife betrayed him? What were the chain of events occurring that day sequentially connecting behaviors and consequences that resulted in his retrieving and using the gun? And, to add a twist to the plot, did his wife and her lover twice attempt to murder Sam before he acted in self-defense? All of these transactions, proceeding through *segments of behavior in a causal continuum,* separate a traditional from a behavioral analysis.

Dissemination of ABA into other disciplines of psychology or human services is not new and of course did not start with this author. Calls for accurate depictions of behavior modification and behavior therapy started as early as the mid 1970s, to counter the media distortion of behavior modification as mind-control and unethical manipulation (cf. Davidson, 2016; Davidson & Stuart, 1975). The caricature of abuse epitomized in Stanley Kubrick's 1972 dystopian crime film, *A Clockwork Orange,* symbolized this merciless pillorizing on the behavioral movement. Here, a violent and psychopathic delinquent Alex (played by a young Malcolm McDowell) gets arrested and undergoes "behavior modification" (actually, respondent conditioning) to pair visual scenes of crime and mayhem with painful eye drops while his lids are clamped open, and while listening to Beethoven's ninth symphony. The association of the symphony music with his pain subsequently triggers aversion to crime scenes. Kubrick's drama spread outrage in the mental health community over patient helplessness and loss of dignity and humanity when treatment involved behavioral methods (Newman, 1991; Strange, 2011). The kickback was a media campaign launched by the formation of two major national organizations—The Association for the Advancement of Behavior Therapy (AABT) and Association for Behavior Analysis (ABA)—both drawing membership from the cadre of highly talented researchers and scholars who were first-year generation disciples of B.F. Skinner, J.R. Kantor and their associates. The organizations later expanded internationally (e.g., Association for Behavior Analysis International-ABAI) and became more inclusive of cognitive therapists and scientists (Association for Behavioral and Cognitive Therapies–ABCT). Despite this diversified growth, ABCT never lost its fervor to debunk myths, prejudice, and misleading media presentations of the ABA.

In short, bringing ABA to the forefront of other professions and disciplines has been a robust process. The irony is that one highly visible discipline overlooked in this franchise expansion of ABA is *forensic psychology.* In all fairness, ABCT does offer a special interest group called *Forensic Issues and Externalizing Behaviors.* Its ambitious aim is to explore the application of cognitive-behavioral principles to the understanding, prevention, assessment and treatment of externalizing behaviors that put individuals at risk for harming others and themselves, and for criminal justice involvement. Likewise, ABAI follows suit by their special interest group called *Crime, Delinquency, and Forensic Behavior Analysis.* Less elegantly articulated, their mission is to ensure that those in the criminal justice fields have access to appropriate, evidence-based behavior analytic therapy to reduce crime and delinquency. At one time, this special interest group published the *Journal of Behavior Analysis of*

*Offender and Victim: Treatment and Prevention,* until it was sold to the American Psychological Association. Despite loss of this precious publishing outlet, the surge of research innovations and behavioral applications in *criminal justice in general* continued (Braukmann, Fixsen, Phillips, & Wolf, 1975; Morris, 1980; Morris & Braukmann, 1987).

Closer to forensic applications was Joseph Wyatt's workshop called *Behavioral Practice in the Forensic Arena* (2010). This workshop impressively addressed the marriage of behavioral principles with court-ordered psychological evaluations. He introduced conceptual and applicational guidelines on converting cumbersome legal definitions of insanity, criminal responsibility, and trial competency into more operational language. His workshop, offered mostly to Board Certified Behavior Analysts (BCBA) for continuing education, was a brief intra-disciplinary window for behaviorally-trained specialists to see how the science of behavior blends coherently into the world of jurisprudence. Historically, forensic evaluations prototypically reflected a hybrid of psychoanalytical, humanistic, and other "cognitive" psychological interpretation of abnormal personality. Hypotheses from test results typically focused on the criminal mind, antisocial personality, and precursors in childhood predating juvenile or adult crimes. Analyses rarely considered the *contingencies of behavior, functional repertoires, motivational properties (i.e., conditioned or unconditioned motivational operations), and inter- and intra-relationships among behavioral segments.*

One argument for this omission might be the incompatibility between ABA assessment and traditional psychometric testing. But literature previously existed extolling the value of cognitive, learning, and personality measures in behavioral assessment (Silva, 1993). This melange of measures sampled a more diverse cross-section of behavior pathology; more importantly, it allowed traditional-trained psychologists a gateway to crossover or broaden their heuristic perspective on discernment of behavior causes and effects. A similar clarion call for merging science and clinical practice recently was offered by Reardon, Corker, and Tackett (2018). Clinical psychologists, insists the authors, may be lagging behind in transparency of their case studies demonstrating evidence-based approaches and replicability of measured outcomes. Despite this imperative for openness and embracement of science, organizations principally promoting ABA research and practice have been delinquent in recent years to offer workshops, webinars, or other educational training to help practitioners make this crossover in forensic psychology. For example, in the ABCT's Annual Convention (2018) list of Institutes, Clinician Seminars, Workshops, General Sessions, Mini-Workshop, Panel Discussions, Symposia, Research and Professional Development (poster sessions), Spotlight Research, and Invited Addressess—about 456 presentation in total—*none were about using ABA in court or forensic evaluations.*

This embarrassing dearth of representation is likely reflective of two disturbing trends in ABA professional development. First, among the reduced number of admitted students into accredited clinical psychology programs, only a handful of these programs offer comprehensive specialization in cognitive behavior therapy or applied behavior analysis (cf. Heatherington et al., 2013; Woods, Miltenberger, & Carr, 2006); the exception may be in Australian and New Zealand Universities (Kazantzis & Munro, 2011). Second, a mixed blessing in proliferation of ABA training programs. On the one hand, ABA graduate programs nationwide spiked in the last 5 years, propelled by (a) profusion of two-year programs certifying masters-level students in Applied Behavior Analysis (i.e., Board Certified Behavior Analyst), (b) third-party payers (Aetna, Blue Cross Blue Shield, United Behavior Health, etc.) reimbursing BCBAs, and (c) a burgeoning employment market offering competitively high salaries to BCBAs. On the other hand, few if any of these brilliantly trained behavior specialists are clinical psychologists, the most common subspeciality in psychology typically called upon for forensic psychological evaluations.

But this exclusivity of clinical psychologists as the only licensed evaluator in court cases is likely to change. A new army of highly trained behavior analysts (clinically trained and non-clinically trained) now work in agencies, homes, hospitals, and the criminal justice system, all excited to integrate behavioral assessment into other disciplines unaccustomed to applied behavior theory and practice. Disciplines, like forensic psychology, were kept in the dark ages of psychoanalytic profiling of personalities as prognosticators of criminal behavior. Changing this antideluvian model of analysis requires a guidebook that shows current clinical psychologists, psychiatrists, mental health specialists, social workers, or BCBAs, and graduate students the invaluable role of behavioral analysis in decision making about criminal risk behaviors.

***Behavioral Forensics: Using applied behavior analysis in psychological court evaluations*** attempts this mission. It presents the first compendia on the application of behavioral principles for assessment and analysis of criminal behavior in court-ordered psychological evaluations. ***Behavioral Forensics*** is divided into two sections. The first section introduces evidence-based concepts and principles of behavioral forensics compared to obsolete forensic evaluation models. The second section offers twelve case studies illustrating the intricate surgery of using ABA in pre-sentencing and post-sentencing evaluations that determine risk of criminal recidivism or competency for such common offenses. Chapters describe and employ principles and techniques of behavioral assessments in deducing causal evidence from interview and psychometric data. The process is usually twofold. First, self-reported data of complex psychopathology is operationalized into concrete and measurable units of stimulus-response and integrative-field contingencies. Second, corroborative data (police reports, witness statements, school records, etc.) are considered alongside other (anecdotal) observational information to form functional analyses in diagnostic evaluations.

Captured in these chapters are snapshots of real-life forensic cases disguised by anonymous names, genders, and locations. Chapter 3 on Sexual proclivity demonstrates applications of motivating operations and reinforcement schedules in understanding criminal acts of a severe pedophile. Chapter 4 also looks at the unregulated pathology of establishing operations in other sexual predators. Chapter 5 combines an interbehavioral (behavioral systems theory) and radical behavior analysis perspective of *intracontingencies* underlying the successive planning and commission of murder in a criminal responsibility evaluation. Chapter 6 examines the significance of continuous and linked behavior segments that revealed additive behavior patterns contradicting alleged reports of sustainable sobriety; the individual applying for vehicular license reinstatement was still engaged in high behavior potentials or risk of alcohol recidivism. Chapter 7 offers an operationalization of the competency to stand trial standards and shows basic match-to-sample methods to identify court concepts that replace hypothetical constructs on the defendant's state of mind or "capacity" to participate in court. Chapter 8 looks at social contingencies likely potentiating community vandalism an how to present steps for behavior amelioration to the courts. Chapter 9 examines the unusual rule-governed and operant contingencies motivating repeat embezzlement in a highly trusted administrator in a nonprofit agency revered for her efficiency; behavior patterns show how insularity effects of continuous self-reinforcement dulls or lessens adverse effects of variable-interval schedules of punishment. Chapter 10 considers the generalization effects of violent behavior indigenously accepted in one subculture (set of contingencies) but forbidden in other cultural contexts (set of contingencies), Stimuli in both environments may present relevant properties (i.e., metaphorical extension) evocative of identical aggressive (domestic abusive) behaviors, and the nuances for discriminative control (i.e., separating the environments) are very hard to separate.

Chapters 11–13 explore more advanced applications of behavior analysis to forensic cases. Chapter 11 is a court-ordered parental competency evaluation, based on preliminary investigative reports from a child protective agency, that a parent coached a child to make sexual allegations. The parent, experiencing sexual abuse herself in childhood, possibly jaded her consolation of her children by "vicariously" sharing contingencies believed to have occurred. The assessment looks at fabrication of allegations, and possibly instilling the falsehoods into the children's verbal statements. Such "coaching" served to increase the children's emotional dependence on the mother and made her the heroine, a common phenomenon in forensic court cases called Munchausen by proxy. Chapter 12 ventures into the ethically and legally precarious territory of custody evaluations, long viewed as the highest risk for malpractice for forensic evaluators. Custody evaluations are initially a last resort between two disputing parties after failing repeatedly at settlements through mediation, Friend of the Court (FOC) referees, attorney negotiation, and even direct testimony in front of the judge. Parents undergo evaluations to rule out compromising psychopathology undermining their parental skills and to advance an opinion on which parent, if any, best serves the best interests of the minor children. Since interviewed parents often promote their own virtues and decry the other parent's vices, the job of a forensic examiner is to remain objectively operational in answering the basic questions: (a) why should there be a change in custody? and (b) what adverse or positive value does a change of custody have for the minor children? The chapter offers a rare look into the intrafamily contingencies and contradictory testimonies of two incompetent parents pushing their agendas unrelated to the children's best interests.

Chapter 13 looks at the intermingling of respondent and operant conditioning effects on an adolescent arsonist in contrast to dual diagnoses of conduct disorder and reactive attachment disorder. A final chapter covers the strategies, word translations, and general guidelines to transform the often complex lexicon of ABA vernacular into comprehensible language for a jury, judge, prosecutors and defendant attorney, and other personnel in the judiciary. Communication of technical jargon outside of the insular behavioral community and into the vast multidisciplinary forensic community is no easy task. Parsimonious explanations may seem too superficial or may weaken the scientific integrity of principles enunciated by certain technical words or phrases. But, as with writing for lay audiences, this is not true. Language simplification is a matter of altering grammar and using single bytes of phrases, not of "dumbing down" the context. Court testimony by behaviorally-trained forensic evaluators is the pulpit from which to introduce and teach an attentive audience the fascination and genius of using applied and basic science to understand criminal behavior. This chapter equips the expert witness with concrete tools to successfully bridge this technical-to-public educator gap.

Considering the unprecedented numbers of mental health specialists turning to forensic work, and influx of graduate programs offering degrees in criminal behavior analysis, ***Behavioral Forensics*** offers a promising blueprint for the next generation of ABA scientists conducting court psychological evaluations.

## References


ABCT. (2018). 52nd annual convention preview. *The Behavior Therapist, 41*, i–xxiv.

Braukmann, C. J., Fixsen, D. L., Phillips, E. L., & Wolf, M. M. (1975). Behavioral approaches to treatment in the crime and delinquency field. *Criminology, 13*, 299–331.

Davidson, G. C. (2016). Some reflections on the evolution of behavior therapy during ABCT's first 50 years. *Cognitive and Behavioral Practice, 23*, 420–425.

Davidson, G. C., & Stuart, R. B. (1975). Behavior therapy and civil liberties. *American Psychologist, 30*, 755–763.

Heatherington, L., Messer, S. B., Angus, L., Strauman, T. J., Friedlander, M. L., & Kolden, G. (2013). The narrowing of theoretical orientations in clinical psychology doctoral training. *Clinical Psychology Science and Practice, 19*, 364–374.

Kantor, J. R. (1987). What qualifies interbehavioral psychology as an approach to treatment? In D. H. Ruben, & D. J. Delprato (Eds.), *New ideas in therapy: Introduction to an interdisciplinary approach* (pp. 3–8). Westport, CT: Greenwood Press.

Kantor, J. R., & Smith, N. W. (1975). *The science of psychology: An interbehavioral Survey*. Chicago, IL: The Principia Press.

Kazantzis, N., & Munro, M. (2011). The emphasis on cognitive-behavioural therapy within clinical psychology training at Australian and New Zealand universities: A survey of program directors. Australian Psychologist, *46*, 49–54.

Morris, E. K. (1980). Applied behavior analysis for criminal justice practice. *Criminal Justice and Behavior, 2*, 131–145.

Morris, E. K., & Braukmann, C. J. (Eds.). (1987). *Behavioral approaches to crime and delinquency: A handbook of application, research, and concepts*. NY: Springer.

Newman, B. (1991). A Clockwork Orange: Burgess and behavioral interventions. *Behavior and Social Issues, 1*, 61–70.

Reardon, K. W., Corker, K. S., & Tackett, J. L. (2018). The emerging relationship between clinical psychology and the credibility movement. *The Behavior Therapist, 41*, 307–313.

Ruben, D. H. (2001). *Treating adult children of alcoholics: A behavioral approach*. NY: Academic Press.

Ruben, D. H. (2015). *Behavioral guide to personality disorders (DSM-5)*. Springfield, IL: Charles C. Thomas Publishers.

Silva, F. (1993). *Psychometric foundations and behavioral assessment*. CA: Sage Publications.

Smith, N. W., Mountjoy, P. T., & Ruben, D. H. (Eds.). (1983). *Reassessment in psychology: The interbehavioral alternative*. Washington, DC: University Press of America.

Strange, C. (2011). Stanley Kubrick's a Clockwork Orange as art against torture. *Crime, Media, Culture: An International Journal, 6*, 267–284.

Woods, D. W., Miltenberger, R. G., & Carr, J. E. (2006). Introduction to the special section on clinical behavior analysis. *Journal of Applied Behavior Analysis, 39*, 407–411.

Wyatt, W. J. (2010). *Behavioral practice in the forensic arena*. FL Tech ABA Professional Development Program (BEHP 1049).

SECTION I

# Concepts of behavioral forensic assessment

CHAPTER

# 1

# What is behavioral forensic assessment (BFA)? The role of applied behavior analysis in psychological evaluation

Utilization of Applied Behavior Analysis (ABA) in the criminal justice field is not new. Innovations first appeared for behavioral approaches in crime and delinquency in the mid 1970's and 1980's (Braukmann, Fixsen, Phillips, Montrosem & Wolf, 1975; Morris, 1980; Neitzel, 1979). These radical approaches called for humane models of "behavior modification" as safeguards against cruelty and non-educational prison reform. Morris and Braukmann (1987), as well, argued eloquently how cognitive behavior therapy in only 20 years (since 1967) contributed to prevention and correction of adult and youth crime, referencing systemic changes in sentencing guidelines for parole and probation, token economics inside prison walls, and programs for alcohol, and drug abuse. Stone (1975) and Everstine and Everstine (1986) returned to conceptual basics, reminding eager practitioners entering into the forensic field of ethical and legal dilemmas that separate confidentiality in individual behavior therapy from public domain court knowledge. In each of these scholarly treatise, outstanding advice advanced ABA to the forefront of criminal justice. Ironically, none of these seminal works addressed the systematic application of principles, procedures, or techniques involved with *forensic psychological evaluations.* Even in prototype books on Behavioral Assessment (Cone & Hawkins, 1977; Hersen & Bellack, 1981), none of the invited contributors addressed the delicate balance between performing behavioral interviewing and data collection with forensic objectives. More contemporaneously, Mcleod, Jensen-Doss, and Ollendick (2013) updated applications of behavioral assessment for children and adolescents; again, focus remained conceptual, procedurally related to schools, agencies, homes and naturalistic settings; but coverage fell short of interventions in the criminal forensic domain.

Lately, hints of applied behavior analysis in forensic psychology surfaced in evidence-based approaches to criminal profiling (Bartol & Bartol, 2012; Turvey, 2012). But there is an inherent limitation with behavioral profiling. It only assists with initial police investigation

*Behavioral Forensics*
https://doi.org/10.1016/B978-0-12-819805-6.00001-4

in the accumulation of facts *before the arrest of a suspect*. Behavioral forensic evaluations, by contrast, *are a posteriori or after the arrest of the suspect*. Forensic examinations do not aim to prove or disprove the suspect committed a crime; the aim is to determine state of mind (behavior) or other aspects of risk and psychopathology contributing to the crime. How would that be done, *behaviorally?* One hunch is that it might involve reductionism and operationalism of heretofore mentalistic concepts such as personality traits, intrapsychic dynamics, cognitive reasoning, and motivation dynamics. The language of re-defining patterns of behavior might change from nebulous generalizations to succinct behavioral jargon, using common words such as "response topographies," "stimulus conditions," and "contingencies." But is changing the lexicon the only reform needed when crossing the threshold from traditional forensic analysis to a behavioral forensic analysis? No, there is more.

The transformation of criminal behavior patterns from a descriptive or qualitative analysis to a functional and potentially quantitative analysis requires revision of two parts. First is the perspective from which the behavioral examiner views and interprets connections of behaviors to events. The second is how the analysis is used in a criminal psychological evaluation. Traditional forensic approaches try to weave the thread of behavior through the fabric of internal mechanisms of emotions, behaviors, and personality typologies to predict future crimes. They explain the suspect's inner tendencies, habits, thoughts, and feelings, all toward better appreciating "who the suspects is." Behavioral approaches go inside or outside the so-called personality (i.e., constellation of behavior), emotions, and behavior and precisely identify cause-and-effect relationships directly correlated with similar or different events in a behavioral segment. Behavioral perspective are less phenomenological on describing the inner being of the suspect, and more focused on why his criminal behavior occurred, what actually triggered it, and what conditions are likely to evoke it again. Both perspectives contribute valuable knowledge to the jurisprudence process. Traditional analyses give a characterological or larger profile of how such criminals act and might repeat similar crimes if returned to civilization. Behavioral perspectives go one step farther; the perspective scientifically frames the exact sequence of stimulus and response conditions likely to explain *why the character of the criminal might repeat the crime.*

To appreciate this distinction, and by way of introducing forensic behavior analysis, this chapter allows the reader to witness the conspicuous transformation from non-scientific to scientific explanations of the same phenomena in a suspect undergoing a forensic evaluation. First, the case is presented briefly for an overview of the crimes accused of a suspect, and how the suspect responded during the evaluation. Second, analysis follows of the suspect's behavior through the eyes of traditional forensic interpretation. Focus is more on personological variables. A third section introduce concepts and principles of operant, respondent, and systems (interbehavioral) conditioning. This primer of behavioral terms is certainly not exhaustive and readers may wish to have included other terms or principles that represent a wider kaleidoscope of ABA technology. Despite this obvious limitation, the defined lexicon amply lays the foundation for any non-behavioral reader to grasp, apply, and witness the make-over effect of criminal behavior transformed into operational precision, measurability, and predictability. Fourth, using the wisdom of this primer, we return to the case study viewed through the optics of behavior forensic analysis.

## The case of murder during domestic violence

A 45- year old married female held for Assault with Intent to Commit Bodily Harm pled not-guilty, claiming she suffered trauma from the "battered-woman syndrome." Battered-woman syndrome is not a DSM-5 code or uncodified psychiatric diagnoses, but has gained court recognition as a legitimate argument for somebody using self-defense with a reasonable and proportional amount of violence in response to excessive domestic abuse (Downs, 1996). She chronicled repeated domestic violence incidents, perpetrated by her husband, leaving her physically scarred, injured, and requiring urgent medical care. Abusive attacks frequently occurred after he drank alcohol, at night, while he ranted in a low-bass voice about her inadequacies. His tirades were a sign that physical abuse might follow. Hearing his tirades, inside she stated feeling terror, panic, shaking, and contemplating escape routes in case his violence got out of control. During a recent assault, she reported self-defense by plunging a knife into her husband's upper right chest. He stumbled out of the house bleeding and drove away. Within blocks, entry of the puncture wound caused collapse of his lung, cutting off respiration. He lost consciousness, as his car jumped a residential neighborhood curb and raced onto a front porch killing one child and critically injuring another child.

During the clinical interview of the psychological forensic evaluation, the suspect sat across from the examiner in an attorney-room surrounded by transparent windows on the unit of a county jail, in full view of other inmates walking by. Insulation from ambient noises was poor. Voices of male and female correction officers standing outside the door having conversations could be heard. Within 15 min of the interview, the Examiner observed the suspect's shoulder blades quiver, her body abruptly shifted to an erect position, and her breathing become arrhythmic. She gasped for air twice, then recoiled to a relaxed posture. Twice again the same sequential pattern of visceral arousal occurred lasting 30 s, both with the suspect apparently unaware of her movements. Ambient noises emanated from two low-bass voices of male correction officers laughing together. After the male correction officers left, tremors and irregular breathing ceased, and the suspect's body rested more normally. Forty-minutes later, two other male corrections officers stood proximal to the exam room, talking in loud enough voices permeating in the exam room. The suspect's arms and legs noticeably cramped, she stood erect in her chair again, coughed irregularly, and her eyes watered. The forensic examiner interrupted the testing and asked the subject to deliberately listen to the male corrections officers, not informing her of behavior movements she made. Her face turned pale and she held her breath for seconds but remained inhaling in short breaths until the male corrections officers' voices trailed off. Asked directly why she withheld her breath, the suspect unequivocally said the male corrections officers' voices sounded exactly like the voice of her husband.

## Traditional forensic psychological evaluations

The ubiquitous goal of forensic psychological evaluations has been the intersection between psychological theory, science, and the justice system. Theory, more than science, however, presided over the assessment of past, current, and future actions of the criminal suspect to make tenable predictions about risk of repeated crimes. Based on one-on-one interviews, review of collateral evidence, and use of personality measurement tests, traditional forensic evaluators arrive at conclusions about personality typologies and how these typologies interact with or manifest cognitive or emotional parameters. Based on these parameters or markers, a diagnosis is identified that consolidates personality parameters into a unified category, from which reasonable predictions follow on the proclivity of the same or similar crimes. Proclivity is a barometer that aides the court after arraignment and during discovery to help prosecutor or defense bolster their arguments.

In post-verdict cases, diagnostic predictors help to guide pre-sentencing negotiations among all the legal parties. In the case cited above, a traditional forensic evaluator performed the protocol steps of clinical interview, document review, and administration of personality testing. Scores on the MMPI-2-RF revealed several factors. First, her test profile was valid, reliable, and interpretable. Second, on validity scales, High F-r scores signified deflators, self-deprecators, and individuals who over-humble their circumstances with an underlying victimization theme. They feel inferior, useless, and internally defective. They are anxious, self-devalued and perceive self as undeserving of approval and peripheral to mainstream life. Over-reporters frequently will overstate their negative features while downplay or completely omit any positive features. They are bad fakers about happiness, energy, intelligence, optimism, and ambition. They make hollow promises to appease their listeners and their actions show profound alacrity (lack of follow through). Since she presents an elaborate version of bad events, and overlooks any redemptive features, the suspect may not be a credible historian.

Third, on the Higher-Order scale, elevated EID and THD scores signify thought internalizers. She is quiet, shy, unassertive, introversive, and privately withholds her thoughts for fear of negative judgment. She is hypersensitive to feeling rejected, criticized, or an impending conflict arising from her expression of opinions. Internalizers frequently are ruminators, obsessing over past mishandled situation or reasons about people's behavior and motivations. She infers quickly people are adversaries, distrusting most men and some male authorities. Internalizers struggle with mild paranoid ideations of being randomly persecuted for untraceable reasons, and always feeling guilty for others blaming her. She is susceptible to self-demoralization, agreeing with people's unfounded accusations about her behavior. Her hypervigilance also accounts for pre-emptive or anticipatory anxiety. She can become inaccurately alert to minor details in her environment misinterpreted as threatening imminent danger. Anticipators over-react with anger, irritability, and aggression in response to distorted or irrational thoughts about situations. For example, her tremors, sweating, chocking, and tearing in response to ambient noises of hearing the two correction officers talking suggested a perceptual distortion and over-reaction. She misperceived the correction officers, like all men, were potential threats to her safety. She experienced profound cognitive dissonance between affection and hatred of men (her husband), and between hope for reconciliation with her husband and her contradictory morals and beliefs on the wrongness of physical abuse. Further, her misandrous thoughts contradicted her severe umbilical dependence on her husband (or other men), through whom she feels emboldened. She needs male companions and may unknowingly be attracted to another domestic abuser, partly to eliminate her anxiety of being lonely, and partly to fulfill a normalcy of being mistreated and victimized.

Fourth, on the Internalizing scale, elevated scores among depression and anxiety subscales denotes a cyclical mood or cyclothymic disturbed individual. She descends to self-defeated anguish for extended periods, feeling victimized, overwhelmed and helpless. Pervasive patterns of depression probably interfered continuously with her job and unsuccessful interpersonal relationships. In such depressed states, she may cocoon in her house for several days to avoid social contact, insulating herself from risks of public anxiety. While not agoraphobic, her spiked social anxiety or discomfort emerges when she doubts her words communicates her thoughts accurately or that she may be misinterpreted as incompetent. Recovery from depression is slow, sluggish, and may require intervention of friends or family drawing her out into a semi-structured activity. Even when she mixes with the public, she is cautious, guarded, unassertive, easily intimidated, and over-thinking the consequences of her every spoken word. For this reason, her incapacity to handle her husband's alleged physical violence reflects her paralyzing anxiety and helplessness evolved from chronic depression. The depression was likely premorbid to her cited incidents of spousal violence against her. Her helplessness was likely present before she got married, before her husband physically abused her, and before she resorted to self-defense of stabbing her husband. Diagnostically, she meets the DSM-V criteria for (300.02) Generalized Anxiety Disorder, (301.13) Cyclothymic Disorder, with anxious distress, (301.82) Avoidant Personality Disorder, and (301.60) Dependent Personality Disorder.

## Behavioral forensic assessment (BFA)

Edens and Boccaccini (2017) cleverly framed this unmet need of ABA regarding forensics as taking evaluation "out of the lab" (2017). They called for increased reliability and replicability of forensic science in field settings using evidence-based technology. An evidence-based assessment technology is where data measurement methods derive largely from research showing the efficacy, reliability, and validity of these methods. Data collection may consist of diverse types from direct observation, objective-based (forensic) interviewing, to video or audio (or equivalent) recording of discrete and continuous samples of behavior. *This is what Behavioral Forensic Assessment* (BFA) is all about. *Samples gathered from collection of data from interviews, collaborative documents, and testing make up the initial formulation of operational hypotheses regarding cause-and-effect interrelations of behavior with its surrounding environment.* For example, a suspect arrested for homicide may say he or she blacked out and suffered amnesia about the crime; they blame their documented medical diagnosis of the flu and sedative effects of prescribed amoxicillin for unusual and erratic aggression escalated into physical abuse. While outwardly these reasons sound plausible and even acquittable, data reviewed from past police records might show the defendant was a habitual offender of eight assault convictions in the last 5 years, none of which involved the flu or taking sedative-producing medications. Facing this discrepancy—the defendant's report marginalizing the crime versus police records attesting to prior violence—the challenge is for the evaluator to formulate an operational definition that might reconcile the contradictions.

Unlike mentalistic forensic evaluators who might turn to personality disorders or transdiagnostic categories for solutions, behavioral forensic scientists are still in scientific mode.

They are not quick to label criminal behaviors with personality traits or emotional dispositions, or borrow codes from classificatory schemes like the *Diagnostic and Statistical Manual of Mental Disorders* (APA, 2013). For example, Skinner (1953) talked about inner cause of behavior. "Every science has at one time or other looked for causes of action inside the things it has studied...the practice of looking inside the organism for an explanation of behavior has tended to obscure the variables which are immediately available for a scientific analysis." (pp. 27–31). Attributing anger, for example, to antisocial or Narcissistic personality disorders, or to Disruptive Mood Dysregulation Disorder is a masquerade. It disguises the dynamics of a psychological field in which the offender performed criminal actions. The DSM-5 codes unfortunately are still the protocol used in psychological evaluations, as well as serve for communication clarity in explaining *some criminal behavior during expert testimony in the courtroom.* Since DSM-5 codes are admissible and even conventional, more details must surface during the behavioral-based evaluation to shift from focus on intrapsychic dynamics to focus on stimulus-response conditioning effects. Behavioral interviewing searches answers to such questions as:

1. "What antecedents triggered the response sequence leading to murder?"
2. "Was the response sequence (pattern) self-reinforcing or produce terminal reinforcement effects?"
3. "Are the victims identical, different, or bear similar verbal and nonverbal behavior properties?"
4. "Does the suspect show repeated or habitual aggressions since childhood (behavior repertoire)?"
5. "Was the (conditioned, unconditioned) motivating operators unique to the homicide incident or identical under all prior acts of violent aggression?"

Data assembled for these questions permit formulation of a working (provisional) functional analysis, with which the behavioral forensic evaluator can run further observational experiments before drawing final conclusions. Such reductionism from ambiguous (molar) to specific (molecular) and measurable behaviors follow the seven common steps of the scientific method. These include: (a) observing an occurrence, (b) asking questions, (c) researching the topic (d) forming an hypothesis, (e) designing and conducting an experiment, (f) drawing conclusions and (g) reporting results.

Baum (2018) explained these steps more succinctly when he described the ubiquitous laws of behavior emanating from basic research. These include *allocation, induction,* and *covariance.* First, the *law of allocation* refers to the amount of time allocated for competition among contingencies under limited time durations. Motivating operations (i.e., establishing operations), for example, may generate responses due to simultaneously conflicting and intense contingencies that increase limited access to reinforcement. Second, the *law of induction* is the organism's choice to act based on phylogenetic and ontogenetic variables, analogous to *natural selection of behavior.* For example, the homicide suspect hypothetically chose to get angry when provoked by another person consistent with his or her interbehavioral history (behavior repertoire) of anger since childhood. Third, the *law of covariance* replaces contiguity and explores both the acquisition of new cues and the cues inducing operant activities. That is, stimulus events and responses (operant or respondent) do not just occur coincidentally, contiguously, or in isolation. They occur *reciprocally* and *transactionally.* They are interdependent; stimulus functions and response functions interact together, in sequence across time, and may directly influence outcomes of multiple contingencies.

Kantor (1959, pp. 70–71) captured the essence of Behavioral Forensic Evaluation in his conceptualization of interbehavioral (field systems) psychology. He identified 10 protoposulates (assumptions) conveying the integrity, depth, and meaning of behavioral sciences applied to interdisciplinary sciences (like forensics). His fundamentals nicely speak to the improvements of behavioral over traditional analyses in any scientific (forensic) enterprise. These protopostulates include:

Protopostulates in the logic of science:

*Protopostulate 1*: Science is an enterprise of interbehaving with specific things and events which leads to a definite and precise orientation with respect to those things and events.

*Protopostulate 2*: Scientific orientation concerns (a) the existence and identity of things and events or their components of things and events, or between either the components of things and events, or between the various thing and events themselves.

*Protopostulate 3*: No science is concerned with existence or processes transcend the boundaries of scientific enterprises. No scientific problem is concerned with a "Reality" beyond events and their investigation.

*Protopostulate 4*: Scientific orientation requires specialized instruments and methods depending upon (a) the specific characteristics of the events interacted with and (b) the specific problems formulated about them.

*Protopostulate 5*: Scientific interactions eventuate in protocols (records), hypotheses, theories, and laws.

*Protopostulate 6*: Scientific construction—the formulation of (a) hypotheses and (b) theories and laws—must be derived from itnerbehavior with events and not imposed upon the events or scientific enterprise from nonscientific cultural sources.

*Protopostulate 7*: Culture consists of the events and institutions (religion, art, economics,technology, social organization, and laws) of a specific group of people.

*Protopostulate 8*: Scientific enterprises are evolutional; they develop in cultural situations as complex institutions. Scientific domains are cumulative and corrigible. They are completely free from all absolutes, ultimates, and universals.

*Protopostulate 9*: Scientific enterprises can be and sometimes are specific enterprises and fundamental within a cultural complex. Only specific enterprises may cooperate and mutually influence each other with respect to basic investigational and interpretive procedures.

*Protoposultae 10*: Applications of (a) scientific findings (records concerning events and their investigation), (b) investigative results (laws and theories), may be localized within scientific enterprises or in the larger cultural setting of such enterprises. Suh applications constitute the authentic basis for scientific prediction and control.

Kantor's predated notions of integrating behavioral science with other disciplines, such as the marriage between behavioral psychology and forensic psychology, echoes a common belief that Kantor's works either instrumentally influenced or is consonant with a growing body of contemporaneous research in behavioral analytic theory (Fryling & Hayes, 2018; Morris, Higgins, & Bickel, 1982; Ruben, 1984). For example, field or systems analysis, inspired by Kantor, readily has been the compass to navigate through, understand, and formulate empirical interventions for complex patterns of behavior as in alcohol and drug addiction (Ruben, 1992). His precepts of *how behavioral science can help specific scientific enterprises in a culture (i.e., the legal system)* paints a new picture on the old canvass of traditional forensic enterprises. Kantor's paradigm, combined with some of his principles and basic principles of operant and respondent conditioning, are the next topic to consider as we continue the transformation of a forensic case from mentalistic to behavioral.

## Basic behavioral structure and concepts

Essentially, modern learning theorists define the structure of personality as a composite of the following critical variables: stimuli, responses, history of behavior or "repertoire," media of contact, deprivational states, and propensity for behavior, also known as interbehavioral potentials. The structure consists of:

### Behavior segment

A unit of behavior along a stream of multiple segments flowing in succession. A unit is a field consisting of stimuli, responses, media of contact, and setting factors. Types of segments include operation behavior segments, process behavior segments, witting behavior segments, and unwitting behavior segments. Operation segments are responses acting on the environment. Process behavior segments entail more complex responses engaged in multiple operations. Witting behavior segments is the organism responding to his or her own behavior (e.g., self-monitoring). Unwitting behavior segments also involves reacting to one's own behavior without awareness of it (e.g., hair pulling, nail biting).

*Reaction System Components* consist of the lowest analyzable action the organism performs. Components in response to some stimulus consist of *attending, perceiving and consummatory responses.* Attending begins the behavior segment when the organism and object first interact. Perceiving is an orientation around the stimulus object and setting, involving alertness to its parametric features of shape, size, color, intensity, and familiarity (i.e., discriminative cues). Both attending and perceiving are precurrent phases while the organism is still detached from the stimulus object and independent from effects from it. Consummatory responses are subtle or covert acts as soft smiles or "appreciating" the compliment one receives. Less observable, these responses begin a more dynamic interactive process with stimuli, the impact of which may increase the topography, frequency, intensity, or duration of responses that evolve from consummatory behaviors.

*Reactional Biography* is the totality of behavioral events connected with a single individual. Ideally, a complete reactional biography includes every nose blow, scratch, smell, touch, or miniscule transaction in the organism's life up to a certain point. Their psychological history, from implicit to explicit events, goes beyond their cumulative record of conditioned and unconditioned behavior (i.e., behavior repertoire) and involves diversely complex inheritable (genetic) and adventitious biological changes transmuting the organism (Delprato, 1980).

*History of behavior or behavior repertoire* means what it suggests–that a human organism develops a cumulative past of interactions with the environment that is predictive of its current and future behavior (Rutter, 1980).

The repertoire is one of the few reified concepts in behavioral psychology, largely tolerated because it suggests learning is measurable and contained "in the personality." Inside the personality is analogous to players on a football field. Each player represents a learnable behavior; players on defense or players on offense go on or off the field as team possession of the football changes. Likewise, learnable behaviors enter or exit the stimulus field based on changing interactions.

*Stimuli* (stimulus functions) refer to current or impending events evoking action in a person. External or internal stimuli, also known as *cues*, can prompt any variety of behavior. Stimuli occurring before behavior arises are known as *antecedents*. When they follow behavior and either increase or decrease the likelihood of that behavior occurring again, they are called *consequences* (e.g., Matson & DiLorenzo, 1984).

*Responses* (response functions) are the biological configurations that an organism takes when interacting with stimuli (stimulus objects). Response features may vary from shape and size (topography) to speed and impact (intensity, magnitude) to length (duration). Responses are voluntary (conditioned) and involuntary (reflex, or involuntary). Response form may be simple (one action occurs), complex (sequence, concurrent, adjunctive responses), functional (mands, enjoining another organism), or implicit (detached from the stimuli, inside the organism such as having a vivid imagery of food in the absence of that food).

Learned responses also fall into three operant subcategories consisting of *Evocative, repertoire-altering, and rule-governed behaviors.* Evocative behavior refers to immediate, abrupt, or instant changes in response form typically triggered by preceding discriminative or other stimuli. Yelled at for swearing, the toddler immediately stops talking and emits the phrase, "I'm sorry." Repertoire-altering responses are more durable and usually products of direct or repeated contingency contacts. Lasting or "residual" effects in the toddler's behavior, for example, is that he does not swear again under similar conditions in the future (e.g., when told to wait in line), and instead emits incompatible behaviors ("Okay, I'll wait) replacing the profanity. Rule-governed behavior is a very complex set of externalized verbal operant repertoires eloquently analyzed by Hayes (2004). Efforts appeared later to operationalize childhood punishment contingencies and show how the contingencies morphed into telegraphic self-statements, sounding like beliefs or values, which dictated self-monitored adult behaviors (Ruben, 2001). For example, a self-deprecatory adult male saying to himself, "I really should not brag (i.e., don't toot your horn), is the adult's description of punishment given to him in childhood whenever bragging about his sports triumphs. The punishment of a parent condemning the child with "Don't boast or put yourself above others" later is truncated into self-reminder or colloquial expressions in adulthood such as "bragging is bad," and "only people who brag are selfish."

## Verbal behavior

Verbal behavior or "operants" represent a unique subset of organismic response repertoires mediated by other persons. Functionally, verbal responses are definable by interrelations with antecedents and consequences than purely by its topographical properties. By contrast, traditional linguistics interpret language by word meaning and syntactical structure independent of response functions or stimulus functions (cf. Sautter & LeBlanc, 2002). Primary verbal operants, first introduced by Skinner (1957), include mand, tact, intraverbal, autoclitic, and echoic. Mands are verbal behaviors enjoining another person or oneself (autoclitic mand) to respond based on unconditioned or conditioned establishing operations. Saying, "Hey, can you come here?" is a mand. Tacts are verbal response to nonverbal verbal stimuli (an object, action, relation, or property). Calling the canine a "dog" aloud is a tact. Intraverbal behaviors are in response to someone's verbal behavior that do not have point-to-point correspondence to what a person says. Asked, "How are you doing today," you respond, "Fine, yourself?" portrays an intraverbal exchange. Echoic behavior is a duplicate or has point-to-point correspondence to the antecedent speaker's verbal response. Repeating verbatim what somebody says is echoic behavior.

Variations include Copying a text, taking dictation, autoclitic, and public accompaniment. Copying a text are written verbal answers matching (having point-to-point correspondence) what somebody wrote. Taking dictation is writing down what somebody says. Public Accompaniment describes a community using verbal behavior to describe covert, cognitive or affective behaviors, such as "I see you feel sad today." Autoclitic is a unit of verbal behavior that depends on other verbal behavior for its occurrence and modifies the effects of that other verbal behavior on the listener. *Descriptive autoclitics* involve discrimination of one's own behavior. For example, when a person speaks loudly in a library, stops suddenly, and says, "Oh sorry for talking so loud." *Relational autoclitics* are supplemental verbal behavior coordinated with other verbal behavior for grammatical or temporal accuracy. Saying, "Eric, you stole the merchandise, *when you went to the store yesterday*. The proper syntax of using the past tense, *when you went* instead of present tense, *when you go to the store now*, conjugates the phrase correctly, in response to the first phrase, *Eric, you stole the merchandise.*

Michael (1982a, 1982b) and Vargas (1982) expanded elementary verbal relations to include *codic behavior, duplic behavior, and sequelic subtypes.* Codic verbal behavior has point-to-point correspondence, is triggered by the antecedent stimulus, and has no formal similarity (does not have to all visual or auditory). Taking dictation is an example, but so is finger spelling prompting another speaker to say what the spelling means. Duplic verbal behavior, unlike codic, does have formal similarity, such as two people finger signing to one another. Sequelic subtypes are when neither the verbal stimuli nor response correspond, nor do they co-exist in the same behavior segment. A person watching a comedian on HBO tell a joke might not think "it is funny" until two days later when the listener can "relate to it." That is, when the listener directly contacts contingencies directly or indirectly producing reinforcement or punishment resembling the comedian's punch line.

*Media of contact* refer to the intervening factors between stimuli and human organism that account for responses. Light and dark affect visual responses; hot and cold affect thermal responses; sour and sweet affect gustatory responses, and the list of sensory receptors goes on. Each mediating factor in the environment either enables or disables responses. Media of contact ingeniously provide the "missing link" in many multivariate contingency analyses. Take, for example, repeated mistakes copying notes from a chalkboard by a 21-year-old male college student whose academic history was exemplary. Operational analysis ruled out historical variables such as poor study skills and aversiveness to the classroom. Weak notetaking skills actually befuddled clinicians, who were searching for salient external stimulus-response cues. Closer inspection of variables showed it was not a repertoire impairment but visual impairment causing the skill disruption. The student recently underwent cataract surgery that reduced visual acuity in short- or long-distance reading when the ambiance was dark. Increasing illumination (i.e., media of contact for photoreception) immediately restored visual clarity and permitted the student to copy correct information from the board. As this example of *behavioral ophthalmology* shows, new variables not only are important additions to the traditional "S-R model," but frequently these variables help explain why the S-R model works.

## Principles of conditioning

This basic structure sets the stage for principles of operant and respondent conditioning. Operant and respondent conditioning are two scientific (lawful) systems engineered to construct, alter, and maintain organismic behavior through a series of systematic manipulations. This section reviews these basic principles as examples of how experimental science can advance our understanding of common responses in everyday life, and particularly as references in performing behavioral forensic evaluations.

### Stimulus cues

Cues make it possible to see the world in a natural way. All actions have a starting point, and with human behavior the starting point involves objects or things preceding behavior. There are two ways these events precede behavior. First is through respondent conditioning. The second is through operant conditioning. However, bear in mind that separating each type of conditioning is only an academic task. Most human interaction is a hybrid of operant and respondent learning (e.g., Rehfeldt & Hayes, 1998; Rescorla, 1988).

### Respondent conditioning

Respondent conditioning follows very simple principles of association. It deals primarily with the sympathetic and parasympathetic nervous system. Historically, Pavlov started by conditioning the salivary response. Meat powder (unlearned stimulus) presented to a dog produces salivation (unlearned responses). If a bell (neutral stimulus) rings prior to presenting meat powder (unlearned stimulus), pairings between the bell and meat powder change the properties of the bell. Now the bell alone can produce salivation. The bell, acquiring *elicitive properties,* is called a conditioned stimulus. Many events trigger direct reflexes in people such as onion odors causing tear duct reflexes or puffs of air across the face causing an eyeblink reflex. Biologically, the sensory systems react involuntarily to stimuli as a normal process of daily living. For example, when onion odors are paired with seeing an onion, crying might occur even before the person slices the onion; just looking at the onion might trigger crying.

This harmless process of natural conditioning involves biology and learning on simple and complex levels. Order from simple to complex learning involves: (a) conditioned emotional responses, (b) simultaneous conditioning, and (c) higher order conditioning.

## Conditioned emotional responses

Respondent conditioning explains how early fears are learned. Continuous pairings of an unlearned or unconditioned fear (stimulus) and a neutral stimulus can suppress a behavior. Usually the unlearned fear occurs first, warning of the onset of another fearful stimulus. This creates instant anxiety and the need for avoidance and escape. Yelling and screaming, for example, are loud sounds to an infant's ear. This is an unlearned fear. But then something happens. Yelling pairs with many neutral stimuli preceding the yelling. The infant hears footsteps or the voice of a parent coming in the bedroom before yelling happens. Such "neutral stimuli" used to mean nothing. Now these stimuli warn the infant that yelling is about to occur.

## Simultaneous conditioning

This is when two stimuli, unlearned and neutral, occur at exactly the same time. These simultaneous pairings usually produce more abrupt, stronger, and longer lasting conditioning effects.

## Higher order conditioning

Conditioning on simple levels occurs between an unlearned and neutral stimulus. This is the first level of conditioning. A higher order of conditioning starts with the neutral stimulus that is now a "learned" stimulus. Now the stimulus triggers behavior in a person, where before it did not. This learned event pairs with even more neutral situations. The link is endless. For example, first yelling scared the infant. Then hearing footsteps of the parent (before yelling) scared the infant. Now, smelling the father's aftershave or mother's perfume (both once neutral stimuli) before hearing the footsteps scares the infant. New links are called "second levels of conditioning." Conditioning on second and higher levels generates weaker and weaker fears. Pairings get lost between old and new stimuli. As the hierarchy of conditioned stimuli rise, all paired to other conditioned stimuli, pairings must occur continuously or intermittent between all of the conditioned stimuli and the original unconditioned stimuli. Interruption of this pairing deteriorates the elicitive function of the stimulus over a response. A response no longer triggered or decreasing around one conditioned stimulus that lost its properties, is called *respondent extinction*. For example, eating food at MacDonalds (unconditioned stimulus) may pair with the seeing the iconic golden arches (neutral turned conditioned stimulus). Later that night, pictures of the golden arches in a book may stimulate or elicit hunger. But the book (its cover, binding, location in the room) in which the picture of golden arches appears may be less elicitive of hunger since it is farther removed from the smell (olfactory) sense of food and hunger inside the Macdonald restaurant that first aroused the unconditioned response.

## Operant conditioning

Operant conditioning, also historically called "instrumental conditioning" is when discriminative stimuli and consequence stimuli are change agents in controlling organismic behavior. Components inside the bilateral and continuous field are preceding events, called "antecedents" and "consequences," each serving distinct and overlapping properties. Antecedents both evoke voluntary or involuntary behaviors to start off a sequential chain of a standard contingency (S-R), *and serve as consequences shaping or conditioning the response preceding them.* Functioning in two roles eliminates the mistaken notion that an S-R model is purely isolative, discrete, and independent from interactive behavior segments. For example, take stopping at a traffic light. The red light cues a person to apply the brakes and stop the car. Force on the brakes before the intersection has multiple consequences shaping this behavior to occur in the future. First, slowing down reduces or avoids going through the intersection and colliding with oncoming traffic; this avoidance reinforces the act of slowing down in the future (i.e., negative reinforcement, see below); Second, slowing down increases alertness to auditory or sensory cues generated from the car motor both reinforcing the deceleration is done accurately (i.e., positive reinforcement, see below), and also doubling as antecedent to continue applying pressure to the brake. Of interest is the hybrid effect of respondent conditioning in this example of associating autonomic arousal with anticipatory fear as the driver approaches the intersection too quickly and must apply the brakes intensely. Respondent influence is even more salient for Midwest drivers negotiating winter weather and who frequently lose momentary control over their vehicles as it hydroplanes over ice.

*Operant extinction* is decline and eventual cessation of some response controlled by a discriminative stimulus and consequential stimulus, when separation increases between the response and original contingency. Jake, for example buys his girlfriend a dozen roses on her birthday. He stops buying her roses when she no longer compliments him after she changed religions and (a) no longer celebrated her birthday, and (b) no longer accepts compliments or gifts from her boyfriend. Operant extinction presumes a unilateral or isolated unit of events that involves withdrawing or terminating both antecedent and consequence. This removal reduces and eliminates the response frequency of another organism. But his elementary or unilateral flow of events is not representative of real events in a behavior segment. In an integrative-field of setting events, the extinguished response is highly malleable, receives competing (concurrent) reinforcers from other sources, and is likely to remain strong under different stimulus conditions. For example, the boyfriend stops buying his girlfriend roses and now buys roses for his siblings on their birthdays. Competing contingencies support or maintain response strength of buying roses. For example, his best friend buys roses for his girlfriend and told Jake he is a real "jerk" unless he buy roses. Jake follows his best friend's advice, avoiding criticism of being a jerk, and oversteps his girlfriend's contingency to buy her roses again. This is called *spontaneous recovery. Spontaneous recovery,* in other words, depends on many uninterrupted sources of contingencies within the psychological field.

## Types of consequences

Outcomes or consequences apply to both respondent and operant conditioning. Respondent outcomes are the conversion from a neutral to a learned stimulus. Operant outcomes are a little more complex. As people behave, the world responds according to four different types of consequences: positive reinforcement, negative reinforcement, positive punishment, and negative punishment.

## Positive and negative reinforcement

To say outcomes are "reinforcers" means they can increase a particular behavior (Bolles, 1972). Positive reinforcers are events or objects given to a person after some behavior increases in the future. Examples of positive reinforcers surround all of us. A smiling child receives affection from her parent. This increases the future probability of that child smiling again at the parent. Money, food, material goods, status–all are powerful rewards exchanged on a daily basis.

However, reinforcers that are desirable and effective under one situation might be ineffective under different situations. For example, under deprivation (hunger, thirst, etc.), urges for reinforcers strongly motivate behavior. But remove deprivation, and motivation disappears; this is due to the presence or absence of motivating operations (discussed below). People do not want the reinforcer anymore. So, events surrounding the behaver determines the effectiveness of the reinforcers.

This is uniquely so for negative reinforcement. A negative reinforcer removes something after the person responds. This increases future responses of the same type. Negative reinforcers also enter into daily routines. Take a panic attack. Escaping a panic attack by rushing out of the mall removes the fear and increases the future probability of escaping again under like situations. Events clearly signal negative reinforcement if they achieve the following:

1. Delay the fearful person, place or thing, until later.
2. Remove the fearful person, place, or thing.
3. Produce behavior that delays or eliminates the fearful person, place or thing.

## Positive and negative punishment

"Punishment" conceptually is a misleading term, conjuring up ideas ranging from cruelty and corporal discipline to traumatic physical and sexual assault. None of these are correct. Punishment instead means the opposite of reinforcement; it decreases behavior. Two types of punishment are positive punishment and negative punishment (Crosbie, 1998; Matson & DiLorenzo, 1984). Positive punishment occurs after a person responds, and it decreases some response in the future. Yelled at for talking loudly, a frightened child learns quickly not to repeat loud talking in the future and risk being yelled at again.

Negative punishment delays or removes things after a person behaves. If the person who fears panic attacks refuses to go to the mall, panic is avoided. But, so are all the normal behaviors causing anxiety: traveling by car, entering public places, and talking to strangers. Not going to the mall, in other words, causes more problems than bargained for. It also decreases routine social behaviors to the point of the person refusing to go anywhere where there is high risk of anxiety. All of the responses interdependent on the fear response, equally receive punishment. Punishment account for emergence of strange or collateral behaviors not directly exposed to the fearful consequences. The agoraphobic person, fearing to drive to the mall, now *develops a habit* of previewing Youtube weather reports and *cleaning the house excessively*. These newly manifested set of responses are *superstitious behaviors* since they indirectly or continuously come close to the reinforcer or punisher but were not part of the original contingency. Baseball players may go through hand or body "rituals" before standing in the batter's box as part of a response sequence hoping to hit a homerun. The ritual is superstitious in that it only remotely and independently associated with the batter's sequence in the batter's box to prepare for the incoming pitch. The ritual itself is not a reliable functional response producing the batter's contact with the ball.

Positive and negative reinforcement and positive and negative punishment follow simple rules in assessing behavior changes. These include:

1. If behavior increases, it means the behavior is reinforced.
2. If behavior decreases, it is means the behavior is punished.
3. If behavior increases because of things received or given, it means there was positive reinforcement.
4. If behavior increases because of things removed, it means there was negative reinforcement.
5. If behavior decreases because of things received or given, it means there was positive punishment.
6. If behavior decreases because of things removed, it means there was negative punishment.

## Schedules of consequences

Positive and negative reinforcement are lawful operations to response outcomes. However, they are the first of many variables interacting with the organism in determining response form. These operations are more effective or less effective on the organism depending on how frequently the consequences occur and whether consequence delivery is time-based and response-frequency based. The *schedule* of reinforcement or punishment, in other words, is just as important in shaping forensic outcomes as the consequences implicated in the crime scene. The four most common schedules of consequences include: Fixed ratio, variable ratio, fixed interval, and variable interval.

*Fixed ratio* is when reinforcement or punishment occurs after a fixed number of responses. It produces a high rate of responses, followed by a burst-pause, burst pattern (called *post-reinforcement pause*). Judy knew to greet her husband after she (a) woke him up in the morning, (b) made him breakfast, and (c) placed out his clothing. She never received attention in between these tasks, only at end of her ritual efforts. Her fixed number of responses produced her husband's reinforcing remarks.

*Variable ratio* is when reinforcement or punishment occurs after an average number of responses, which varies from trial to trial. Sometimes Judy wakes him up, sometimes all she does is place out his clothing—it changes day by day; still, her husband thanks her before he leaves for work. Variable ration schedules produce a high, steady rate of responses (in Judy).

*Fixed interval* is when reinforcement or punishment occurs for the first response emitted after a preset time has elapsed. The schedule increases procrastination or a sudden surge of responses just before the reinforcer or punisher is available. Judy does some or all of the ritual of steps to help her husband but the time spent on her husband is *always the same, about 20 min.* Just before 20 min elapse, she makes sure her husband's clothes are laid out; this last effort proximal to time lapsing assures her husband acknowledgment of her.

*Variable interval* is when reinforcement or punishment occurs for the first response emitted after an average amount of time has elapsed, but the interval of time varies from trial to trial. This schedule produces a moderate, steady rate or responses. Judy is not on a stringent time schedules. Sometimes her helpfulness to her husband varies by what she does, and how little or how much she does for him. Her husband rewards her nonetheless before he leaves to work in the morning regardless of the time schedule.

The precision of contingency schedules in basic research helps to pinpoint the cause-effect unilateral relationships formed between organism and stimulus conditions. But as suggested above, interactions between organism and stimuli are multi-causal, reciprocal, and entail a progression of variables equally potentiating response probability. In the example of Judy, what if Judy did not get her husband's loving acknowledgment for all of her efforts before he left for work? What if the consequences were punishment? She yells or hits her unless she completes the ritual of chores for him. According to punishment theory, fixed time schedules may vary her efforts but her overall tendency is to do less, since punishment *decreases behaviors*. However, Judy shows no sign of behavior abatement. What maintains her moderate to high response frequency, duration, and intensity despite punishment for her efforts? The answer lies with how fixed and interval schedules are a subclass of seven larger matrices for understanding the unique interaction between operant stimuli, responses, and consequences. These molar schedules include: chained, mixed, concurrent, tandem, alternative, multiple, and conjunctive (cf. Lyon, 1982).

*Chained schedules* are when the response requirements of two or more basic schedules must be met in a specific sequence before reinforcers are delivered. Each sequence has its own antecedent or discriminative stimulus. For example, Rick has to buy the cocaine and then buy paraphernalia to prepare the cocaine before he can smoke the cocaine. While each schedule in the sequential chain probably has other consequences (reinforcer or punishers) maintaining its operation, a terminal reinforcer is still desired after one, two, or multiple chains connect contingencies.

*Mixed schedules* is when two or more basic schedules of reinforcement (or punishment) occur in an alternating, usually random sequence. No discriminative stimuli are correlated with the presence or absence of each element of the schedule, and reinforcers (punishers) are delivered for meeting the response requirements of the contingencies *at any time.* For example, the alcohol-abusing, and domestically violent spouse may wake up everybody in the household early, yell at or physically strike family members, and then go on a tirade about the messy house, all on a random schedule without warning (discriminative stimuli). Random (mixed) punishment schedules frequently induce unpredictable outcomes in traumatically exposed family members. These outcome behaviors often become the source of child and adult psychopathology (Kazdin, 1994, 1995; Ruben, 2001). Such manifestations of traumatic behaviors in adults and children include:

1. *Family members learn to react to punishment for attention.* Attention-seeking responses are instantly fueled by negative or aggressive reactions by the aggressor.
2. *Family members learn to pair or "associate" the properties of punishment with the person administering the punishment.* Repeated anger, aggression or negativity by the aggressor turns the aggressor himself or herself into an aversive event. Properties defining the aggressor

such as tone of voice, physical stature, odor, and facial features acquire threatening messages avoided by other family members.

3. *Family members learn to stay away (avoid) anticipated or actual punishment.* Repeated exposure to aversive situations oversensitizes family members to obvious and subtle stimuli surrounding the aggressor or punishing situation.
4. *Family members inhibit appropriate behaviors in anticipation of punishment.* Anticipation of aversive situations interrupts appropriate and inappropriate behaviors. For example, not only does the frightened child hide underneath his bed during a loud marital argument, but the avoidance prevents him from also (a) saying goodnight to his parents, (b) brushing his teeth or going to the bathroom, and (c) changing clothing. That is, appropriate behaviors that never were punished but are collateral or sequential to punished (avoidance) behaviors now are inhibited. Unless corrected, inhibitions develop into routines where that child simply omits steps (a) through (c), even into adulthood, whenever he goes asleep.
5. *Family members learn inappropriate behavior in anticipation of punishment.* Suppression of some inappropriate behavior from punishment does not prevent the spontaneous learning of other, more discrete inappropriate behaviors. Inappropriate behaviors "spontaneously" arise for two reasons. First is to replace necessary *appropriate* behaviors that are inhibited. Second is to replace *inappropriate* behaviors receiving punishment.

*Concurrent schedules* are two or more contingencies of punishment or reinforcement that operate independently and simultaneously for two or more behaviors. Dara, for example, anticipating her husband's physical abusive assaults at night, observes two simultaneous contingencies she abides by. First, she can remain silent when she sees him (discriminative stimulus), withhold her remarks, or just decrease her talking to her husband, thereby delaying or avoiding his angry reaction (negative punishment). Simultaneously, she can put off making dinner and decide to be amorous with her husband while he is inebriated, since intoxication makes him more romantic, sensual, and more amenable to tenderness (positive reinforcement). There are other contingencies likely at play here, namely, that lovemaking further avoids or delays violent behaviors against Dara for two days (negative reinforcement). Faced with these choices of contingencies, why would Darla select one contingency over the other? Is she just intuitively prone to reinforcement contingencies over punishment contingencies, or vice versa?

One operant (or scientific) law to help understand Darla's dilemma of concurrent contingencies is the *matching (or generalized matching) law.* Matching laws, first formulated by Herrnstein (1961, 1970), originally involved an experiment with pigeons pushing two buttons on concurrent and variable interval schedules. The pigeons pecked the button that produced the greater food reward more often than the other button. Rates of button pushing were matched against the rates of reinforcement on both buttons. Ratios can be predictors of how people respond favorably and frequently to one set of circumstances while are less partial to another set of circumstances. For children and adults, high rates of behavior should "match" the relative amount of reinforcement associated with each response (cf. Horne & Lowe, 1993; Poling, Edwards, Weeden, & Foster, 2011). Ratios also may determine how people maximize or minimize reinforcement in three ways: molecular maximizing, molar maximizing, and melioration. Spelled out simply.

- *Molecular maximizing*: organisms always choose whichever response alternative is most likely to be reinforced at the time.
- *Molar maximizing*: organisms distribute their responses among various alternatives so as to maximize the amount of reinforcement they earn over the long run.
- *Melioration*: literally means to "make better"; organisms respond so as to improve the local rates of reinforcement for response alternatives. Behavior keeps shifting toward the better of two alternatives until ratios are equal-which makes matching.

In other words, Darla quickly compares the *probabilistic ratio* of each contingency's impending or immediate impact on her behaviors. If she thinks her husband will respond more favorably and immediately to her amorous overtures, she selects that contingency over the one of withholding her remarks (i.e., molecular maximizing). Alternatively, she may partition her behaviors amid both contingencies—acting amorous, and withdrawing her remarks—proves more effective in the short-run or long-run (i.e., molar maximizing). Or, a more efficient use of behavior may be to first withdraw from her husband except to make amorous overtures. Once she observes his responsiveness to her overtures, she shifts distribution of responses more to the sexual repertoire and less to the verbal withholding, until only her sexual responses are dominant. The matching law explains the "decision making" organisms go through in determining viability of response execution in concurrent contingencies.

*Tandem schedules* are schedules of reinforcement or punishment identical to chained schedules except, like the mixed schedule, the tandem schedule does not use discriminative stimuli to start, prompt, or reinforce responses. Tandem schedules risk imposition of randomness with two or more schedules for which there are predictable outcomes. Darla has no idea what time her inebriated husband will return home that night, nor whether his agitation might evolve quickly into violent aggression. Her reactional biography does prepare her to survive against either contingency once it occurs, despite the ambiguity of setting events (absence of discriminative stimuli); she can prepare to protect herself knowing her husband's sequence of responses, and usual consequence of outcome of his behaviors.

*Alternative schedules* provide reinforcement or punishment whenever the requirement of either a ratio or interval schedule is met, regardless of which of the component schedule's requirement is met first. Here the difference in Darla's calculated response patterns can determine her husband's pleasant or unpleasant outcome. She observes he takes 20 min to shower when he gets home (fixed interval) and can have his meal ready for him. Or, she can display a ritual of several sexual responses in precise order occurring fluidly and continuously from the moment her husband steps out of the shower. Her husband's receptiveness reinforces her repetition of the same sexual response ritual and estimation of time-related behaviors in the future.

*Multiple schedules* is a compound schedule of reinforcement or punishment consisting of two or more basic contingencies that occur in an alternating, usually random sequence. A discriminative stimulus is associated with the presence or absence of each contingency and predicts the inevitability of reinforcers. Combine all of the contingencies discussed above affecting Darla, from the moment her husband enters the house, and it represents the totality of a psychological field progressing through multiple schedules.

*Conjunctive schedules* are in effect whenever reinforcement or punishment follows the *completion* of response requirements for both a ratio schedule and an interval schedule. In other words, Darla lacks outcome prediction of her response choices—either to be romantic or withdrawal completely from her husband—since the consequences, good or bad, only appear *after she emits responses in each of the concurrent contingencies.* In real life, conjunctive schedules that require production of high and durable responses for prolonged periods (30 min to an hour), without the organism having a clear history of expected outcomes, create anxiety, response decay, and collateral aggressive behavior. Darla, for example, not knowing if everything she does, from being romantic or talking minimally to her husband (for several hours), may delay or avoid his wrath, may manifest irritability, agitation, sarcasm, extreme nervousness's or even anticipatory aggressive behaviors. Anticipatory aggression is a pre-emptive emission of anger that enjoins her husband to delay, mitigate, or cease angry behavior toward her.

## Social exchange of reinforcement and punishment schedules

In an integrative-field or ecological perspective, prediction of behavior outcomes from reinforcement or punishment schedules requires more than parameters of rate, contiguity, or locality of antecedent stimuli and consequences in one or multiple sequences. Included is also the *reciprocity or exchange of reinforcers or punishers between two organisms.* Amount and frequency of consequation between two individuals determines critical family dynamics of (a) cohesion (closeness vs. detachment), (b) trust (vs., distrust), (c) sensitivity (vs. indifference), and (d) risk of approach (vs. avoidance/escape behaviors). *Effective* and *reciprocal* exchanges maintain equilibrium. *Ineffective and inconsistent* exchanges disrupt the family balance causing gradually progressive deterioration in interpersonal relationships (Foa & Foa, 1974, 1980). Ruben (1998) revised the Foa & Foa model of social exchange, converting resources of love, money and status into positive resources and forming rewarding exchanges. Likewise, physical abuse, verbal abuse, or aversive resources constituted negative resources, or *punishing resources,* The revised rules of exchange, based on operant and respondent conditioning, included the following:

1. *The larger the amount of rewards possessed by a person, the more likely it is to be given to others.* By this is meant supply. Quantity of resource supply selfishly guarded by one spouse is a form of control. In dysfunctional families, abundance of supplies does not threaten resource shortages and selfish spouses can to give rewards to partners or children without feeling robbed or sacrificed. Self-sacrificing love, money or other accolades is inconsistent with dysfunctional family members strongly protective of their own resources. For example, Marilyn refuses to let her boyfriend Jack drive her car when his car is in repair. She trusts his driving but is reticent to sacrifice or release this rewarding resource.
2. *The smaller the amount of rewards possessed by a person, the more he or she is likely to take resources away from others.* Limited resources in a selfish family member's cache are guarded. Family members are greedy, fearful of losing their supply, and selective of which resources are denotable. Hoarding resources, in effect, protects a family member from feeling vulnerable, out of control, and risking another family member may exceed their allotment of resources. For example, Marilyn hates that her boyfriend stores extra cash in the house they share; she secretly embezzles his money to balance out resources and prevent him from gaining a reward supply advantage.

3. *The nearer two rewarding resources are, the more likely they are to be exchanged with one another. The nearer two punishing resources are, the more they are to be avoided.* Rewarding resources never occur in isolation. Money and love, for example, become united holistically as a larger reward. Spouses may grow accustomed to receiving one rewarding resource with another rewarding resource. Failure to supply one rewarding resource without its Gemini feels unnatural. For example, frequently dysfunctional partners show their love exclusively through gifts rather than physical or verbal affection. Gifts paired with "love" are dually exchanged, where the occurrence of one reward invokes expectations to receive the other reward.

   By contrast are punishers. Exchange of punishers may occur by proximity and contiguity. Proximity refers spatially to object closeness, whereby one punisher sequentially precedes or follows another punisher. Verbal yelling, for example, may precede physical abuse, or vice versa. Contiguity refers to simultaneity. Two punishing resources co-existing simultaneously in time and space exert greater impact on receivers. Yelling and spanking occurring together, for example, frightens a partner more than when both punishers are sequential.

   Still, sequentially or simultaneously, receivers (e.g., battered partners) are prone to avoid the punishing resources. Avoidance may take several forms. One form is silence, withdrawal, and recession of any behavior to private levels. A second, typically oppositional form is outward aggression; victimized partners who argue, debate, or passively-aggressively sabotage communication attempt to escape from punishing resources.

4. *The nearer to love a rewarding resource is, the more likely it is to be exchanged with the same resource. The near to love a punishing resource is, the more love and the punishing resource will be avoided. Love is exchanged for love except if punishers are present.* Love displayed as physical, verbal or material resource along with another rewarding resource is apt to be mutually exchanged between giver and receiver. These rewards carry similar *weight (i.e., intensity, magnitude)* and pose little risk for a partner to give to another partner, knowing in return the same amount of reward will be given back. When love is contiguous or proximal with punishers, partners (or children) avoid both rewarding and punishing resources in spite of a past history seeking and attaining the rewarding resource. Eating a meal, for instance, is a rewarding resource (e.g., food). However, when food intake frequently coincides with angry parents scolding a child at the mealtime table, food is avoided. Decreased food intake or development of idiosyncracies (superstitious behaviors) accompanying food avoidance, like rituals of overcutting food or counting calories, are the forerunner to eating disorders such as anorexia nervosa. The adjunctive or superstitious behavior coincide with food-avoidance to delay, attenuate, or eliminate impending criticism by parents at mealtime (cf. Altier & Ruben, 1984).

   Varying conditions may increase or decrease this propensity for avoidance. For example, children or partners who are extremely hungry (i.e., state of deprivation) may approach the punisher faster and endure the punisher for longer durations than non-hungry (satiated) children.

5. *The nearer to love a punishing resource is, the narrower the range of resources with which it is likely to be exchanged.* Love paired with punishing resources discourages a family

member to exchange that love for another resource. Avoidance of punishing resources not only prevents contact with family members giving those punishers, it also suppresses love, affection or any rewarding resource typically exchanged for love. Punishment inadvertently has three effects, none of which encourage love: (a) it decreases overall effort and caring; (b) it inhibits asking the punishing resource giver anything; and (c) it produces inappropriate, aggressive or passive-aggressive responses further replacing love and affection (see above).

6. *For resources closer to money or any other rewards, the amount lost by the giver tends to approach the amount gained by the receiver (so that one's gain is the other's loss).* A serious problem in dysfunctional families is resource imbalance. Breakdowns in family economic systems occur when a disproportionate amount of rewarding resources are allocated to only one family member. One partner may receive more love, gifts, privileges, and accommodations (i.e., fly first class, get maid to clean house), whereas the giver receives a paucity or disproportionate allocation of love (rewarding resources). Distribution of rewarding resources is random, in particular, in response to individuals with addictive or impulsive lifestyles.
7. *When a rewarding resource is not available for exchange, it is more likely to be submitted by a less particularistic person than by a more particularistic person.* Rewarding resources are rare commodities in a dysfunctional family economy. When they are presented, rewards are superficial, temporary, and lack enthusiasm. Less particularistic in a giver means the resource is uneventful and that givers are casual, nonchalant, or even aloof about reward exchanges. In healthy families, rewards are given with intentionality, caring, and affection. Reward distribution that lacks "genuineness" or "meaningfulness" also relates to receivers not regarding the rewards as valuable in their lives; it neither generates motivation nor increase some property of responses (e.g., frequency, duration, intensity, topography, etc.). For example, a spouse buying a birthday card featuring animals on it for a receiver who hates animals may seem ingenuous. The receiver "feels" neither joy, gratefulness, nor excitement around the card-buyer and may even misinterpret the giver as naively selfish.
8. *The simultaneous transmission of love and rewarding resource increases the value of this other resource, or facilitates its transmission. The simultaneous transmission of love and punishing resource decreases the value of both resources, or terminates its transmission.* As suggested earlier, variables of simultaneity and proximity greatly determine the value of resources exchanged. Rewarding resources paired with love intensify the rewarding resources, further drawing interest to it and enabling equitable transfers of this rewarding resource between family members. Love paired with punishment has the opposite effect. Punishers delay and prevent family members to want an exchange; they avoid exchanges in spite of their state of deprivation for it. The traditional model of domestic abuse cycle between couples illustrates this problem. A physically violent partner's assault may pair with his or her verbal reminders that "I do this because I love you," or the attack episodes may follow with purchase of gifts to the victims and sincere promises never to act abusive again. Unconditional acceptance of these love-gestures, after suffering abuse, may decrease the value of the resources for the victim (i.e., the victim distrusts the honesty of promises made), but may also interrupt, delay, or temporarily terminate repetitive episodes of the spousal abuse.

9. *Taking away any resource (including love) produces a loss of love and produces punishers.* Families who place a premium on resources instead of sharing them equally are prone to penalize members who jeopardize the resources. When rewarding resources are limited, removed, or contaminated (e.g., ruined), the penalty is retribution. Dysfunctional parents or families aggressively blame, shame, and physically torment family members believed to be the culprits of reward cessation. Take, for example, affection neglect in couples who began their nuptials enjoying frequent presexual touching or sexual relations. When one partner observes unilateral cessation of physical intimacy by the other partner, barring significant medical or life-altering problems (e.g., pregnancy, dementia, and recent family deaths), extinction effects in the deprived partner may appear twofold. First are repetitive solicitations (mands) to resume affection or conjugal activity. Second, when repeated mands for affection fail, response escalation into anger may include accusing the affection neglector of having ulterior motives (holding grudges) or deceptive acts (infidelity).
10. *The optimal range (neither too little nor too much) of a resource is narrowest for rewards, and increases progressively for resources closest to money. Punishers in the way of money decreases exchange of resources closest to money.* Rewarding resources are distributed sparingly. Optimal ranges of resource exchange in dysfunctional or functional families is either too little or too much depending on the person's impulsive needs (motivation operations). Parents who run out of marijuana, for example, may spend money replenishing their supply rather than on dinner for the kids. Other expenditures of money are just as calculated. As money in the family decreases, dispersions are selective and decrease over time. When family income or money access increases, rewarding resources are more generously given and, for example, both purchases of marijuana and dinner occur. Gifts of money accompanied by punishers, for example, buying dinner while yelling at the kids, decreases the reciprocal exchange of resources as receivers withdraw from the exchange and disregard the value of money.
11. *In the absence of an exchange, the amount of love possessed and rewarding resources decreases, and the amount of love is lower for people closer to love.* Troubled families scarcely show exchanges of love. Reduction of love exchanges to the point of extinction produces common outcomes. First, any rewarding resource, absent of repeated pairings with love (i.e., respondent conditioning), loses its elicitive properties to generate interest (a motivation operation) in the receiver. It simply loses its potency and no longer functionally occurs between family members. Second, loss of love, affection or compassion in the primary family prompts a search for rewarding resources outside families. Examples are when neglected and abused children adopt surrogate parents or "friends' parents" who generously invites the child over frequently for meals and nights. Or, displaced reactions in spouses neglected of love when they engage in extramarital affairs to fill a void of love in their marriage.
12. *Other conditions being equal, the probability of occurrence of a given exchange (rewards and punishers) is contingent upon the family economy in which it may take place.* This is a general postulate stating that family dynamics entirely control the frequency and value of rewarding and punishing reward exchanges. In troubled families, exchanges are unilateral, inconsistent, unreliable, and primarily with punishing resources based on a context of distrust, greed, and impulsivity. In non-dysfunctional families, balanced

exchanges derive from a cohesion between family members and equal use of punishing and rewarding resources.

**13.** *The probability of reward and punisher exchange is higher in small families. The opposite is true for larger families. In the latter, different members of the family may serve as surrogate-parent givers of rewards and punishers.* Size of the family is a critical variable in predicting distribution of resources. Small, close families of four people (parents, two children) risk little competition and obstacles in equally benefiting from resources. Members receive individualized exchanges from the primary parent. In larger families, distribution of resources from primary parent may be tedious and resources can be exhausted before all the children receive equal amounts. In dysfunctional families, size of family also plays a role but is complicated by nepotism. A child from either large or small family perceived as "the helper" will be given preference and receive resources before another member perceived as "the scapegoat." Labeled children who fall out of favor are relegated less number of resources and fewer rewarding resources.

In sum, social exchange theory provides a viable paradigm to explore the interplay of economic and social factors in family life from a systems behavioral perspective. Love, fear, and other qualities transfer from one family member to the next, with expectations that similar qualities will be equally reciprocal. Failure of this reciprocity means there is family disparity, marked not only by poor communication, but by decomposition of love, affection, and general caring. In the case of dysfunctional families, resources deliberately withheld or randomly allocated disrupts family trust and inherently engenders a search outside the family for rewarding resources.

## Functional stimulus properties

Cues or "antecedent stimuli" make it easier to trace roots of people's behavior. Even complex cues are easy to trace. Cues take on many properties from texture and shape to function. Properties define the cue and can be relevant or irrelevant. Relevant properties are obvious features that most people consider when picturing the cue. Dogs, for instance, have four legs, fur, a tail, and bark. Cars have four wheels, a chassis, hood, trunk, passengers, and are for transportation. Irrelevant properties, not defining a dog include how fast it licks the owner, or whether it responds quickly to commands. Likewise, irrelevant properties of a car are its trim resembling colors of a flag, the high pitch or low pitch sound of its horn, and whether passengers inside the car wear blue or red sweaters. So, why is it that people who see cars think of dogs, or people who see dogs think of cars? Why is it that a car reminds a person of good and bad memories of other cars? Peculiar conditioning of this sort occurs due to external and internal cues. External or internal stimuli may control behavior directly because of very relevant properties of that stimulus; properties previously associated with the stimulus trigger reactions, such as an alarm-clock arousing a sleeper. Sounds, sights, smells, and tastes conveniently familiar to behavers appear to *belong to the stimuli.* Onset of familiar cues "instinctively" evokes a repertoire of conditioned behaviors that seem logical to the naive observer.

The trouble is that units of conditioning are never that simple. Complexly integrated contingencies blur the origins of stimulus-response connections, confusing both behavers and observers of behavior. Parents of oppositionally defiant children, for example, may insist their children's tantrums really are inherited from family genes. Parents think a spouse's temper "somehow" seems to transmit genetic codes of behavior from one generation to the next generation. Phylogenetic reasons often replace other salient ontogenetic reasons for Johnny's tantrum behavior when no "obvious" antecedents or consequences are present. Similarly, classroom teachers fed up with Johnny's oppositional behavior in class accuse Johnny of having Attention Deficit Hyperactivity Disorder (ADHD)—a label for a supposed biological condition conveniently explaining Johnny's disruptive misbehavior. All of these iatrogenic explanations are bogus and invent or *reify* a concept—genetics, or ADHD—as the magical depository for otherwise unexplained reasons for behavior.

Mythical explanations for behavior have been a tradition in pseudo-psychology and often relieve explainers of the anxiously disturbing mystery behind the origins and persistence of culturally strange behaviors (cf. Moore, 1980; Ruben, 1988; Skinner, 1974). But environmental cues really do exist-there is traceable evidence showing connections between responses and antecedents (or consequences). The reason cues seem to "disappear" or seem "elusive" is due to an unusual form of higher order conditioning, in which both *relevant* and *irrelevant* stimulus properties may functionally exert control over behavior. Stimulus properties may share: (a) the same things (generic extension); (b) similar things (metaphorical extension); or (c) different things (metonymical extension) (Hayes & Chase, 1991; Skinner, 1957; Sundberg & Partington, 1983).

## Generic extension (same things)

Cues that have all the relevant properties so that one cue looks exactly like another cue, are called similar things (generic extension). Fear of hearing the same loud noise each time, despite when or where one hears it, is due to the noise having all of the relevant properties for fear.

## Metaphorical extension (similar things)

Cues that have some but not all of the relevant properties and still produce fear are called similar things (metaphorical extension). Loud noises vary by intensity, duration, and quality. But they may still invoke fear exactly as if the noises were identical. A Vietnam Vet exposed to traumatic artillery fire in wartime may be startled when mowing the lawn and hears the engine sputter and backfire loudly. It is not fear of a lawnmower. Fear comes from the sounds being similar to the storm of artillery fire in wartime.

## Metonymical extension (different things)

Cues that have none of the relevant properties but still produce fear or pleasant responses are called "different things" (metonymical extension). People react to irrelevant properties of the cue, as well as to relevant properties of competing cues. *Irrelevant* means properties are hidden, vague, or not the typical things people react to in that cue. For example, nothing about a shower curtain should produce anxiety. But some shower curtains that are hooked above showers in small motels may remind people of the scene from the Alfred Hitchcock classic movie, *Psycho*–the shower curtain in the Bates Motel, torn down before a female was stabbed in the shower. Viewers who see shower curtains designed similar to the "Psycho" shower may shiver (experience autonomic arousal) at the "memory" associated with the shower curtain of traumatically seeing the victim murdered. Likewise, people who think they see ghosts may be looking at irrelevant or different things. Ghosts that appear in the house they lived in may not be ghosts at all, but rather objects that remind the perceiver of the deceased person. If, say, the deceased person used to stand by the Christmas tree on Christmas Eve, seeing that tree and its shadows may trigger strong memories of the deceased person. Shadows of the tree thrown upon the wall may look like the person being thought of. The silhouette may resemble somebody standing there (Ruben, 1987).

Kantor's version of memory (1922) predated the concept of metonymical extension, by cleverly explaining reactions to ominous or obsolete events; he called them *Recollective Memory Acts*. He classified recollective memory acts under three subtypes, *casual remembering of reminiscence, direct recollection, and memorial recovery*. Casual remembering of reminiscence is when the organisms recalls some unimportant or obscure stimulus, but is tied to consummation (interaction with) stimulus-response connections. Direct recollection is more intentional and allows retrieval of archival facts needed at the moment or to achieve a practical result. A witness in court testimony, for example, may be called upon to recall abstract or obscure facts from direct experience occurring months or years earlier. The only stimulus cue prompting memory may be stark pieces of evidence loosely or irrelevantly connected to the direct (relevant) eye-witness encounter the victim had during the crime. The third subtype, memorial recovery, operates to affect some change in the person, whether a thought or feeling. Sadness, for instance, over the death of a sister who physically decayed over months in hospice, may be changed by imagining more pleasant times enjoyed in the decedent's earlier life. Retrieval of these memories seems difficult without reminder cues such as pictures of her or from souvenirs to re-construct the happy events. These are all relevant properties of stimulus cues. Instead, the bereaved person relies on irrelevant properties of stimulus cues—the season or day of the week. For example, memory of weekends trigger internal biophysical cues of happiness. This association of happiness with weekends represents different events in the transactional psychological field of the sad person's reactional biography. However, none of these properties were relevant or prominent during the original stimulus-response conditioning with that sister.

## Motivating operations

Another functional stimulus property deals with motivation. Traditional psychology relegates motivation or drive to intrapsychic reasons of personality, intentionality, or biological conditions underlying the intensity and fulfillment of immediate gratification. While theses inner psychological factors are pertinent in behavioral analysis, interpretation of their functionality is different and more focus is upon the organism's reciprocal interaction with multiple stimulus conditions. This environmental approach is legendary. Learning theory always viewed motivation a function of deprivation states around antecedent or consequential stimuli; it explained organismic responses based on fluctuations that partially or completely terminated the deprivation of states. Keller and Schoenfeld (1950) first introduced experimental analogues of motivation; they showed the evocative effects of stimuli on response accretion or deceleration during deprivation. Their research helped to move the term "motivation" from a psychoanalytical or humanistic realm into a conditioning realm; they called this motivation an "establishing operation." Michael (1982a, 1982b, 1988, 1993) refined the term *establishing operation* to describe the effectiveness of some stimulus, object, or event to become a reinforcer based in states of deprivation. Typically low rates of responses under an establishing operation (EO) would increase in rate or frequency to the extent deprivation could be eliminated within a time limit.

Expansion of Michael's pioneering reconceptualization has been an asset in the assessment, treatment, and prevention of problem behaviors with autism and related populations (e.g. Iwata, Smith, & Michael, 2000; Langthorne & McGill, 2009; McGill, 1999; Miguel, 2013; Nosik & Carr, 2015; Thomas & Frasier, 2005). Applied research with various adult and child populations, in particular, narrowed the EO lexicon into eight classifications. These include the Abative effects (of motivation operation), Establishing Operation (EO), Abolishing Operation (AO), Motivating Operations (MOs), Reflexive Conditioned Motivating Operations (CMO-Rs), Transitive Conditioned Motivating Operation (CMO-T), Surrogate Conditioned Motivating Operation (CMO-S), and Unconditioned Motivating Operation (UMO).

## Abative Effects (of a motivating operation)

This describes a decreased frequency in responses reinforced by stimuli functionally connected with the *same Motivation Operation.* A child raising her hand to be the next one receiving food decreases if food already was distributed by row. The food already being served through another contingency reduces (abates) the hand-raising to relieve hunger (motivating operation).

*Establishing* operation *(EO):* A state of deprivation that increase the effectiveness of some stimulus, object, or event as a reinforcer. Missing the school bus and threat of arriving late a school *increases the probability of a friend calling another friend to drive him or her to school.*

*Abolishing* operation *(AO):* A motivating operation that decrease the reinforcing effectiveness (value) of a stimulus, objects, or event. Food ingestion, for example, eliminates hunger and the immediacy of food reinforcer value. Abolishing operations also vary by degree based on the organism's physiology, reactional biography, and competing motivating operations. For example, food ingestion may produce satiation (abolishing operation) but not in food-deprived children who over-eat (exceed satiation) to eliminate anxiety. They over-eat to feel "stuffed" under fear that they may wait several hours or days before eating again. Addiction to heroin, in another example, may involve intravenous injection to momentarily relieve heroin withdrawal symptoms. But when withdrawal symptoms occur eventually, restorative use of heroin may or may not effectively abolish the urges depending on one's physical tolerance threshold, history of metabolism of opioids, and stash of other prescriptive opioids co-occurring with heroin.

*Motivating* operations *(MOs):* An environmental variable that (a) alters (increases or decreases) the reinforcing effectiveness of some stimulus, object, or event, and (b) alters (increases or decreases) the current frequency (or some other property) of responses reinforced by the stimulus, object, or event. Dusk, for example, may signify the best opportunity after work for high rate buyers of cocaine and marijuana to meet with drug dealers. Drug dealers use this environmental event (time of day) as antecedents that increase urgency of drug sales under a limited time period (i.e., limited hold). Drug dealers find, during dusk, when streets are empty with people at home eating dinner or returning home from work, there is less risk of unscrupulous buyers or undercover police officers disguised as buyers. When dusk turns to darkness, a period deemed more dangerous to be outside due to robberies of drug dealers, the brief window of sales opportunity (establishing operation) ends.

*Reflexive conditioned motivating operation (CMO-R)* is a stimulus that acquires motivational properties by preceding some form of reinforcement or punishment contingencies. It alone triggers or forewarns of upcoming contingencies and establishes an operation under which the organism can function either to facilitate or delay (avert) onset of the forewarned contingency. This "warning stimulus" is illustrated by a fired worker calling his former employer, threatening to take revenge for his job termination. The threat describes an impending contingency of the fired worker bringing his handgun to work and unloading rounds at co-workers. Taking the threat seriously, the former employer *acts immediately under the establishing operation of fear to contact building security and the police department* to avert or terminate the imminent punishment event. Predictably, in the future, similar cues of disgruntled or fired employees making threats *evoke the same establishing operation* for that employer.

*Transitive conditioned motivating operation (CMO-T)*, similar to reflexive conditioned motivating operation, is an environmental variable that, as a result of some learning history, establishes or abolishes the reinforcing effectiveness of another stimulus (or set of stimulus conditions); it also doubles as a cue to evoke (or abate) the behavior that has been reinforced by the other stimulus. Called the "blocked response," since it obstructs, alters or changes the valence of ensuing contingencies, transitive conditioned motivating operations can actually take precedent or carry more value for the organism in a field succession of contingencies. A disloyal husband taking his wife out for New Years later that evening, for example, receives an earlier text from his extramarital partner who requests him for a sexual rendezvous. Historically, the girlfriend's erotic prompts superseded any activity planned that evening with his wife. The extramarital partner's persistent desire to meet the husband *abates his behavior of going out with his wife, reinforced in the past.* In the future, when the girlfriend calls, whether the unfaithful husband already planned or was going to plan outings with his wife, the girlfriend's request *has a higher probability of evoking (controlling) the husband's behavior.*

*Surrogate conditioned motivating operation (CMO-S)* is a stimulus that acquires motivating properties by being paired (prior, during, or immediately after) with another motivating operation. The surrogate motivating operation has the same value-altering and behavior-altering effects as the motivating operation with which it is paired. This process is functionally equivalent to the symbiotic relationship between an unconditioned and neutral stimulus in respondent conditioning, where the neutral stimulus gains elicitive properties over the reflex behavior just as the unconditioned stimulus it was paired with. In the surrogate variation, using operant conditioning, an *entire set of stimulus conditions correlates contiguously with one or many pre-existing motivating operations*. The interesting feature of surrogate contingencies is that, while the form (topography) or function (mechanics) of the contingency may resemble its original contingency being paired with it, the outcome behavior can be different. For example, an office manager accused of embezzling $100,000 from her employer, a physician, explained the contingencies though which she pulled off her heist. First, the physician gave the office manager carte blanche to collect patient copayments, open the mail of insurance checks, endorse the checks, and make bank deposits. These events represent the original contingency. After 1 month, the physician granted more privileges to the office manager of organizing staff payroll and bonuses based on a percentage of the weekly receivables. This was the second or surrogate contingency. Combined together, both contingencies evoked the office manager to collect, manage, and distribute the money (either in a bank or as dispersions for payroll or bonuses. *However, once the office manager was free to calculate payroll and bonuses unmonitored, she inflated the calculation for her share and began embezzling funds. The surrogate motivating operation actually evoked spontaneous responses beyond the original motivating operation*. The effectiveness of this surrogate (conditioned) motivating operation lies in the unique reactional biography of the office manager. A manager raised piously, with strong rule-governed behaviors (morals) dictating prudent decision-making may be less susceptible to embezzlement than a manager with a juvenile and adult criminal record, polydrug abuse, weak rule-governed behaviors, and raised by neglectful parents.

*Unconditioned Motivating Operation* is as motivating operation whose value or altering effects do not depend on a learning history. Malleability of responses is more phylogenetic. Deprivation of food (hunger) is likely to increase the reinforcing effectiveness of buying food at the moment. *But not always*. When there are competing unconditioned motivating operations at work, the choice of one reinforcer over the other depends either on (a) the *matching theory* (described above) or (b) the probability of avoidance/escape; let's consider the latter. Sarah's addiction to nonprescriptive Adderall for its stimulant effects helps her cram for college tests. She enjoys the autonomic arousal to increase her focus, information retention, and the high energy that allows her to be socially assertive. When she feels sleepy, labile, or bored, she ingests the Adderall for rapid onset alertness and the internal effusiveness with which she feels productive. However, lately, on the weekends, she also smoked 1–2 joints (marijuana) on Saturday and Sunday to socialize with her friends. Sarah did not realize cannabis blunts the effects of Adderall, lowering the amount of stimulation she expected. She then took more Adderall to achieve the desired drug effects and was surprised how she felt when the marijuana wore off. Effects of the Adderall were more noticeable, doubled in intensity, and caused her uncontrolled anxiety bordering on panic attacks. She became frightened and immediately ceased taking the Adderall. *She avoided and escaped from the sensory anxiety (panic) produced by Adderall despite her body previously craving Adderall when she felt low energy or boredom*. Altering the physically addictive effects of a drug by diluting the effect with unpleasant or noxious stimulation is not always accidental, as in the case of Sarah. It can be deliberately done such as in the well-researched relapse prevention method called *aversion conditioning* (Fralwey and Howard, 2009).

## Functional response properties

Responses involve what people do and how they behave after cues occur. In both cases, responses vary by their topography and function. Topography refers to the shape, form, or movement of behavior in space and time. An example is anxiety. Topography asks: (a) how many times does the behavior occur (frequency); (b) how long does each behavior last (duration); (c) how intense is the anxiety (magnitude/intensity)? Function of behavior describes how the behavior impacts the environment: (a) what events caused the anxiety (cues); (b) what effect did anxiety cause upon others around the person (outcomes); and (c) is the anxiety a recurrent or one-time problem? Using "topography" is like reading a map. Reactions further divide into two types of patterns: simultaneous (concurrent) response patterns, and sequential response patterns (Delprato, 1986; Delprato & McGlynn, 1988; Ray & Delprato, 1989).

### Simultaneous (concurrent) response patterns

Responding never occurs in isolation. It occurs instead in connection to other responses. Behavior is like a constellation of stars all strung together, so that changes in one behavior have specific or broad effects upon linked behaviors. One constellation is called simultaneous or "concurrent" response patterns (Lyon, 1982), involving two or more behaviors that occur simultaneously. Anxiety, for example, consists of many simultaneous behaviors. These include respiratory elevation, increased glandular secretions, increased muscular contractions, and private, self-defeating thoughts. Patterns interconnected can be mutually reinforcing, evocative, or elicitive. Respiratory elevation, for example, may elicit glandular secretion due to stimulation of the adrenal glands. Activation of the endocrine system releasing hormones, among them, noradrenaline (adrenaline), also may have an evocative function. It may trigger increased negative or self-debasing statements spiraling a person into panic. This spiral of panic reinforces both the labeling of the adrenaline sensations as "anxiety," and progression into a fury of negative self-statements.

### Sequential response patterns

A response sequence is a series of linked behaviors like a row of dominos. Knocking one will tumble the rest in the chain. This means that removal of one response in the sequence will directly affect the remaining behaviors. Fear follows sequential response patterns. For example, a rapid heart-beat (tachycardia) sweaty palms, and dizziness nearly always increase action, usually by avoiding or escaping the fearful situation (Reiss, 1987). Or, fear can immobilize the person; in which case, sequential response patterns might consist of silence, withdrawal (retreat), and indifference. Response sequential analysis is particularly germane to the evolution of addictive behaviors. In alcohol use, for example, onset of drinking typically is not confined to the temporal unit or time period during which the person imbibes. Segments of behaviors linked by a common thread, namely, the motivating operation, spread out across several hours and entail discrete actions leading up to the eclipse of weekend drinking. For example, for college students who go tail-gating before Saturday football games, plans for the beer drinking pre-exist several hours or days before tail-gating commences. Students may coordinate who buys the beer and snacks, who drives the vehicles, and who is the Facebook wizard sending out group invitations to the tail-gating. Each of these steps are recurrent segments forming and strengthening the behaviors of a response constellation, the interruption of any particular one may have consequences for the individual's drinking (or interbehavioral) potential. If Bill, for example, buys the beer and plans the tailgating but gets the flu on Friday night (before tailgating Saturday), his illness interrupts part of the chain precluding drinking. Similarly, in behavioral forensic assessment, response sequential analysis can prove invaluable in chronicling precipitant behaviors to a crime, the criminal chain of events itself, and chain of behavioral events following the crime.

Other properties defining the structure of responses include:

*Rate* defines the speed of responses. For example, the burglary occurred between 1:00 a.m. and 1:30 a.m. Thirty-minutes was the time frame for sequential or chained responses from entering the store, breaking into the cash register, and leaving the store. The shorter the time, the more likely responses (a) were well-established (i.e., crime has been done before), (b) occurred with precision (were rehearsed), (c) encountered few obstacles, and (d) were executed by one versus several suspects.

*Latency* refers to a time lapse between some precipitating stimulus and onset of first response in the sequence of responses within a psychological or field segment. The store closed that evening only for 10 min, for example, before robbers broke in and stole the money. Shorter latency might implicate (a) pre-existing familiarity with the store and location of money (i.e., an inside job), (b) motivational operating conditions, either intentional or unintentional, accelerating onset of responses. Thieve, for example, entered the store rapidly under a limited hold of knowing the alarm activates within 30 min of store closing. They wanted to complete the job undetected before he alarm was set.

*Frequency* is a measure of number of response occurrences. For example, the offender was a habitual sexual offender committing 10 acts of child molestation within the last 5 years. Here, response recurrence offers not only a gauge of *how many crimes of the same type, but also the severity of unmanaged urges compelling the sexual offense.* Ten acts of sexual molestation spread out over 10 years, on the other hand, may still fall within the statutes of limitations in a particular state, but may mean *the suspect's motivation or proclivity for crime was less intense and even reduced as time passed.*

*Duration* is a measure of response time from onset to offset or *termination* of the response. In behavioral forensics, duration can be a reliable predictor in perpetration of domestic violence. For instance, the female suspect punched, slugged, and kicked the victim for 10 min. Then, after a 3 min pause to smoke a cigarette, returned to the beating for 5 min until the victim went into a coma. Duration speaks to several properties about the response such as *response strength (history or strong repertoire of response), response discrimination (only occurring for this situation), and sequential response patterns (inter-response connections serving as cue and reinforcer for responses preceding and following other responses).* In the latter case of response patterns, the order of responses from kicking to punching involved the victim bleeding. Once bleeding appeared, that visual stimuli evoked a faster and more intense emission of beating behavior by the suspect.

*Intensity* is a measure of magnitude or strength of the response. In the above example of domestic abuse, rougher hitting after the victim bled possibly involved (a) more rapid punches delivered, (b) impact intensity of punches was stronger, and (c) hitting intensity possibly combined with collateral or other aggressive behaviors with similar force. *Inter-response time (IRT)* is the time elapsed between responses in a sequential response pattern. In the above example of domestic violence, interruptions of the beating to smoke a cigarette *slows down the IRT*. A slower IRT usually implicates several other possible variables operating in the psychological segment. First, there are less number and less intense motivating operations (other than urge to smoke the cigarettes). Second, concurrent or sequential responses may be tiring, difficult, or arouse other (physical or emotional) aversive consequences regarded as aversive by the organism. For example, each assault on the victim lasted 3 min before the suspect took a cigarette break. The 3 min of punching aggravated a pre-existing arthritis in the knuckles causing severe pain for the suspect. The cigarette breaks also doubled as relief time to escape the excruciating pain and let he inflamed knuckles relax. By contrast, a faster IRT means rapidity and high frequency of response units, likely interdependent or functionally increasing through automatic reinforcement or self-stimulation (cf. Anger, 1956)

## Excesses/deficits

This is a twofold measurement. First, it measures how much or how little a response occurs relative to some stimulus conditions. In jail, for example, Marcus incurred five violation tickets in two months. The citations always occurred for talking back (disrespecting) to the corrections officers. If other inmates received similar numbers of citations, his amount appears normative. If the amount is way beyond the norm, his number of citations is excessive. If the average citation rate is 30 per month per each inmate, Marcus' low amount seems like a deficit.

Second, determination of whether this frequency is high (excess) or low (deficit) depends on the cultural matrix (e.g., Kantor, 1982). Kantor classified cultural values or norms into (1) idiosyncratic psychological values, (2) contingential psychological values, and (3) cultural psychological values (pp. 323–324). Idiosyncratic values are those satisfying the needs of the organism, such as talking politely to people to foster reciprocal kindness from listeners. "Thank you Sir," or "Yes, ma'am." Contingential values depend on the exigencies or needs of a moment requiring some tool or property of the environment with which to achieve the need. One takes an umbrella to protect from the rain. But so does one say, "Yes, Sir, or yes Ma'am" to acquire favorable responses (i.e., manding) from another person if living in Macon, Georgia. Similarly, cultural values describe institutional stimuli derived from the heritage from earlier periods of psychological contact with things and events. In Macon, Georgia, as with many places geographically in the south, customary linguistic practices are to address adults formidably with "Yes, Sir" and Yes, Ma'am." However, transplant that same person from Macon, Georgia, to Lansing, Michigan, and the cultural linguistic norms deviate drastically and may even backfire aversively. For example, in a high school classroom in Lansing, a young 16 year old recently relocated from Charlotte, North Carolina to Lansing greeted her 30-year old teacher with "Yes, Ma'am." The teacher took offense and openly scolded the child for insulting her, treating her like an old woman by calling her "Ma'am." Here, the adolescent's response was normal for one culture but regarded as an excess for another culture.

*Predictive Response Patterns (interbehavioral potentials)* is a way to speak mathematically or probabilistically about the future likelihood of some behavior. Ruben (1983) first functionally described interbehavioral potentials as "a nonmetric predictive measure of probability regarding the chance that some behavior may bring about changes in the environment (p. 457). They are confrontable, tangible behaviors about which some history (in our case, criminally) shows a very high risk of recidivism. Janet, a domestically violent, adult offender, slugged her boyfriend in the middle of a grocery store when she found out he was unfaithful. She often hits whenever she is jealous or thinks he lied to her about women. But Janet began hitting people in elementary school, which continued through high school. She over-reacted to anybody misinterpreting her actions or for whom she felt was disloyal to her. Four times arrested as a juvenile for assault, and five times arrested for adult domestic violence, her tirades escalated quickly and violently. Faced with a new boyfriend's unfaithfulness, one could estimate she had a *high interbehavioral potential to commit domestic abuse with that new boyfriend.*

*Implicit response interactions* are responses that involve an absent stimulus object, and both the organism's participation or the participation of the substitute stimulus function can be subtle or invisible (Delprato, 2008; Kantor, 1976). "Thinking," hypothetically, might fit this characterization. It is a mediated activity in that an inapparent response (thought) occurs without surrounding events cuing the thoughts. Given that any psychological field always involves stimulus-response interactions, the explanation offered for an absent stimulus is that there is a *substitute stimulus.* Substitute stimuli resemble the operational definition given earlier for Skinner's analysis (1957) of stimuli for verbal behavior; this consisted of generic, metaphorical, and metonymical types. The latter two types present some relevant but mostly irrelevant properties under which verbal responses occur. The irrelevant properties of stimuli are analogous to Kantor's concept of *inapparent, subtle, or invisible cues.* Confusion naturally arises, then, when implicit responses are responsible for organsimic action for which no immediate traceable stimuli can be found in the environment. For example, Jack overate food every day after work, claiming his work made him hungry. Hunger pangs (i.e., gustatory sensations from food deprivation) seemed an obvious reason for his eating, but not an obvious causal analysis for overeating. Variables considered were motivational operations, behavior repertoire history (reactional biography), and implicit series of responses. Jack's history of previous work was during incarceration, when he finished a job followed by eating very small portions of food for dinner. He constantly felt food deprived, associated with anxiety about losing too much weight (emaciation) or growing sick from starvation. Now, after work in the civilian world, he *becomes famished and urgently overeats food. He responds to metaphorical stimuli (gustatory receptors fooling him of being hungry) reminiscent of his food deprivation in jail.* The excessive eating functions as implicit responses.

*Response induction* is a process through which a response changes its frequency, rate (or some probability) due to associating with another response which also changed its probability of rate, frequency, or other properties. Simultaneous or concurrent responses patterns are notorious for this untoward effect. For example, Mark fully intended on making love to Lucinda until Lucinda, inebriated at the time, unloaded on Mark about his uselessness, impotence, and her multiple affairs with better lovers than Mark. Mark's overtures to lovemaking ceased abruptly (due to positive punishment), and so did his patience of withholding any faults or comments to Luncida. Both responses were interdependent, such that when lovemaking initiatives ended, so did his quiet tolerance about Lucinda's comments. Mark shifted from passively timid and self-restrained to loudly belligerent, and blaming; he escalated a fight with Lucinda, which resulted in him murdering her by strangulation. Response induction becomes the scientific smoking gun to help explain how two or more responses linked in a sequential chain deviated so quickly.

*Adjunctive (collateral) responses* are sequentially or concurrently related responses or other responses contingently available in the psychological field; they are influenced by consequences for some other organismic response. *Adjunctive means it is tagged onto or adjoins another reinforced behavior due to contiguity or proximity.* An employee in a telephone call-in-center for passports, for example, is scolded verbally for spending too much time (over 8 min) on the phone troubleshooting the customer's concerns. Corrective action included steps to shorten the call (a) eliminating words, (b) eliminating empathy, and (c) fast-tracking solutions. Collateral responses, not directly taught in the corrective action, but associated with shortening calls include (1) bluntness, (b) interrupting customers, (c) ignoring customer requests, (d) callousness or coldness, and (e) anger when customers talk too long. Trainers of corrective action, in other words, had no idea they were fostering aggressive customer service in employees by reducing the rate and duration of answered calls.

Adjunctive behaviors in retail fraud is even more conspicuous. Gary frequently stole merchandise from a department store. After stealing the clothing, he sold it for a profit in his "store." His store is a boutique or tailor-made request service where customers request an item, and he sells it to them for a higher price than sold in the store. After Gary gets an order, he plans out his sequential steps of the theft including getaway exists in the store should he get caught. *He also observes the stores at different hours of the day to determine less traffic flow. He goes in for practice-runs, finds the merchandise, and rehearses exactly how to discretely remove the item to avert security cameras or in-store detectives.* These practices of rehearsal and checking the store at different hours are adjunctive behaviors, since they relate to but are not operationally definable in the stepwise series of committing the actual retail fraud.

*Response generalization* is spontaneous or taught variations of response strength in the presence of stimuli under which the original response occurred. A simple case is a child taught to say "good-bye" to his mother when she leaves him at daycare and two days later says, "Hope to see you soon, I'll be okay." Expansion of his first response from "good-bye" to "hope to see you soon," shows the response generalizing. Such intraverbal behavior is also significant in collecting witness testimony from suspects after they have given repeated testimony to the arresting police, the state forensic evaluator, and their attorneys. Each class of responses occurs in front of slightly different stimulus conditions, although the inquiry prompt is the exactly same, "What happened on the night of July 4th, 2007?" However, testimonial bias can occur in the form of under-reporting (elliptical), over-reporting (hyperbole), or by inventing data (fabricating, malingering). A misleading testimony can mand (enjoin) the listener to respond effectively, such as persuading the defendant attorney to drop the charges or bargain to a lesser charge. Response generalization, in this case, *was not taught, did occur spontaneously, and was a variation of response strength in front of the original or very similar stimuli; however, content of the response altered significantly depending on the motivating operations.*

## Forensic behavior assessment

The exigency for behavioral forensic assessment is to increase precision and predictability of offender/suspect's behavior based on a functional analysis of pre-criminal, criminal, and post-criminal behaviors. After reviewing the case of a woman flinching in a test-exam room during a psychological evaluation, the first analysis given was a traditional, intrapsychic, or "mentalistic" profile, featuring aspects inside the suspect, such as her personality, that might account for the phenomena observed during the interview. Followed was a glossary of behavioral concepts and principles most likely retrieved to translate the same phenomenon into, not just behavioral language, but into a more scientific perspective more easily understood by prosecution and the defense. Below is a table (see Table 1.1) showing a behavioral concept or principle relevant to the case. Across from the concept or principle is the translation of behavior patterns from the case into functional or operational analysis.

The foregoing chart captures the mindset of a behavioral forensic examiner ordered to conduct psychological evaluations on criminal suspects. They are scientists, first–examiners of facts and interpreters of multicausal interactions across the psychological field continuum. The case of the women charged with Assault with Intent to Commit Bodily Harm was a snapshot of transactional events across not only behavior segments of the crime itself, but also of behavior segments that occurred *during the clinical interview and evaluation.* Her unusual reaction to the external noise of male correction officers talking in a low voice provided a window into her reactional biography. Her multiple response sequences, repeated twice with two sets of correction officers, added validation to her claims of intrapartner domestic violence. It also provided a blueprint to systematically compute functional variables that were possibly causal in her pre-criminal and criminal behaviors.

Detection and measurement of these variables does not reflect on her guilt or innocence of the crime, since the investigation of culpability is left to detectives, prosecutors and defendant attorneys. If the preliminary hearing concludes the case goes to trial, adjudicators of her crime will be the judge and jury. The role of evaluator in jurisprudence clearly limits duties to determine the human psyche or mental capacity responsible for an offender's *commission of a crime.* But *how evaluators execute the job of assessing human psyche and mental capacity is what delineates the scientific from pseudo-scientific approach.* In behavioral forensics, and in performing behavioral forensic assessments, focus is never on human psyche and mental capacity. These terms are explanatory fictions departing from the underlying truths and concrete facts defining human behavior. Focus instead is on *natural* events. Natural events are concrete, confrontable, measurable, replicable, and conform to laws governing behavior. A morbid reminder to replace mentalism with empirical principles was a note that J.R. Kantor's daughter, Helene, found on Kantor's nightstand after his death in 1984. On the piece of paper was written the words, "No spirits, wraiths, hobgoblins, spooks, noumena, superstitions, transcendentals, mystics, invisible hands, supreme creator, angels, demons ..." (Fryling & Hayes, 2018). Kantor rejected these myths of traditional psychology. His legacy was to assure the study of behavior remained a natural and interdisciplinary science. Behavioral forensic assessment preserves this direction that Kantor, Skinner, and many of their disciples clearly have shepherded into a modern era of applied behavior analysis.

**TABLE 1.1** Sample demonstration of translating prisoner behaviors during a psychological evaluation into predictors of a functional analysis.

| Behavioral concept or principle | Translation of behavior patterns into functional or operational analysis |
|---|---|
| Behavior segment | Sitting in a transparent room with low noise insulation involving the Examiner asking questions of a female suspect. |
| Reaction system | Suspect attends, perceives, and engages in consummatory responses by facial expressions (subtle) and actual verbal vocal and written responses. Precurrent behaviors are suspect's eye contact gazing out the transparent windows, increased perspiration. |
| Reactional biography | Suspect's total history preceding, during, and after her marriage including reported and unreported incidents of domestic abuse paired with husband's drinking, her reactivity to abuse, her collateral or compensatory behaviors (getting angry, concessions to husband, cleaning up her injuries), and negative reinforcement history of avoiding abuse by withholding comments or submission to husband's spoken and unspoken (inferred) needs. |
| History of behavior (repertoire) | Suspect's recurrent passivity, submissiveness, and avoidance-escape behavior patterns around conflict including anticipatory anxiety over impending conflict. She never engaged in self-protective, self-defense behavior except to exit escape routes. |
| Verbal behavior | Engages in mands to enjoin her husband to walk away, not hurt her; engages in tacts to identify properties of nonverbal stimuli associated with or likely to evoke fears and anticipation of impending conflict; engages in autoclitic mands to correct herself (aloud). She constantly apologizes, and makes self-debasing statements. Her emotional conditioned response (of fear) occurs around *her husband anytime he approached her (generic extension).* Metaphorical extension is her fear around the low vocal intonation of two male correction officers talking outside the exam room. Metonymical extension is her fear response to male correction officers who largely showed irrelevant properties (not similar clothing, name, size or shape of husband). |
| Media of contact | Poor sound insulation, ample light to see correction officers, light and loose clothing to allow (not block) sensory (visceral) feedback to suspect. |
| Respondent conditioning | Conditioned stimulus of low-bass voice of correction officers eliciting arrhythmic breathing, visceral arousal, interruptive breathing, shoulder blade tremors, abrupt postural shifting, irregular coughing, and eyes-tearing (conditioned emotional response). Conditioned stimulus at one time was neutral stimulus (tone of voice) paired with unconditioned stimulus of physical assault causing muscular contractions and glandular secretions. Higher order conditioning occurred between low-bass voices (conditioned stimulus) paired with laughter (neutral stimulus), eliciting similar fear behaviors just from correction officers laughing. Husband's laughter likely was an antecedent stimulus preceding the battery of abuse. |
| Operant conditioning | Discriminative stimulus of low-bass voices sets occasion for viscerally driven avoidance and escape behaviors. When avoidance/escape behaviors were not possible (suspect locked inside an exam room), she increased sitting in an erect position and became hyperalert to her surrounds. Increased alertness momentarily reduced visceral or fear response (negative reinforcement). |

(Continued)

**TABLE 1.1** Sample demonstration of translating prisoner behaviors during a psychological evaluation into predictors of a functional analysis.—cont'd

| Behavioral concept or principle | Translation of behavior patterns into functional or operational analysis |
|---|---|
| Positive and negative reinforcement | Negative reinforcement seen in the increase of such sequential and concurrent responses as face turning pale, breath-holding, inhaling short-breaths, grasping for air, posture shifting, and leg cramping—all serving as avoidance and escape behaviors—to reduce, avert, or terminate aversiveness of impending violence expected from the low-bass voices of correction officers. History implicated of positive reinforcement for suspect's cumulatory response history of repeating (a) cowering, idleness, or submission when physically assaulted, and (b) verbally apologizing, accommodating her husband, and hiding injuries after assaulted. |
| Positive and negative punishment | Negative punishment observed in an abrupt deceleration of collateral behaviors from verbalizing to silence, smiles to frowns, and energy to hypo-energy, all toward averting, reducing, or eliminating the impending violence triggered by the low-bass voices. |
| Simple schedules of consequences | Husband's delivery of abuse was on variable interval and variable ratio schedules. Both produce a steady state of autonomic arousal (constant fear). The interval schedule also creates superstitious behaviors in suspect such as anticipatory caretaking or efforts to placate husband (her sitting erect in chair ready to respond). |
| Complex schedules of consequences | *Chained and tandem* schedules consists of emission of the multiple response sequences with one discriminative stimulus of the correction officers talking in low-bass voices. *Mixed* schedule occurred in two or more response sequences triggered either by presence of male correction officers, low-bass voices of correction officers, laughter of correction officers, and when first group of two male correction officers left. Schedule of fear arousal was intermixed and random. *Concurrent and multiple* schedules occurred by the simultaneous effects of positive reinforcement, negative reinforcement, and negative punishment (see above). *Conjunctive* schedule did not occur since the primary simple schedules in her natural environment were variable interval and variable ratio. Also, around the correction officers (in the exam room), she also responded on a variable interval/random schedule (her autonomic responses occurred non-contingently with the correction officers' behaviors). |
| Social exchange of reinforcement/punishment schedules | *The smaller the amount of rewards possessed by a person, the more he or she is likely to take resources away from others.* Suspect's reactional biography suggested a paucity of family or partner resources, and constant deprivation of thee resources contingent on the suspect's submission/compliance to her husband. *Exchange of punishers may occur by proximity and contiguity.* Self-history showed alcohol, husband's verbal tirades, and talking in low-bass voice all precipitating exchange (delivery) of punishers (abuse). *The simultaneous transmission of love and punishing resource decreases the value of both resources, or terminates its transmission.* Husband's offer of fondness or tenderness, coupled with verbal tirades, low-bass vocal statements, and alcohol aroused anxiety. His traumatic threats of assault numbed the receiver to idleness, immovability, emotional paralysis, helplessness, and state of hypervigilance (arrhythmic breathing, interruptive breathing, shoulder blade tremors, abrupt postural shifting, irregular coughing, eyes-tearing, etc.). *Taking away any resource (including love) produces a loss of love and produces punishers.* Proportionality of more punishers to love or husbands' removal of love eventually fostered resentment, anger, and interbehavioral potentials for self-defensiveness. Suspect explained she plunged the knife into her husband's upper right chest after unable to avoid/escape the situation, while husband's violence escalated. Unlike in the past, when escape routes were accessible, absence of a route now *increased the suspect's potential for maladaptive behaviors.* Noteworthy is the high probability of children or adults imitating the physical punishment on other people that was inflicted on them. |

| | |
|---|---|
| Motivational operations | Abative effects seen when suspect wishes to talk but remains silent to avoid/escape from aversive sound of male voices; Motivating operations were continuous in risk-reduction scenarios (opportunities) to respond with a limited hold, against several obstacles, under multiple contingencies, with a limited repertoire producing brief anxiety relief on a variable ratio or variable interval schedule. Abolishing operation pertains to suspect's history of mitigating husband's violence by accommodations. Or, if she altered his environment to delay or eliminate any patterns precurrent to violence such as hiding his alcohol. Reflexive conditioned motivating operations appeared at night or when he ranted. The rampages served as "warnings" preparing the suspect for impending violence and increased the urgency to engage in fear-inoculation behaviors (apologies, accommodations, escape from household). Transitive conditioned motivating operations (CMO-Ts) were also ongoing as abolishers or strengtheners of contiguous motivational operations. Husband's alcohol use during the daytime, rather than at night, was less likely to produce violence (at the moment) and provided an opportunity for suspect to deter or eliminate night-time drinking, which did produce aggression. Also, during physical battery, the injured suspect remained quiet and silent, producing a new motivational operation for her husband, competing with his delivery of abuse. Abolishing effect was that he walked away. Surrogate conditioned motivating operations (CMO-Ss) involved her pairing two or more motivating operations in temporal sequence either preceding, during, or after the abuse. Husband's low-bass voice (during tirades) established one operation (for avoidance behavior); his onset of drinking established another operation (for avoidance); her husband seeing her injured produced still a third operation. Occurrence of any of these operations, together or alone, with short or long time intervals between each stimulus condition, was likely to evoke the same sequential response pattern in the suspect. Unconditioned Motivating Operations refer to the biological response of pain, unconsciousness (near-fainting), tearfulness or other sympathetic nervous system reactions after infliction of bodily injury. Pain can induce either paralysis or rapid-onset aggression. This suspect likely emitted paralysis to avoid/escape further physical beatings. |
| Simultaneous (concurrent) response patterns | Concurrent response patterns included the suspect's chain of obstructive breathing, crying, suppression of verbal behavior, sitting erect, cramped muscles, and shoulder blades quivering (tremors). |
| Sequential response patterns | Sequential response patterns, while similar to the list of aforementioned responses, also included autonomic responses followed by stating she felt terror, and stating the low-bass voices sounded like her husband's voice. |
| Rule governed behavior | Rule governed behaviors were any self-statements in response to being asked about the two sets of correction officers talking in low-bass voices. Self-talk about the officers' voices is shorter, and truncated from the longer version describing punishment contingencies. The longer version of punishing contingencies, hypothetically, entailed her recollection of the cycle consisting of (a) antecedent drinking over some period of time, (b) progression of verbal and physical response escalation, (c) delivery of violence on her, and (d) violence reduction after her injury (e.g., bleeding) was evident. She now abbreviates this entire sequence of events and its adverse impact using the rule-governed phrase, "he drinks and gets violent." |

(Continued)

**TABLE 1.1** Sample demonstration of translating prisoner behaviors during a psychological evaluation into predictors of a functional analysis.—cont'd

| Behavioral concept or principle | Translation of behavior patterns into functional or operational analysis |
|---|---|
| Response rate | Vital signs observed in increased respiratory rate, arrhythmic breathing including deep breaths; increases in throat-clearing coughs, abrupt postural shifts into erect position, eyes-tearing, held breath, turned pale, and muscular cramps. |
| Response frequency | Respondent and operant response units recurred twice in sequence elicited/evoked from identical stimulus conditions of two male correction officers talking and laughing outside of the exam room. |
| Response intensity | Elevation of response magnitude observed for 1–2 min while the two male correction officers' voices were in background. Suspect inhaled more deeply, cried more intensely, coughed louder and repeated throat-clearing spaced only 2–3 s apart, while holding her breath twice to three times during the 1–2 min duration of the entire response sequence. |
| Inter-response time | Time observed (recorded) in between chained or sequential responses or between aggregates of concurrent responses was 1–2 s. Her fluid pace rapidly moved from one response to another, without pause or return to calmness. Faster IRTs suggest response interdependence, concurrence, or duel role as cue and reinforcer. For example, autonomic arousal co-exists with coughing and throat-clearing, which also triggers crying and sitting erect in her chair. Her last behavior in the sequence, that of sitting, temporarily relieves (negatively reinforces) anxiety and conditions the entire chain of autonomic responses. Faster IRT's also implicate continuous contact with impacting contingencies and multiple motivating operations. |
| Response duration | Length of each response unit and response chains in any behavior segment varied from 30 s to 1 min. Time variability was due to response permutations; she did not display the exact (ritualistic) order of chained or singular responses each time. By changing the order of responses in the chain, with each response doubling as reinforcer and antecedent (for previous and new responses, respectively), durations also changed across the response sequence. However, the longer the duration, the higher the number and more complex the aggregate of responses. Longer response duration also appears a function of longer exposure time to punishment contingencies. Meaning, she has to emit more behaviors to survive (adapt to) the beatings. |
| Latency | Elapsed time between onset of correction officers' talking and suspect's first autonomic response was less than 2 s. Elapsed time of 20 s occurred, however, between termination of bass-sounding voices and the suspect ending her autonomic responses. This 20-s (slower) delay suggests the suspect has (a) a history of anticipatory arousal that similar voice sounds may recur instantly or sporadically, and (b) self-stimulatory or self-reinforcing functions. Such self-stimulatory (self-reinforcing) functions might include (1) negative rule-governed behaviors (i.e., fear-induced self-statements), and (2) adventitious (accidental) negative reinforcement from removal of anxiety after she completes a ritual chain of fear-behaviors (e.g., cough excessively, cry, breath irregularly, and sit up in chair). |

| | |
|---|---|
| Excess-deficit | Behavior excesses observed in the suspect included her multiple response concurrence and sequence of autonomic (and somatic responses). Her deficits were verbal inabilities to describe her anxiety while it occurred (i.e., to engage in autoclitic verbal behavior). High frequency of autonomic responses often correlates with deficits in assertiveness, communication, or even in anger expression. One hypothetical functional analysis might be that she lacked an effective verbal repertoire to counter her husband's physical and verbal abuse. |
| Interbehavioral potentials | The suspect showed a high probability of repeating same or similar response sequences under same or similar conditions. The *interbehavioral* parameters include a likelihood this response sequence transacted across a field of psychological events in many behavior segments involving her husband's physical and verbal abuse. The strength of her repeating this behavior, given the right cues, appears unabated by any competing learning or set of skills. |
| Implicit response interactions | The suspect showed evidence of implicit response occurrence in her continuing autonomic responses for 20 s after offset of the low-bass-sounding noises. Implicit responses occurred despite absent stimuli and no apparent correspondence to metaphorical or metonymical stimuli. After 20 s elapsed, she resumed normal intraverbal exchanges observed during baseline conversation (i.e., before the first two correction officers were talking). |
| Superstitious behaviors | The suspect's entire response class of autonomic reactions are artifacts produced by adventitious (accidental) conditioning. Her reactions formed like phobias to neutral objects that become terrifying objects. The low-bass voice of her husband, years ago when she first met him, probably did not evoke autonomic responses. She probably paid no attention to his natural modulation of voice tones. However, when he drank, alcohol dried the vocal chords and without proper lubrication, his voice worked poorly or swelled up; it sounded lower, like he had a cold. That low-bass voice (a neutral stimulus) *was paired by accident* with the husband's volatility, eliciting the suspect's autonomic response and evoking tendencies for avoidance and escape. By the phenomenon of stimulus generalization (i.e., metaphorical extension), the suspect responded to vocal cues (in the correction officers) having nearly the same or very similar relevant properties as the original cues first triggering her phobic behaviors. Higher-order conditioning of superstitious behavior is also very likely. Here, the suspect might associate elicitive properties of low-bass voices in *men and women, across different races or ethnicities, and across settings atypical for fear*. For example, suppose the suspect attends a church service during Christmas eve and listens to a coed choir singing holiday music. One song involves a bass solo of *Ave Maria*. Hearing the solo, she panics with autonomic arousal, and suddenly motions to leave the church. |
| Response induction | Her class of visceral responses may be all linked to the same contingency or diversely spread across different contingencies. If alternative contingencies affect response strength of one or more of the chained responses, it may induce broad or specific effects in responses unconnected to those alternative contingencies. For example, suppose the suspect engaged in arrhythmic breathing, paleness, tearfulness, and excessive coughing when both male correction officer (in low voices) were talking. When they were gone, she breathed normally, was energetic, and talked at an uninterrupted pace. Now, say, she overhears two female correction officers talking and laughing, in alto-soprano range of pitch. The suspect says, "those woman are rude and should be quieter for us to concentrate in this exam room." Ten minutes later, another two male correction officers begin talking in low −bass voices outside the room. The suspect *now verbally says aloud, "Those men are rude and should be quieter for us to concentrate in this exam room."* Her new responses evoked by a different contingency (the women) gained strength and transferred to another contingency (the men). |

*(Continued)*

**TABLE 1.1** Sample demonstration of translating prisoner behaviors during a psychological evaluation into predictors of a functional analysis.—cont'd

| Behavioral concept or principle | Translation of behavior patterns into functional or operational analysis |
|---|---|
| Adjunctive responses | Adjunctive behaviors are common in fear-induced or obsessive-compulsive behaviors. One class of behaviors already occurs. Each response in that class may adjoin or be tagged by a subsidiary response affected by the same contingencies. When the suspect coughs excessively, for example, she hurts her chest muscles causing pain and chest tremors (sensations). This quivering sensation and pain quickly permeated down her arms, legs, chest, and into her abdomen. Subsequently, she now finds when she coughs excessively (anticipating physical abuse), she also gets a jolt of consecutive spasms (tremors) and pain in her lower torso. These adjunctive responses all conform to the same contingencies initially controlling her coughing (and other autonomic responses). |
| Response generalization | One example of response generalization was shown above with adjunctive responses. The suspect also showed several response variations of fear, mostly all from the peripheral nervous system. A reasonable functional hypothesis is that, when physical beatings first began, the suspect suffered one or possibly two autonomic reactions as long as she could avoid or escape the aversive situation. As beatings intensified in frequency and intensity (severity) to 1 h, the contingencies seemed unavoidable and inescapable for longer periods of time. This delay of escape formed longer durations of, and more complex (integrated) response chains to adapt to pain and to survive the 1-h ordeal. Her *adaptation* involved generating new (adjunctive) behaviors. These autonomic behaviors included faster respiration, rapid breathing (before hyperventilation), and hypervigilance (fight or flight response). |

## References


Altier, D. T., & Ruben, D. H. (1984). The real events of anorexia nervosa. In *Readings in anorexia nervosa and eating disorders* (pp. 39–41). Guilford, CT: Special Leaning Corporation.

American Psychiatric Association. (2013). *Diagnostic and statistical manual of mental disorder.* Arlington, VA: American Psychiatric Association.

Anger, D. (1956). The dependence of interresponse times upon the relative reinforcement of different interresponse times. *Journal of Experimental Psychology, 52*, 145–161.

Bartol, C., & Bartol, A. (2012). *Criminal and behavioral profiling.* NY: Sage.

Baum, W. (2018). Three laws of behavior: Allocation, induction, and covariance. *Behavior Analysis: Research and Practice, 18*, 239–251.

Bolles, R. C. (1972). Reinforcement expectancy and learning. *Psychological Review, 79*, 394–409.

Braukmann, C. J., Fixsen, D. L., Phillips, E. L., & Wolf, M. (1975). Behavioral approaches in the crime and delinquency field. *Criminology, 13*, 299-231.

Cone, J. D., & Hawkins, R. P. (Eds.). (1977). *Behavioral assessment: New directions in clinical psychology.* NY: Brunner/Mazel.

Crosbie, J. (1998). Negative reinforcement and punishment. In K. A. Lattal, & M. Perone (Eds.), *Handbook of human operant behavior research methods* (pp. 163–189). NY: Plenum.

Delprato, D. J. (1980). The reactional biography concept: Early contribution to a perspective for the psychology of aging. *Human Development, 23*, 314–322.

Delprato, D. J. (1986). Response patterns. In H. W. Reese, & L. J. Parrott (Eds.), *Behavior science: Philosophical, methodological, and empirical advances* (pp. 61–113). Hillsdale, NJ: Lawrence Erlbaum Associates.

Delprato, D. J. (2008). Book review: Mind and its evolution: A dual coding theoretical approach. *The Psychological Record, 59*, 295–300.

Delprato, D. J., & McGlynn, F. D. (1988). Interactions of response patterns and their implications for behavior therapy. *Journal of Behavior Therapy and Experimental Psychiatry, 19*, 199–205.

Downs, D. A. (1996). *More than victims: Battered women, the syndrome society, and the law.* Chicago, IL: University of Chicago Press.

Edens, J. F., & Boccaccini, M. T. (2017). Taking forensic mental health assessment "out of the lab" and into the "real world." *Psychological Assessment, 29*, 599–610.

Everstine, L., & Everstine, D. S. (1986). *Psychotherapy and the law.* NY: Grune & Stratton Inc.

Foa, U., & Foa, E. (1974). *Societal structures of the mind.* IL: Charles Thomas.

Foa, E., & Foa, U. (1980). Resource theory: Interpersonal behavior as exchange. In T. Gergen, S. Greenberg, & R. Willis (Eds.), *Social exchange: Advances in theory and research* (pp. 77–94). NY: Plenum.

Fralwey, P. J., & Howard, M. O. (2009). Aversion therapies. In K. Richard, D. A. Fiellin, S. C. Miller, & R. Saitz (Eds.), *Principles of addiction medicine* (4th ed., pp. 843–844). Philadelphia: Lippincott, Williams and Wilkins.

Fryling, M. J., & Hayes, L. J. (2018). J.R. Kantor and behavior analysis. *Conductual, 6*, 86–94.

Hayes, S. (2004). *Rule-governed behavior: Cognition, contingencies, and instructional control.* Las Vegas, NV: Context Press.

Hayes, L., & Chase, P. N. (Eds.). (1991). *Dialogues on verbal behavior.* Reno, NV: Context Press.

Herrnstein, R. J. (1961). Relative and absolute strength of responses as a function of frequency of reinforcement. *Journal of the Experimental Analysis of Behavior, 4*, 267–272.

Herrnstein, R. J. (1970). On the law of effect. *Journal of the Experimental Analysis of Behavior, 13*, 243–266.

Hersen, M., & Bellack, A. S. (1981). *Behavioral assessment: A practical handbook.* NY: Pergamon Press.

Horne, P. J., & Lowe, C. F. (1993). Determinants of human performance on concurrent schedules. *Journal of the Experimental Analysis of Behavior, 59*, 29–60.

Iwata, B. A., Smith, R. G., & Michael, J. (2000). Current research on the influence of establishing operations on behavior in applied settings. *Journal of Applied Behavior Analysis, 33*, 411–418.

Kantor, J. R. (1922). Memory: A triphase objective action. *Journal of Philosophy*, 624–639.

Kantor, J. R. (1959). *Interbehavioral psychology.* Granville, OH: Principia Press.

Kantor, J. R. (1976). Cognition as events and as psychic constructions. *Psychological Record, 28*, 329–342.

Kantor, J. R. (1982). *Cultural psychology.* Chicago, IL: Principia Press.

Kazdin, A. E. (1994). Models of dysfunction in developmental psychopathology. *Clinical Psychology: Science and Practice, 1*, 35–52.

Kazdin, A. E. (1995). Child, parent and family dysfunction as predictors of outcome in cognitive-behavioral treatment of antisocial children. *Behaviour Research and Therapy, 33*, 271–283.

Keller, F. S., & Schoenfeld, W. N. (1950). *Principles of psychology*. E. Norwalk: Appleton-Century-Crofts.

Langthorne, P., & McGill, P. (2009). A tutorial on the concept of motivating operation and its importance to application. *Behavior Analyst in Practice, 2*, 22–31.

Lyon, D. O. (1982). Concurrent behavior: Are the interpretations mutually exclusive? *The Behavior Analyst, 5*, 175–187.

Matson, J. L., & DiLorenzo, T. M. (1984). *Punishment and its alternatives*. NY: Springer.

McGill, P. (1999). Establishing operations: Implications for the assessment, treatment, and prevention of problem behavior. *Journal of Applied Behavior Analysis, 32*, 393–418.

Mcleod, B. D., Jensen-Doss, A., & Ollendick, T. H. (2013). *Diagnostic and behavioral assessment in children and adolescents*. NY: Guilford Press.

Michael, J. (1982a). Skinner's elementary verbal relations: Some new categories. *The Analysis of Verbal Behavior, 1*, 1–3.

Michael, J. (1982b). Distinguishing between discriminative and motivational functions of stimuli. *Journal of the Experimental Analysis of Behavior, 37*, 149–155.

Michael, J. (1988). Establishing operations and the mand. *The Analysis of Verbal Behavior, 6*, 3–9.

Michael, J. (1993). Establishing operations. *The Behavior Analyst, 16*, 191–206.

Miguel, C. F. (2013). Jack Michael's motivation. *The Analysis of Verbal Behavior, 29*, 3–11.

Moore, J. (1980). On behaviorism and private events. *The Psychological Record, 30*, 459–475.

Morris, E. K. (1980). Applied behavior analysis for criminal justice practice: Some current dimensions. *Criminal Justice and Behavior, 7*, 131–145.

Morris, E. K., & Braukmann, C. J. (Eds.). (1987). *Behavioral approaches to crime and delinquency: A handbook of application, research, and concepts*. CA: Springer.

Morris, E. K., Higgins, S. T., & Bickel, W. B. (1982). The influence of Kantor's interbehavioral psychology on behavior analysis. *The Behavior Analyst, 5*, 159–173.

Neitzel, M. (1979). *Crime and its modification: A social learning perspective*. NY: Pergamon Press.

Nosik, M. R., & Carr, J. E. (2015). On the distinction between the motivating operation and setting event concepts. *The Behavior Analyst, 38*, 219–223.

Poling, A., Edwards, T. L., Weeden, M., & Foster, T. (2011). The matching law. *Psychological Record, 61*(2), 313–322.

Ray, R., & Delprato, D. J. (1989). Behavioral systems analysis: Methodological strategies and tactics. *Behavioral Science, 34*, 81–127.

Rehfeldt, R. A., & Hayes, L. J. (1998). The operant-respondent distinction revisted: Toward an understanding of stimulus equivalence. *Psychological Record, 48*, 187–210.

Reiss, S. (1987). Theoretical perspectives on the fear of anxiety. *Clinical Psychology Review, 7*, 585–596.

Rescorla, R. (1988). Pavlovian conditioning: It's not what you think. *American Psychologist, 43*, 151–160.

Ruben, D. H. (1983). Interbehavioral implications for behavior therapy: Clinical perspectives. In N. W. Smith, P. T. Mountjoy, & D. H. Ruben (Eds.), *Reassessment in psychology: The interbehavioral alternative* (pp. 445–469). Washington, D.C.: University Press of America.

Ruben, D. H. (1984). Major trends in interbehavioral psychology from articles published in the psychological record. *The Psychological Record, 34*, 589–617.

Ruben, D. H. (1987). Epilogue: Science, myth, and magic...and then what? In J. Hagelthorn, & M. J. Ruben (Eds.), *I've never told anyone but...exploring the hidden reality of natural events* (pp. 157–161). Lincoln, NE: Media Publishing.

Ruben, D. H. (1992). Behavioral systems approach. In C. Stout, J. Levitt, & D. H. Ruben (Eds.), *Handbook for assessing and treating addictive disorders* (pp. 3–24). Westport, CT: Greenwood Press.

Ruben, D. H. (1998). Social exchange theory: Dynamics of a system governing the dysfunctional family and guide to assessment. *Journal of Contemporary Psychotherapy, 28*, 307–325.

Ruben, D. H. (2001). *Treating adult children of alcoholics: A behavioral approach*. NY: Academic Press.

Ruben, D. H. (1988). Private events revisted: Does unobservable mean private? *Journal of Contemporary Psychotherapy, 18*, 16–27.

Rutter, M. (1980). The long-term effects of early experience. *Developmental Medicine and Child Neurology, 22*, 800–815.

Sautter, R. A., & LeBlanc, L. A. (2002). Empirical applications of Skinner's analysis of verbal behavior with humans. *The Analysis of Verbal Behavior, 22*, 35–48.

Skinner, B. F. (1953). *Science and human behavior*. NY: the Free Press.

Skinner, B. F. (1957). *Verbal behavior*. Cambridge, MA: Prentice-Hall.

Skinner, B. F. (1974). *About behaviorism*. NY: Alfred Knopf Publishers.
Stone, A. (1975). *Mental health and law: A system in transition*. Washington, DC: US Dept of Health, Education & Welfare.
Sundberg, M. L., & Partington, J. W. (1983). Skinner's verbal behavior: An update of the reference list. *Verbal Behavior News, 2*, 10–13.
Thomas, C. A., & Frasier, J. (2005). The effects of establishing operations on functional analyses conditions. *Journal of Early and Intensive Behavior Intervention, 2*, 74–78.
Turvey, B. (2012). *Criminal and behavioral profiling*. NY: Sage Publications.
Vargas, E. (1982). Intraverbal behavior: The Codic, duplic, and sequelic subtypes. *The Analysis of Verbal Behavior, 1*, 5–7.

CHAPTER

# 2

# The paradigm shift from traditional models to behavioral forensic model of forensic psychological assessment

Calls for unity within any scientific discipline typically come after a history of separationism, isolationism, and provincialism. Separationism is the radical departure from the mother-ship or charter paradigm in which basic concepts and principles formed a movement and recruitment of loyalists, many being researchers eager to revolutionize some antiquated system. Once they branch off into independent franchises, some borrowing tenets of the charter foundation, while others creating new foundations, leaders assemble in private, hiding their newly developed system. They fear infiltration from rival factions, who also defected from the charter paradigm group, and seek to preserve novelty of their individualist efforts. Inside their faction they grow exponentially and believe their insightful contributions are precocious, invaluable. Outside of their faction, with some exception, they seem strange, cannot relate to other burgeoning factions, and view these rivals as naïve, primitive, lacking forethought, and regressing. Insularity replaces interdisciplinary. The group isolates itself from threats of criticism, intrusion, and merger with other factions it once shared ideas with. In its microcosm, creativity continues to flourish with remarkable efficiency and industry using only the concepts, principles, and ground-breaking research endemic to its provincial mind-set. Upset that other factions may triumph with greater public notoriety, the group dismisses this positive reputation by downplaying the legitimacy of rival organizations and invalidating their research through meticulously scathing reviews. Demonization of rival factions is the mainstream approach, while the group arrogantly galvanizes its own base membership by claiming unimpeachable uniqueness in their role in society. They unabashedly idealize their philosophical ideas as superior to all other systems and revel in their self-efficacy. But once this group reaches its zenith of self-importance, and different members believe they deserve credit for this quantum achievement, resentment inherently grows like a contagion. All the members view self as authorities and are less inclined to subscribe to the communal beliefs once motivating the group's annexation from the mother-ship. Anarchy rises among dissenting leaders who feel their role in research went unappreciated. Not surprisingly,

*Behavioral Forensics*
https://doi.org/10.1016/B978-0-12-819805-6.00002-6

they imagine a fertile land outside of the faction to plant their own crop of ideas, and contemplate separation from the polarizing group they once felt security in.

This cycle in the evolution of scientific systems was articulated so brilliantly by philosopher Thomas Kuhn (1962). He viewed progress as "development-by-accumulation" as anomalies in revolutions prompted new paradigms that replaced old paradigms. Normal science, insisted Kuhn, proceeds by working out the unsolved problems posed by the paradigm. But when factions internally riot and stall resolutions of anomalies, while its members vie for individual recognition, the system implodes and from the rubble emerges growth of new scientific ideas promising even better innovations for society (cf. Lundin, 1985; Marx & Hillix, 1963). A similar revolutionary cycle progressed through the venerable corridors of the first, second, and third generations of behavioral psychology. After J.B. Watson borrowed concepts and technology from Associationism (i.e., Thorndike, Ebbinghaus) and Classical Conditioning (Pavlov), offering a methodological slant, Skinner and his disciples advanced the science of behavior using operant conditioning, calling it a more "radical behavioral approach" (Schneider & Morris, 1987; Skinner, 1974). Concurrent with Kantor's field system theory called "interbehaviorism," the momentum increased to broaden the scope of theory and practice in behavior analysis (Reese & Parrott, 1986). Undeterred by its cognitivist's opposition, the most formidable being Noam Chomsky's assailment of Skinner's *Verbal Behavior* (Chomsky, 1959, 1967), the second generation yielded a third generation of behaviorism, unofficially claimed by Staats, called *psychological (social) behaviorism* (e.g., Staats, 1975, 1996a, 1996b). Staats' reason for calling for a unified science was in part responding to Skinner's complaint that, "psychology as a basic has failed has failed to supply a conception which recommends itself to specialists in other fields of human behavior" (1969, p. 96). Staats also sought convergence of mini-sciences lacking a common set of principles to apply across many boundaries of learning theory (cf. Holt, 2003).

Staats' self-proclaimed third generation is different from the *third wave of behavior therapy*. Hayes and Hoffman (2017) essentially argued for this third wave of behavioral methods (not necessarily applied behavior analysis techniques) focusing on the role of maladaptive thinking patterns in emotion and behavior. Supposedly this new wave era started 13 years ago, hailed by the use of contextual concepts centered on mindfulness, acceptance, value goals, and meta-cognition (Hayes, 2004). Contextual approaches are reminiscent of Eastern approaches to psychology and return a different spin on interpreting cognitive events. Contextual-type therapy may well reconcile the dualism between mentalists and behaviorists, and even service a clinical population more completely. But the contextualism Hayes speaks about is very different from the contextual field of events vividly revealed in Kantor's interbehaviorism; that context is a marriage between Tolman's field theory, William James' applied philosophy, Bentley's psychophysical philosophy, and Skinner's radical behaviorism; cognitive events are a subclass of operant and respondent behaviors and not sacrosanct as highly powerful, soulful, or more transcendental entities affecting the organism. They are *behavioral events, the totality of complete events.* Just the same, Kantor, Skinner, James, Bentley, Staats, Hayes, and many other defectors, disenfranchised by the prevailing disciplines of scientific psychology, branched out on their own to revitalize lawful behavior principles and to broaden the scope of phenomena studied (cf. O'Donohue, Henderson, Hayes, Fisher & Hayes, 2001).

These visionaries are the inspiration behind this chapter. Behavioral Forensic analysis only can claim credible aptitude when it can humbly show its advantages and disadvantages against competing models of forensic psychological evaluation. This chapter surveys prevailing models of forensic psychological evaluation in comparison to the behavioral forensic model. First explored is the traditional paradigm focused on only criminal history, personality, and proclivity or probability for offense recidivism. The second model explored is the scientific-criminal perspective. Here, optics shift to a rudimentary stimulus-response model, but not in an operant or respondent sense. The stimulus, or preceding event, represents the evidence around which the responder (suspect) interacts, producing a crime based on multifaceted traits of the suspect (history, physiology, personality, and proclivity). Within the scientific-criminal model lies three contemporary empirical approaches called the *(a) risk-need responsivity model, (b) actuarial model, and (c) structured professional case formulation.* A fourth model, the most evidence-based approach to formulate operational analyses, is the behavioral forensic model.

## Traditional model

Criminal behavior has a long history of being a manifestation of inner defective personality traits. Inside the suspect, in other words, lies the pandoras box of immoral, unethical, or asocial patterns traceable to childhood and adult years of maladjustment. The specific conditions under which maladjustment occurred are less isolated or important as the cumulative linearity of social problems encountered by the offender. They are the product of nameless, countless, and ambiguous situations through which conduct disorder and antisocial behaviors predominated over healthy behaviors and made the criminal prone to violate cultural and social laws. This macrocosmic perspective begins with the underlying assumption of dysfunctionality in offenders and proceeds to explain a trajectory of likely crimes based on certain personality typologies regardless of the shifting environmental contingencies shaping the suspect's life.

### Focus

The subject of analysis undertaken in the traditional model is one's temperament (in childhood) and personality (in adulthood) Facets of personality are combined together into broad or super-traits defining a pervasive pattern of action. Traits shape the emotional or experiential spheres of individual history, determining how the person perceives, thinks, or reacts at any given time. Four models of personality models applied to criminology included the five-factor model (McCrae & Costa, 1990), the PEN model (Eysenck, 1977, 1997), Tellegen's three-factor model (1985), and Cloninger's temperament and character model (Cloninger, Dragan, Svraki, & Przybeck, 1993). Subtypes of personality classified within each model appear in Table 2.1 below (Miller & Lynam, 2001):

The archetypical typology of criminal personality has been the *psychopath, or antisocial personality disorder*. The distinguishing characteristics of psychopaths, according to Hare (1993, 1996) are absolute self-centeredness, grandiosity, callousness, and lack of remorse or empathy

TABLE 2.1 Subtypes of personality in four models.

| *Definitions* | |
|---|---|
| **Five-factor model** | |
| Neuroticism | Emotional stability and adjustment versus instability and maladjustment |
| Extraversion | Sociability and agency |
| Openness to experience | Interest and willingness to try or consider new activities, ideas, beliefs; intellectual curiosity |
| Agreeableness | Interpersonal strategies: Agreeableness versus Antagonism |
| Conscientiousness | Ability to control impulses, carry out plans and tasks, organizational skills, follow one's internal moral code |
| **Eysenck** | |
| Psychoticism | Egocentricity, interpersonal coldness and disconnectedness, lack of empathy, and impulsiveness |
| Extraversion | Sociability and agency |
| Neuroticism | Emotional stability and adjustment versus instability and maladjustment |
| **Tellegen** | |
| Positive emotionality | Sociability, tendency to experience positive emotions, assertiveness, achievement orientation |
| Negative emotionality | Tendency to experience negative emotions; one's ability to handle stress |
| Constraint | Ability to control impulses, avoid potentially dangerous situations, and endorse traditional values and standards |
| **Cloninger** | |
| Novelty seeking | Tendency toward intense exhilaration or excitement in response to novel stimuli |
| Harm avoidance | Tendency to respond intensely to aversive stimuli |
| Reward dependence | Tendency to respond intensely to signals of reward |
| Persistence | Perseverance despite frustration and fatigue |
| Self-directedness | Self-determination and willpower |
| Cooperativeness | Tendency to be agreeable versus antagonistic and hostile |
| Self-transcendence | Involvement with spirituality |

for others coupled with a charismatic, charming, and manipulative superficiality. An agreement eludes personality theorists on whether psychopaths or antisocial personalities are stand-alone dimensions or overlap with indiscriminable traits in less pernicious personalities, such as Borderline Personality Disorder. Borderline personalities, for example, are also prone to unremorseful juvenile and adult crimes due cyclical mood swings (bipolarity), reckless impulsiveness befitting of random crimes, and can be retaliatory in their pendulum shift between adoration and demonization of people (e.g., "splitting"). Borderline types can be aggressive, volatile, reactionary, and may even possess more psychopathology than their antisocial personality counterparts (Sansone, Sellbom, & Songer, 2016). Likewise, narcissists have been equally notorious as crime perpetrators, with their unabashingly egocentric needs, disregard for other people's feelings, and fulfillment of gratification (Sinha, 2016; Stone, 2009). Their domineering and exploitive traits–anchored in the seven deadly sins of gluttony, lust, laziness, wrath, envy and pride—control their prey with unflattering vigilance and persistence.

Underneath these personological traits lay many assumptions on the cause and effect of their behaviors in the commission of crimes. Assumptions imply, in other words, a universally fundamental correlation between *what traits or behaviors the person might do, and the behaviors they actually do given underlying proclivities or tendencies for that particular personality type.* This unusual leap from anecdotal or correlational evidence to causal inferences represents a serious flaw in the scientific deduction process. Blesk-Rechek, Gunseor & Maly (2018) correctly pointed out the plethora of unwarranted causal language found in scholarly and media publications touting "amazing" research findings. Misrepresentation of scientific findings occurs in conflating correlation with causation, not only in allied fields like education and medicine, but inside the reverent disciplines of psychology. Particular in nomothetic studies, data misrepresentation that shows up in criminal profiles of personalities imply causality without valid experimental data or with *no experimental data.* When assumptions of personality type are disseminated without legitimate casual analysis, the predictions made about crime will appeal to some vague reasons why human behavior occur. But these reasons will lack specification to the environmental conditions or variables directly influential on the behaviors making up the personality.

Contrary to Blek-Rechek et al.'s caveat, traditional models of forensic psychological assessment view criminal acts through the eyes of the suspect. Execution of the crime is explainable by looking at three subcomponents of the suspect relative to the crime: His or her *history, personality, and proclivity* (see Fig. 2.1 below).

## History

In personality trait theories of criminality, history is an important archive of key precipitants forming the nucleus of malcontent behaviors. Childhood through early adult influences in family, school, the community, and the court system are the microsystem. In school, records document qualification for special education services, psychological testing, misconduct (suspensions, detentions, and expulsions), earned grades, and extracurricular activities. A recent domestic terrorist threat to harm elementary school children, for example, came from a local honors student who graduated sum cum laude, was on the debate team,

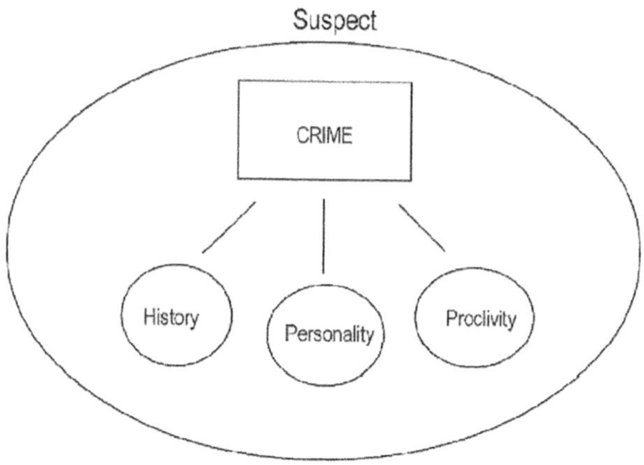


FIG. 2.1 Traditional model.

played tennis and football, and was the president of his local church youth group. Consideration of these educational assets may throw discrepant light on the sinister or malicious intentionality underlying his crime compared to a less academic and enriched student. Then, too, the Unabomber Ted Kaczynski, was a former mathematics professor, a math prodigy, and graduated with a Bachelors from Harvard University and Masters from University of Michigan. His academic acumen was not a reliable predictor of his later mail bomb detonations killing 3 people and injuring 23 other people.

Other biodata collected in support of the criminal personality type is (a) substance abuse history, (b) crimes, and (c) psychiatric treatment. Substance abuse is a precarious criteria since there is multivariance on what constitutes impairment despite the legal and physiological guidelines. While "addiction" usually implicates physical or psychological dependence, violation of the legal guidelines may not necessarily mean the user has physical or psychological dependence. A recent positive drug screen for cannabis suspended a UPS driver under the mandatory Department of Transportation rules. His explanation, later corroborated, was that he was at a party consuming edibles unknowingly prepared with THC. He reported *no other history of ever smoking or using cannabis.* His illegal act of a positive drug screen, which nearly cost him his job, *was not a predictor of any drug addiction or of personality types associated with polyaddiction.* Crimes follow a similar misleading pattern but can be a measuring stick of some recurrent deviant social behavior. Arrested twice in adolescence for larceny to a building, a young adult may graduate to Breaking and Entering or armed robbery. Accretion to a more serious crime might be a progressive and desensitization process or sign of depravity. Then, too, retail or building crimes may reflect financial family hardships in the suspect who stole from stores to help feed his siblings and parents. While his indigence is not an excuse for crime, there is a difference between stealing for survival and stealing to pay for cocaine or because of the impulsive adrenaline-rush. In the latter, the impulsiveness adds more prerequisites to the precriminal personality.

Likewise, psychiatric history includes admission into facilities, youth detention centers, outpatient counseling, the polymorbid diagnoses given, and recurrent use of psychopharmacology. Consider a 4-year old diagnosed with Attention Deficit Hyperactivity Disorder

(ADHD, combined type), placed on Adderall, who is severely oppositional requiring three psychiatric hospitalizations before he turns 5 years old. While personality theorists might conjecture his early recalcitrant behaviors are clear antecedents to adult antisocial behavior, more of his history may veto that assumption. For example, add this to the mix: He was born cocaine-positive, removed from his biological parents by 6 months old, transitioned through 5 sets of foster parents by age 3, and spent 6 months on a long-term children's psychiatric unit. Circumstances of his debacle unfold with a different image of a child who was possibly helpless, abandoned, and lacked any consistent structure or surrogate parent. Diagnostically, he probably met criteria for Reactive Attachment Disorder, a trauma-and-stress related disorder characterized by disruption or disturbance of developmentally inappropriate attachments (APA, 2013, p. 266). Does his absent-parent trauma fuel a course of adult mental illness that shapes the cavilarity, incorrigibility, and reckless impulses leading to adult criminality? Maybe, but not always. On the one hand, manifestations of childhood disorder in adult life are indisputably common. But to say early, mid-, or late-childhood misconduct links to adult criminality automatically is to play the fate card of determinism. Personality theorists often embody a biological-deterministic position that childhood demeanor sets the stage for adult demeanor regardless of environmental (nurture-like) influences.

Such life-course persistent antisocial behaviors are often distinguished from *adolescence-limited antisocial behaviors,* which are momentary oppositional behaviors that mimic antisocial behavior but are normal and adjustive (Moffitt, 1993). In the former, antisocial behavior is stable and consistent. In the latter, antisocial behavior is temporary and situational. A learning curve of crime over age depends on frequency and severity of recidivistic crimes. More callously violent, rule-violating, and authority-disregarding the crime, the more there is cumulative continuity. Childhood predispositions for adult crime seem longitudinally possible providing the adult lives in an isolated bubble or is confined to an institution such as adolescents imprisoned for murder awaiting re-sentencing as adults. But most evidence-based research debunks this early child predisposition theory. Early rebelliousness just does not instinctively cause criminal personalities (cf. Caspi, Moffitt, Silva, and Krueger, 1994).

## Personality

The binding ties between crime and personality traits are theoretical at best and emerged from a stunning absence of calculated methods to understand, isolate, identify, and measure units of behavior transacted across several psychological fields. The traditional model emphasized personality as an aggregate or composite of many behaviors, all interrelated and less important to study separately than to study collectively. Take the fusion of narcissism and antisocial personality—diplomatically referred to as the syndrome called *malignant narcissism* (Gerberth & Turco, 1997; Lenzenweger, Clarkin, Caligor, Cain, & Kernberg, 2018). The trait-mix additionally consists of sadism, aggression, and grandiosity. Malignant narcissists, among them criminal headliners such as Jim Jones, O.J. Simpson, and Ted Bundy, all supposedly share five immutable behaviors predisposing them to commit crimes. These include:

1. Success at any cost
2. Hypersexuality

3. Incessant Blaming
4. Violence
5. Manipulation

Measurement of all five traits on, for example, the Hare Psychopathy Checklist (cf. Hare, 1991; Hare & Neumann, 2006) supposedly will positively correlate high scores with criminal potential. High score also associate with collateral traits of impulsivity and Machiavellianism, both the antithesis to empathy and affiliation. Hare's attempt to objectify these composites of behavior provide an acceptable blueprint for personality theorists to postulate the absurdity and morbidity of serial and horrific criminal acts. When a well-educated, high community profile entrepreneur in towns yells out obscenities at college coeds and stalks other females, for example, personification of the *malignant narcissist* makes it easy to explain his ulterior motives or other underlying etiologies. He wanted to upset the woman at any cost, felt hypersexual, blamed them for his own failed marriage, felt viciously angry at them, and manipulated his authority in town to stalk the coeds. All five reasons incorporate the broad definition of malignant narcissist, offering some atlas for prediction of the suspect's future behavior.

## Proclivity

Proclivity or *likelihood of committing the same or similar crimes,* is a natural outgrowth of personality measurements of criminal behavior, but can result in unwarranted conclusions of causation. When groups of criminal behaviors are predictors of violence, no matter the mathematical algorithms calculated, the explanatory power of outcomes is weak and compromised by assumptions about trait correlations. Some criminological studies (e.g., Chaiken, Chaiken, & Rhodes, 1994; Delisi & Scherer, 2006) used comparison groups of offenders to offset methodological bias and tried to frame criminal behavior, and how criminal careers begin, evolve, and end. By their own admission, the limitations of such studies always rest with clustering typologies of offenders, despite subclassifications used to reduce this compression of behaviors (e.g., murderers trichotomized into serial killers, mass killers, and spree killers). Propensity measures, then, fail to give idiographic projections; they lack the statistical and theoretical precision to code individual behaviors in response to observable parameters in the environment controlling the onset, maintenance, and termination of at-risk behaviors.

## Evaluation resources

Data sources used in the traditional model are protocol for most police or psychological investigations. Records of past police arrests, of mental health treatment and prior psychological evaluations, educational records, of collaborative witness testimony (i.e., forensic interviews), crime-scene analyses, medical autopsy or past medical reports (including psychotropics prescribed), and logs of behavior while incarcerated, all represent the snapshots of the suspect's pre-criminal and criminal world. The advantage of these data are their tangible, confrontable and mensurational value. Collection of facts in a case is like taking a biopsy of the real (not simulated) skin. Peterson, Sommers, Baskin, and Johnson (2010), for example, published an impressively comprehensive treatise on scientific investigation of police crimes in which they argue for analyses of objective forms of physical evidence using state-of-the-art laboratory techniques. Meaning, data sources accrued in the early stages of criminal psychological assessment are congruent with canons of behavioral science. But how these data samples get lifted from the substratum of science into the hypothetical stratosphere eludes the personality criminologist and can ruin the validity of their conclusions about behavior.

## Flaws with model

Several flaws inherent in the traditional personality model already were discussed heretofore. Three additional fatal flaws potentially contaminating the mental health (forensic) evaluation and subsequent projections of future crime include (a) expediency of heuristics, (b) omission of interactive effects between stimulus and response, and (c) unilaterality of cause.

## Expediency of heuristics

A heuristic is an imperfect approach to problem solving to amply reach tentative findings or a desirable research goal. *Expediency* means the clock-ticking time restrictions under which psychological or mental health reports must be completed and submitted timely for an arraignment, hearing, trial, or sentencing. Report completion, in other words, is often at the mercy of a random adjudicative process notorious for last-minute ("the 11th hour") requests for documents. When pressured for results, mental health forensic specialists may take short-cuts in data assembly and interpretation, the most common of which is repeating conclusions from earlier psychological reports or synthesizing prior data with abbreviated coverage of new information. Truncation of new data means making generalizations about personality traits that are probabilistic, at best, and completely incongruent with facts at worst. The best "guestimates" are when mental health reports catalog behaviors into a personality typology and make actuarial predictions of crime for this typology. For example, *dependent personality types are likely to be aiding and abetting the larcenist* (e.g., Stone, 2007). The worst estimates is when personality typologies logically and theoretically correlate with high-risk crimes accused of the suspect, but the police or other investigative data contradict the personality schema, and the personality schema still prevails in court. For example, a 25 year old was arrested for indecent exposure at a county swimming pool. Eye-witness accounts and interviews with his peer characterized him as selfish, exploitive, and careless; mental health and educational documents also documented incidents of opposition and diagnosis of ADHD. Conclusions were that his ADHD and conduct disorder preceded his adult antisocial and narcissistic personality disorders, both prototypically involved uncontrolled hypersexuality. In truth, and after a closer reading of the police report, a different story emerged. He took his brother's oversized bathing suit that day to the county pool and wore it. A female onlooker observed his genitals "slipping out" of the wide leg openings instead of being tucked inside the suit. She contacted the police authorities and filed a complaint. There is a big difference between outfit neglect (wearing oversized clothing) and a deliberate intent to exhibit his genitals.

## Omission of interactive effects between stimulus and response

The logic implicit in personality theories is that pervasive patterns of behavior are likely to occur regardless of situational variables. A person simply follows a life cycle of criminal acts enabled by the cognitive, emotional, or behavioral traits of some personality. While certain environmental conditions, inarguably, may propagate or suppress personality traits, details of these conditions are nebulous and relegated to a minor role in the overall etiology. Stimulus functions and response functions are subordinate, unimportant, and less explanatory of criminal intent, responsibility, trial competence, and culpability than the amalgam of behaviors inside a high-risk personality. The upside of omitting the interplay between stimulus and response properties is a simple, straight-forward, and layman-friendly presentation of criminal action based on generalized results. The downside of omitting stimulus-response transactions is manifold. First, the judge, jury, attorneys, or parole/probation officers never know about extenuating circumstances of the current crime or if conditions exist under which the suspect *would never or be very unlikely to commit a crime.* Second, in retelling his or her side of the crime, the suspect's chronology of events go unrecognized or marginalized, although self-witness information can be fertile ground either to contradict or complement police (and other) records. Third, without knowing specific contingencies, predictions of future crime entirely lay with stereotyped, hyperbolic, and non-causal speculations.

## Unilaterality of cause

Personality criminologists locate the smoking —gun for any crime inside the person. The unidirectional flow of behavior events proceeds either from without or within. If it comes from without, such as the checkbook lying visibly on the table, it may occasion theft and later writing a bad check (uttering and publishing). The stolen checks, after all, were *only* coincidental artifacts, according to the notion of lifelong criminals and the obviation of individual characteristics to understand the full deviance spectrum (Walters, 2012, 2104). Off the shoreline, and closer to bilateral thinking, was Wilson and Herrnstein's *Net-Advantage Theory* (1985). It is loosely based on operant and respondent conditioning principles in which personality "traits" (not behaviors) are reinforced to facilitate better emotional decisions in life. Underlying their inclusion of reinforcement is that crime is inherently rewarding, since it allows the action-taker to get something at little or no cost. That some people rewarded by criminal behavior are different from people unaffected by the enticements (motivating operations) of rewards. While lip-service is paid to learning theory, in a pseudo-empirical way, the logistics of net-advantage theory are still inferior to scientific paradigms employing the conventions of applied behavior analysis. A bilateral (behavioral) or multilateral (interbehavioral) approach does not presume antecedents and consequences impact a pack of behaviors called traits. Even in the behavioral vernacular when referring to a "class of response," the experimental assumption is that *each response in a class, no matter how similar, dependent or interdependent, operates as discrete units of action under similar, different, or contiguous stimulus conditions.*

## Scientific-criminal model

The scientist-criminal model made its debut about 35 years ago amid the invention of DNA profiling and it advanced over the last decade of technological proliferation. Forensic assessment uses lasers, drones, genetic code analysis, and refined forensic interviewing strategies for adults and children. Forensic science became interdisciplinary, in solving criminal activity persistent in the fields of art, anthropology, astrology, accounting, botany, dentistry, engineering, entomology, geology, limnology, linguistics, medicine, psychiatry, psychology, to name only a few. The subdivisions of forensic research officially organized and gained momentum as advantages abound on the economic and legal benefits of solving crimes, and restoring dignity back to the disciplines. In mental health assessments, the scientific-criminal model acknowledged the multifarious effects of environment (stimulus evidence) on the suspect (response). This reciprocal relationship permitted a better "bird's eye" perspective on the crime scene as depicted in Fig. 2.2 below.

### Focus

Focus of the scientific-criminal model is on *the crime scene*. Not just the physical evidence—for the example, the corpse, the blood stains, broken glass, upside down furniture, and emptying of drawers—but the psychological evidence—cell phone, Facebook account, work calendar, contents of laundry, google search engine history, contents of refrigerator, and wardrobe in the closet. Artifacts are objects that may or may not be immediately relevant to the investigation—keys, files, stamps, piano. Evidence, on the other, implies relevancy to solving crimes and understanding intentionality. In cyber/digital forensics, for example, "artifact" is obsolete and replaced with the term cyber observable expression, since the latter is a more accurate and rigorous classification of forensic objects (Harichandran, Walnycky, Baggili, & Breitinger, 2016). In forensic psychology, evidence and artifacts belong to the stimulus function, an umbrella term under which lies (a) collateral data, (b) the crime science,

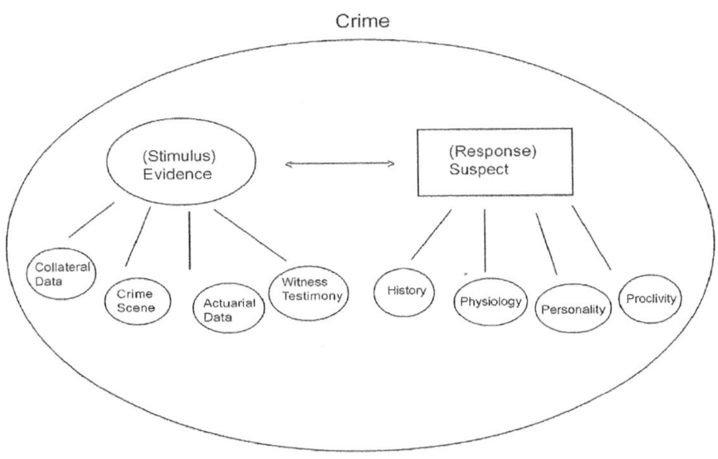


FIG. 2.2 Scientific-criminal model.

(c) actuarial data, and (d) witness testimony. Bilaterally interacting with the stimulus (evidence) is the response (suspect). Dissection of the response is in four subcomponents: (a) history, (b) physiology, (c) personality, and (d) proclivity.

## Collateral data

Stimulus events, in forensic terms, are *evidentiary products*. Products vary by relevance and contiguity with the pre-crime, crime, and post-crime scenes, consisting of concrete, measurable, confrontable, observable, and functional properties. Even when properties are partly or entirely unobservable or indiscernible, computer or chemical detection procedures can illuminate facts for analysis. Forensic anthropologists, for example, in determining the age of decomposed corpses, apply osteology, the scientific study of bones, to clarify sex, age, and ancestry. Forensic odontology, as well, in collecting amortum data (i.e., before postmortem autopsy), can examine oral structure or decay of ruminant teeth for both age estimates and identification, particularly in the aftermaths of disasters (mass murders, fires, tsunamis, earthquakes, floods, etc.). Both allied health disciplines purvey reasonable causal explanations of behavior based on collateral data sampled from the crime scene.

Lee and Harris (2000) further classified physical evidence into four types. These include *Transient evidence, pattern evidence, conditional evidence,* and *transfer evidence.* Transient evidence is any product which is temporary in nature and can be easily changed or lost. Examples include odor, temperature, imprints and indentations, and markings. Pattern evidence are products induced by forcible, direct contact between persons and objects within varying durations of time. In many cases, multiple types of pattern evidence overlap in crime scenes, among them including blood spatter patterns, glass fracture patterns, fire burn patterns, furniture position patterns, track-trail patterns, powder residue patterns, body position patterns, and shoe or boot print patterns. Pattern evidence, like transient evidence, also risks a short shelf-life and requires urgency of photo or other samples made proximal to the crime. A third type of physical evidence is conditional. Such evidence is the consequence of certain events or actions. Examples of conditional evidence, also subject to attrition, include light, smoke, fire, location, vehicle status, and body status. For example, light is a factor in whether headlights of a vehicle were on or off prior to an accident or to throw light on a homicide scene. A fourth form is transfer evidence. Here, contact occurs between physical objects and people or between two objects or between two people. Skin debris attached to crevices in the wood floor might reflect the supine position of a victim beaten until he collapsed. Similarly, destroyed door frames and broken door locks are contingent on burglars using a crowbar. The malleability and transitory nature of products all depends on objects- or people-evoking the contact interaction.

## Crime scene

The role of physical product evidence as collateral data in psychological or mental health evaluations also clearly depends on the crime scene itself. Former head of the FBI's investigative Support Unit, Dr. John Douglas, a famous criminal profiler, claimed that any hunt for the "rogue's gallery of assailants" largely begins with recognition and respect for crime scene context (cf. Douglas, 2000). Unlike fictional portrays of crime scenes in such popular TV shows as *Law and Order, True Detective, or Battle Creek,* its real-time counterparts are more serious and naturalistic labs are meticulous to collect undisturbed evidence. For mental health evaluators, crime scenes offer a peak into behavior segments in the suspect's biography otherwise missed from scanning police documents or past educational and psychiatric reports. For example, a man arrested for soliciting sex for money (i.e., prostitution) pre-arranged to meet his female prospect in an elite hotel to deflect suspicion of the women's illicit intentions. His pre-arrangement constituted a sex-trafficking operation. But it was the *crime scene that drew unusual attention to the man because it was an atypical location for sexual meetups, and the man rarely frequented the hotel except for these affairs.* Beside location, naturalistic properties of crime scenes important for (behavioral) psychological analysis are (a) time of day, (b) weather, (c) reward or punishment potentials in that setting, and (d) susceptibility of the suspect to behave in a certain way unlike in other settings (e.g., what motivational operations or discriminative stimuli are unique in this setting). The sex solicitor, for example, chose this hotel for another reason; he had accumulated membership honor points for staying at this hotel chain nationwide and could get rooms for free.

## Actuarial data

Actuarial data are not directly part of a crime scene. They are statistics generated over the course of time from multiple crime scenes identical or similar to the one in question, from which predictions of behavior are possible. Risk probability charts, geographic risk charts, demographic crime charts, among hundreds of numerical prognosticators. The advantage of this data is having prior research showing preponderance or high tendencies of behavior under certain parameters. The downside is obvious. Indirect statistical data my lead to actuarially derived decisions that replace clinical and police investigations and decisions (cf. Sreenivasan, Kirkish, Garrick, Weinberger, & Phenix, 2000). When statistically identified factors determine high risk versus low risk sex offenders, for example, the cost of false negatives or false positives weighs against the validity and economy of using these actuarial devices. Incorrectly predicting high recidivism in a sex offender, for example, despite clinical or other documentation to the contrary, may results in imprisonment or lifetime listing on a state or federal sex registry. On the obverse, incorrectly concluding low recidivism rates, despite multiple arrests and witness testimony challenging the actuarial data, may result in exculpation and unmonitored freedom to possibly commit the same or related crimes. While actuarial estimates may seem problematic, they serve a vital role in summation of crime scene and criminal behaviors as a compass to begin navigating through the morass of direct evidence.

## Witness testimony

One of the valuable assets of stimulus evidence is witness testimony. Witness testimony are retrospective accounts provided by the suspect, victims, and other observers directly or indirectly exposed to the crime. Direct witness testimony from victims offers a perspective of crime impact. Suspects who provide parallel or discrepant storylines from the victim's statements give a different perceptual angle on the same setting events. Likewise, direct (eye-) witnesses offer a third lens through which to observe the crime. Indirect witnesses such as parents of victims or suspects, educators, and therapists offer anecdotal information elaborating on or confirming eye-witness impressions. Witnesses also must be compellable and competent. They either are asked or forced into court via a subpoena, but at least have the cognitive and behavioral facility to comply with the court order. Likewise, while witness testimony may vary profoundly, the person offering testimony must be shown as competent. Once these judicial criteria are met, inclusion of testimonies into the police or court records supplies two behaviorally important sources of information. First, as direct or indirect observers, estimates of interreliability help to determine the veracity of coding (interpreting) the behaviors sampled. Two or more eye-witnesses of the assault occurring on the baseball field likely reflect a higher percentage of inter-reliability than if witnesses have diametrically different stories.

A second behavioral value is samples of cultural contingencies. Racism and ethnocentricity, for example, may bias the testimonies of observers in rural counties compared to their counterparts in sprawling urban counties. The *norms or tolerance for certain cultural contingencies* resonates Kantor's conceptual scheme of cultural matrix, important for forensic analysis (1982, pp. 164–166; Mountjoy & Ruben, 1983). The problem is that intrinsic characteristics of cultural interbehavior may be in concert or contrast to the suspect's own reactional biography and therefore cannot be an accurate gauge of his or her actions. An assailant, for example, from the United Kingdom and a professional cricket player (bowler), was now on American soil pitching in a professional baseball game. His style of releasing the ball in American baseball was very different from being delivered in Great Britain. When he released (bowled) the ball, making it bounce first before reaching the batter (as done in cricket), the batter presumed his throw was deliberately wild and meant to hit him. The batter charged out to the mound to physically strike the pitcher, who retaliated in aggression. Differences in the two games aside, the norms governing the pitchers were not consistent with the norms (contingencies) governing the batter. Consequently, eye-witness testimony of their interactions grouping their behaviors under one standard (the American norm or contingency) is an inaccurate account of the psychological events.

## History

History, in the scientific-criminal model, goes beyond classifications of personality as seen above in the traditional model. It considers diagnostic markers or milestones in a person's life demarcating their development, underdevelopment, and experientially traumatic events contributing to pre-criminalistic behaviors. This reactional biography covers substance abuse, peaks and lows of achievement or success (e.g., in sports, fine arts, or other extracurricular or volunteer groups), education, criminal background, education, and evolution of signifying behaviors through childhood and adulthood relative to different setting events. A female arrested for carrying a Taser, for instance, had exemplary academic achievement, a pedigree education, was oldest of two professional parents, and held leadership roles in Girl Scouts, Future Farmers of America, and debate club. She went to summer camps, studied abroad during her junior year of college, and advanced to a Masters degree in special education, the career she currently works in. A nondrug user, her trauma-free childhood and adulthood, and social competence in most circumstances stumped forensic evaluators as to why she carried a weapon. She even claimed uncertainty and vagueness of motives, problems with her memory, and denied any fears of predatory or stalking attacks. She also denied any head injuries. But she did not object to undergoing Explicit Alternative Testing (EAT), a type of forced testing using binomial probability distribution to assess deception (cf. Hall & Thompson, 2007). Deception, or *malingering*, is the deliberate distortion, omission, or exaggeration of recall deficits. While a variety of methods are viable to detect faked memory impairment of confusion (e.g., Hall & Poirier, 2001), the EAT is unique in its use of sensory stimulus cues which the testee denies or confirms he or she can confirm and recall. Applied to the female suspect, EAT results detected her faking "bad memory" and she later confessed about other undisclosed events when confronted. Among these "new facts" presented was that her ex-boyfriend was violent and she feared all men might hurt her again.

## Physiology

Biochemical and physiological events are response units identified with the same interrelationship with other changes inside and outside of the body. Sensations generated by the central and peripheral nervous system, by muscular contractions and glandular secretions, by receptor mechanics, by cranial nerves, and within vital body systems (e.g., lymphatic network, respiratory system, endocrine system, digestive system, urinary system, reproductive system, etc.) all comprise continuous interactions studied as subjects in the same naturalistic world as other interbehavioral events (cf. Kantor, 1947; Ruben, 1986). As such, they are under the common microscope of psychology and particularly in behavior analysis during forensic evaluations. Biophysiological disorders contribute significantly to the panoramic landscape of variables surveyed in the understanding and interpretation of offender's criminal behaviors. A Traumatically Brain Injured (TBI) suspect claiming amnesia during a homicide may be reliable historian, and less likely of malingering (deception). If a recent neuropsychological evaluation attests to anterograde interference (amnesia)—the loss of ability to create new memories (i.e., damage to temporal lobe, limbic system)—that *physiological response* becomes revealing evidence to possibly prove diminished capacity in criminal responsibility. Similar evidence for forensic consideration includes neuro-imaging lab tests results, and medical records showing congenital or adventitious disorders.

Recently, for example, innovations in olfaction detection technology helped to solve forensic cases (e.g., Wasterson, Blackmore, & Bagby, 2006). Schuh and Porter, in particular, outlined contemporary uses of olfaction evidence in scientific forensic evaluations. Also part of the limbic system, the olfactory bulb closely associates with the amygdala, responsible for facilitating (a medium of contact for) memory and emotions. Smell, in other words, can serve as discriminative stimuli evoking conditioned responses in the recall of events as part of witness testimony and withstanding and cross examination. Distortion of smell, as well, is often associated with TBI, nutritional deficiency, and certain medications. When scent is taken up by the nostrils, receptor cells send an electrical impulse to the olfactory bulb through the axon at its base, Together with the fifth cranial, or trigeminal nerve, impulses signal adverse or other reactions impacting emotional arousal, like from smelling ammonia. The resultant emotion or behavior from scent is likely to correspond to the original smell reaction during initial exposure of the odor, such as in a crime scene. Using tests to gauge smelling ability, many calibrated to rule out artifact or confounding variables, the witness can better rate the accuracy of the smell, giving greater validity to details recalled in a case.

## Personality

Similar to the traditional model, personalities included in this category prototypically derive from the ten personality disorders defined in the DSM-V (APA, 2013, p. 266). Higher social risk personalities in Cluster B (e.g., Antisocial, Borderline, Histrionic, Narcissistic), historically associate with criminally deviant behaviors both at home and in the workplace (Ruben, 2015). In a scientific-criminal model, the role of personalities is more of a conglomerate of behaviors responsive to the environment than intrapsychic dynamics explaining inner traits of the person's character. Antisocial personality disorder, for example, equates to higher frequency of aggressive or violent and risk-taking behaviors, and overall excessive behaviors in response to basic social contingencies (cf. Connor, 2002; Nelson-Gray et al., 2002). A suspect scoring positive for cannabis on a random drug test, who claims a psychiatrist diagnosed him with Antisocial Personality Disorder, may seek exemption from the test, saying his medical marijuana card (in states of cannabis illegality) entitles him to unrestricted use. However, he also climbs cell towers and repairs them for a living, regardless of his diagnosis. At that height, impaired visuo-spatial judgment may disorient him, jeopardize his safety, and consequently cause him to fall, incurring abominable liability expenses for the employer. His antisocial personality disorder is not the problem; it simply offers a class of responses explaining his tenacity for reckless risk-taking behaviors, accelerating the likelihood of his disregard for safety-protection standards and disregard for his cannabis use.

## Proclivity

Proclivity is a probabilistic estimation of cause and effect. The marijuana smoker *has a higher proclivity for repeating cannabis use despite scoring positive on a random drug test.* The next step is showing how past interactions between the stimulus evidence and response suspect prove this causal theory. Four times before the positive drug test, eye-witnesses, for example, corroborated the suspect was "high" from cannabis when climbing up the tower. On two of these occasions, he nearly lost his balance and received a written reprimand for neglecting to fasten his harness immediately and correctly. The stimulus evidence is the job site (the tower), around which the employee indiscriminately and frequently worked while impaired by cannabis. Collateral data brought into the causal formula, like other positive drug tests, eye-witness accounts, and even similar injuries sustained at home from disturbed perception and judgment after smoking cannabis, all increase the sample size of evidence. It strengthens the statistical power to make predictions about the suspect's behavior.

## Evaluation resources

In the traditional model, evaluation resources were corroborators confirming the underlying personality construct of a suspect. Prior police records, for example, offered confirmatory evidence of rule violations, authority-challenges, and repeat unremorseful violence, all subsumed under the umbrella of antisocial personality disorder. Slightly different in the scientific-criminal model, collaborative resources are still historical markers of psychopathology, but in relationship to certain stimulus events, namely, events resembling the stimulus evidence. For example a medical report from a pain management clinic documenting chronic sacrolumbar pain from degenerative (and herniated) discs showed the suspect was prescribed Oxycodone and Valium. During pain breakthrough cycles, when the suspect usually would take her next dose of pain medicine to transition through pain onset, she found she was out of Oxycodone and Valium. Apart from the flu-like withdrawal syndrome, pain increased to unbearable levels, making her viciously angry over any disruption of her day, let alone when she was under urges (motivating operations). She flew into a tirade and punched her 10 year old in the face for noncompliance. Subsequently, Children's protective services charged her with first degree child abuse. While mistreatment of her child is not impunible, and enough discolored facial skin imprint evidence on her child proved the crime did occur, the medical documentation suggests the abuse may be situational, related to unmedicated pain and withdrawal syndrome aggravating anger levels (cf. Ulrich, Wolf & Dulaney, 1969). The documents shed light on the interplay between the child (evidence) and the parent's (suspect's) responses (actual behaviors, physiology) at the time.

## Flaws with model

Enhancement of stimulus-response interactions, particularly between suspect and its immediate surrounds, makes the scientific-criminal model more conducive to forensic science and research. By isolating hypothetical causal variables, and exfoliating personality-trait constructs, reasonable conclusions about criminal events remain tangibly and coherently connected to natural events. Natural (observable) events are more amenable to scientific (laboratory) analysis, more evidence-based in formulating linear response patterns of crimes, and more persuasive in expert testimony, explaining complex behaviors to a judge or jury. For its clear empirical advantages over the traditional model, three flaws still obstruct its approximation to a pristine scientific approach. First, causal analyses are molar, inferential, or too broad. Clustered into assessments are generalized statements about behaviors and presumptive or universal expectations of *multiple contingencies interacting simultaneously or inextricably*. Investigative behavioral processing, using interrogation, interviews, polygraph exams, photographs sketches, and observations may increase thoroughness of details recorded of crimes, but the *functionality of behavior on stimulus events* is less priority. A second flaw is overuse of actuarial data aggregated into statistical estimates (inferences) of behavior probability, instead of measures of molecular or specific relations between events showing direct, causal, and reciprocal stimulus-response effects. A similar objection, expressed almost 45 years ago, condemned the harmfulness of group designs and statistical analyses in losing experimental control, compared to collections of directly observed data to better understand matrices of complex behavior. (cf. Michael, 1974; Shadish, 2014). The argument plainly predicted that more time would be spent by researchers learning about the judgment aids (statistical methods) than on the experimental variables in question.

A third flaw is sacrificing a formal behavioral analysis for correlations among groups of suspect behavior (response) and evidence (stimulus). Behaviors are collapsed into classifications of personality typology, with inferred profiles predicting the individual's likely decisions, emotions, and reactions relative to stimuli. This error is most conspicuous in the endeavors undertaken by the Behavioral Science Unit in the Federal Bureau of Investigation, who touts a behavioral analysis approach to crime investigation. However, their descriptive analyses are neither situation-specific, measurably quantifiable in units of behavior, nor consisting of causal connections between antecedent, consequent, or intermediary events surrounding the sexual criminal offenses (see Chapter 3 for elaboration on this problem). Forensic behavior analysis, by contrast, while not discarding personality as mystic, supernatural, or inaccessible to science, focuses more on the unique contingencies transacted between specific behaviors and its surrounds across a time continuum of multiple behavior segments (the psychological field).

## Risk-need responsivity model for offender assessment

Reliable prediction of offender's current and recidivistic behaviors becomes the hallmark of a highly feasible, scientific-criminal model. But the road to pristine science has been long and difficult. Traditional forensic psychological models, which reached its nadir in the mid 1980s, enjoyed a brief renaissance after it was conceptually reformulated into the *Need-responsivity model,* an innovative approach predicated on three principles (Blanchette & Brown, 2006; Ward, Mesler, & Yates, 2007). First is the *risk*-principle, which asserts that criminal behavior is predictable and treatable and thus focus should be upon more complex, higher-risk offenders. Second is the *need*-principle, which highlights the value of criminogenic needs in the design and delivery of offender rehabilitation or treatment. A third is *responsivity* principle, a blueprint for how the treatment should be provided. Using actuarial risk assessment instruments, statistical information allowed measures of general trends of offender populations given similar legal or social conditions. Measurement instruments underwent thorough renovation in the last twenty years to collect data beyond simple demography and to include employment, family relationships, criminal friends, types of rehabilitation programs attended and completed, and repetition of offenses (Andrews, Bonta, & Wormith, 2006). Deduced from statistical samples are summative behavior indicators or markers corresponding to types of high risks. The seven major risks universally identified include:

1. Antisocial personality patterns
2. Procriminal attitudes
3. Social supports for crime
4. Substance abuse
5. Family and marital relationships
6. School./work
7. Prosocial recreational activities.

The model also adds non-criminogenic, minor needs impacting the at-risk offender. These markers include:

1. Self-esteem
2. Vague feelings of personal distress

3. Major mental disorder
4. Physical health

Classification of suspect or offender by his or her marker affords a mechanism to tailor-make the treatment interventions. As the individual's world changes, particularly on probation or parole, markers also may vary or become obsolete, all of which allows for a flexible, fluid, and up-to-date profiling process. Treatment, in this respect, remains relevant to the offender's urgent needs and not based on assumptive or universal predilections on what may benefit offenders.

For the triumphant credibility this evidence-based assessment offers over non-psychometric systems or psychometric systems based in theoretical inferences (personality trait theorist), it has serious limitations for forensic psychological evaluation. First, group statistical trends, despite how accurately collected or predictive of behaviors in similarly profiled individuals, lack specificity to the criminal context of a case. The particular details in a robbery incident, for example, may broadly fit the spectrum of attributes of criminals sampled who commit such crimes. But the ubiquitous samples may overlook the suspect's reactional biography of (a) taking Ritalin since 6 years old, (b) aggressively fighting classmates, (c) titrating to amphetamines to spike the autonomic arousal first experienced post-puberty when the paradoxical psychostimulant Ritalin now acted like a stimulant, (d) engaging in hypomanic behavior to induce the euphoria similar to amphetamine drug-use, and (e) in states of hypomania, committing armed robbery. These factors, while perhaps discernible in one or two crimes, are unlikely the prototype of the suspect in this case, for whom an idiographic operational analysis is more appropriate.

A second limitation is correlation versus causation. The vast actuarial data assembled on relevant populations may show remarkable similarities or non-statistical correlations with a particular criminal. Correlations may even provide a flow-chart of decisions to design a treatment regimen for one offender. But somewhere in the pre-treatment (baseline) to treatment continuum, intake information will be taken that deviates from the perfunctory, sociologic databanks and identifies a more causal connection between criminal behavior, the antecedents, consequences, and entire psychological field responsible for illegal action. The correlations are a powerful first step to qualify the offender in naturalistic terms of many environmental variables impacting pre-crime, crime, and post-crime behaviors. But risk-need-responsibility model falls short of a molecular analysis in isolating and measuring the precise conditioning processes (operant, respondent, other), which increase or decrease offender risk for recidivism.

## Structured professional judgment model and actuarial forensic science model

Evidence-based guidelines are paramount to any analytical or taxonomous method of systematically identifying offenders at risk for repeated interpersonal violence, and related crimes. The *Structured Professional Judgment Model (SPJ)* undertakes this very task of isolating, predicting, and managing offender risk using assessments tools such as the *Sexual Violence Risk-20* (Boer, Hart, Kropp, & Webster, 2015) and the *Risk for Sexual Violence Protocol* (Hart, Kropp, Laws, Logan, & Watt 2003). Both of these test devices are actuarial violence risk measures designed as decision-making aids for expert evaluators, after statistically profiling high probable offenders. More succinct than encyclopedic, the measures correlate the most documented personalities traits or behaviors with crime typology, such as sexual or domestic abuse. Factor analyses, by comparison to unstructured protocols, feature (a) inclusion of a fixed set of risk factors, (b) operational definitions of risk factors, (c) scoring or coding procedures for risk factors, (d) direction on how to integrate risk factors to reach a final decision about risk, and (e) higher interrater reliability and predictive validity. With this information, the structured assessment fosters strong generalizability as well as comprehensiveness of the set of risk factors (Douglas & Kropp, 2002).

The *Actuarial Forensic Science Model* also applies mathematics and statistics to assess deterministic and risk behaviors in a wide variety of discipline as insurance, finance, economics, and computer science. In criminal forensic capacities, the model can assist to set up sentencing guidelines for convicted felons (Harcourt, 2003; Silver & Chow-Martin, 2002). Tables of aggregated data on highly probabilistic (serial or habitual) offenders cover their type of crime, age, educational background, and ethnicity—all matched against a current suspect's offense. Traits correlating with a current offender's legal record and background provide justification to be used a prognosticators on rate, frequency, and other dimensions regarding the offender's chance of future crimes. Since accuracy of inferential comparisons is also questionable and may be unethical, adjustments calibrated in the actuarial comparison can reduce or compensate for false negatives and false positives. For example, in assessing recidivism risk rates of sexual offenders, classification accuracy can be improved by using sensitive-specific cut-off scores and more relevant information to a specific offender case (Campbell, 2003). The adjusted actuarial assessment gains more predictive validity by controlling for intravening factors likely to vary risks such as the individual offender's biographical differences.

Just the same, limitations of both models are mathematical and practical. First, these devices lower reliability and validity through allowance of discretion at the variable integration phase of decision making. This discretion leads to contamination. Unanticipated threats to data validity are common in weakening any group design or statistical analysis, including:

*History effects:* Events may occur outside of the locality, setting events, or temporal period in which demographic or other data were sampled that influence the subjects' behaviors, biasing the sample. For example, an individual arrest record showed habitual offense, but only when incarcerated not when on probation or parole for long durations.

*Maturation effects:* Normal developmental processes occur that influence the behaviors samples over one or two weeks or months, unaccounted for in the trajectory of behavior predicted by the sample. For example, a juvenile adjudicated for homicide is now 30 years old and is very unlikely to commit the same crime or present the same proclivity for crime sampled during his youth.

*Instrumentation effects:* Over- and under-estimations of data subjectively sampled from traits or qualifiers may deviate from the actual behaviors upon which these traits are based. For example, statistical data showing that habitual larcenists repeat similar or other offenses within a 6-month period after conviction and probation may be an overestimation of criminal activity if other variables, like motivating operations, change significantly. The offender stole merchandise while addicted to heroin and was a scavenger for money to supply his opiate addiction. When his addiction ends, propensity for similar crimes reduces or ceases entirely.

*Regression to Mean:* Phenomenon in which some outliner variables occur in a normal distribution (population) but not in the sample of offenders measured. Outliners, behaviorally, means competing behaviors shaped by other contingencies that moderate or mediate effects on the sample. For example, only half of the DUIL offenders sampled partook in Sobriety Court, an accelerated and highly monitored abstinence-based completion program. Those in Sobriety court directly has less risk of alcohol use and alcohol-driving offenses, whereas nonparticipants risked higher rates of recidivism. Likewise, still another unstamped population may be on the waiting list for Sobriety Court and given the option to waive it if they demonstrate 6 months sobriety. This motivating operation, while not directly a variable evoked from Sobriety court, can still impact recurrence or attenuation of alcohol use.

Second, echoing a limitation shown with the Risk-Need Responsivity Model, assessment devices largely or exclusively derived from data on personality clusters lose the pristine measurement of specific cause and effect relations among behavior and stimuli. Extrapolation from actuarial data as a baseline measure makes assumptions about the common traits or characteristics inside the person that offer tenuous and unfounded predictions of crime recidivism. Searching inside the organism for an explanation of behavior also may obscure naturalistic variables, which are more valuable for a scientific analysis. These variables, whether they lie outside or inside the organism, are operationally definable by their interrelationship with events in any psychological field (cf. Pierce & Cheney, 2017; Skinner, 1976). Personality development, and how it evolves to influence an offender's criminal behaviors, is a collection of responses to various stimuli across a continuum of time from childhood to adulthood. While personality is an important adjunct to data collection, it offers little concise information unless analysis is possible of the behaviors comprising personality. Personality is better seen as a hierarchy of complex responses retrieved from a history of conditioning which makes the person more or less malleable in facing identical, similar, or completely new circumstances in the future.

## Behavioral forensic model

In the movie, *Catch Me If You Can* (2002), the dramatic bio-documentary, prodigy teen criminal, Frank Abagnale Jr., showed a rare blend of knowledge and expertise in pulling off forgery and embezzlement. Frank Abagnale Jr.'s amazing journey from convicted felon to FBI consultant showed the benefit of using an insider's direct contact with environmental contingencies. Unlike non-criminal experts, inferring personality profiles or speculating cause and effect based on actuarial data, Frank Abagnale Jr., helped federal law enforcement agencies apprehend offenders who responded to contingencies as he did. Frank *became a scientific examiner of behavior patterns interacting with a sequence of events in the commission of financial crimes* (cf. Abagnale, 2002). Forensic entomologists do the same thing. Similar to Frank Abagnale Jr., they are inspectors of *natural events transacted across temporal and spatial fields in which a recovered human body decomposes and the estimated time of death can be determined from the successive invasion of anthropoids.* Using insect biology to uncover elusive criminal facts, police investigators can build a plausible case for murder. Here, too, analysis is *not a psychological autopsy of the deceased victim's personality and how it drove him or her to death.* Analysis stays clear of transcendental, metaphysical, or mythical constructs personifying personality as the underlying causes.

The behavioral forensic model instead embraces a naturalistic confrontation with concrete events not only in isolating artifacts or evidence from the crime scene in two ways. First, it is naturalistic in the architecture of reconstructing human behavior from its outcome of conditioning transacted over time, under diverse contingencies within the psychological matrix. Second, the model expands on the extensive body of research in applied behavior analysis, the experimental analysis of behavior, and interbehavioral psychology—all of the foundations of a behavioral revolution in scientific psychology since the early 1960s (Mountjoy & Cone, 2006).

## Focus

The primary focus of the behavioral forensic model is on the *operational (functional) relationship in a continuity of interactions over time between environments, crime, victim and suspect* (see Fig. 2.3). The figure depicts a procession of intermingling events within three segments. Each segment, hypothetically, contains stimulus and response variables and setting events. Blend between segments suggests permeability across boundaries, or a constant, overlapping flow of one segment into the next segment. Segment 1, Segment 2, and Segment 3, while pictured as discrete components, are actually transient where responses produced in Segment 1 generate operant or respondent consequences doubling as antecedents prompting onset of Segment 2, and so forth. Each segment may entail one or multiple contingencies (i.e., motivating operations, stimulus cues, responses, consequences, unconditioned stimuli, etc.), either completed in a segment or continued uninterrupted into a second segment. Response patterns in one or many segments persist either in the same or different form, generating same, similar, or different contingencies in each segment. Setting events, described in Chapter 1, are the specific environmental conditions around which behavior patterns occur. Setting

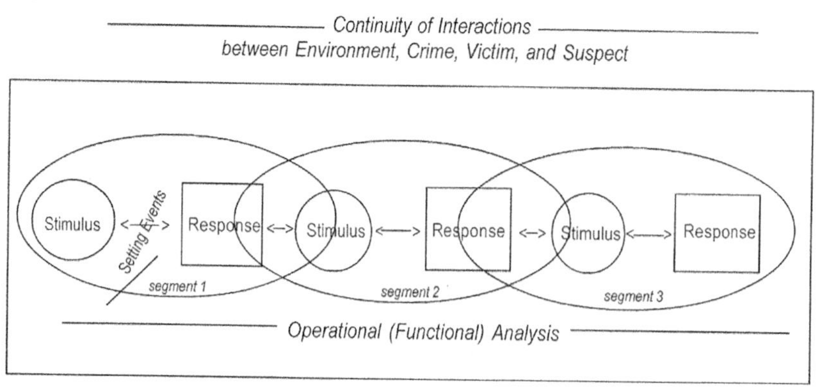


FIG. 2.3 Behavioral forensic model.

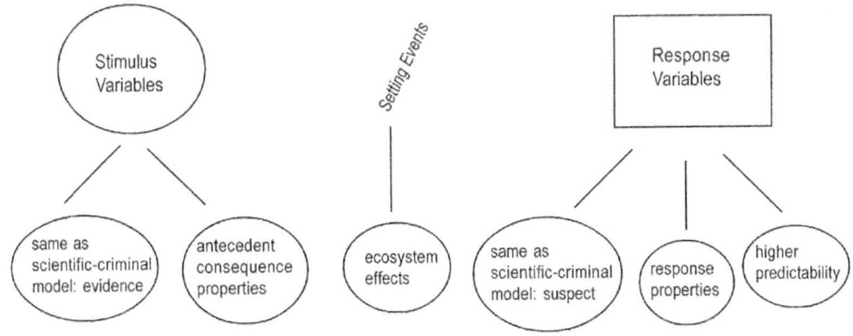


**FIG. 2.4** Stimulus and response variables.

events range from time of day, motivational operations of the organism, physical location, the people (accomplices) associated with the offender, or accessibility of physical objects. For example, in arson cases, placement of ignition devices, accelerants, and trailers to the fire's point of origin depends on entry into the house. If building access is difficult, entails too many obstacles, or occupants in the building stay longer than expected, altering the criminal's schedule, the crime does not get committed, *at least not in that behavior segment.* These confounding events delaying or preventing a crime or forcing production of new pre-criminal behaviors are not just coincidental. They are invaluable specimens in the biopsy of an ecosystem to investigate why the suspect *waited, chose another motivation and sequence for the crime, or committed the crime despite obstacles compromising success of the crime.* A better breakdown in the transaction of events can be explained by stimulus variables and response variables (see Fig. 2.4).

## Stimulus variables

Stimulus variables are functional properties directly impacting evocation, elicitation, or consequation of behaviors. Properties may be physical (corporeal) evidence found in a crime scene as discussed in the scientific-criminal model. For example, a UPS driver arrives at a customer's house to deliver a package. The house, its exterior or interior, constitutes stimulus conditions with which the driver may interact. As an *antecedent,* it may arouse operant or respondent patterns depending on the motivating operations or reactional biography of the UPS driver. In the past, for example, by the hour in the day, the driver needs to use the bathroom and spotted inside the house an accessible bathroom. Under similar circumstances historically, the driver politely asked to use the customer's bathroom. Affirmation of this request relieved the unconditional motivating operation and strengthened similar manding in the future.

## Response variables

Response variables factor into similar features of the offender investigated in the scientific-criminal model: (a) history, (b) physiology, (C) personality, and (d) proclivity. That is, the UPS driver had a (a) history of asking customers to use their bathrooms, (b) often experienced urgency (motivating operations) for urination at certain times of the day owing to taking anti-hypertensive medications, (c) was assertive or "confident" to ask the question, and (d) demonstrated a high probability of repeating same or similar questions under successively equal stimulus conditions. *Reponses properties* also consider novel or concurrent patterns deviating from the suspect's response history that make the current interaction more curious or sometimes difficult to account for a crime. For example, after the UPS driver exited the bathroom, he "accidently" left his pants zipper open exposing his genitalia. The female customer witnessing this "exposure" immediately drew it to the UPS driver's attention but also filed a police report, charging the UPS driver with indecent exposure.

A closer *behavioral analysis* of the offender's reactional biography goes beyond the simple stimulus-response relationship of his asking to use the bathroom. Response properties, in this case, also may involve his history of never wearing underwear after years of Olympic training for men's gymnastics. He shaved his pubic hair, and always wore a unitard without underwear to allow for unencumbered waist movement flexibility. His lack of wearing underwear meant one less insulator blocking the view of his genitals if he left his zipper open. Combined with his noncriminal background and absence of any sexual paraphelias (i.e., exhibitionism), the contingencies governing his genital exposure behavior seemed less a case of sexual deviance and more a case of bad judgment on wardrobe when going to customers' houses. His crime was reduced from Indecent Exposure to Disturbing the Peace.

The UPS driver is one example of using ABA principles (see Chapter 1) in the employment of a behavioral forensic assessment of stimulus and response variables. Notice the perspective of assessment shifts from personological variables characterizing, for example, traits of sexual abnormality or narcissism of not wearing underwear, to functional explanations. The functional explanations, culling from real events, are not always exculpatory. On the contrary, elucidation of behavior events, from one segment to another segment, may be the *tour de force* in unequivocally showing a cause and effect relationship for criminal responsibility, intentionality, and proclivity for recidivism.

## Flaws with model

Advantages of using the behavioral forensic model abound procedurally, pragmatically, and adjudicatively. Procedural or methodological steps to conduct functional analyses of controlling variables are easy, efficient, easy to teach, inexpensive, predictable, directly confrontable with naturalistic events, replicable, and offer high inter-rater reliability. Pragmatic advantages are the operational benefits of bypassing ominously-clustered personality traits or statistically compounded data that broadly profile criminal actions. Ambiguity is replaced with concise, situationally specific contingencies of cause-effect relationships explained through scientific principles. Adjudicative advantages are the clarification, precision, and better prediction of criminal intentionality, responsibility, and proclivity. A judicial process works more fairly, in other words, when the playbook of defendant's motives and behaviors are understandable by judge, jury, and attorney.

But these benefits compete with a legacy of criticisms, from predictability raising fears of losing freedom of choice (cf. Zamir & Teichamn, 2014), to exclusion of mediating events such as cognition and emotion, which are conventionally considered innate in advanced hominoids. The latter argument is more paramount and reverberates the cognitivists continuous caveat that applied behavior analysis, even *cognitive-behavior analysis*, is myopic in overlooking the richness and uniqueness of an individual (cf. Phelps, 2007; Skinner, 1977). Dehumanization already exists in some measure in jurisprudence. Arrested suspects, from the moment of being read their *Miranda rights* are de-individualized into homogenous classifications of crime for which laws, statutes and precedents exist to prosecute them. Loss of identity, and assimilation into the vast morass of crime profiles, admittedly has serious drawbacks. A 17 year old male arrested for Criminal Sexual Conduct (CSC) for performing sexual acts with his 16 year old girlfriend (who turned 17 years old in 2 months) *may be automatically classified under an adult-level first-degree rape offense.* If convicted, this offense carries a life-maximum prison sentence, depending on the state and inevitable entry on the state sexual registry. Prosecutors, charging him with this heinous act, expected the 17 year old to understand that a minor's (his girlfriend's) consent for sexuality is impermissible in court. The older teen, the statute implies, should be properly educated on legal parameters affecting his choices. The older adolescent loses opportunities accorded to pre-teen or mid-teen offenders, of performing community service or restitution to the harmed family. None of these proactive steps of rehabilitation are optional when the prosecution lumps this older teen into the category of antisocial psychopathology as an adult violent sex offender (Becroft, 2006; Kurlychek & Johnson, 2010). The label itself iatrogenically typecasts him as reckless, ruthless, remorseless, and predatory. His identity evaporates into a faceless and amorphous grouping of high-risk criminals. Any vestige of his redemptive and healthy behaviors also vanish. He is simply prisoner #174356 blended invisibly into an anonymous aggregate whose life, behaviors, and purpose in the world are obviated.

The prosecutory lynching of this young offender not only demoralizes his character and marginalizes his existence, it also prejudices any discovery attempted by the public defender. Without knowing the facts of his case, he can be railroaded into an unfair plea bargaining where he accepts a lesser offense but still serves jail time and enters the national sex registry, scarring him for life and nearly destroying any hope for gainful career employment. Grandstanding his CSC case as a bad example to follow may be a scare-tactic to deter other older adolescents from similar crimes. But it may not. Nazi commandants of concentration camps employed similar tactics when they hung a child thief to warn other children not to steal. The children stole anyway. They were hungry. Is there a way to prevent or even stall de-individuation of this CSC adolescent or of other arrested suspects? If so, one viable way is widening the angle on investigating and assessing the behavior patterns unique to his behavior segments precurrent to and including the criminal acts.

Assessments that focus on empirically-measured subcomponents of a field, including widely diverse parameters of response and stimulus functions, avoid this homogenization of arrested suspects into nebulous personality categories or stereotyped psychological profiles. Behavioral forensic analysis may be radical, even inhospitable to the courts. The approach at first may snub the powerhouse of traditional models of forensic science. It may shutout non-measurable or inferential traits of human behavior that some consider sacrosanct to criminal investigation (e.g., inheritable genes, personality traits, etc.). More controversially, it may introduce uncomfortable language with its vocabulary of concepts and principles, all of which deviates from the normative landscape of psychodynamic or humanistic language on the court lawn. But this is how behavioral forensic analysis makes its debut, not its last curtain call. The breakout success of the behavioral forensic model will not be to comfort the jurisprudence process by speaking in intuitive language. The model is not a marketing campaign advertising a consumer product to the masses. Instead it is an empirical model showing how principles of science link cause and effect relationships to better isolate, measure, predict, and prevent criminal recidivism.

## Eight parts of a functional analysis

Performing the first steps of behavioral forensic analysis begins with revising the optics on how to look at suspect's behavior. In Chapter 1, concepts and principles of applied behavior analysis and interbehavioral analysis introduced a basic lexicon to follow the discourse on forensic case examples. Here, similar concepts and principles re-appear, without definition, in a series of interrogatories or questions the behavioral forensic examiner asks in laying out the investigatory landscape of a criminal evaluation. Fig. 2.5 (below) identifies the main categories into which questions appear orderly and logically. These categories include *Preliminary analysis, Clarification of Problem, Analysis of Consequences, Analysis of Responses, Developmental Analysis, Social Change History, Self-control, and Analysis of Setting Events.*

### Preliminary analysis of the problem

Here, basic data collection occurs on the simple aspects of behavior. Questions asked include:

1. What are the behavior deficits?
2. What are the behavior excesses?
3. What are the suspect's assets and liabilities?

**FIG. 2.5** Eight parts of a functional analysis.

*Example and explanation: A hoarder sued by this condominium association who retaliates with physical violence.* He is a quiet, reserved, asocial person who stays indoors unless he works. He has inherited wealth but never spends it. His house is over-cluttered, filthy, inhabitable, and he sleeps in a small space on the floor surrounded by his nest of blankets while the remainder of 1700 square feet is filled with debris.

## Clarification of the problem

Clarification questions get a perspective on who filed the complaint, why the complaint or crime a violation is or culturally inappropriate, and simple troubleshooting about the antecedents and consequences. Questions asked include:

1. What is the arrest for and did it match the conviction?
2. Who viewed the problem as objectionable? Who filed the complaint?
3. Is this a recurrent complaint or did circumstances warrant police or some agency intervention?
4. What are the consequences of the problem for the suspect, complainant (victim), or other people impacted by the arrest, investigation, or conviction outcome?
5. What would the consequence be for the suspect or victim if the problem was eliminated?
6. What are the antecedents of the problem? Is provocation unilateral or bilateral?
7. Was there a long-term delay between provocations or between provocations and criminal act? What antecedents occurred in between to sustain criminal behavior?
8. Would the suspect still have problems if the antecedents never occurred? Are victims responsible for producing high risk or illegal behavior in the suspect?
9. How would changing the suspect's environment reduce or accelerate the crime in question or in subsequent repeated offenses?

*Explanation:* The arrest of clutter and inhabitable housing matched the complaint of violating the condo association rules for sanitary dwellings. Removal of the suspect or clutter from the condo eliminates the violation, but also alerts other condo owners of the association's vigilance in enforcing this rule. Once the condo is clean, condo neighbors are still unlikely to accept the suspect's continued residence fearing repetition of the crime. Had his condo never been unsanitary or cluttered, his isolationism and non-friendliness still ostracized him from the condo community, raising suspicion about his behavior. More importantly, cleaning his condo would not immediately prevent future episodes of clutter since the suspect hates living alone, never developed a sense of enjoyable home-life, and sees his house as a warehouse.

## Analysis of the consequences

Closer inspection of consequences means putting the frequency, schedule, and other parameters of reinforcement and punishment under the microscope for a magnified reading of causal implications it has for the crime in question. Questions asked include:

1. What kind of reinforcers are most effective for this offender?
2. Were the reinforcers absent, in abundance, jeopardized, or removed under threatening circumstances?

3. What has been the suspect's experience with these reinforces? Are they rapidly accessible, consumable, dispensable, disseminable, or exchanged for more desirable reinforcers?
4. What groups exert the most control over this offender? Do they withhold reinforcers or punishers contingent upon the offender's compliance? Is accepting a plea of guilty or going to jail an example of offender compliance (loyalty)?
5. Does the offender understand the effects of the consequences?
6. How impervious is the offender to a past history of correctional system punishment, police authority, or social and civil rules?
7. Is the offender resourceful, resilient, and efficient at cultivating self-reinforces to re-start criminal behaviors either in the same setting or in another setting?
8. What is the offender's historical ratio of reinforcers to punishers relative to appropriate behaviors?
9. Are the consequences supporting deviant behavior ensconced in the behavior segments and supplant reinforcers for appropriate, crime-free behaviors?
10. What combination of contingencies (concurrent, mixed, tandem, etc.) motivate criminal behavior and noncriminal behaviors?

*Explanation:* Reinforcers for the offender are staying home or working. He is listless, indifferent, depressed, stays in one spot in the house watching YouTube videos. He can watch the videos for 5–6 h mixed with drifting into sleep. Except for bathroom and eating needs, he stays in this cocoon. The suspect grew accustomed to his self-restricted arrangement, not only in the condo, but from a 20 year history of living in apartments or basement of his mother's house. The same pattern occurs of messing up his surrounds and nesting in one spot. Once his routine begins, he is not resourceful and poor at cultivating new self-reinforcers for prosocial or healthier behaviors. Part of this is due not having or not knowing how to get a repertoire of socially healthy behaviors. Part of his routine is also due to complacency and self-debasement for living in such unsanitary conditions, figuring he deserves this dilapidation. His self-punishment contingencies far exceed any awareness of or use of self-reinforcing contingencies to shape appropriate behaviors (maintenance of healthy condo living). His motivating operations to sustain filth and clutter are avoidance/escape from any effort to face and clean his insurmountable pyramid of debris, and avoidance to face the morbid embarrassment of having a professional organizer enter his premises to facilitate evacuation of his mess.

## Analysis of responses

Properties of responses such as current or sequential, rate or frequency, topography, inter-response time, and intensity, duration, and latency from stimulus, while essential to measurement, are equally as important as adjunctive or collateral behaviors occurring either historically or in the current behavior segments. Adjunctive behaviors are the ethical, moral, cultural, religious, or other behaviors compatible with or co-occurring with criminal behavior offering a potential estimate of crime severity and risk of repeat offenses. Such questions include:

1. Has the criminal act occurred previously?

2. Does it associate with similar behavior patterns or it is unique or occur under very specific stimulus conditions?
3. Are the responses consistent with the offender's routines, rituals, or lifestyle patterns? If not, how did the offender learn this behavior and for what purpose?
4. Is the topography incompatible with moral, religious, pacifist, or docile behaviors?
5. Is the topography of behavior appropriate, but its function is not because of poor stimulus discrimination?
6. Has the response regularly or historically occurred without incident, and is even the normative behavior under certain circumstances or with certain peers?
7. Was the offense act benign and resolvable but aggravated when police or other authorities (or victim) intervened?
8. Did the crime require response such as language, rituals, or other patterns endemic to particular cultures, ethnicities, religious, nations, cults, gangs, or other factions? If the offender was not a member of these factions, did they have access to or relevant knowledge of these responses?
9. In cases of excessive behaviors, did impulsivity interfere with prudent judgment as it has in the past?

*Explanation:* The hoarder has a documented history of repeated voluntary psychiatric admissions for major depression when he ceases to take antidepressant medications, decompensates to a point of pre-suicidal thoughts, and neglect self-hygiene. His inertia in the house (not cleaning, just sitting in filth) co-exists with withdrawal, anhedonia, dysphoria, detachment, and asocialization. At work, his behavior is diametrical; he is highly efficient, organized, calculated, over-active, eager for work, and takes enormous pride in job completion beyond standards. Cross over of this work response class into his home-life is rare, since the stimulus conditions in the house immediately trigger apathy and response incapacitation. That is, he is very discriminative in responding one way under one set of conditions, and one way under another set of conditions, no matter the obvious metaphorical extension between both stimulus conditions conducive for stimulus generalization. His pattern of household neglect and clutter is neither new, nor manifested from aggravation of neighbors or current outside forces (creditors, lawyers for the condo association) regarding his household negligence.

## Developmental analysis

The reactional biography, as explained in Chapter 1, ideally, represents the totality of every unit of biophysical and behavioral occurrence through the transaction of many psychological fields. Since monitoring every discrete unit is technically or methodologically difficult and probably not even necessary for estimations of potential responses (interbehavioral potentials), a reactional biography is more of a sample of past response patterns and functions, inclusive of one's medical history. A developmental analysis asks questions about this reactional biography to see how it influenced current criminal behavior or may predict future crime recidivism. Questions frequently asked include:

1. Does the offender have physiological or medical limitations that affected judgment or response continuity?

2. Doe the response history show recurrent or similar offenses by significant family members during the offender's lifespan?
3. Is the offense affected by any learning, cognitive, or educational deficits or excesses?
4. Was the offender's criminal behavior due to errors in medication or drug-taking overuse, underuse, use?
5. Is the offense likely to occur more when the offender is hungry, thirsty, without medicine, inebriated, or using other illicit drugs (motivating operations)?
6. Is the offender too young or significantly aged to have committed the crime according to the police report, victim's testimony, or seen the offender's confession?
7. Is the suspect physically unable to commit the offense of which he or she was accused?

*Explanation:* Analysis of the behavior repertoire (reactional biography) does raise some concerns. First, on higher doses of the antidepressant and antipsychotic medications taken for 5 years, the offender is sleepy, sluggish, hypo-energetic, forgetful, and despondent. He is morbidly overweight, moves slowly, and cannot easily bend down to clean floors, collect empty bottles, and gather laundry sprawled on furniture. His history of high productivity relates to highly structured environments with clearly definable rules and stimulus conditions promising tight concurrent schedules of reinforcement and punishment for compliance or noncompliance. By contrast, at home, he lives in a free-operant environment and lacks self-management skills to install behavior contingencies or rely on rule-governed behaviors to keep busy and clean his domicile. Educationally, he was a college graduate scoring honor grades in calculus and science, with as premed major and career expectation of pursuing medical school. That is, *he has the acumen and skill potential to change inappropriate behaviors.* He also accepted underemployment at a retail store (for over 20 years) requiring elementary and mundane routines that he delights in mastering and outshining his coworkers. He regularly take his psychotropic medications. But when lapses occur in routine, particularly with antidepressants, abrupt withdrawal produce pre-treatment symptoms of severe depression and anxiety disabling his behavior and increasing self-confinement in his condo.

## Social change history

Setting events—the social and cultural matrix consisting of complex stimulus conditions—are tantamount to the fuel energizing an automobile. Events provide the opportunity for behavior occurrence, or mediate behavior changes from 1 s to the next. Criminal behavior may seem outwardly like a one-time accident, but it breaks down into sub-responses or precurrents that evolve slowly, with some spikes, over the offender's history. Increases in spikes, just as decreases in behavior, entirely depend on where the offender is, how he or she responds to discernible stimulus cues, and the consequences generated from his behavior relative to same, similar, or different setting events. Questions often asked about social change (setting events) include:

1. What is the offender's current social and cultural situation (rural, urban, and financially solvent)?
2. Did the offender recently relocate in housing, cities, or dramatically shift to a difficult or challenging environment inconsistent with the offender's past. Did he act this way before this transition?

3. Can these social situations be changed to affect immediate improvement in the offender's behavior?
4. As there been recent deaths, job loss, job jeopardy, family or partner disturbance, or financial pressures affecting the offender's behavior?

*Explanation:* Five years ago, the offender bought a condo 3-times the size of his prior apartments or living space in the basement of his parent. He never properly cleaned, decorated, or personalized prior housing spaces and was equally delinquent in disconnecting from his current living condo space. When his overwhelming clutter and debris eclipsed to a panic level upsetting other inhabitants of a house or apartment complex, he delayed any self-clean-up until forced into cleaning by legal order or a parent, brother, or trusted family member. Procrastination of house maintenance grew longer over time when fewer family members or authorities imposed a penalty (i.e., eviction, shame, etc.) for his filth and coerced his decluttering. As the schedule of punishment, in other words, grew thinner, his duration increased of tolerating and habituating to his stockpile of indoor garbage. With his mother's early onset dementia, his father's death two years ago, and brother living in another state, he lacks any contacts with people historically imposing contingencies for rapid clean up.

## Self-control analysis

Self-management, at any level, is the tour de force of maximal human performance. Developing independence in functional behavior is optimal using applied behavior analysis (Southall & Gast, 2011), and has been the measure in forensic evaluations of self-regulation, confidence, purposefulness, and control over one's world. Discernment of self-control in criminal cases helps determine awareness between right and wrong, or acting in conformity with laws in cases of criminal responsibility. In parental competency evaluations, degree of self-control favorably suggests anger regulation and prudent choices of positive behavior management methods. In the hoarder's case, baseline data or pre-criminal history of self-control indicates awareness of the household filth, prerequisite abilities to initiate and execute house rehabilitation, and capacity to use preventive maintenance steps to keep the household clean. Questions frequently asked include:

1. Are there any situations in which the offender can control the problem and reform?
2. What are those situations and how does he or she control behavior?
3. Does the offender's perception of the criminal behavior correspond with observations by others—defendant attorney, prosecutor, judge, jury?
4. Does offender show self-discipline in other areas of life?
5. Can this self-discipline be employed within offender rehabilitation?
6. What variables eroded, obstructed, or eliminated self-discipline causing the current crime?
7. Are there adult or other role models (clergy, close friends, family members) exerting contingency control over self-discipline responses?
8. Do acts of self-control generate continuous, variable, or random schedules of punishment?

9. Do these schedules of punishment compete with reinforcement schedules for appropriate behavior or no-crime behaviors?
10. Does the offender display the skills, personal or community resources, motivating operations, and history of resilience allow for self-discipline skill development?

*Explanation:* Erosion of self-discipline since college years contributed significantly to the offender's repeated hoarding and household clutter. Before college years, he kept his room meticulously clean, with obsessive-compulsive daily rituals of making his bed, removing clothing from the floor, and dusting furniture. He also studied for tests and completed homework in his impeccably clean room. His mother, a high achiever, scolded the offender incessantly in childhood and adolescence for his underachievement of A's, when he regularly earned high B grades. She denigrated his intelligence, claimed he would fail high school, and ultimately shame his family with a useless career. He already recognized his father's professional job as lawyer required college and new the family expected both completion of undergraduate and graduate school. By his first year of college at a big-ten school, he aced his grades but got no reprieve from his mother's torrent of sordidly insulting remarks about his character. He hated living at home and commuting to college. His room maintenance deteriorated extensively. He continued to live in the basement room in the house after dropping out of college, but left the room in a state of constant disarray. When he moved out into his own apartment, household clutter quickly increased to unlivable levels ignored by the offender. The only contingencies forcing his rapid and last-minute (procrastinative) cleaning is when his father or mother came to visit. After they left, decomposition of the room was within the week. No matter the apartment or houses he visited that were neat, clean, and cleverly decorated, the offender never imitated the images of their apartments into altering his own apartment. However, he demonstrated infinitesimal self-discipline in his methodical design of templates and other prompts to help him complete his job at work and share with other people. He became the reliable worker depended on by many staff in the retail store to efficiently trouble-shoot, solve, and prevent recurrence of warehouse-related messes and product re-ordering obstacles. His acumen to foresee retail operations problems and intervene on them with unbelievable speed, accuracy, and proficiency earned him promotions and favor among coworkers. History of his employment showed he demonstrated similar remarkable industriousness in all of the jobs he held, from restaurant to retail. This preexisting repertoire of self-discipline was mature, well-integrated, and passed the test of generalization across many *job settings*.

However, *he could not generalize this exceptional response class into his home setting*. Obstacles blocking generality was a psychological field of many behavior segments involving parental punishment for his intelligence, his house care, and of him personally. Delivery of punishment from his mother occurred randomly, which resulted in constant anxiety or anticipation of awful comments (foreboding). His echoic or self-repeating of these remarks (rule-governed statements) served further as punishment decreasing his home-cleaning efforts to the point of response cessation; the punishment contingencies competed with and exceeded the reinforcing contingencies gained from the work environment from employee and employer kudos. Stimulus control of self-discipline behaviors at work was absent at home, replaced with a different stimulus control over complacent, avoidance-escape (non-cleaning) behaviors. This example of alternating stimulus conditions—one generating crime-free behavior, the other generating criminal behavior—shows the special insight a behavioral approach brings to the case.

## Analysis of setting events

Under "Social History" described above, analysis of setting events covered the cultural and social matrices controlling the contingencies of reinforcement and punishment affecting the hoarder. Where he lived, where he worked, the time of day—or environmental variables—randomly or predictably shaping the psychological field around which clutter escalation persisted. The external "forces" or consequences crossing over from one setting to the next explained the offender's unabated house neglect and risk for condominium rule violations. Contingencies also pertain to his biophysical, or unique social and family rules governing his verbal behavior spoken aloud and to himself (e.g., rule-governed behavior). Social and family rules are moral, religious, and ethical beliefs, values, attitudes, or self-expressions about the appropriateness of certain behaviors proportional to some promulgated standard. Common questions asked include:

1. What is the offender's religious or family-moral beliefs? How do they affect problem behavior maintenance or encourage reform?
2. Does the offender adhere to some moral or other principles (statements) against which he compares himself negatively or interferes with motivational operations for correcting behavior?
3. Are legal threats restricting self-disciplined behavior changes or posing threats for reform maintenance?
4. Does the offender suffer any medical problems or drug side-effects impairing progress on behavior change efforts? Will altering the drugs or curing the medical problem relieve or exacerbate problems with cluttering?

*Explanation:* Self-imposed moral judgments are the product of echoic, tacts, mands, or intraverbal exchanges between child and parent during childhood and adolescence. A parent repeatedly tells his 6-year old daughter "it is good to help people to their seat," while she joins him ushering congregants into the pews before church service. The same daughter observes her mother, after the church service, serve congregants coffee and pastries. She imitates her mother's behavior by bringing over a doughnut to an elderly man, greeting him with, "I know it's nice to bring you this doughnut." Once these verbal responses are frequent, earn excessive attention, and in effect become *part of the child's repertoire*, their topography changes. Verbal responses are less wordy, or truncated to succinctly describe the contingencies impacted by the verbal response. For example, on subsequent days serving as usher, the 6 year may see an elderly person and say to herself, "it's good to usher." This is an autoclitic mand enjoining or urging the youngster to step toward the infirmed congregant and help him to his seat. Likewise, helping her mother with the fellowship hour after the service, the 6-year old may engage in another autoclitic mand, "I need to serve this lady sitting at the table." The autoclitic mand enjoins her to walk over to the pastry table, pick up a doughnut on a paper-plate, and serve it to a woman sitting there. That is a primary way rule-governed behaviors or "beliefs" form.

But evolution of beliefs are not always a function of reinforcement. The offender of house violations learned a litany of rule-governed statements during childhood and adolescence preserving his delinquency of cleaning. Unfiltered criticism bombarded in his ears included "You are a slob and will always be messy," You will always need somebody to clean up after you," "Smart people are clean, you are dumb and messy." Verbal battery decreased the hoarder's time at home, eliminated his bedroom cleaning and built a complex hierarchy of avoidance and escape behavior involving more time spent *anywhere but home.* For example, when he worked at a horse stable in his teens, he stayed after his work shift, worked a double shift and even offered a triple shift around malodorous manure just to avoid going home. He repeated the same disproportionate amount of time spent at jobs than at home into his adulthood. Derived from these punishment contingencies were such rule-governed statesman (beliefs) as "I hate home," "My work is my home," "home is bad, aversive, or threatening, and I don't want to be there." Consequently, his disastrously filthy and uninhabitable condo eliminates any semblance of the place being "home." He may stay there but does not interact with it in productive ways (clean it, use it functionally except to sleep, take a shower, or use the restroom).

Besides taking antidepressant medications, he suffers polymorbid obesity, hypertension, high cholesterol, and type 1 diabetes requiring self-administered insulin injections. His failure to routinely administer the injection or take medication for his medical conditions can cause malaise, indifference, and aggravate his depression. But even when he takes the insulin, for example, if he takes Lantus, predictable side-effects such as headaches, insatiable hunger, weakness, poor concentration, rapid heartbeat, and fainting might discourage undertakings to clean his condo. He sits motionless, catatonically, in a state of disorientation or fugue, disconnected from the reality of his condo's debris.

When analysis of interoceptive and exteroceptive setting events shows there are salient impediments to self-cleaning the condo, resilience, and offender rehabilitation, it changes the perspective of the forensic etiology of the hoarder's behaviors. He is not just a complacent, sloppy, rule-deviant, and self-neglectful adult with a diagnosis of major depression. Instead, inside his psychological field lies a very complex series of setting events empirically explaining previous and current antecedents under which he is more probable to commit the household neglect crimes. Collection of this biodata during clinical inquiry of the offender's background or from collaborative reports is also not atypical for psychological evaluations. The first hour or two of meeting with an offender consists of gathering a biographic history and their perception of the crime. Questions are protocol about childhood, adolescence, geographic displacements, juvenile and adult crimes, education (e.g., grades, special education), social and school activities, military experience, substance abuse, psychiatric and drug abuse residential and outpatient treatment, psychotropic or other medications taken, social and sexual experiences, partner relationships, past head trauma and surgeries, genetic or developmental anomalies, and abuses by parents. Answers to these questions appear in every properly executed psychological evaluation. *The difference in preparing a behavioral forensic analysis report* is *how this information is interpreted using behavioral standards guiding an objective person-environment interaction.*

## Behavioral standards

In every profession, standards provide general principles of practice by which to uniformly establish a common philosophy or pragmatic model recommended to its users. In the discipline of applied behavior analysis, standards may vary, but largely the focus is on objectively defined, observable behaviors of social significance. "It seeks to improve the behavior under study while demonstrating a reliable relationship between the procedures employed and the behavioral improvement; and it uses the method of science—description, quantification, and analysis" (Cooper, Heron, & Heward, 1987, p. 2). Derivatives of ABA–in cognitive behavior therapy, dialectical behavior, Acceptance and Commitment Therapy, Rational Emotive Therapy—and the list is endless, all share the common denominators of scientific constructs, objectification, and functionality of variables. In behavioral *forensic analysis,* similar standards act as aspirations for the examiner to move closer to switching from traditional optics to behavioral optics. The six standards facilitating this new perspective include the following:

1. Examinations include objectively quantifiable and reproducible data generated from reliable measurement instruments. Multiple measures consist of standardized tests, direct observation and analogue tests, and case document reviews.
2. Testing should be within a context best representing or simulating the offender's natural environment. When natural environment access is impossible (e.g., in jail, prison), ambient conditions of testing including the role of examiner should reduce sources of error, bias, artificiality, or intimidation causing expectancy (demand) effects, which may lower or contaminate scoring.
3. Assessment of criminal behavior, and contingencies under which it occurs, remain within the canons of scientific deduction. Conclusions do not transcend the boundaries of science, such as using invented (reified) concepts or unproven ideas beyond events under investigation.
4. Behavioral forensic assessment considers past, current, and potential events impacting criminal behavior. Behavior is among a larger constellation of responses, and is not consolidated into one target pathology. Events directly relate to individual repertoires (reactional biographies), effectiveness at performing behaviors compatible or incompatible to criminal acts, and habituation to contingencies delimiting or precluding success of offender rehabilitation.
5. Assessment facts consist of interrelated factors that have been a reciprocal or "symmetrical" relationship instead of an asymmetrical relationship. Events measured in one behavior segment of time are interpreted in connection to preceding and succeeding behavior segments. This way, a more accurate etiology/diagnosis arises regarding whether the crime was isolated or resulted from repetitive incidents.
6. Behavioral segments represent the totality of person-environment interactions at any given time. Relevant factors in a behavioral segment go beyond traditional psychological data to include sociocultural, physiological, domestic, educational, climatological, and physical structure of the setting. Assessment, in other words, entails a multidisciplinary approach.

## Commentary on the standards

Recognition of a more powerful scientific approach to criminal assessment means its standards must align with a pre-existing evidence-based model in the natural sciences. Behavior analysis is an example of such an empirical model. From its inception in basic or infrahuman experimentation–with pigeons, rats, dogs, chickens, and rats–to its naturalistic applications with human beings– in education, prisons, homes, industry, and clinical settings—*applied behavior analysis* has been at the nexus of a systems revolution in psychology to be more lawful and a gemini to its allied scientific fields in, for example, chemistry, physics, biology, and anthropology. Each of allied scientific field operate on the general postulate that scientific construction constitute "descriptions of things and events as they interbehave with each other and with the investigating scientist" (Kantor, 1971, p. 19). Kantor's articulates the homogeneity of psychology with other sciences in his example of studying electricity. Since electricity cannot be seen, but must be revealed (observed) by visible galvanometer deflections, so naturalistic psychology studies effects in organic action by measuring the behavior of the organism (p. 29).

All six standards prescribe a conceptual scheme consistent with this multidisciplinary naturalistic science. The first and second standards are consistent with ethical forensic practice of using the most updated, objectively normative, and court-accepted measurement instrument in data collection. Use of the MMPI-2-RF, for example, over using the MMPI-2, relies on current and reliably sampled norm and enhanced specificity of behavior pathology. Direct observation measurement also means data gathering is not purely at the mercy of standardized questionnaires. Behavioral forensic examiners, as scientific investigators, observe and record putative behaviors of the offender during the pre-interview, interview, and post-interview process; they incorporate and study records taken of offender's actions in jail, prison, school, or in environments simulating the environment around which the crime occurs. The third standard prescribes a restriction on information collected from the offender. Observations and interpretations remain inherently connected to the naturalistic facts showing interactions between behavior and events. Deductive reasoning stays within the limits of what *the offender did, not what he or she thought or some other aspects of personality*. Conclusions extract from isolated or multi-transactional instances of criminal action within certain contexts, the stimuli and responses acting as the core source of assessment, rather than it being underlying hypothetical or reified constructs lacking correspondence to the actual data. The fourth standard speaks to the spatial-temporal continuum of behaviors under investigation from childhood to adulthood. Access to the reactional biography offers a glimpse into the window of behaviors compatible and incompatible with the criminal actions and events likely responsible for causation of these behaviors. Psychological history, as different from *psychohistory* (a psychoanalytical endeavor), can show cumulative response sequences of behavior influenced by operant, respondent, or other stimulus influences resembling the contingencies during the crime. Congruence between the nascent behavior identified historically and its advance stages currently can show the probability of risk behavior, criminal recidivism, and the conditions most conducive for production of criminal actions.

The fifth standard reminds the evaluator that measured behaviors or past records of behavior (e.g., in education or medial documents) are not idiographic or asymmetrical products of behavior. The data describing an offender's action, instead, is a snapshot in time of symmetrical, reciprocal, and a multivariance of stimulus conditions impinging on the offender. For example, in love-triangle murders, where the jealous spouse kills his unfaithful spouse or the lover, events surrounding the eventual homicide directly shape motivation and actual behavior in the assailant than any personality or internal character flaw identified in testing. As interactive species, human beings collude with their environment in generating same, similar, or very different behaviors from their history or recent past, the distinction between which proves essential in estimating recidivistic rates or foundations for mitigating circumstances on criminal behavior. The sixth standard also addresses the transactional scope of confrontable data. For example, suppose the homicide occurred in a Midwestern town inside a motel room, when the town was under a winter storm warning and freezing temperatures. Suppose further the offender suffered fibromyalgia and greater skeleton-muscular pain at higher barometric pressures. He also underwent an epidermal cyst removal one day ago and the bandaged left-sided scar still residually hurt from the lidocaine injection numbing the site. Climate, time of year, location, and predisposition to physical pain now become valuable variables in operationalizing the pre-criminal and criminal behaviors. For example, consider that: (a) offender is confined in an unheated motel room under a state-declared winter emergency forbidding road travel, (b) offender's pain escalation is intolerable without any over-the-counter or prescribed painkillers, (c) historically pain intensity associated with the offender's proclivity for aggression, (d) the woman inside the same motel room, with whom offender is having an affair, is under a motivational operation to return home within the next 20 min before her husband arrives from work, and (e) she threatens exposure of her affair to her husband, who is the offender's brother. Convergence of these *mutually interactive stimuli and responses constitute unusual contingencies that produce outcome effects otherwise unlikely to occur under less adverse conditions.* The functional conclusions tentatively deduced are neither declarations nor exculpations of offender guilt; the analysis simply considers the confluence of naturalistic events as further evidence in the investigation of behavior causality.

## Threats of despecialization

In the brutally competitive health service business, the economics of service delivery demand an efficient system to reach larger numbers of patients without losing money and not taxing the providers. Calculated into the mathematics of this business model is costs expended in paying primary providers, support staff, and regular overhead fees (building maintenance, utilities, etc.). Within the last 10 years, service agencies came up with the idea of reducing the patient load from the primary provider and dividing it among, not just other equally licensed providers, but among subspecialists subordinate to the primary provider. Delegation of service tasks to less trained or subspecialists working under the supervision on primary specialists was not new but not an accepted standard. Dentists, for example, utilized dental hygienists since 1914, then called dental nurses. Hygienists took over the role of dentists in examining and polishing teeth and extended duties ensued in x-ray administration. In the last twenty years, dentistry services expanded subspecializations to Dental Assistant, who helps the dentist or hygienist in procedures such as fillings, crowns, and extractions they also take and pour dental impressions, and now operate the x-ray computer systems. With this hierarchy of staff came profound different levels of training and education from the dentists, who requires four post-bachelors years either for Doctor of Dental Medicine or Doctor of Dental Surgery, to the hygienist, who requires a 2-year Associates Degree, to the Dental Assistant, who needs 6-months to one year for certification.

The hierarchy of dental or any human service staff *reflects a current trend for significantly less educated staff to be given exponentially more responsibility in patient care.* Performing the complex tasks of dentistry among less specialized staff achieves the goal of servicing more clients in a practice or in outlining or rural areas where dentists may be scarce. It re-invents health service into a more turnkey operation where complete needs are met by less specialized staff treating patients as if patients were seen by the specialized staff. Medical assistants, for example, while at one time relegated to the unsavory tasks of bedpan removal, now are assisting nurses and physician's assistants in outpatient diagnoses, injections, and simple produces. The bedpan and primordial tasks fell to a lower subspecialty called Certified Nurse Assistant (C N A). The C N A's also recently elevated their duties to administration of medications, patient monitoring, and taking vitals. Their custodial duties, including the role of comforter to patients, is now part of training for Patient Care Technicians. The de-escalation of education, training, experience, from primary provider to assistant, with the latter assuming key duties once performed by the primary specialist, reflects a disturbing cultural trend called *despecialization.*

Despecialization is not a derogatory term. It describes the progressively increasing delegation of human service delivery from specialists to subspecialists, with the expectation that consumers are receiving equal care. *And this expectation is a false assumption.* Physician's Assistants and Nurse Practitioners, for example, fill the gaps of physician shortages in the healthcare system (cf. Gerrie & Holbrook, 2013). They meet the inundation of patients doubled in the last four years from medical access through the Affordable Care Act. Their overarching knowledge, flexibility, and contributions, without doubt, is no longer seen as a band-aid for missing physicians. Likewise, innovations in technology to correct human error in misdiagnoses are even replacing nurse practitioners and physician's assistants with artificial intelligence—robots who can analyze eye scans for hemorrhages lesions, or detect common childhood conditions after processing the patient's symptoms, history, lab results, and other clinical data (He et al., 2019). Artificial intelligence aside, limitations in education and breadth of problem assessment may narrow these subspecialists' perspective and their depth with which they can formulate organic causes in the body's complex biological system. But they are not alone. Most allied health fields employ different levels of professionals eroding the *scientific integrity of investigation required to garner a proper functional analysis of particular situations.* Veterinarians now delegate tasks to Veterinary technicians and Veterinary Assistants. Occupational and physical therapists delegate tasks to Occupational Therapist Technician, and Physical Therapy Aids and Assistant. Ophthalmologist delegate tasks to Ophthalmological Assistants. Cardiologists permit Certified Cardiographic Technicians to run Electrocardiograms. Pharmacists use pharmacy technicians to fill prescription orders and communicate basic answers to medication questions to consumers. The list of subspecialty professionals and certified technicians endlessly abounds.

The practice of psychology also has not been spared this propagation of subspecialists and technicians. Interstate debates, more recently, called into question the Masters- (limited) Licensure level in clinical psychology being permitted to work independently in a practice, except they had to report to a licensed psychologist. A bill nearly passed in Michigan, for example, would amend this privilege and relegate Masters-level (clinical) psychologists to "Psychology Associates" (State of Michigan, 2017). The Psychology Associate would continue privileges to administer psychotherapy, but could not practice applied behavior analysis unless licensed or certified to engage in that practice. Similarly, stripped from their options for service would be more complex forensic and neuropsychological assessments, the very tools they likely received training in during graduate school. By juxtaposition, compare the pruning of service tools for a Masters-level psychologist with the plethora of tools afforded to the Master-degree "Forensic Psychologists" who works in the criminal justice field. Forensic psychologists consult judges and juries on behavior motivation, help conduct assessments, provide rehabilitative treatment, and consult state and federal agencies on criminal profiles. Curricula for the Masters programs vary considerably and always cover conventional courses on criminal behavior, abnormal behavior, victimology, forensic research, law, violence and threat assessment, and some clinical courses to meet a professional counselor licensure track. But without the counselor licensure track, forensic psychologists are not a licensable profession. The Masters level clinical psychologist takes extensively more classes on abnormal psychology, psychometrics, therapy interventions, basic and applied research, statistics and research models (single and group design), and service one or two practica with diverse populations. The irony is that this sprawling discipline of forensic psychology can harvest therapists, educators, and consultants, who are less trained than Masters-level psychologists and are not qualified for licensure. But, to their advantage, they have more community and professional support and recognition to be called *psychologists*.

Another disturbing trend in despecialization that hits more closer to home is the subclassifications of service delivery in Applied Behavior Analysis. When the author received his doctoral training in Applied Behavior Analysis (ABA) and Clinical Psychology in the late 1970s to early 1980s, doctoral-level and even Masters-level psychologists in ABA were venerable professionals. They gained respect for their cleverly analytical acumen to functionally assess any behavior problem within seconds and instantly retrieve from memory a trove of baseline-recording methods and possible interventions. Their wizardry in decontextualizing a complex behavior segment into succinct operational definitions was uncanny and almost "magical." This is because ABA education from bachelors, through Masters, and into Doctoral level courses entailed comprehensive study of the history of the science, and conducting basic and applied research. Students learned upfront and live, how the principles of conditioning really worked, how experimental analogues related to naturalistic field behaviors, and what common contravening variables may sabotage the best interventions. They also learned to scrutinize articles in *Journal of Applied Behavior Analysis and Journal of Experimental Analysis of Behavior,* from the research review through to the discussion of research limitations and implications for future research. Given this regal training, ABA professionals became impeccable at assessment not only of the target behaviors, but also in assessing problems; they were rapid troubleshooters in identifying and fixing ineffective strategies, human errors, and the conduciveness of an environment to support successful implementation of ABA methods.

This elite group of skillful ABA professionals still exists and proudly teach at universities, consults for schools, industries, or families benefiting from their razer-sharp precision of logical details in behavior assessment and modification. But they are the minority. In the last 10 years, inspired by a sweeping advocacy campaign nationwide calling for insurance coverage of ABA services for Autism Spectrum Disorder, the need for ABA-delivery specialist has skyrocketed. Lobbyists like attorney Lorri Unumb and her associates barnstormed the country to teach state politicians what ABA therapy was, and pushed for landmark legislation compelling Medicaid and commercial insurance benefits (cf. Baller et al., 2015). In just 4 years, plans covering ABA therapy from Blue Cross Blue Shield, Aetna, United Health, and others—now provide reimbursement for onsite assessment and intervention for at-risk children. Rapid uptake of these laws spun the state public health licensing boards into a frenzy of how to oversee professionals qualified to deliver these services. This exigency sparked the re-birth of statewide or national bills favoring licensure of ABA therapists, echoing the sentiments of behavioral practitioners some 10 years earlier (Dorsey, Weinberg, Zane, & Guidi, 2009). To ensure consumer protection of ABA services and regulate practitioners, many state licensing boards proposed educational training and competency exams. But passing these licensing standards into law was slow, laborious, and muddled through the morass of debates and hearings through endless subcommittees and think-tank lobbying. In the interim, a national organization located in Florida, the *Behavior Analysts Certification Board (BACB),* founded in 1998, figured it could get a head start on credentialing ABA specialists. They created the certification called Board Certified Behavior Analysts (BCBA). Qualifications for this credential were very specific and entailed (a) graduate level (Masters or Doctorate) training in ABA, and (b) passing a board exam.

At first, credentialing was only open to pre-existing masters-level and doctoral-level ABA psychologists. The credential option seemed a win-win situation. Codify their educational training with a nationally recognized credential to deliver services privately (and be paid for it) instead of publicly through agencies, school systems, state, county, and federal governments. Practitioners saw a mecca of opportunities in the private sector, coupled with their "day-jobs" of college faculty or behavioral consultant for community mental health. Excitement over this capitalistic market for ABA entrepreneurs exploded; it was not only ideal for ABA clinical and nonclinical psychologists to expand their services, it also was ideal for *development of fast-rack ABA programs to flourish. Programs that can expedite education for freshman ABA trainees to share the insurance coffers available for ABA therapy.* University-sponsored programs sprouted (what seemed like) overnight, offering a two-year certification or masters-terminal programs in ABA. The underlying strategy was simple: Recruit and train *students who already have a graduate degree in some other discipline and offer ABA training to enhance their career options and income.* In Michigan alone, eight universities rapidly joined the bandwagon of this fashionable trend—Wayne State University, Grand Valley University, Eastern Michiana University, Western Michigan University, Oakland University, University of Michigan, Michigan State University, Central Michigan University, and Northern Michigan University. Each university offered almost an identical online or onsite curricula involving a minimum of 18 credit hours and practica. Required courses uniformly covered (1) foundational principles, (2) applications of behavior change, (3) specialty populations, (4) ethics and diversity, (5) research, and (6) behavioral assessment. Elective courses covered more measurement methods, behavior changes systems, and implementation-management, and supervision. Course content *fulfilled the perquisites for state licensing or the BCBA credential.* Students who applied to the program were very diverse—occupational therapists, physical therapists, recreational therapists, social workers, school counselors, special education teachers, nurses, but mostly all from health allied fields. Each candidate either earned a master's degree in their own specialty or elected the program track to earn a Master's degree combined with ABA training.

Proliferation of these *boutique* academic programs lured high enrollments and pumped out graduates with basic knowledge and skills to pass the BCBA exam. In less than two decades, BACB has credentialed over 50,000 behavior analysts (and technicians) in more than 70 countries, propelling this outgrowth beyond expectations (cf. Carr & Carr, 2016). This new class of ABA specialist also sought a role in the forensic side of ABA practice. Cautiously, a minor footnote about these two-year ABA programs, and one gaining concern among the ABA community, is this: Just how in-depth where the courses taught on research, theory, and practice of behavioral methods? Did courses cover the same caliber of information previously taught to masters and doctoral students in traditional ABA-psychology programs? Or, are the courses supplying cookie-cutter techniques, with little understanding of underlying philosophy, analysis, and history of experimental research? Add to these questions a small detail most practicing ABA professionals or even the forefathers of BCBA credentialing never anticipated—most of these boutique programs are not offered in the psychology departments of the host university. Many of the ABA programs reside in departments of counseling, special education, or education. Instructors are usually doctoral level trained in ABA, but not all are psychologists or schooled in psychology departments. Psychology departments naturally do not own the domain of ABA, given its multidisciplinary branches in education and allied human services. But basic research in operant and respondent conditioning does emanate from the science of psychology and should have some of its roots planted in the coursework. This cascade of unsettling issues can be summed up by two points. First, how does watering-down the courses cheapen the BCBA credential? Second, as needs for BCBAs grow, is the answer to really create subordinate credentials such as the Registered Behavior Technician and Board Certified Assistant Behavior Analyst?

*Does lowering the standard cheapen the credential?* In surveying business managers, Livingston (1971) worried that managers were less effective trained in accelerated MBA training programs (on weekends, once weekly for one year) compared to managers trained in formal two year programs. The fads of pushing through graduates to meet current industry needs were ephemeral, and likely in the long-run to diminish the quality and integrity of managers. In accelerated ABA programs, a similar mechanism is in effect to rapidly build foundational skills in awareness and applications of behavioral principles, behavior change procedures, measurement procedure, and ethical standards governing practice. The immersion-like programs also rush through one or two practica in naturalistic settings for students to directly sample their knowledge under supervision. Under the pretense that most behavioral procedures are crafted in specific self-help manual terms, which are easy to follow and implement, application of procedures then should be easy. For example, in teaching joint attention in autism kids (Baron-Cohen, Cox, Baird, & Drew, 1997), steps shown on building two repertoires—imitating joint attention and responding joint attention—follows a calibrated use of reinforcement contingencies to shape such behaviors as shared gaze, dyadic eye gaze, triadic eye gaze, gate following, eye-gaze shifting, and pointing. Once the steps proceed in order, like following a recipe when baking a cake, behavior outcomes should match the picture of a child sharing attention shown in the training manual.

The problem with this sterile and robotic process is that it presumes a perfect psychological field, no abnormalities in the reactional biography, and uninterrupted precision in the application steps. However, baseline measures of children with poor join attention may show otherwise. They are easily distracted, receive constant redirection (positive reinforcers for bad behavior), often engage in self-injurious behaviors, lack verbal repertoires (for tacting, manding, etc.), poorly manage their motivating operations, and lack stimulus opportunities for joint attention with people. This "baggage" the children bring with them into the clinical setting cannot be swept under the rug or marginalized when ABA therapists visit the household. Manualized procedures are simply templates or outlines of proposed steps once the environment is ready for those steps. But it becomes the *genius* of ABA therapists to (a) assess the problems in the environment, (b) design ways to mend or solve the problems, (c) adapt the (joint-attention) procedure to the amended environment, and (d) monitor progress accrued from the procedure under both the amended environment and non-amended (chaotic naturalistic environment), just in case the psychological field reverts to pretreatment setting events when the ABA therapists leaves that day.

ABA therapists equipped with practical knowledge on using procedures, like joint attention methods, may not have the panoramic knowledge to look beyond the box of the procedure to spot and correct contravening variables. This wider perspective *is gained, not just from experience, but also from courses such as "rat-lab," where the student directly observes under controlled environmental conditions how extraneous variables can upset the most precise experiments.* The goal of rat-lab or of any research lab with infrahuman subjects is to discern breakdowns in procedure and to creatively adapt to the breakdowns using scientific principles. However, since ABA therapists are not in rat-lab, and instead in real-life households servicing special needs children and families, this lacuna means therapists may lack expertise to adjust the procedure or brainstorm ways to alter other contravening variables.

*Does creating subordinate classifications of ABA therapists really meet the growing consumer needs for ABA?* The foregoing argument that cookie-cutter trained ABA therapists may lack a panoramic view of and not know how to modify contravening variables also applies to subordinate classifications of BCBAs. Pressure to expand the fleet of behaviorally-trained specialists receiving third-party payment progressed to the next step of inventing lower levels of training as assistants and technicians. Just as a stepdown of training went from physicians to physician's assistant and then to medical assistant (and even to certified nurse assistant), so has the ABA industry imitated this model by offering certifications for Board Certified Assistant Behavior Analyst (BCABA) and Registered Behavior Technician (RBT). BCABAs require a minimum of a Bachelors degree and meet the Fourth-Edition Task List of core area courses (taken online or in college courses). Core content areas covered include basic behavior analytic skills, client-centered responsibilities, and foundational knowledge. Passing an exam shows mastery of these core topics and ensures a level of competency to work under the supervision of BCBAs. Likewise, RBTs only require a high school diploma and act as paraprofessional under the close supervision of BCBAs or BCABAs. They receive 40 h of online or in-class training and also must pass competency tests and the RBT examination. In other words, if a 35 year old homemaker with a high school diploma, who only worked retail jobs, takes 40 h of coursework in the Task List and passes the examinations, this individual can now enter the arena of a highly complex self-injurious, and tantrum explosive child who engages in pica (eating nonedible food), and smears feces on the wall. Incidentally, this is precisely the polymorbid behaviors this author confronted during his freshman year practicum after only 2 weeks of learning some behavioral principles. The author's reaction, who probably was more into psychology than the retail homemaker was, likely equaled the homemaker's reaction: "What the heck do I do?"

It is absurd to expect under-trained paraprofessionals to perform operationally accurate analyses, remain objectively detached and poised, and intuitively retrieve plausible evidence-based methods to implement or to correct flawed interventions. It is equally absurd for the RBT to seek advice from a BCABA, who is also in the dark, or who consults the BCBA, who may not be in the dark, but has no idea where to turn the light on. That is, the BCBA, or authority at the top of the pyramid, already works in a black box confined by a very limited selection of problem solving tools and understanding of experimental and applied behavior analysis. For example, the procedure for "calm counts," involves therapists coaching an agitated child to defuse anger through a desensitization-like self-calming process (Ward, 2013). Caveats explicitly stated in the method include (a) never use this procedure when child is already severely upset, (b) when counting acts as reinforcers, and (c) when the child depends on parent for counting. Further advised are the baseline prerequisites in the repertoire a child must have for the procedure, which include (a) instructional compliance, (b) proper visual alertness to fingers, (c) counting skills, and (d) able to imitate models. These preconditions aside, the ABA therapist *must be proficient in motivating operations and also other concurrent procedures for tantrum extinction and control over self-injurious behaviors.* Competency in these skills will avert a crisis when the procedure backfires in child behavior escalation. Unfortunately, these therapist competencies are unlikely part of the nascent and paraprofessional repertories of RBTs and BCABAs. Whether the two-year trained BCBA also has this expertise is also doubtful. The reason why subclassifications of ABA therapy is discussed here is due to its implications for forensic behavior analysis. Despecialized ABA therapists certified as RBTs and BCABAs already realize and navigate around the sensitive ethics of entering the privacy of family's household. Observations deliberately recorded as part of baseline measures or inadvertently witnessed during intervention sessions may go beyond the target behavior data and raise suspicions of parental abuse and neglect. For example, a parent of an emaciated child being deprived of food as punishment for misbehavior may raise red flags. Under state compulsory laws for reporting child abuse, ABA therapists, governed by the same standards, must notify the local Children's Protective Services or similar authority or be liable for negligence should that abuse persist and cause harm to the child. After filing the report, that RBT and BCABA may subsequently receive a subpoena to testify at a deposition or court about the witnessed incidents of abuse. Since they are called "therapists," and legitimized by professional certifications, defense attorneys and prosecution may presume they have a level of competency to serve as fact witness or expert witness about the case. A fact witness confines testimony only to the objective data of facts pertaining to the incident in questions under the assumption a therapeutic or biased relationship exists with the accused. An expert witness presumes the testimony is bias-free of any pre-existing or current relationship with the accused or incident. The expert specializes in the abuse, neglect or area examined based on his or her years of experience, notoriety, published articles and books, or previous court approval as expert. The latter qualifiers for expert witness clearly derive from the Daubert Standards, or *rules of evidence regarding admissibility of expert witnesses' testimony* (Tancredi & Giannini, 1994). These standards consist of:

1. The expert's scientific, technical, or other specialized knowledge will help the trier of fact to understand the evidence or to determine a fact in issue;
2. The testimony is based on sufficient facts or data;
3. The testimony is the product of reliable principles and methods;
4. The expert has reliably applied the principles and methods to the facts of the case.

Subordinate-level ABA therapists mandated by legal defense or prosectuon to testify under the Daubert rule of expert testimony may be imposters. They may actually lack the thoroughness and acumen expected of experts whose opinions are the product of reliable principles and methods stemming from basic and applied research. For example, on a superficial level, speaking about a father using corporal punishment (severe physical punishment) or noncompliance at the dinner table, the under-experienced ABA therapist may explain the adverse side effects of punishment decreasing appropriate behaviors. While this point is true—punishment can decelerate appropriate and inappropriate behaviors– it is just barely scratching the surface on why the father's punishment is dangerous. By comparison, the masters- or doctoral-level psychologist trained in the formal scientist-practitioner model of ABA may expound upon effects of continuous or random punishment (a) not only suppressing target behavior but also engendering anticipatory anxiety and aggression (Ruben, 2001); (b) fostering learned helplessness, based on Seligman's experimental research on conditioned suppression with dogs (Seligman, Maier, & Geer, 1968) or Radner's tonic immobility research with chickens (Ratner & Thompson, 1960), (c) increasing pain-related aggression based on Ulrich's research on reflexive fighting and cooperative escape (1967), and (d) fostering reciprocal aggressive behavior as the primary attention-seeking for the youngers, based on Patterson's theory of reciprocal exchange (1982) and Wahler's insularity theory related to setting events (1980), and Fox, (1981). Inclusion of published research buttresses the validity of opinions given and enhances the credibility of the expert—the very reason why the Daubert criteria prevails as a yardstick for acceptable professional court testimony. By contrast, under-reporting effects of punishment, especially if the cursory testimony is irrelevant to the case, may portray a false negative impact. The uninformed ABA specialist's lackluster testimony may marginalize victim effects of punishment or even imply the procedure of punishment delivery did not deviate widely from established scientific conventions. The result can be tragic. Misleading expert testimony dilutes the integrity of a behavioral science and can inadvertently exculpate perpetrators of physical abuse. Consequently, ABA's venerable image as the savior for children with Autism Spectrum Disorder may be compromised or perilously shattered.

## Use of social media and virtual evaluations

Recent advances in the speed and scope of digitization, connectivity, big data, artificial intelligence, and social media are taking consumers deep into places and powers never experienced before. Some media-platform technologies offer unprecedented promises and unprecedented peril, both depending on the user's age, amenability to digital systems, and risk-benefit ratio estimated from using online versus offline (face to face) communication. From Facebook and Twitter to E-commerce platforms of E-learning, the absorbing complexity of worldwide connectivity oversteps the bounds of privacy, changes the language of interpersonal communication, and impersonalizes human contact from intimacy to impartiality. Abundant use of *mobile apps* has further decentralized human beings from direct contact; one-on-one contact in real time is replaced by face-time and remote or virtual contact between students and educators, or between therapists and clients. The digital-age revolution, as behemoth as its spiraling impact on children and adults, is still in germinal stages for the discipline of mental health.

The accessibility of reaching therapists in cyberspace has sparked a torrent of online therapy shops offering 24-h appointments through video-conferencing, skype, or facetime. The no-boundary availability of therapists, theoretically, means a patient living in Detroit can counsel with providers in Kentucky. Of course, less known is that the therapist in Kentucky *must be licensed to also practice in Michigan, or wherever remotely the nationwide or worldwide client reside.* Online therapy also provides mobile apps allowing instant therapist contact that replaces the traditional tedium of scheduling appointments. Popular online therapy services such as Better Help, Regain, My Therapist, Talk Space, and Breakthrough all share common denominators in per hour pricing, protection of confidentiality, and even the option for services to be covered by major insurance companies. For the vast promoters of online counseling (Alleman, 2002; Maheu & Gordon, 2000), the "telepresence" of therapists offering empathy and behavioral advice seems unequivocal. Opponents of cyber-therapy are less enthusiastic, admonishing the ethical ramifications of professional misrepresentation, underdevelopment of clinical rapport, and overlooking poor suitability of clients for the simulated platform (Rochlen, Zack, & Speyer, 2004; Suler, Barak, Chechele, Fenichel, et al., 2001). Regardless of its controversy, commercial hype over its wide-reaching resourcefulness has increased its popularity second to online dating apps.

A natural progression from cyber marketing for online therapy is integrating digital technology into assessment and enhancement of treatment effectiveness. For example Lebowitz and Francois (2019) ingenuously used motion tracking to measure subtle avoidance behaviors in children. The cost and time-effectiveness, and high inter-reliability of recording typically covert or ominous behaviors had a third advantage; it made computer programs user friendly. Likewise, consumers who are routine web scanners were ideal subjects for a 3-session, web-based, therapist-assisted, acceptance-based behavioral intervention targeting anxiety (Eustis, Hayes-Skelton, Orsillo, & Roemer, 2019). Using similar methods, consumers adroit with mobile apps, who had children with delayed or underdeveloped speech, were subjects in a two-session hierarchy for augmenting their children's speech and desensitizing anxiety associated with non-speech (Bunnell, Mesa, & Beidel, 2019). Here, the technology of smartphones, tablets, cellphones, and laptops accessing the mobile device, gave parents the portability to procedures to develop and maintain a commonly difficult behavior problem (selective mutism in children). In all, the seamless integration of internet into consumers' lives appears to be an implicitly new setting event in a vastly wider psychological field; a psychological field consisting of multiple behavior segments measurably transacting over unlimited time and unlimited space in a virtual interaction with the consumer-user. Tapping this treasure chest of virtual interactions seems a logical next step in capturing instances of behavior related to crime and making predictions about criminal behavior.

Riva (1997), in campaigning for virtual environments for psychological (forensic) assessments, warns of an important distinction. A distinction between *psychological testing and psychological assessment*. Testing, the more objectively-technical or mechanistic option, employs rigorous methods with clearly definable and uniform parameters. For example, most forensic examiners administering the WAIS-IV follow specific instructions to assure test delivery is reliably similar from one examiner to the next. Assessment, argues Riva, is not synonymous with testing. Psychometrics may "miss" critical idiographic variables in the person's life showing connections to stimulus and response events or shedding light on the mysteries of the examinee's reactional biography. Assessment, he argues, must assure conclusions about behavior or personality are broader than the statistics representing normative scores. Parsons and Phillips (2016) concurred with this sentiment, further showing how new virtual reality technology can be panoramic in broadly sweeping the psychological field of a subject's life, while preserving the objectivity and precision of data collection (cf. Villani, Cipresso, Gaggioli, & Riva, 2016). They showed how testing is embedded in assessment and not a separable function. For example, in performing functional behavior assessments in the classroom, an offsite school psychologist may use multi-site and portable videocams to capture and record discrete units of target behavior of a student in a classroom. Then, using teletherapy, the school psychologist accesses the examinee student virtually during administration of testing. Materials on which the student writes are duplicated and appear live on the student's table while visually assailable through a close up feature in the remote examiner's laptop monitor control panel. Follow up of test results with the students' parents also can be virtual and especially for parents living in remote rural areas with limited internet service.

In behavioral forensic assessment, advantages of using virtual technology for assessment and testing are manifold. First, the problem of examiners missing an inmate due to frequent transferability to another facility is overcome. The examiner stays in one place, his or her office, while verifies locality of the inmate before connecting virtually to commence the test battery in that facility. Second, test interruption variables are less disruptive or do not irrevocably end the testing battery. If, for example, during testing the prison or jail commences a lock-down, testing can be easily suspended for 1 h or 1 day without inconvenience imposed on the examiner, trapped in the prison or re-driving to the facility. Likewise, in assessing an inmate held on the psychiatric unit who is sedated on antipsychotic medications, the effects of which preclude coherency for valid test responses, the examinee can reschedule the assessment at little or no cost and inconvenience to both parties. Third, behavioral assessments can be more diversifiable and repeatable. Since contact between examiner and examinee or examinee's behaviors can occur repeatedly, instead of just once, evaluations can now include multiple-day recording of inmate behavior across different settings. Correction officers (guards) can send momentary time-sampling records of the examinee's behaviors in his or her cell, cafeteria, or other locality. That data, transmitted immediately to a program calculating percentage of occurrences for some target behavior, adds to the scientific validity of cause-effect analysis in the psychological report. In this way, not only does the examination offer operational analysis of behavior during the crime itself, that analysis now gains data (empirical) support by testing the hypothesis in how the examinee behaves while incarcerated. For example, a middle-aged adult defendant awaiting trial in jail for criminal sexual conduct on a younger male adult is monitored using an interval recording method. Two days of sample data showed he made sexual advances to younger inmates and even exposed his genitals in the shower room. The data offers evidence of response generalizability and further strengthens the prediction of high risk of offender recidivism.

In the best of all worlds, then, virtual reality assessments can be conduits to more efficient behavioral forensic assessments. For their technical, time-saving, and empirical advantages, there will be lingering mentalistic arguments that remote testing is a modern day lab treating human beings as infrahuman organisms and undermining their dignity. Sterilizing human worth by removing one-on-one direct (genuine emotive) contact and replacing it with artificial, unemotional exchanges may violate rights of patient care and dignity. This argument echoes the public outcry regarding the insensitivity and inhumane applications of behavior modification nearly 50 years ago. The same argument airs during routine medical exams, when a physician assistant, nurse practitioner, medical assistant, paramedic, or some other specialist, robotically takes vitals and blandly inquiries about symptoms. The same indignity supposedly occurs when lying naked on the table while the throbbing noise and imposing fixture of a MRI crosses over a person's body.

In a new era of scientific advancements, violations of human dignity may be outweighed by the benefits that science brings, namely, more effective diagnoses and treatments of heretofore incurable and inapproachable problems. In forensic science as well, embracing virtual portholes to assessment outwardly may seem impersonal and futuristic. The absent or remote examiner hidden inside a television monitor may seem elusive or from a dystopic world of Big Brother omnipotently controlling the inmate—an eerie feeling lifted from the pages of George Orwell's classic book *1984*. But the paranoia of being miniaturized by imposing technology is not all bad. It is a small price to pay for its comprehensiveness and precision in sampling larger behavior segments more representative of the defendant's life transactions. This wider angle captures behaviors in naturalistic settings previously unseen during the snapshot of a one-day, 3-h interview held in an office interview. Additional footage of naturalistic behaviors, courtesy of virtual connectivity, also provides a rare window into seeing the defendant's world. A world revealing whether the accused really engaged in illegal or inappropriate behaviors over time and under multiple contingencies.

## References


Abagnale, F. (2002). *The art of the steal*. NY: Crown Publishers.

Alleman, J. R. (2002). Online counseling: The internet and mental health treatment. *Psychotherapy, 39*, 199–209.

American Psychiatric Association. (2013). *Diagnostic and statistical manual of mental disorders: DSM-5* (p. 266). Arlington, VA: APA.

Andrews, D. A., Bonta, J., & Wormith, S. J. (2006). The recent past and near future of risk and/or need assessment. *Crime & Delinquency, 52*, 7–27.

Baller, J. B., Barry, C. K., Shea, K., Walker, M. M., Ouellette, R., & Mandell, D. S. (2015). Assessing early implementation of state autism insurance mandates. *Autism, 20*, 796–807.

Baron-Cohen, S., Cox, A., Baird, G., & Drew, A. (1997). Infants with autism: An investigation of empathy, pretend play, joint attention, and imitation. *Developmental Psychology, 33*, 781–789.

Becroft, A. J. (2006). Children and young people in conflict with the law: Asking the hard question. *Juvenile and Family Court Journal, 57*(4), 1–37.

Blanchette, K., & Brown, S. L. (2006). *The assessment and treatment of women offenders: An integrative perspective*. NY: John Wiley & Sons.

Bleske-Rechek, A., Gunseor, M. M., & Maly, J. R. (2018). Does the language fit the evidence? Unwarranted causal language in psychological scientists' scholarly work. *The Behavior Therapist, 41*, 341–352.

Boer, D. P., Hart, S. D., Kropp, P. R., & Webster, C. D. (2015). *Sexual violence risk-20*. Version 2. Burnaby, Canada: Mental Health, Law & Policy Institute.

Bunnell, B. E., Mesa, F., & Beidel, D. C. (2019). A two-session hierarchy for shaping successive approximations of speech in selective mutism: A pilot study of mobile apps and mechanisms of behavior change. *Behavior Therapy, 49*, 966–980.

Campbell, T. W. (2003). Sex offenders and actuarial risk assessments: Ethical considerations. *Behavioral Sciences & the Law, 21*, 269–279.

Carr, J. E., & Carr, M. R. (2016). Professional credentialing of practicing behavior analysts. In *Policy insights from the behavioral and brain sciences, 4* pp. 3–8).

Caspi, A., Moffitt, T. E., Silva, P. A., & Krueger, R. F. (1994). Are some people crime-prone? Replications of the personality-crime relationship across countries, genders, races, and methods. *Criminology, 32*, 163–170.

Chaiken, J., Chaiken, M., & Rhodes, W. (1994). Predicting violent behavior and classifying violent offenders. In *National research council. Understanding and preventing violene* (pp. 217–295). Washington DC: National Research Council.

Chompsky, N. (1959). A review of B.F. Skinner's Verbal Behavior. *Language, 35*, 26–58.

Chompsky, N. (1967). A review of B.F. Skinner's Verbal Behavior. In L. A. Jakobovits, & M. M. Miron (Eds.), *Readings in the psychology of language* (pp. 142–143). NY: Prentice Hall.

Cloninger, C. R., Dragan, M. S., & Thomas, R. P. (1993). A psychobiological model of temperament and character. *Archives of General Psychiatry, 50*, 975–990.

Connor, D. (2002). *Aggression and antisocial behavior in children and adolescents: Research and treatment*. NY: Guilford Press.

Cooper, J. O., Heron, T. E., & Heward, W. L. (1987). *Applied behavior analysis*. Columbus, OH: Merrill Publishing Company.

Delisi, M., & Scherer, A. M. (2006). Multiple homicide offenders: Offense characteristics, correlates and criminal careers. *Criminal Justice and Behavior, 33*, 367–391.

Dorsey, M. F., Weinberg, M., Zane, T., & Guidi, M. (2009). The case for licensure of applied behavior analysts. *Behavior Analyst in Practice, 2*, 53–58.

Douglas, J. (2000). *The anatomy of motive*. NY: Pocket Books.

Douglas, K. S., & Kropp, P. R. (2002). A prevention-based paradigm for violence risk assessment: Clinical and research applications. *Criminal Justice and Behavior, 29*, 617–658.

Eustis, E. H., Hayes-Skelton, S. A., Orsillo, S. M., & Roemer, L. (2019). Surviving and thriving during stress: A randomized clinical trial comparing a brief web-based, therapist-assisted, acceptance-based behavioral intervention versus waitlist control for college students. *Behavior Therapy, 49*, 889–903.

Eysenck, H. J. (1977). *Crime and personality*. London: Routledge and Kegan Paul.

Eysenck, H. J. (1997). Personality and the biosocial model of antisocial and criminal behavior. In A. Raine, P. A. Brennan, D. P. Farrington, & S. A. Mednick (Eds.), *Biosocial bases of violence* (pp. 21–37). New York: Plenum.

Gerberth, V., & Turco, R. (1997). Antisocial personality disorder, sexual sadism, malignant narcissism, and serial murder. *Journal of Forensic Sciences, 42*, 49–60.

Gerrie, B., & Holbrook, E. A. (2013). The evolutionary role of physicians assistants across the United States, Canada, and the United Kingdom. *International Journal of Exercise Science, 6*, 1–8.

Hall, H. V., & Poirier, J. G. (2001). *Detecting malingering and deception: Forensic distortion analysis*. Boca Raton, FL: CRC Press.

Hall, H. V., & Thompson, J. (2007). Explicit alternative testing: Applications of the binomial probability distribution to clinical-forensic evaluations. *Forensic Examiner, 16*, 39–43.

Harcourt, B. E. (2003). The shaping of chance: Actuarial models and criminal profiling as the turn of the twenty-first-century. *University of Chicago Law Review, 70*, 105–128.

Hare, R. D. (1991). *The hare psychopathy checklist-revised*. North Tonawanda, New York: Multi-Health Systems.

Hare, R. D. (1993). *Without conscience: The disturbing world of psychopaths among us*. New York: Guilford Press.

Hare, R. D. (1996). Psychopathy: A clinical construct whose time has come. *Criminal Justice and Behavior, 23*, 25–54.

Hare, R. D., & Neumann, C. N. (2006). The PCL-R assessment of Psychopathy: Development, structural properties, and new directions. In C. Patrick (Ed.), *Handbook of psychopathy* (pp. 58–88). New York: Guilford.

Harichandran, V. S., Walnycky, D., Baggili, I., & Breitinger, F. (2016). CuFA: A more formal definition for digital forensic artifacts. *Digital Investigation, 18*, 125–137.

Hart, S. D., Kropp, P. R., Laws, D. R., Klaver, J., Logan, C., & Watt, K. A. (2003). *The risk for sexual violence protocol: Structured professional guidelines for assessing risk of sexual violence*. Bunaby, Canada: Mental Health, Law, and Policy Institute.

Hayes, S. C. (2004). Acceptance and commitment therapy, relational frame theory, and the third wave of behavioral and cognitive therapies. *Behavior Therapy, 35*, 639–665.

Hayes, S. C., & Hoffman, S. G. (2017). The third wave of cognitive behavioral therapy and the rise of process-based care. *World Psychiatry, 16*, 245–246.

He, J., Baxter, S., Xu, J., Xu, J., Zhou, X., & Zhang, K. (2019). The practical implementation of artificial intelligence technologies in medicine. *Nature Medicine, 25*, 30–36.

Holt, P. (2003). Psychological behaviorism: A path to the grand reunification of psychology and behavior analysis? *Behavior Analyst Today, 4*, 306–317.

Kantor, J. R. (1947). *Problems of physiological psychology*. Bloomington, IN: Principia Press.

Kantor, J. R. (1971). *The aim and progress of psychology and other sciences*. Chicago, IL: The Principia Press.

Kantor, J. R. (1982). *Cultural psychology*. Chicago, IL: Principia Press.

Kuhn, T. S. (1962). *The structure of scientific revolutions*. Chicago IL: University of Chicago Press.

Kurlychek, M. C., & Johnson, B. D. (2010). Juvenility and punishment: Sentencing juveniles in adult criminal court. *Criminology, 48*, 725–758.

Lebowitz, E. R., & Francois, B. (2019). Using motion tracking to measure avoidance in children and adults: Psychometric properties, associations with clinical characteristics, and treatment related changes. *Behavior Therapy, 49*, 853–865.

Lee, H. C., & Harris, H. A. (2000). *Physical evidence in forensic science*. Tucson, AZ: Lawyers & Judges Publishing Company.

Lenzenweger, M. F., Clarkin, J. F., Caligor, E., Cain, N. M., & Kernberg, O. F. (2018). Malignant narcissism in relation to clinical change in borderline personality disorder: An exploratory study. *Psychopathology, 51*, 318–325.

Livingston, J. S. (1971). Myth of the well-educated manager. *Harvard Business Review, 49*, 79–89.

Lundin, R. W. (1985). *Theories and systems of psychology*. Lexington, MA: DC Heath and Company.

Maheu, M., & Gordon, B. L. (2000). Counseling and therapy on the internet. *Professional Psychology: Research and Practice, 31*, 484–489.

Marx, M. H., & Hillix, W. A. (1963). *Systems and theories in psychology*. NY: McGraw-Hill.

McCrae, R. R., & Costa, P. T. (1990). *Personality in adulthood*. New York: Guilford Press.

Michael, J. (1974). Statistical inference for individual organism research: Mixed blessing or curse? *Journal of Applied Behavior Analysis, 7*, 647–653.

Miller, J. D., & Lynam, D. (2001). Structural models of personality and their relation to antisocial behavior: A meta-analytic review. *Criminology, 39*, 769.

Moffitt, T. E. (1993). Adolescence-limited and life-course persistent antisocial behavior: A developmental taxonomy. *Psychological Review, 100*, 674–701.

Mountjoy, P. T., & Cone, D. M. (2006). Biographical sketch of Jacob Robert Kantor. In B. D. Midgley, & E. K. Morris (Eds.), *Modern perspectives on J. R. Kantor and interbehaviorism* (pp. 15–38). Reno, NV: Context Press.

Mountjoy, P. T., & Ruben, D. H. (1983). J.R. Kantor's cultural psychology. *Psychological Record, 33*, 285–287.

Nelson-Gray, R. C., Lootens, J. T., Mitchell, C. D., Robertson, N. E., Hundt, N. A., & Kimbrel, T. (2012). Assessment and treatment of personality disorders: A behavioral perspective. *Behavior Analyst Today, 10*, 7–45.

O'Donohue, W. T., Henderson, D. A., Hayes, S. C., Fisher, J. E., & Hayes, L. J. (2001). *A history of the behavioral therapies: Founder's personal histories*. Reno, Nevada: Context Press.

Parsons, T. D., & Phillips, A. S. (2016). Virtual reality for psychological assessment in clinical practice. *Practice Innovations, 1*, 197–217.

Patterson, G. R. (1982). *Coercive family process*. Eugene, OR: Castalia Press.

Peterson, J., Sommers, I., Baskin, D., & Johnson, D. (2010). *The role and impact of forensic evidence in the criminal justice process*. Washington, DC: National Institute of Justice.

Phelps, B. J. (2007). Why we are still not cognitive psychologist. A review of why i am not a cognitive psychologist.: A tribute to B.F. Skinner. *The Behavior Analyst, 30*, 217–226.

Pierce, W. D., & Cheney, C. D. (2017). *Behavior analysis and learning: A biobehavioral approach* (6th ed.). NY: Routledge.

Ratner, S. C., & Thompson, R. W. (1960). Immobility reactions (fear) of domestic fowl as a function of age and prior experience. *Animal Behaviour, 8*, 186–191.

Reese, H. W., & Parrott, L. J. (1986). *Behavior science: Philosophical, methodological, and empirical advances*. Hillsdale, NJ: Lawrence Erlbaum Associates.

Riva, G. (1997). Virtual reality assessment tool in psychology. *Studies in Health Technology and Informatics, 44*, 71–79.

Rochlen, A. B., Zack, J. S., & Speyer, C. (2004). Online therapy: Review of relevant definitions, debates, and current empirical support. *Journal of Clinical Psychology, 60*, 269–283.

Ruben, D. H. (1986). The "interbehavioral" approach to treatment. *Journal of Contemporary Psychotherapy, 16*, 62–71.

Ruben, D. H. (2001). *Treating adult children of alcoholics: A behavioral approach*. NY: Academic Press.

Ruben, D. H. (2015). *Behavioral guide to personality disorders: DSM-5*. Springfield, IL: Charles Thomas Publishers.

Sansone, R. A., Sellbom, M., & Songer, D. A. (2016). Criminal behavior and borderline personality: Correlations among four measures. *Innovations in Clinical Neuroscience, 13*, 14–16.

Schneider, S. M., & Morris, E. K. (1987). A history of the term *radical behaviorism* from Watson to Skinner. *The Behavior Analyst, 10*, 27–39.

Schuh, A. J., & Porter, E. A. (2012). The forensic psychology of olfaction evidence. *Forensic Examiner*, 35–47.

Seligman, M. E. P., Maier, S. F., & Geer, J. (1968). The alleviation of learned helplessness in the dog. *Journal of Abnormal and Social Psychology, 73*, 256–262.

Skinner, B. F. (1974). *About Behaviorism*. Knopf: NY.

Shadish, W. R. (2014). Statistical analyses of single case designs: The shape of things to come. *Current Directions in Psychological Science, 23*, 139–146.

Silver, E., & Chow-Martin, L. (2002). A multiple models approach to assessing recidivism risk: Implications for judicial decision making. *Criminal Justice and Behavior, 29*, 538–568.

Sinha, S. (2016). Personality correlates of criminals: A comparative study between normal controls and criminals. *Industrial Psychiatry Journal, 25*, 41–46.

Skinner, B. F. (1969). *Contingencies of reinforcement*. New York: Prentice Hall.

Skinner, B. F. (1976). *About behaviorism*. NY: Vintage Books.

Skinner, B. F. (1977). Why I am not a cognitive psychologist. *Behaviorism, 5*, 1–10.

Southall, C. M., & Gast, D. L. (2011). Self-management procedures: A comparison across the autism spectrum. *Education and Training in Autism and Developmental Disabilities, 46*, 155–171.

Sreenivasan, S., Kirkish, P., Garrick, T., Weinberger, L., & Phenix, A. (2000). Actuarial risk assessment models: A review of critical issues related to violence and sex offender recidivism assessments. *Journal of the American Academy of Psychiatry & the Law Online, 28*, 438–448.

Staats, A. W. (1975). *Social behaviorism*. Homewood, IL: Dorsey Press.

Staats, A. W. (1996a). Aberrance in Science: Should behavior analysts know about psychological behaviorism? *The Behavior Analyst, 19*, 121–124.

Staats, A. W. (1996b). *Behavior and personality: Psychological behaviorism*. New York: Springer.

State of Michigan. (2017). *Senate bill No. 641 (draft)*. Legislative Service Bureau.

Stone, M. H. (2007). Violent crimes and their relationship to personality disorders. *Personality and Mental Health, 1*, 138–153.

Stone, M. H. (2009). Narcissism and criminality. *Psychiatric Annals, 39*, 130–135.

Suller, J., Barak, A., Chechele, P., Fenichel, M., Hsiung, R., Maguire, J., et al. (2001). Assessing a person's suitability for online therapy. *Cyber Psychology and Behavior, 4*, 675–679.

Tancredi, L. R., & Giannini, A. J. (1994). The admissibility of scientific evidence in psychiatric malpractice: Junk science and the Daubert case. *Journal of Clinical Forensic Medicine, 1*, 145–148.

Tellegen, A. (1985). Structures of mood and personality and their relevance to assessing anxiety with an emphasis on self-report. In A. H. Tuma, & J. D. Maser (Eds.), *Anxiety and the anxiety disorders*. Hillsdale, NJ: Lawrence Erlbaum Associates.

Ulrich, R. (1967). Interactions between reflexive fighting and cooperative escape. *Journal of the Experimental Analysis of Behavior, 10*, 311–317.

Ulrich, R., Wolfe, M., & Delaney, S. (1969). Punishment of shock-induced aggression. *Journal of the Experimental Analysis of Behavior, 12*, 1009–1015.

Villani, D., Cipresso, P., Gaggioli, A., & Riva, G. (2016). *Integrating technology into positive psychology practice*. Hershey, PA: IGI Global.

Wahler, R. G. (1980). The insular mother: Her problems in parent-child treatment. *Journal of Applied Behavior Analysis, 13*, 207–219.

Wahler, R. G., & Fox, J. J. (1981). Setting events in applied behavior analysis: Toward a conceptual and methodological expansion. *Journal of Applied Behavior Analysis, 14*, 327–338.

Walters, G. D. (2012). *Crime in a psychological context: From career criminals to criminal careers*. Thousand Oaks, CA: Sage.

Walters, G. D. (2014). *Drugs, crime, and their relationships: Theory, research, practice, and policy*. Sudbury, MA: Jones and Bartlett.

Ward, S. (2013). *Teaching good learner repertoires*. Private Publishing.

Ward, T., Mesler, J., & Yates, P. (2007). Reconstructing the risk-need-responsivity model: A theoretical elaboration and evaluation. *Aggression and Violent Behavior, 12*, 208–225.

Watterson, J., Blackmore, V., & Bagby, D. (2006). Considerations for the analysis of forensic samples following extended exposure to the environment. *Forensic Examiner, 15*, 19–26.

Wilson, J. Q., & Herrnstein, R. (1985). *Crime and human nature*. NY: Simon & Schuster.

Zamir, E., & Teichman, D. (Eds.). (2014). *The oxford handbook of behavior economics and the law*. England: Oxford Press.

SECTION II

# Case studies in behavioral forensic assessment

CHAPTER

# 3

# Behavioral predictors of sexual proclivity in a sexual offender

Criminal sexual conduct represents a subcategory of adult legal offenses frequently demonized as the epitome of amorality and sociopathy. In recent months, media exposure of celebrity figures exploiting women opened Pandora's Box to a secret society of hidden sexual harassment and abuse plaguing the motion picture industry. Denigration of high profile offenders focused on their misuse of power, authority, accessibility to, and unrestrained predation of susceptible victims. Similar typologies existed before this media frenzy in describing adult (male) molesters of children (see Prentky & Knight, 1991). Among the most definitive classificatory system using personality typologies has been the FBI's document on *Child Molesters: A Behavioral Analysis* (1992, Hazelwood & Burgess, 1987). This handbook was prepared for law-enforcement officers investigating cases of child sexual exploitation. The report presents a taxonomy of adult offenders divided by their behavior types, their modus operandi, and the age of their victims.

Descriptions of behavior typologies are broad, nomothetic, and presume ubiquitous etiologies and actions in the adult (male) offenders. Descriptions are neither situation-specific, measurably quantifiable in units of behavior, nor consisting of causal connections between antecedent, consequent, or intermediary events surrounding the sexual criminal offenses. In other words, the FBI's taxonomy called a *Behavioral Analysis* lacks any of the scientific principles, methods, or conceptual schemes prototypically used in an *applied behavior analysis (ABA) or a behavioral systems approach (BSA) to understanding criminal behavior* (Emery & Marholin, 1977; Neitzel, 1979; Ruben, 1992; Ruben, 2017). The reasons for this misuse of language and omission of scientific framework is not entirely surprising. Morris explained this omission nearly 30 years ago (Morris, 1987), opining "...although many theories of social deviance are somewhat compatible with a 'learning theory' orientation, applied behavior analysis has not been as effective or widespread as originally envisioned" (p. 67, see also Morris & Braukmann, 1987). Morris elaborated his point by identifying pitfalls of applied behavior analysis including (a) the conception of ill-conceived behavioral programs in corrections, (b) misuse of behavioral programs, and (c) the philosophy underlying ABA of determinism and free will at odds with the philosophy of freedom-denial and punishment (anti-rehabilitation) enmeshed in the correctional system. Morris echoed the clarion call for the corrections field to embrace ABA and

*Behavioral Forensics*
https://doi.org/10.1016/B978-0-12-819805-6.00003-8

learning theory, first articulated over 5 decades ago by Sutherland and Cressey (1955) and Jeffrey (1965).

Despite the torrent of behavioral interest in sexual offenders and victims sparked from 2008 to 2010, in the short-lived publication of *Journal of Behavior Analysis of Offender and Victim Treatment and Prevention*, ABA or BSA have remained unpopular in corrections research. One explanation has been the seemingly incompatible philosophies with anti-rehabilitation. Another reason lies in the dearth of effective dissemination and implementation of learning theory ideas and technology in the corrections system (cf. Bearman & Ward, 2017; Rotheram-Borus, Swendeman, & Chorpita, 2012). Just the same, the use of ABA techniques and principles in the operational (functional) formation of behavior still reign as the most empirically-validated predictors in the science of human behavior (cf. Burton, Miller, & Shill, 2002). In expanding BSA, in particular, to one subcomponent of the criminal justice system, that of forensic evaluations, Ruben (2017) showed the value of shifting focus away from personality typologies and toward a functional relationship between crime, suspect, victim, and setting events over time. His analyses incorporated six widely held standards in collecting premorbid or pre-assessment data, before the forensic evaluation occurred, and how to integrate that data in forming probabilistic statements about criminal propensity. These six principles included:

1. Examinations include objectively quantifiable and reproducible data.
2. Testing should represent or simulate the offender's natural environment.
3. Assessment of criminal behavior conforms to canons of scientific deduction.
4. Inquiries consider past, current, and potential events impacting crime.
5. Assessed facts are interrelated or have reciprocal-symmetrical relationships, not asymmetrical.
6. Behavioral segments represent the totality of person-environmental variables that interact with human variables.

Assessment is molecular in dissecting the continuous behavior segments of pre-criminal or criminal behavior into three common groups, the same groups used in performing *Functional Behavioral Assessments* (Cooper, Heward, & Heron, 2007; Drasgow & Yell, 2001). These groups, spun slightly differently for BSA applications, include Stimulus properties, Response properties, and Consequence properties. Stimulus properties consist of (intensity/duration) of evocative effects, motivating operations (unconditioned, conditioned) (Laraway, Snycerski, Michael, & Poling, 2003; Michael, 1982), and similar/dissimilar stimuli and latency (i.e., classifications of stimulus generalization a la Skinner's *Verbal Behavior*, 1957). Response properties include topography, frequency, duration, concurrent response patterns, sequential response patterns, excesses and deficits, assets and liabilities, and predictive response patterns. Consequent properties include the operations of positive and negative reinforcement, and positive and negative punishment, realizing they are frequently intermingling. Assessment of these properties, together in a total behavioral segment, cover seven type of possible interactive relationships between a criminal and the environment. These compound schedules or relationships include: (1) functional relationships, (2) concurrent schedules, (3) mixed schedules, (4) tandem schedules, (5) conjunctive schedules, (6) multiple schedules, and (7) alternative schedules (Lyon, 1982). Careful use of these contingencies can simplify deductions about the behavioral *potentials* or trajectories of highly probable criminal action (see Ruben, 1983, Ruben, 2015). The probable behaviors or predictors also provide a blueprint to prevent criminal recidivism (e.g., Furby, Weinrott, & Blackshaw, 1989). This article provides one example or case study of a severely complex sequence of sexual behavioral pathology assessed during the examination of criminal responsibility in an accused child molester. Following the case study, implications are offered on reasonable steps for the amalgam of the FBI typologies and behavioral systems or ABA models.

## Case of John Doe

John Doe represents a fictional name of a 28 year old single male Caucasian currently held in a Midwestern Jail for 8 months pending a trial for the felony charge of Criminal Sexual Conduct (CSC). He worked very few hourly-wage jobs, each lasting 1–2 months in restaurants. By first grade (age 6), he qualified for an IEP (special education) certified under Otherwise Health Impaired (OHI) for Attention Deficit Hyperactivity Disorder (ADHD, predominately hyperactive/impulsive presentation) and Oppositional Defiance Disorder. He received the pediatric co-diagnosis premorbid to any psychoeducational testing and was prescribed the psychostimulant Ritalin. When formal school testing occurred (second grade, age 7), scores on standard intelligence and achievement batteries yielded no evidence of specific learning disabilities. However, in his triennial re-resting, scores revealed significant deficits in Mathematics Calculation. Mathematics Problem Solving, and Reading Comprehension. Re-testing, administered 22 years later (by the author), showed cognitive deficits in Working Memory, Perceptual Reasoning, and Processing Speed. Learning deficits recurred for Mathematics Calculation, Mathematics Problem Solving, and Reading Comprehension. Additional deficits appeared in Listening Comprehension.

He graduated high school and advanced 2 years in college. He reportedly was bullied severely in primary and secondary school, called racial slurs, microaggressions, and either cowered defenselessly or accepted the slurs as truth, similar to blunt insults heard from his biological father. By middle school, he over-reacted to peer harassment with *anticipatory aggression* (Ruben, 1993, 2015). Anticipatory aggression consists of pre-emptive responses before the presentation of aversive conditions, in hopes of avoidance or escape from those stimulus conditions (e.g., peer harassment). Pre-emptive response sequences included three types. First, he voluntarily helped other students seen as taunted physically or verbally by peers. Second, he showed aggression toward animals anticipated as threatening. He threw puppies against the wall, suffocated cats, and harmed other pets, initially, when expecting the pets to attack him; in adolescence, violence and cruelty toward animals occurred for self-reinforcement. Third, he acted verbally and physically defiant in school.

Infliction of verbal and physical pain onto people or animals progressed chronologically from mild to severe from age 6 to his mid-twenties. The response frequency and magnitude, in other words, intensified as a function of consecutive school and home-based incidents of receiving either parental scolding and corporal punishment or removal (escape) from the classroom or school. A series of documented behavior incidents recording his aggression followed this timeline:

1. At age 6, he was noncompliant, verbally aggressive; stabbed a teacher with a pencil.

2. At age 7, he showed severe school noncompliance, arguing with authorities. He Cut the hand of his sibling and threw puppies against the wall until they died. He choked a cat until its eyes pop out.
3. At age 8, he bullied and hurt females. He threw a student against the wall; suspended for repeated in-school fighting. He developed a fascination for weapons.
4. At age 9 to 10, he described fascination with watching people in pain.
5. At age 12, he entered a residential school placement.
6. At ages 13 to 14, he regularly strikes people and claims he hears voices of devil inside of him.
7. At ages 14 to 15 (2005), he enters a second residential psychiatric/educational placement.
8. In his 20s, he pushes his niece (3–4 years old) very high on a swing and releases the swing, causing her to fly off the swing and suffer chest injury from crashing on the ground.

Regarding alcohol and drug abuse, John Doe's recreational experimentation was extensive. He co-abused cannabis and alcohol, and later titrated to opiate synthetics for enhanced sedative-hypnotic effects. Alcohol and drug use, however, did not always precipitate or accompany his oppositional and pain-inflictive behaviors. Aggression frequently occurred absent of any self-induced drug or alcohol condition. Medically, documented reports showed two mild head-injuries causing intracranial temporal hematoma. However, neuro-imaging testing ruled out post-injury neuropathology. His only minor surgery was in childhood incurring no post-operative complications with anesthesia or from taking prescriptive analgesic medications. His only residual medical condition was asthma.

Family history, the common hallmark of child sexual abusers, was indeed fraught with verbal and physical maltreatment. His unmarried parents separated at his birth. His mother, a prostitute and polydrug (cocaine, cannabis, alcohol) abuser, barely managed the household. His father, a pimp, when seen, displayed a volatile temper when inebriated. His father's escalations frequently included corporal punishment for random household infractions. Exposure to this arbitrary and capricious punishment increased the subject's hypervigilance (high anxiety), helplessness, and expectancy of being mistreated. Frequently battered, his father's beatings persisted until the subject yelled or cried in pain. Over time, the subject associated his cries of pain with the father's cessation of violence (negative reinforcement). This negative reinforcement not only shaped the subject's production of tearfulness to stop the aggression, but it also became a rule governed (self-) statement that "when people cry in pain, it means they really feel the effects of his father's (perpetrator's) actions. Years later, when inflicting sexual pain on children, the children's crying and yelling in pain served a similar cue for the subject. It signaled to the subject the children were really feeling effects of sexual assault intensity, positively reinforcing the subject's persistence.

## Documented history of crime

Records reviewed included a litany of court-accessible documents from police arrests, school incident reports, letters written by his parents, previous psychoeducational and psychological evaluations, medical treatment, witness and victim testimonies, crime scene reports, and incarceration reports. Analyses of these data, along with self-reported data, provided a *reactional biography* or approximate summation of the subject's interbehavioral criminal history from the perspective of authoritative observers (Kantor, 1933; Ruben, 1983). It provided a vivid window of historical interactions between a multiplicity of stimuli and the subject, and allowed for relocation of controlling variables from inside the organism (subject) to outside in the environment. The reactional biography showed a bevy of juvenile and adult crimes ranging from domestic abuse to retail fraud, involving placement in residential psychiatric hospitals, juvenile detention centers, and county jail.

## Behavioral analysis and history of sexual behavior

In his sexually perpetrative behaviors, initiation of contact was unilateral, entirely prompted by the subject. His sexual actions also depended on varying motivating operations, setting events, reinforcement schedules, and continuity of events transacted between victim and the subject through successive segments of conditioning. These factors further constitute an operational or functional analysis between environment, crime, victim, and suspect (subject). Below is a time series of such successive events in the subject's sexual activity from age 6 to 28, reflecting the evolution of his sexual behavior pathology:

1. At 6 years old, subject was molested by his $^1/_2$ brother.
2. At 7–8 years old, subject digitally penetrated and attempted intercourse with his $^1/_2$ sister and made his brother perform oral sex on him.
3. At 7 years old, subject discovered and frequently looked through Penthouse and Playboy magazines.
4. At 7–8 years old, subject began performing oral and anal sex on children he babysat for. Subject says it reminds him of the intense excitement he felt when penetrated by his $^1/_2$ brother.
5. At 7 or 8 years old, he begins sexual harassment of female classmates and taunting pets by touching their genitals.
6. At age 12, subject began having anal sex with a Pitbull. He enjoyed the soft, hairless buttocks of the Pitbull and replicated it by shaving his own anus before letting partners perform anal sex on him.
7. At age 12 and 13, teachers observe his making sexual overtures to males.
8. At age 12, subject becomes the victim of alleged sexual molestation by adult perpetrator.
9. At age 12, subject shows a picture of a naked boy to a female classmate and asks her if this makes her sexually aroused.
10. At age 12, The Behavioral Intervention Plan instituted at his school specified, among other target behaviors, that subject will refrain from using sexually inappropriate gestures or obscene language.
11. At age 14 (2002), A metropolitan Assessment Center found his "eroticization and sexualization includes sexual preoccupation, alleged sexual victimization of others, and precocious sexual activity.

12. At ages 18 to 19, subject regularly visited topless bars. He also paired masturbation in the shower with defecating or urinating in the shower.
13. At ages 18 to 22, subject frequently masturbates (covertly) in college classes.
14. At ages 22 to 24, subject regularly uses internet pornography to build fantasies and intensify his masturbation.
15. From ages 14 to his recent incarceration, subject is bisexually promiscuous with over 80 casual adult partners.
16. At age 26 to 27, subject begins frequent sexual activity over a two month period of time with a 3 year old (boy), 5 year old (girl), and 6 year old (boy) involving anal and oral sex, and intercourse.
17. At ages 26 to 28, interval time in between sexual acts (through masturbation to partner-sex) is short, 1–2 h, with strong withdrawal symptoms arising during longer latencies without sexual relief.
18. At age 28 to present (while incarcerated), subject solicits other inmates to expose their genitals (penis) to him; subject said he would concede to performing oral on the inmate if prompted.

One way of quantifying his progression of actions is by two classifications: *Cognitive and behavioral progression of sexual behaviors. Cognitive progression* consists of self-reported or publicly stated thoughts (verbal mands, tacts, autoclitics, intraverbals), serving the function to motivate or enjoin the subject to engage in precurrent sexual or actual sexual behaviors. His cognitive progression consisted of (a) antecedent thoughts about the victim, (b) reasons to see or visit the victim beyond normal family interactions (c) favors or demands made of the victim, (d) any scheming to systematically or methodically lure the victim, or (e) the belief that his sexual offense could be achieved (i.e., optimize reinforcers) without incurring punishment. The *behavioral progression* consists of publicly directive and predatory behaviors imposed on the victim and reliably observed by other people. Such behavioral progression involved (a) stalking, cruising, or hunting the victim through any compulsive act in which he must be in control, (b) playing with or grooming the victim to the point of the victim's submission, and (c) sexual assault, either from a distance or close up in touching the victim.

The chronological progression of sexual behaviors also reflects, in this case, the adventitious (superstitious) conditioning of fetishes. Fetishes, or paraphelias, are abnormal sexual behaviors characterized by intense sexual arousal to atypical objects, fantasies, situations, or individuals. The fundamental conditioning principles of how these paraphelias or fetishes develop are simple in concept but can become very complex in real life and evolve into very strong urges that supersede logic or awareness of the wrongness of an act during the commission of the act. Paraphelias develop in one of three ways and often these three ways intermingle. First, sexual arousal is repeatedly paired with neutral or insignificant objects or people, and properties of these objects or people acquire or "take on" sexual-arousal triggers. For example, the subject paired masturbation in the shower with defecating or urinating in the shower. Any neutral objects he added to the shower ritual, such as taking showers with children, also became a sexual cue. Another example is his pairing the sound of his victims' painful or pleasurable noises with engaging in anal or oral sex with them. The noises itself subsequently evoked sexual arousal cues. Although these cues might deteriorate after repeated extinction and communication training (Fyffe, Kahng, Fittro, & Russell, 2004), the subject quickly generalized his responses to multiple and diversified settings, increasing his resistance to extinction. He performed similar acts with different children, in different households, and at different times of the day.

Second, sexual arousal also triggers a sequence or ritual of steps chained together to produce a very gratifying outcome. For example, the subject followed a certain *predictable* order or habit when engaging sexually with the children, different from his sexual acts with adults his age or older. With children, he frequently had them perform oral sex, and did not withdraw his penis when ejaculating; with adults, the subject either was the one performing oral sex on them (male or female) or if the partner performed fallatio, the subject *always withdrew his penis before or during ejaculation*. Other rituals involved a combination of oral and anal sex with children before the subject completed his ejaculation. The subject varied the schedule of reinforcement from concurrent (e.g., each stimulus produces a consequences) to mixed (e.g., two stimulus options night produce a consequence), to multiple (e.g., two stimulus options do produce same consequence), to conjunctive (e.g., one of four stimuli may produce consequence), and to Tandem (two behaviors needed to produce a consequence). After each stimulus-response chain, he achieved climax (release of oxytocin) that strengthened the interrelated links in the chain and increased the future probability of ritual repetition. The longer the chain, the more diverse the response topography, and the more reinforcing each link in the chain was to propel the chain, the more difficult it became to interrupt the entire sequential response pattern.

Third, repeated climax at the terminal point of the chain built a tolerance. Like drug or alcohol addiction, it took more erotic arousal to produce satisfying sexual outcome. A sexually evocative object, for example, a young boy victim, may generate strong sexual arousal at first. But, after a month or after consecutive oral and anal sex with that victim, the sex arousal threshold reached a plateau and the victim child alone was inadequate as the discriminative stimulus to sexually excite the subject; new and more exciting properties were needed. Enhancement of erotic properties required pairing the child with new arousing properties or seeking new objects of stimulation. The subject, for example, went from anal sex with minors to anal sex with dogs. He went from oral sex of swallowing semen (of boys) to drinking urine (of the children). The thrill of the new sensations intensified sexual arousal to a higher level that, ultimately, would evoke orgasm. A hierarchy developed of gradually incremental erotic properties paired with the rituals, operating on compound reinforcement schedules (e.g., concurrent, mixed, interval, ratio, etc.).

A better schematic understanding of the subject's recurrent sexual behaviors may be possible by coding the environment and his actions with the operation it produces. Below appears a description of coded variables in the subject's behavioral context, placed into four classifications: Stimulus properties, response properties, consequence properties, and total behavior segment properties.

## Stimulus properties

*Setting Events:* Children's house.
*Establishing operation (EO):*Baby-sit for the children.
*Abolishing operation:* Risk of children disclosing incidents to their parents.

*Motivating operation:* Desire to achieve climax via ritual.

*Surrogate (EO):* Rotation among different children producing similar sexual acts.

*Reflexive (EO):* Temporary absence of desired child delays, interrupts, or deprives onset of sexual ritual; increases the establishing operation for wanting same or other children.

*Transitive (EO):* One victim child performing sex act *makes another child desirable to perform* Similar acts.

*Evocative/Elicitive Effects*: Presence of children (their words, noises, etc.) are discriminative cues triggering onset of ritual sequence. Presence of children and their initial contact (oral, anal sex) are unconditioned/conditioned stimuli eliciting subject's erection, autonomic (erotic) arousal. (Operant/respondent effects are intermingling).

*Generic Extension:* Repeating similar sexual acts with same child.

*Metaphorical Extension:* Repeating similar sexual acts with same gender or age.

*Metonymical Extension:* Repeating similar sexual acts with varying gender or age but of victims who dress alike or have similar hair-color or facial features associated with the child that are irrelevant properties (i.e., not the properties per se that evoke/elicit predatory, grooming, and perpetrative behaviors).

## Response properties

*Topography:* The ritualistic sequence consisting of predictive response from having child perform fallatio to taking showers with children, to urinating or defecating in the shower.

*Frequency:* Once or twice weekly to monthly.

*Duration:* Rituals lasted 30 min to 1 h.

*Concurrent response patterns:* Subject's talking to (approving, affirming) the child while the child performed sexual acts on him; the subject promising rewards/favors following completion of the sexual acts.

*Sequential response patterns:* Events preceding baby-sitting (contacting the family to arrange baby-sitting, remarks made to parents before leaving children alone with subject), the ritual sexual sequence itself, and events succeeding the sexual ritual (e.g., activities with children after sexual acts occurred).

*Excesses/Deficits:* Subject's high demand for sexual acts; high desirability for children victims; weak interpersonal skills; cognitive and learning disabilities.

*Predictive Response Patterns:* High probability of repeating ritualistic behaviors given consistently dense reinforcement schedules (rich variable schedules produce higher ratio schedules produce higher rates). Variable ratio schedule, for example, was that every fourth or fifth time he asked to baby-sit, the parents would agree. Variable interval schedules, for example, were that for every fourth or fifth day he baby-sat for the children, it produced a steady, moderate rate of the subject repeating both his inquiry to baby-sit and also execution of the sexual rituals with the victims.

## Consequence properties

*Positive reinforcement:* (e.g., forward and backward conditioning (successive approximations) on a fixed or variable schedule shaped the sexual ritual).

*Negative reinforcement:* (e.g., withdrawal/removal of subject's penis before ejaculation in adult partner's mouth increased the precipitating erotic arousal and potency of the orgasm).

*Positive punishment:* (e.g., a child protesting, resisting, or refusing compliance with oral or anal sex immediately interrupted and ceased the progression of ritualistic patterns. Repeated interruptions ceased (or decreased) enlistment of the noncompliant child and prompted grooming for a replacement child).

*Negative punishment:* (e.g., removal or prevention of baby-sitting opportunities with children also decreased incidents of molestation since subject's actions largely occurred in the household context of babysitting while the children's parents were absent).

## Total behavior segment properties

*Concurrent Schedules:* (e.g., subject masturbates while defecating or urinating in the shower, all three of which produce separate but concurrent sensory reinforcers.)

*Multiple Schedules:* (e.g., child performs oral sex on the subject; he delays ejaculation and switches or alternates to perform anal sex on another child, the outcome being the same reinforcing consequences of orgasm.)

*Tandem Schedules:* (e.g., subject performs oral sex on adult, then shortly thereafter has oral sex performed on him by child, the completion of both enabling the subject to experience orgasm.)

*Conjunctive Schedules:* (e.g., subject anally penetrates two children (ratio schedule), then waits 20 min before another child performs fallatio on him (interval schedule), producing the subject's orgasm.)

*Mixed Schedules:* (e.g., similar to multiple schedules, above, but the discriminative cue starting the ritual chain for either child is unclear and may even interrupt execution of the entire ritual.)

*Alternative Schedules:* (subject either achieves orgasm from anal/oral sex with children or from adult partners, whichever occurs faster when both options are equally available.)

The above coding of sexual responses within a behavioral field samples a causal or operational explanation of why the subject is more or less likely to engage in predatory, precurrent, or the actual sexual ritual. Variations in response choice and intensity also are subject to the valence or value of past reinforcers matched against competing reinforcers. This is called the *Matching Law* (Borrero et al., 2010; Herrnsetein, 1961; Poling, Edwards, Weeden, & Foster, 2011). According to this law, rates of responding typically are proportional to the rate of reinforcement received from each choice alternative. For example, if performing fallatio on a male adult generated a higher rate or richness of reinforcers for the subject, compared to anally penetrating a child, especially if the availability of children was intermittent (interval schedule), the subject's sexual preference may lean toward the adult partner. On concurrent *ratio* schedules, to spin this differently, responders tend to almost always choose the more reinforcing schedule.

The subject, in our example, choose accessible male adult partners to perform oral sex on. However, in concurrent *interval* schedules, responders do not typically choose or allocate all of their efforts to the richer, more reinforcing schedule. Here, by contrast, with time passage, the subject's motivating operations are already delayed and he may weigh other factors into the formula to calculate which schedule (partners) to pursue. For instance, if he babysits for the children *or* can rendezvous with a male partner both in 3 h, with his urgency postponed (abolishing operation), the subject may choose more spuriously the option of the subject's history of erotic arousal with either victims. He may choose the children, for example, if it means he can eat dinner at their house when he babysits; he may choose the adult male, on the other han, if the male partner promises to watch a movie with him. The varying motivational operations affecting the subject's later choice, in other words, can be less certain and more impulsive.

Another variable imposing on the setting events are mediating psychophysical sensations. Suggested earlier was the evolving tolerance the subject develops to erotic stimuli, forcing the response sequence to diversity or acquire more intensity as the sensory threshold increases for orgasm. Attention to the role of this mediating sensory response comports with current research on the habituation model (see Cohen & Leckman, 1992). Here, self-monitored sexual cues pertain to certain somatic phenomena, or *premonitory urge severity* (cf. Hougton et al., 2017). Premonitory urges are internal antecedent sensations repeatedly and precurrently associated with the sexual arousal and emission of sexual behavior; they act as evocative cues for subsequent sexual behavior patterns. This proprioceptive feedback (premonitory urges) discriminately arousing the organism is analogous to research previously done on postpartum women, who reported spontaneous crying and depression unrelated to palpable or external stimulus conditions; their internal sensory induction of hormonal changes instead triggered false cues resembling familiar biophysical sensations experienced in nonpostpartum circumstances, such as when the women were sad or borderline tearful (Ruben & Ruben, 1985). Detection of premonitory cues (urges) can both operationally explain the hidden or "private" sensations implicit in the sexual predator, and also help to target and reduce sexual risk habits of adults who were victims of childhood sexual abuse (Senn, Braksmajer, Hutchins, & Carey, 2017).

## Total behavior segment properties implications for offender rehabilitation

A behavioral analysis of this fetish (paraphilia) provides a blueprint for quantitatively measurable and predictable sexual criminal behaviors of a sexually predatory criminal. In nonbehavioral (conventional forensic) investigations, assessment of the predator is to classify him or her into action-outcome categories of sexual molestation or pedophilia. Once classified as *Situational, Regressed, Morally Indiscriminate, Sexually Indiscriminate, Inadequate, Seductive, Introverted,* and *Sadistic,* the typology puts complex behavior into neat categories. But the "neatness" of this taxonomy also invisibly eliminates the intricacy and interrelationships of stimulus-responses from the equation of profiling, predicting, and preventing future criminal incidents. One way to combine the BSA with conventional forensic practice for sexual offenders is to preserve their nosology of labels, with different functional definitions. Definitions that shift from a broad outcome-based typology to more concrete, subcomponental behaviors that interact continuously in a series of behavioral segments; each segment shows more precisely what motivates the offender's actions. Isolation of these multicausal factors would provide distinct advantages to defendant attorneys and prosecutors preparing the case, jurors who hear the case, judges who moderate the cases, and probation/parole officers who monitor the convicted offender for risk of recidivism. For example, jurors could be presented with less hypothetical conjectures about the criminal, and instead with actual cause-effect scenarios, and with mathematical-like probabilities on the propensity for recriminalization. Probation or parole officers, tracking offender compliance, can pinpoint more accurately the actual risk-behaviors likely to recur, and the antecedent and consequent effects increasing risk of probation outcome failure. More importantly, as in medical science when a condition like cardiomyopathy is assailable into verifiable facts about diagnosis and prognosis, so can criminal sexual behavior be profiled with logical and verifiable data that details influences on pathology and exactly how to ameliorate the problem in the future.

## References


Bearman, S. K., & Ward, A. (2017). Coming of age (professionally) in the age of dissemination and implementation. *The Behavior Therapist, 40*, 231–236.

Borrero, C. S., Vollmer, T. R., Borrero, J. C., Bourret, J. C., Sloman, K. N., Samaha, A. L., et al. (2010). Concurrent reinforcement schedules for problem behavior and appropriate behavior: Experimental applications of the matching law. *Journal of Applied Behavior Analysis, 93*, 455–469.

Burton, D. L., Miller, D. L., & Shill, C. T. (2002). A social learning theory comparison of the sexual victimization of adolescent sexual offender and nonsexually offending male delinquents. *Child Abuse & Neglect, 26*, 893–907.

Cohen, A. J., & Leckman, J. F. (1992). Sensory phenomena associated with Gilles de la Tourette's Syndrome. *Journal of Clinical Psychiatry, 53*, 319–323.

Cooper, J. O., Heward, W. L., & Heron, T. E. (2007). *Applied behavior analysis* (2nd ed.). Upper Saddle River, NJ: Pearson Prentice-Hall.

Drasgow, E., & Yell, M. L. (2007). Functional behavioral assessments: legal requirements and challenge. *School Psychology Review, 30*, 239.

Emery, R. E., & Marholin, D. (1977). An applied behavior analysis of delinquency: The irrelevancy of relevant behavior. *American Psychologist, 32*, 860–873.

Furby, L., Weinrott, M. R., & Blackshaw, L. (1989). Sex offender recidivism: A review. *Psychological Bulletin, 105*, 3–30.

Fyffe, C. E., Kahng, S. W., Fittro, E., & Russell, D. (2004). Functional analysis and treatment of inappropriate sexual behavior. *Journal of Applied Behavior Analysis, 37*, 401–404.

Hazelwood, R., & Burgess, A. W. (Eds.). (1987). *Practical aspects of rape investigation: A multidisciplinary approach*. NY: Elsevier.

Herrnstein, R. J. (1961). Relative and absolute strength of response as a function of frequency of reinforcement. *Journal of the Experimental Analysis of Behavior, 4*, 563–573.

Houghton, D. C., Capriotti, M. R., Scahil, L. D., Wilhelm, S., Peterson, A. L., Walkup, J. T., et al. (2017). Investigating habituation to premonitory urges in behavior therapy for tic disorders. *Behavior Therapy, 48*, 834–846.

Jeffrey, C. R. (1965). Criminal behavior and learning theory. *The Journal of Criminal Law, Criminology, and Police Science, 56*, 294–300.

Kantor, J. R. (1933). *A survey of the science of psychology*. Chicago, IL: Principia Press.

Lanning, K. (Ed.). (1992). *Child molesters: A behavior analysis for the law enforcement officers investigating cases of child sexual exploitation*. Quantico, VA: Behavioral Science Unit, Federal Bureau of Investigation.

Laraway, S., Snycerski, S., Michael, J., & Poling, A. (2003). Motivating operations and terms to describe them: Some further refinements. *Journal of Applied Behavior Analysis, 36*, 407–414.

Lyon, D. O. (1982). Concurrent behavior: Are the interpretations mutually exclusive? *The Behavior Analyst, 5*, 175–187.

Michael, J. (1982). Distinguishing between discriminative and motivational functions of stimuli. *Journal of the Experimental Analysis of Behavior, 37*, 149–155.

Morris, E. K. (1987). Introductory comments: Applied behavior analysis in crime and delinquency: Focus on prevention. *The Behavior Analyst, 10*, 67–68.

Morris, E. K., & Braukmann, J. (Eds.). (1987). *Behavioral approaches to crime and delinquency: A handbook of application, research, and concepts*. NY: Plenum Press.

Nietzel, M. T. (1979). *Crime and its modification. A social learning perspective*. Elmsford, NY: Pergamon Press.

Poling, A., Edwards, T. J., Weeden, M., & Foster, T. (2011). The matching law. *Psychological Record, 61*, 313–322.

Prentky, R., & Knight, R. A. (1991). Identifying critical dimensions for discriminating among rapists. *Journal of Consulting and Clinical Psychology, 59*, 643–661.

Rotheram-Borus, M. J., Swendeman, D., & Chorpita, B. F. (2012). Disruptive innovations for designing and diffusing evidence-based interventions. *American Psychologist, 67*, 463–476.

Ruben, D. H. (1983). Interbehavioral implications for behavior therapy: Clinical perspectives. In N. W. Smith, P. T. Mountjoy, & D. H. Ruben (Eds.), *Reassessment in psychology: The interbehavioral alternative* (pp. 445–469). Washington DC: University Press of America.

Ruben, D. H. (1992). Behavioral systems approach. In C. E. Stout, J. L. Levitt, & D. H. Ruben (Eds.), *Handbook for assessing and treating addictive disorders* (pp. 3–39). Westport, CT: Greenwood Press.

Ruben, D. H. (1993). A behavior analysis of impulsive child behavior. In L. Koziol, C. E. Stout, & D. H. Ruben (Eds.), *Handbook of childhood impulse disorders and ADHD* (pp. 78–107). Springfield. IL: Charles Thomas Publishers.

Ruben, D. H. (2015). *Behavioral guide to personality disorders (DSM-5)*. Springfield, IL: Charles Thomas Publishers.

Ruben, D. H. (October 2012). *Behavioral forensic assessment: Using applied behavior analysis in forensic psychology. Originally presented at the 2012 Executive Summit*. American College of Forensic Examiners International. https://youtu.be/zv5SI6KLYLQ.

Ruben, D. H., & Ruben, M. J. (1985). Behavioral implications of the postpartum blues (depression). *Birth Psychology Bulletin, 6*, 1–9.

Senn, T. E., Braksmajer, A., Hutchins, M., & Carey, P. (2017). Development and refinement of a targeted sexual risk reduction intervention for women with a history of childhood sexual abuse. *Cognitive and Behavioral Practice, 24*, 496–507.

Skinner, B. F. (1957). *Verbal behavior*. Englewood Cliffs, NY: Prentice-Hall.

Sutherland, E. H., & Cressey, D. R. (1955). *Principles of criminology*. Philadelphia, PA: Lippincott.

CHAPTER

# 4

# Mis-entitlement of thrill-seeking sexual assaults in individuals with unregulated urges (establishing operations)

The current zeitgeist of whistle-blowing accusations of sexual misconduct among politically or media-powerful males in the United States has reached unprecedented momentum. Afflicted women, banding together under the #MeToo campaign, have opened the flood gates of revelations about their heretofore suppressed experiences of being sexually harassed or mistreated (Khomami, 2017). Allegations cite men in roles of authority who raped, exposed their genitals (and masturbated), or made lewd overtures intimating quid pro quo expectations of their victims. It the last year alone, the war on unscrupulous male offenders intensified in its indiscriminate attacks on politicians and entertainers. While only hints of impropriety tainted the Anita Hill testimony against then Supreme Court nominee Clarence Thomas in October 1991, now the torrent of sordid accusations are bluntly vivid and even abutted with indictable archival pictures retrieved from the clouds of the internet. For example, sexual harassment allegations poured in during the campaign of then Republican presidential candidate Donald Trump; he escaped the carnage of the *Access Hollywood Tape* by diverting attention onto his Democratic opponent Hilary Clinton's private email server scandal.

But other targets of accusations were not as lucky to divert away attention. Among high-profile males facing the aftermath of damaged careers include movie producer Harvey Weinstein, gymnastics doctor Dr. Lawrence Nassar, actor Kevin Spacy, senator Al Franken, television host Charlie Rose, New York Times Reporter Glenn Thrush, Pixar/Walt Disney Manager John Lasseter, comedian Louis C.K. and Bill Cosby, and Alabama politician Roy Moore. The questions raised by this proliferation of female victims is not why they came forward now, or even the veracity of their allegations. The question herein is *what gives the male sex offender the entitlement by his prestige to poorly regulate sexual urges.*

Unrestrained sexual indulgence is not endemic to males. In fact, while the recent outgrowth of female testifiers all named male perpetrators, the percentage of female

*Behavioral Forensics*
https://doi.org/10.1016/B978-0-12-819805-6.00004-X

perpetrators of sexual crimes surprisingly has been steadily increasing (Stemple, Flores, & Meyer, 2017). More androgynously, risk of committing sexual victimization *can be* equally as high for men or women depending on the contingencies of reinforcement and punishment directly impacting on the at-risk individual's life. Contingencies consist of the prototypical tripartite of stimulus-response-consequence, enlarged in a series of behavior segments continuously flowing longitudinally. Each behavior segment inherently contains subproperties of the stimulus, response, and consequence, in addition to mediating variables affecting motivation (motivating operations, setting events), biophysical conditions, cognitions (or rule-governed verbal behaviors), and history of the organism (reactional biography) (see Kantor, 1959, 1976; Ruben, 1992, 2001, 2015). Together these properties *functionally produce a probability of behavior occurrence* that may explain the peculiarly high rate of mis-entitlement of tenacious (rule-violating) sexual behaviors. This paper presents multiple clinical cases of individual overstepping boundaries due to self-privilege or other misconstrued rights. The names in each case are fictional, in some cases their gender changed, and details about their precontemplative or actual sexual acts also modified to protect their identities. Analysis follows each case to identify the operation of behaviors underlying the misconduct and causal variables likely responsible for repetition or cessation of misbehavior in the future.

## Case examples of urge indulgence

Urge indulgence will always raise ethical, moral, or legal flags. A man passing another attractive man and soliciting him for sex is viewed as harassment, stalking, pandering, and sexual assault. An adult over 17 years old approaching a minor online or in person for sex is a criminal offense. Sexually touching a person perceived as attractive and submissive is rape. Using social apps for sexual hook ups, while legal, borders on sleaziness. Acting on immediate sexual impulsiveness means this: It violates the boundaries of other people and falsely inflates a euphoric feeling of invincibility. One feels a grand and fake sense that "I am above the law" and consequently the invincibly-driven person might engage in thrill-seeking sex acts regardless of any outcomes.

Richard, a 40 year old man, absolutely believed that all 20 year old effeminate gay men wanted sex and were frequently subjected to sexual abuse. He felt entitled to some of that abuse and was very aggressive about prospecting perceived effeminate men in public. In bars, at coffee shops, at athletic clubs, and in grocery stores, Richard bluntly approached males and briefly complimented their physical appearance (physique); after minutes, he immediately asked if the man would let Richard perform anal sex on him. When the stranger refused Richard's offer or tried to ignore Richard, Richard erupted in a violent verbal tirade of blaming the stranger man of being a "fag" and deserving to be beat up. Richard rarely acted out his threats of physical violence but often escaped law enforcement who was called by the strangers seconds after being affronted by Richard.

Richard was indiscriminate about asking any man on the street he felt would satisfy sexual urges. He disregarded the legal, social, or moral repercussions of his acts in favor of the intense pleasure he expected once he performed anal sex. Richard's persistence is even more surprising, since it means there were plenty of recipients agreeable to his requests that reinforced his belief that *all effeminate men would want him.* Richard received, in other words, a false verification of a rule governing his behavior; he derived this rule from successful sexual outcomes with anonymously impartial partners agreeing to his demands. Their docile subordination to his persistent (and angry) verbal mands conditioned a (falsely) ubiquitous belief that all men were gay. Rule-governed behaviors derived from false contingencies are the products of superstitious reinforcement. Richard, by some luck, in other words, fulfilled his motivating (establishing) operation by selecting the one prospect who consented; under most circumstances, Richard's precocious sexual request would likely meet severe positive or negative punishment and even draw attention to local police.

Craig did a similar behavior, but with women. He regularly went to adult men's clubs to see naked women dance. He paid extra for lap dancing and knew he could not touch the dancers. So, he touched himself. He masturbated while they danced for him. He also threw money at them, increasing the dancer's lavish attention to him. Outside of the men's club, at work, Craig saw a female around the age of the dancers at the club. He found himself unbelievably attracted to her and compelled to watch her move around the office. After a week of covert stalking, Craig approached the woman with a fifty-dollar bill and asked if she would do a private dance for him at his house. The female coworker immediately filed charges of sexual harassment against Craig.

Craig overstepped moral and legal boundaries when he generalized his solicitation for lap dances from the adult men's club to a civilian female. He did not delineate the two environments as different, since the common denominator between both situations *was his sexual urges. The female coworker aroused him sexually and his desire to masturbate, both sensations frequently associated with paying a female for a lap dance.* Craig got reinforced in one environment for his solicitation but was punished in another environment. He struggled to clearly distinguish the environments and this distinction grew more blurry as his he spent 90% of his free time in adult dance clubs. Similarly, adolescents addictively watching live-stream pornography may "bond with" or mistakenly desensitize toward the dancer/performer in the live video. This artificial intimacy of watching and even communicating "dirty" with the dancer online may generalize to talking "dirty" to female classmates. Stimulus generalization that "goes wrong," or generates unethical or immoral behavior, typically presents some of the relevant (metaphorical) or irrelevant (impure) properties from the original conditioned stimuli (i.e., metonymical stimuli, Skinner, 1957).

Maxine was a sophomore college student who spent Friday nights at a campus bar watching sports or hanging out with friends. She frequently met other male college students there, sharing one or two drinks with them, before they talked about having sex. Maxine enjoyed the sex talk, especially when slightly tipsy, since it made her feel beautiful, wanted, and highly sexually aroused. She frequently went home with the guys she met at the bars and had a one or two-night causal sexual encounters. In class, she also met cute guys and, unthinkingly, slipped into her routine of flirting with them as she did with guys in the bar. But her male classmates were less receptive to her flattery and particularly when she shifted the conversation to having sex with them.

Maxine honestly believes her behavior was normal. She is neither sexually deviant nor aggressive, and her conversations are soft, amiable, and exceptionally personable. The trouble is that her sexual urges, and cues associated with these urges, fool her into thinking she can openly talk about sex to all men. Maxine struggles to make subtle distinctions between environments conducive for sex-talk and environments inappropriate for sex talk. The environments, moreover, are very unclear, since some male classmates may enjoy her advances in class, while other male classmates may find it offensive. When cues are not only unclear but present concurrent contingencies (i.e., solicit and be reinforced or solicit and be punished), the impulsive person may be prone to gamble; she or he will persist with the solicitation for the reinforcing effect. The calculus of which contingency to follow partly emanates from the Matching Law (Herrnstein, 1961). Matching law states that rates of responding typically are proportional to the rate of reinforcement received from each choice alternative. If Maxine discovers a high response return on male classmates complying with her sexual innuendoes, compared to rejections, she will *naturally* act on the higher reinforcement contingency. However, here case is also a good example of motivating operations. She may be under surrogate or transitive operations; the classmates are just as probable as the bar-mates, and soliciting classmates may *increase the reinforcing valence of class attendance,* since she otherwise might not attend class.

A similar behavioral system paradigm appeared for Shelly and Brad. The married couple was heavily into sex. They both enjoyed the spontaneity of fondling each other at home and in public and often used playful touching as warm-ups for foreplay to later have intercourse. For example, Brad often placed his hand inside Shelly's front pants, fingering her vagina, or placed his fingers inside her anus while driving the car or at the movie theater. Shelly, too, was creative. She enjoyed rubbing up against Brad's penis until he became erect, or at a friend's house, she lured him upstairs to the bedroom to perform "quickie" oral sex. After Shelly gave birth to their first child, Brad continued his same sex play and saw it bothered Shelly. Shelly did reciprocate with oral sex but performed it less often and she complained about it. She also was less assertive sexually. Brad felt Shelly's resistance but he kept up the foreplay and ignored her signs of resistance.

Did Shelly and Brad do anything wrong? No, not exactly. They created a private world or microcosm of playful sexual rules (contingencies) and mutually encouraged each other to be spontaneous and creative. The more spontaneous and creative they were, the stronger it reinforced their immediate sexual stimulation and impetus for future public or private foreplay. When Shelly changed the contingencies in postpartum, including diminishment of libido (i.e., low establishing operation or decreased genital sensation), she did not communicate to Brad her altered physical state. Brad, from his history of conditioning, weighed the *probability of Shelly's sexual approval against her sexual disapproval.* He saw Shelly still acted like she used to, spontaneous in public, and figured he play the odds she might accept more than decline.

*Probability* is the issue here. It is the estimated calculation that some outcome is likely given several things. One is the right or familiar cues triggering these outcomes in the past, such as Brad and Shelly visiting a friend's house where Shelly performed oral sex on Brad. Second is the right behaviors (of Shelly) around which Brad expects routines, rituals or amenability to his sexual behaviors. Third is seeing few unpleasant obstacles blocking the path of sex-risk behaviors. Shelly, in other words, is not ranting, threatening him to stay away, and does not put up many barriers between both of them. Fourth, Brad gets sexually aroused under both of these conditions (i.e., his establishing operation). Sexual arousal increases whether Shelly rejects or accepts him, since rejection generates a high response effort (ratio) over time (interval) to repeat the same sexually solicitous behaviors until Shelly relents. In this case, the continuum of behavior segments in Brad's sexual history are very germane. He received a confluence of mixed, concurrent, conjunctive, and tandem reinforcement schedules with low or no punishment consequences; he also transferred (adapted his) sexual acts to exponentially diverse setting events, building a complex and higher response resistance to extinction if just one of the stimulus conditions ceased (e.g., Shelly no longer wants sex at home).

Probability plays many functional roles in sexual impulses, as it does in most behavior. Probability is a gauge of whether to act on risk-behavior; it is a gauge of good and bad consequences; it is a gauge of understanding people; and it is a gauge of understanding ourselves. People suffering chronic pain, for example, use probability to gauge or estimate when narcotic medications will wear off and intolerable pain levels might restore. They synchronize the schedule of taking medications to offset this onset of gradual pain re-intensity, known as breakthrough pain. People suffering Irritable Bowel Syndrome (IBS), likewise, are mindful of probability. They gauge when their intestinal track feels upset or they are prone to need a bathroom. They scope out a new environment for convenient restrooms and choreograph their movements in the setting proximal to the bathrooms.

Probability gives a mathematic reading or estimate about when impulses may produce a reinforcer (or the pleasant outcome desired). But therein lies a problem. Just because the probability *seems* accurate and predicts a reinforcer, it does not mean the probability really *is accurate. It may not be* based on *accurate events that generate the desired reinforcers.*

Jackson preferred blonde ladies with large breasts. He knew it was shallow of him to lust this stereotype but he did not apologize for seeking out this type of woman to date. When meeting these women at proper venues—parties, bars, at work, in stores, at church—he was a metal to their magnet and instantly introduced himself as a segue to flirtation. He never pitched sex with them, unless they did it first, but he did savor the time with them, fantasizing in his mind how sex might feel with them. On one occasion he went to the restaurant Hooters and had a female waitress who fit his stereotype of female physical attributes. He could not concentrate on the food order and started to flirt with her. He found her small-talk diminished quickly as she shifted back to his food order. He asked her to return in a moment while he chose a meal. Nearly 3 min later, a new waitress not fitting Jackson's stereotype appeared, saying she replaced the other waitress. She was there to take his food order.

Jackson's weighed the pros with the cons when he flirted with the waitress. He informally calculated the probability was high of feeling aroused by the blond-hair, large breasted waitress if he postponed his meal order and flirted with her. What he did not anticipate in his probability math formula was that she might be annoyed by his distractions to do her job of waitressing tables. His probability-calculation missed an important fact—it was not based on accurate events of the situation, just on the impure discriminate cues of her being a female waitress. He ignored the relevant environmental cues of her busy table-waiting tasks, or that she completed her work schedule. Jackson focused instead on impure or other cues such as (a) the way the waitress looked, and (b) his sexual urges. While Jackson's error sounds like a typical lack of stimulus control (Cooper, Heron, & Heward, 2007), or inhibition around relevant stimuli (Hearst, Besley, & Farthing, 1970), he indeed did respond discriminately to certain cues that were *relevant to his motivating (establishing) operation at the time.* Relevancy of cues, then, depends on the behavioral context (matrix) of norms, conventions, rule, traditions, values, and other community-defined expectations for Jackson to follow. In a different subculture or community, these social guidelines may be different or more permissive. For example, a 7-year old second grader reading a college-level e-book in class, downloaded from Amazon, shows extremely high discriminative focus. However, the class norm is for all the students to pay attention to the teacher lecturing about math. Jackson does not pay attention to the lecture and is engulfed in reading his book. The establishing operation under which the book reading cues occur exert more discriminative control than do the stimulus cues for Jackson to pay attention to the teacher (cf. Vollmer & Iwata, 1991).

## Masquerade of sexual impulses

Control over sexual impulses really begins, then, with assailing the immediate cues and contingencies to determine if there is a high or low probability of good and bad consequences once the impulse occurs. Around a romantic partner, secure inside a house, probabilities may be higher for good consequences that might outweigh any minor bad consequences. Outside in public, toward the same partner, impulsiveness for sex may backfire immediately. Punitive consequences may overpower the reinforcing consequences. The probability changes even though the person or the behaviors comprising a person's sexual advances may stay the same. It can be very hard to differentiate the right times, right places, and measurements of good reinforcing and punishing consequences, since even consequences will vary depending on the situation. For example, a wife warns her husband to withhold sexually-related, impulsive comments in public. But yesterday, Christmas shopping at Macy's amid a hurricane of people, the wife whispers in her husband's ear how sexually desirous she is of his company. She contradicted her verbal caveat and created paradoxical stimulus conditions.

In view of this ambiguity, how does one learn to make subtle distinctions among situations, and master probability-thinking, when the landscape is always changing and rules about it are inconsistent? The answer is simple; one does not. We make continuous errors in judgment due to unclear cues and contingencies and are forever correcting these navigational decisions. One improper way around this constant GPS recalculation is to mask sexual impulses. The masquerade of sexual impulses means an individual finds alternative ways to express sexual urges bypassing normal routes. The individual nearly or completely abandons conventional routes for sexual behaviors and seek non-conventional outlets with greater probability of highrt success. For example, one pays for a prostitute, engages in affairs, or pre-arranges a safe place for sexual disinhibition.

Carla was tired of her sexless marriage worsened by her husband's dislike of affection and foreplay. She contemplated an affair with a coworker and realized the mess it would cause at the job. She also flirted online using Facebook and Tinder, but felt a connection there might expose her and ruin her marriage and community reputation. Her goal was simple; she wanted sex, not another new relationship. Instead, she found out about a sex resort in Jamaica allowing her to freely engage in unlimited sexual behaviors with her choice of a male. She worried it was a scam, but after some thorough searching, she decided to pay the hefty fee for recreational sex. Carla fulfilled her goal, had incomparably euphoric sex with a male she did not know, and returned home less angry at her husband.

Carla's adventure was very calculated. She planned it out with precision, from taking off time from work and travel arrangements, to self-protection from STDs. She also made excuses to her husband about her reasons for travel to Jamaica. Her impulse control was phenomenal, since she *delayed satisfying her urges for several months until she calibrated the probability of her action to minimize or eliminate bad consequences and maximize good consequences.* Carla engaged in a sophisticated rouse to please her needs; she masked her sexual impulses and frustration by selecting a safe refuge.

Other refuges for sexual release include *the Swinger's Club (or equivalent clubs), escort services, or using discrete online websites catering to affair-prone seekers.* In the recent scandal over hacked-in databases at *Ashley Madison,* the public learned of celebrities or other public figures exposed as members of this discrete club. The most notorious was young evangelist and conservatism reality TV star Josh Duggar, who admitted his infidelity and threw his career into the controversial spotlight (Thomsen, 2015). While risk of hackers has deterred many people from paying monthly fees to similar discrete-affair websites, more websites abound promising Fort Knox data-security systems. A less private route is the Swinger's Club. Meant primarily for couples, Swinger's parties can offer single prime opportunities for discrete, no-strings-attached sex providing the subscriber follows covenanted rules of Swinger's clubs. These rules involve respecting sex refusals, communication, and sensitivity to emotional needs, and self-protection from STDs.

A Swinger's Club, online hookup websites, all-inclusive adult sex resorts, or even engaging prostitutes, are all *sex-relief centers* for the more impulse-controlled person who struggles to navigate the conventional roadways to sexual fulfillment. The problem with selecting these options is not the option itself, but more the seeker's unusual reactions in the aftermath of these pleasure centers.

## How does one reconcile the sexual freedom of using sex-centers with the sexual prohibitions in everyday life?

Like using synthetic or designer drugs like Flakka, Molly, or cracked-cocaine, producing an addictive euphoria, sex centers are euphoric and addictive. After using them once, users return again and become loyal repeat customers. Cost and mild STD-risks aside, the math just makes sense. One pays for a sex service and receives it immediately, or engages with sex-players all passionately sharing the same sex drive. Even in Swinger's clubs, if one partner refuses an individual's advances, other partners there are likely to agree to the individual's terms. There is little rejection and a straight forward blueprint of how to get from A-to-Z on relieving sexual needs. After individuals spends time at the club, or with a prostitute, or returns from a sex resort or legal brothel, what are their behavior like toward existing and new partners? Are they cold, impersonal, and isolate themselves? Do they feel more libido-energy and act hypersexual with partners? Or, are they the same? Do they balance the sexually-satisfied self with similar sexual habits and routines displayed before their pleasure excursions? Or, do you hide their guilt and "immoral" behavior through righteous and ultra-conservative speeches extolling the virtues of abstinence? Let's consider each possibility.

## Cold, impersonal and isolated

Transitioning from sexual autonomy to sexual restriction is like sensory deprivation. One is trapped in a life forbidding certain feelings or behaviors they enjoyed a week earlier. People hate this transition. Abrupt removal of the continuous reinforcement schedule (CRF) and forced inhibition of highly reinforcing behaviors is analogous to the phenomena called *conditioned suppression* (Lyon, 1968; Ray & Stein, 1959). In early experiments of conditioned suppression, electrically shocked animals immediately became subdued or *learned to be helpless* (see Maier & Seligman, 1976). Like infrahumans, human organisms can suddenly become aloof, indifferent and detached. Such dispositions typically produce concurrent responses with sarcasm, cynicism, and fault finding. Each of these reactions mask the anger for being suppressed. A person tunes out his or her current life and replays fantasies of the getaway sex center previously enjoyed; the more these fantasies contrast with the person's mundane, sexless, and maudlin lifestyle, the more a person feels angry, resentful, and impatient. If married or with a partner, the suppressed individual might criticize a partners' subtle flaws, remain distant, quiet, monotone in voice, and outwardly seem depressed.

Another reason for feeling estranged from the partner or family is *betrayal*. The displaced individual feels he or she has *betrayed* the sex partner (i.e., sex surrogate) at the pleasure center, not the home partner. For people unaccustomed to flings, tristes, or other no-strings attached sex, they *attribute meaning to the sex surrogate at the pleasure center. They feel more loyal to the sex surrogate partner than their home partners.* Betrayal in this respect means (a) two or more concurrent (deprivational) states, and (b) memorial behavior (Kantor, 1977) about the unfulfilled state of deprivation or person. That is, the individual "misses" and cannot have sexual relations with the sex surrogate (from a preceding segment), feels erotically aroused and unfulfilled in a current segment, and attributes more reinforcing properties to the sex surrogate than to the current sex partner.

## Hypersexuality

Immersion in sexual autonomy causes another side-effect. A person becomes hungry for more sex. Hypersexual behavior emerges from the increased physical tolerance to orgasm after repeatedly having intense and frequent sex in a short period of time. In the sex resort, for example, one has intercourse six times in a day, combined with multiple anal or oral sex acts. The sex-crave index jumps up several notches overnight and when it drops, as the person returns home, the physical withdrawal is very similar to withdrawal from stimulants; one feels a raging urge to have sex again, followed by hypersomnia (excessive sleep), agitation, apathy, and mood swings. To prevent the negative withdrawal effects, people do several things; they may overcompensate by excessive solicitations for sex from their home partner, or by privately masturbating. Masturbation may occur twice to three times daily to reach and sustain the threshold of arousal sensations enjoyed in the pleasure sex centers. When masturbation is not possible due to the living circumstances or daily schedule, unfulfilled sexual arousal can "leak into" (generalize) into the person's daily life and contaminate interactions with other people.

Katheryn met a male stripper and prostitute at a bachelorette party. She got his name and phone number and privately hired his services on several occasions. Despite the price, she found his passionate love-making was a recharger in her dull life. It enhanced her feeling attractive and built confidence in her sex behaviors. She learned her reliable male stripper moved out of town and left her without a replacement. Her sex withdrawal aroused uncontrollable urges in her body at home and while at work. At home, she struggled unsuccessfully to masturbate when she got a urinary tract infection. Absent of self-relief, she noticed herself frequently flirting with the married and unmarried men at work, and imagined tricking one of the men into having oral sex with her. She played out this fantasy in her thoughts several times at work, imagining the relief-sensation she might feel afterward. This preoccupation with sexual fantasies absorbed huge amounts of time at work and grossly interfered with her job productivity.

Katheryn's loss of a viable sexual outlet—one she cultivated to compensate for a sexless life—spiraled her into a biphasic reaction. First, she suffered an acute withdrawal marked by hypersexual obsessions and strong compulsions to engage in risky behaviors such as approaching married or unmarried men for oral sex; her risk-taking actions spiraled after masturbation was not possible. Ironically, had she tolerated these withdrawal symptoms, resisted the obsession, resisted (attempts at) masturbation, or even ceased flirting with men, urge arousal levels would diminish as a function of disrupting a sequential chain of behavior; the chain consisted of concurrent responses of self-talk, physiological stimulation (pulsing uterus sensations), predatory behavior, and indiscriminately engaging in heterosexual and bisexual behaviors. *That is, Katheryn sought anybody, male or female, at any time for sexual contact.*

Katheryn's ambivalence—do I let withdrawal symptoms pass or do I satisfy them—is very common among people using sex surrogates or sex centers as fixtures in their lives. When this fixed or stable sex outlet is jeopardized, spontaneously generated response may elevate Katheryn to take reckless health and partner risks that deviate significantly from her normal lifestyle.

## Hide your guilt and proselytize abstinence and fidelity

Another very common reaction to masking sexual urges and using sex centers is poorly managing *guilt*. Morally abiding partners may say they place a high premium on relationship fidelity. They are monogamous, supposedly dismissive of invasive thoughts to go astray, and sometimes see masturbation as a cruel betrayal of the partner's trust. However, when these morally-conscious individuals use sex centers, they perceive their acts as violations of this trust and "feel" very sinful. They feel evil, damaged, embraced, and impulsively seek exoneration through different means of contrition. They say they feel *guilty*. After all, in cognitive language, guilt is an emotion characterized by tension, regret, and remorse about a particular action or inaction (Tangney, Wagner, & Gramzow, 1991).

Regret and remorse, seen differently, are really not emotions per se, but are better functionally described as autoclitic verbal mands and tacts which convince (enjoin) us to respond more immediately under the right setting events. They are self-statements responding to verbal or nonverbal properties of our behavior, emitted to either avoid/escape impending punishment or access impending reinforcement. Around congregants, for example, who respect, admire, and revere a Catholic deacon, knowledge that he cheated on his wife may alter their contingencies significantly toward the deacon. He may face public humility and denigration from congregants or be removed from ministry by the deaconate. His later admission of guilt would be less about what he thought or felt, and more about how he overtly responded to the exigency of punishment contingencies. He wants to be exonerated or escape from blame.

There are several ways self-absolution (escapes from blame, or punitive consequences) occur that mask the guilt.

One way is to be over-romantic and generously gift-giving to the partner cheated on. Second, the offender may place himself or herself in solitary confinement, almost like self-administering a time-out. Third, they may immerse in some religious or therapy activity to cleanse clean their bad (sinful) thoughts and action and feel redeemed through self-sacrifice or confession; these are affidavits to reform in the future. For example, Amber Smith, Russel Brand, Tiger Woods, Eliot Spitzer, David Duchovny, Charlie Sheen, and recently Kevin Spacey are among the celebrities and political leaders who went from porn to purity in seeking salvation at treatment centers for sex addiction. Victory over their sex addiction somehow vindicated them from the litany of disgraceful deceptions they perpetrated while dating or married. They escaped extremely punitive contingencies in their careers, from partners, and from a social-media frenzy eagerly waiting to fillet their lives.

When residential treatment in a sex hospital seems a poor solution, turning to faith is always attractive. Religions serve many purposes. Sometimes religion follows the traditions of a subcultural group and has been present in a person's life from childhood through adulthood. It is a staple in their lives just like going to the grocery store. For example, Max was raised conservative Jewish in his homogenously Jewish community and faithfully attended the family synagogue for Shabbat services and on high holy days. He also received his bar mitzvah there. Max simply returned more fervently to a central hub of his cultural and religious identity. Similarly, people return to or seek out religion to help pass through difficult transitions in life such as when family members die or the seeker goes through a divorce, or suffers inoperable medical conditions. However, some people seek religion to disguise terrible behaviors about which they feel mercilessly guilty and feel through worship they can be forgiven.

Similarly, sex cheaters may seek religious sanctuary because *they are expected to by the subcultural group to which they belong or by the public in general.* Gary, a proclaimed atheist, and outspoken antireligious pundit, also happened to be Jewish. After discovery of his sexual practices with clients in his law practice—an ethical and legal transgression—he mitigated the adverse impact of the Board of Professional Conduct disbarring him by seeking private sessions with a local rabbi. The rabbi attested to Gary's sincere reformation and adoption of a Talmudic lifestyle. Without Gary's sexual impropriety exposed, he never would consider counsel with a rabbi. The calculus of contingencies implicit in Gary's reclamation of Jewish Faith relate to the multiple social effects of operant/respondent punishment (Axelrod & Apsche, 1983; Ruben, 2001, pp. 50–52). Among the paramount aversive effects include (a) rapid, intense punishment effectively suppresses behavior, (b) entire situations or the transitions between different situations come to be perceived as entirely aversive, and (c) punished behaviors occurring concurrently with or sequentially to other behaviors may have specific or general effects upon other behaviors. In other words, the permeation of aversive circumstances in a person's life are intense, destructive, and may take extensive time to subside. Against these odds, even non-religious people can become religious zealots.

Still another way to hide sexual behavior is by proselytizing. This is the self-appointed evangelist who disguises sexual vices by hypocritically preaching about the sinfulness of misanthropic sex and its heinous impact on the integrity of mankind. Christian leader Ted Haggard, pastor of New Life Church in Colorado, suffered a nasty scandal about vesting male prostitutes. So did the Bishop Eddie Long, settling out of court over sexual abuse of teens. Televangelist Jimmy Swaggart fell to disgrace after being caught having sex with a prostitute. Leading pastor of Overlake Christian Church Bob Moorehead lost his pulpit after being charged with indecent exposure in a public restroom. And Earl Paulk, founder of Chapel Hill Harvester in Decatur, Georgia, had sex with a number of females in his congregation and was accused of child molestation. The list abounds. The list is not of once pure religious leader's gone rogue. The list is of human beings poorly controlling sexual urges and using religion as a protective shield against feelings of moral repugnance for their actions. They are not authentically religious; they use religion as a decoy to frolic.

## Balance self

The practice of using sex centers and sex surrogates to replace sexual emptiness is as old as the dawn of time. It is a mis-entitled practice unlikely to change as long as people feel sexually deprived, neglected affectionately, and feel their active libidos are unequal to the low libidos of their partners. With advances in social media, more pornographic and hook up websites are very creative at luring sex-hungry buyers into iron-clad guarantees of fantasy fulfillment. The internet accessibility and infomercial-like persuasion of these websites is hard to resist and become the steppingstone to use other sex centers and sex surrogates. Once routinely blended into a person's life, is there way to *balance these acts of cheating with acts of kindness and relationship stability with a sexless partner?* The answer is "yes," but it involves a different perspective on the sexless and sex-fulfilled quadrants of one's life.

Dale married a second time with two intentions in mind. He wanted a friend, and a lover. He did not need the partner's money or want more children. He made his interests boldly clear while dating his girlfriend and seemingly his partner not only agreed to the terms but wanted the same thing. One year into their marriage, his now wife denounced sex as unpleasant, citing some moralistic and religious reasons for celibacy. She emphatically condemned Dale for being hypersexual and disrespecting her lack of libido and new philosophy about sex. This meant Dale's sexual talk, playful romantic advances, and prompt for intimate affection all were rejected; Dale's wife was his soulmate in friendship, and even doted and nurtured him in nonsexual ways. But the marriage turned sexless without Dale having a clue of how to repair it.

Dale's predicament is very common. He loves his wife. His relationship has all of the positively enviable features comprising a solid marriage such as communication, vulnerability, sincerity, minimal conflict, sensitivity, mutual nurturing, and ultimate support. He views his wife as a playmate, close friend, great travel companion, confidence-booster, and fan club admiring him. These were qualities unmatched in his previous marriage and never found in partner relationship before his first marriage. His only objection to his wife, despite her incredible beauty and compassion, was her *extinction of sex.* Dale realized sex was a necessity for close bonding. Absence of it posed a serious problem his wife was unwilling to discuss or seek counseling for.

What did Dale do? Dale was strategic and knew he wanted to maintain the emotional benefits of his marriage while also filling the vacancy of sex in his life. He took on a strange perspective, but one that helped him charter a path toward his calculated solution. He figured, when going to the gas station, he may regularly go to a Mobil station, but if it went out of business or prices skyrocketed, he had no qualms switching to the Sunoco station. Since he needed gas to run his vehicle, it was a matter of selecting which gas station benefited him the most. Dale borrowed this logic and applied it to his marriage. His wife's refusal for sex meant he would find somebody else who supplied sex, since sex was essential in his life. He carefully explored the safest options that did not negatively impact his life or marriage. The answer lied with going out of state. After careful planning and budgeting, for four months, Dale arranged a weekend trip disguised as a conference to a place where prostitution was legal. He spent a weekend paying for a sexual-catering service and fulfilled his unlimited pleasures without feeling rejected, disrespected, or depressed.

When Dale returned home after his erotic weekend, he saw his wife differently. He knew he would. He no longer viewed her with seething resentment, and instead he accepted her no-sex limitations. Dale knew he could be fulfilled in other ways, done discretely, and without it damaging his relationship. His demeanor toward his wife positively improved, and they continued their strong emotional friendship, with smatterings of nonsexual affection. Dale accepted this, knowing he would make that annual pilgrimage to the "conference" for his sexual appeasement.

Dale's solution may seem atypical in that it violates the presumed code of marital monogamy. After all, Dale unilaterally sought sex outside the marriage with another partner rather than to stay sexually loyal to his wife. A moralist may even say Dale was immoral and narcissistic in thinking sex was more important than the sanctity of marriage. But Dale saw it differently. Dale believed his wife violated the moral marital decree early in their marriage by denying and refusing a core part of any relationship. After all, sex was mutually agreed upon in the terms of their commitment before marriage. Dale believed his wife broke that agreement and was arrogantly and sanctimoniously unrelenting. She *unilaterally stopped the gasoline flow in his vehicle, and forced him to go to another gas station; short of another gas station, the only alternative was for Dale to never drive his vehicle again. That was a sacrifice Dale believed was unhealthy, inappropriate, and nobody but Dale had the right to impose it on him.*

## Violent rape

Violent rape is another example of mis-entitlement to sexual pleasure. Predators who stalk innocent victims for surprise attacks are motivated by several (conditioned and unconditioned) establishing operations. These include sexual needs, pre-sexual excitability of a cat-and-mouse chase, the thrill of taunting or luring the victim unobtrusively, and the visceral arousal from the sadistic (pain-inflictive) physical assault. This is different from date-rape or relationship-rape, in which both parties fully know each other, consent to pre-intimacy or intimacy, and there is a supposed breakdown in communication on exactly what foreplay or sex was allowable. The latter cases are very ambiguous forensically, and frequently reveal the victim was premeditative or retaliatory against the date rapist, no matter how little or much he or she exceed the boundaries of touch. While it is difficult to perfectly estimate prevalence of false or misleading accusations, current research reports 8–10% of accusations of forcible rape among known parties may be bogus (Cybulska, 2007; Turvey, 2013).

Sexual molestation of minors is even different. Here, the parties may be consenting or nonconsenting, and at different ages along a continuum. For example, the sexual abuser may be young, middle-aged or older adult who molests a child, preadolescent or adolescent. Or, the sexual abuser may be 18 years old, in a *consenting* relationship with a 16 or 17 year old partner. However, the term "consenting" is misleading, since adult commission of any sexual behaviors with minors is a felony; the laws in several states may uphold consent for ages 16 to 17 and not seek statutory rape charges against the adult perpetrator. However, most state jurisdictions presume a minor is not capable of consent tantamount to adult consent. That is, even if a child or underage teen gives permission or acts willingly, this never implies consent (Abel, Beck, & Cunningham-Rathner 1984). Criminal ambiguity of sex-consent between adult and child is most problematic when the perpetrator is 17 or 18 years old and the victim is 16 years old. The statutory rape laws fall into a gray area metaphorically named, "The Romeo and Juliet laws." Here, a sexually active couple are naïve to the laws forbidding sex with minors, but are both close in age and emotionally act the same. Courts nationwide are inconsistent in their rulings on Romeo & Juliet cases (ages 13–19), often reducing or eliminating the penalty of crime, or reducing the severity of the offense from a felony to a misdemeanor (Bierie & Budd, 2016).

Unlike sexual complicity among two teens, offenses by aggressive (sadistic) stalkers present a case of complex motivating operations. Stalkers can be obsessive, compulsive, ritualistic, and very calculated. Preplanning the attacks is part of the visceral excitement, equal to the viscerality of stalking and eventual execution of the assault. Erotic arousal is both self-induced by rule-governed statements and evoked by highly and diversely generalized stimuli conditioned repeatedly over the assailant's entire reactional biography. One way the courts attempted to control the motivating operations of habitual, aggressive rapists was to administer a drug essentially suppressing the libido or sex drive; this was called chemical castration. The choice of using chemical castration—antiandrogen drugs to impede build-up of testosterone—was to prevent sexual arousal, erection, or any surge of aggression triggered by testosterone (Douglas, Bonte, Focquaert, Devolder, & Sterckx, 2013). Punishment using this drug ran into many problems. The first and foremost was the assumption that all sexual perpetrators were male. *They are not.*

A second problem with using chemical castration was the assumption that libido or sexual arousal was the main variable triggering the predatory and assaultive offense. This is not so. It is the *final or terminal behavior in a chain of behaviors, all operating on different incentives that arouse body stimulation.* Sexually aggressive acts follow a ritual sequence of many smaller acts or behaviors hours before the assault occurs, all linked together with a common thread of stimulation. The stimulants or motivating operations are slightly different for each act in the chain. For example, rapist Nicholas may lay out his clothes for the day, then peruse Tinder-the hook dating site—for 2 h, and then stroll by the house of the person he spoke with on Tinder. After casing the place for 1 h, he calls the Tinder contact to meet her in person. Once he does this, his encounter involves strong innuendos to have sex, or he uses physical force or drugs them into sedation. The motivation in each of these sequential acts include (a) anticipatory arousal (or adrenaline rush from anticipating the crime), (b) the thrill of precision in executing each step the way he wanted, and (c) the imagery or idealism of thinking the victim really wants him sexually. The latter (c) motivator stems from a pathology called erotomania (see Westrup, 2001). In erotomania, a person strongly believes a person he does not know is in love with him or is sending love messages to him via some source. Erotomania derives from inaccurate (impure) stimulus generalization, auto-arousal associated with fantasy images, autoclitic tacts and mands rehearsed repeatedly, and some traceable history of acting on the distorted rule governed statements by literally confronting (or trying to confront) the target person idolized.

The pitfalls of chemical castration, the legal morass of prosecuting teen sex partners, and the conditions under which anybody can regress to morally unconscionable sexual behaviors all seem more understandable through a behavioral systems perspective. Mapping the behavioral segments, forensically speaking, builds causal continuity between precriminal and criminal behaviors. Mapping is reductionistic, in laying out the canvass of behavioral contingencies and setting events more clearly. While a scientific optic of analysis may raise more questions than answers at times, it at least shifts the forensic paradigm from inside the sex offender's mind and personality to the environmental contingencies. These contingencies, when studied under the microscope of science, using the principles of applied behavior analysis in a wider context, can effectively elucidate the etiology and proclivities of mis-entitled sexual actions.

## References

Abel, G. G., Becker, J. V., & Cunningham-Rathner, J. (1984). Complications, consent, and cognitions in sex between children and adults. *International Journal of Law and Psychiatry, 7*, 89–103.

Axelrod, S., & Apsche, J. (1983). *The effects of punishment on human behavior*. Orland, FL: Academic Press.

Bierie, D. M., & Budd, K. M. (2016). Romeo, Juliet, and statutory rape. *Sexual Abuse: A Journal of Research and Treatment, 28*, 135–147.

Cooper, J. O., Heron, T. E., & Heward, W. L. (2007). *Applied behavior analysis* (2nd ed.). Upper Saddle River, NJ: Pearson Education Inc.

Cybulska, B. (2007). Sexual assault: Key issues. *Journal of the Royal Society of Medicine, 100*, 321–324.

Douglas, T., Bonte, P., Focquaert, F., Devolder, K., & Sterckx, S. (2013). Coercion, incarceration, and chemical castration: An argument from autonomy. *Journal of Bioethical Inquiry, 10*, 393–405.

Hearst, E., Besley, S., & Farthing, G. W. (1970). Inhibition and the stimulus control of operant behavior. *Journal of the Experimental Analysis of Behavior, 14*, 373–409.

Herrnstein, R. J. (1961). Relative and absolute strength of response as a function of frequency of reinforcement. *Journal of the Experimental Analysis of Behavior, 4*, 563–573.

Kantor, J. R. (1959). *Interbehavioral psychology*. Granville, OH: Principia Press.

Kantor, J. R. (1976). The origin and evolution of interbehavioral psychology. *Revista Mexicana de Analisis de la Conducta, 2*, 120–136.

Kantor, J. R. (1977). *Psychological linguistics*. Chicago, IL: Principia Press.

Khomami, N. (October 20, 2017). *#MeToo: How a hashtag became a rallying cry against sexual harassment*. The Guardian.

Lyon, D. O. (1968). Conditioned suppression: Operant variables and aversive control. *Psychological Record, 18*, 317–338.

Maier, S. F., & Seligman, M. E. (1976). Learned helplessness: Theory and evidence. *Journal of Experimental Psychology: General, 105*, 3–46.

Ray, O. S., & Stein, L. (1959). Generalization of conditioned suppression. *Journal of the Experimental Analysis of Behavior, 2*, 357–361.

Ruben, D. H. (1992). Behavioral systems approach. In C. E. Stout, J. L. Levitt, & D. H. Ruben (Eds.), *Handbook for assessing and treating addictive disorders* (pp. 3–39). Westport, CT: Greenwood Press.

Ruben, D. H. (2001). *Treating adult children of alcoholics: A behavioral approach*. NY: Academic Press.

Ruben, D. H. (2015). *Behavioral guide to personality disorders (DSM-5)*. Springfield, IL: Charles Thomas Publishers.

Skinner, B. F. (1957). *Verbal behavior*. Englewood Cliffs, NY: Prentice-Hall.

Stemple, L., Flores, A., & Meyer, I. H. (2017). Sexual victimization perpetrated by women: Federal data reveal surprising prevalence. *Aggression and Violent Behavior, 34*, 301–311.

Tangney, J. P., Wagner, P., & Gramzow, R. (1991). Proneness to shame, proneness to guilt, and psychopathology. *Journal of Abnormal Psychology, 101*, 469–478.

Thomsen, S. (2015). Extramarital affair website Ashley Madison has been hacked and attackers are threatening to leak data online. *Business Insider.*

Turvey, B. E. (2013). *Forensic victimology: Examining violent crime Victims in Investigative and legal contexts.* NY: Academic Press.

Vollmer, T. R., & Iwata, B. A. (1991). Establishing operations and reinforcement effects. *Journal of Applied Behavior Analysis, 24*, 279–291.

Westrup, D. (2001). Applying functional analysis to stalking behavior. In R. Melony (Ed.), *The Psychology of stalking: Clinical and forensic perspectives* (pp. 275–293). NY: Academic Press.

CHAPTER

# 5

# Intracontingency variables in criminal responsibility evaluations

Principles of Applied Behavior Analysis (ABA) used in forensic psychology lately have been increasingly prolific (Steel, 2014; Turvey, 2012; Vrij, Mann, & Fisher, 2006; Youngs, 2016). Concepts of positive and negative reinforcement, positive and negative punishment, repertoire-altering effects, rule-governed behaviors, setting events, motivating operations, and functional contingencies provide a welcome scientific alternative to explanations and predictions of crime over pseudo-scientific theories linking reified personality types with criminal behaviors (cf. Codd, 2018; Lillenfeld & Landfield, 2008). In the latter, ambiguously defined typologies offer correlative, often coincidental association with certain criminal acts. However, the acts may vary considerably by context, crime, or complexities in the offender's criminal and personal history. Unlike the mythology of personality profiling that muddles the assessment, a better alternative is behavior analysis.

Its expanded integrative-systems paradigm called *Behavioral Forensic Systems Approach* (Ruben, 2012) offers causal (functional) connections between crime, subject, victim, and setting events over a continuum of time. One principle of ABA, expanded over the last twenty years since its seminal introduction by Michael (1982, 1988, 1993), has been the *Establishing Operation*, or now categorically called *Motivating Operations (MO)* (Laraway, Snycerski, Michael, & Poling, 2003; McGill, 1999). Motivating operations are environmental variables (internal or external to the organism) that alter the effectiveness of some stimulus object or event (acting as reinforcer) and concurrently alter the frequency (or duration, intensity, magnitude, etc.) of some behaviors reinforced by the same stimulus objects or events. If John swims 5 laps and afterward eats lunch daily, but today he missed breakfast and is extra hungry, John might only swim 3 laps, all at record speed, to finish swimming and eat sooner. John's decision to swim less laps, to swim them faster, and to leave the pool quicker, all were a function of Motivating Operations.

This example illustrated *unconditioned and conditioned Motivating Operations.* The unconditioned motivating operation was deprivation of food, the removal (abatement) of which occurred by swimming faster. The desire of food and plan on what to eat, all were *establishing operations,* whereas the removal of hunger (after eating) and feeling satiated related to *abolishing operations.* Both operations changed the stimulus conditions and behaviors across several

*Behavioral Forensics*
https://doi.org/10.1016/B978-0-12-819805-6.00005-1

response segments, all consisting of different contingencies, and accounted for John's change in swim patterns for the day (cf. Kantor, 1959, 1976; Ruben, 1992). Similarly, *conditioned motivating operations* were in effect as well. Each develops in response to the organism's reactional biography or history of conditioning across diverse fields of contingencies over time. For example, before he entered the natatorium, John observed the clock showing it was noon, the time he usually eats; the discriminative cue of the clock frequently paired with hunger in the past and elicited hunger (gustatory responses, gastric juices).

This pairing defines a *surrogate conditioned establishing operation.* John also observed an influx of other swimmers entering the pool, threatening crowdedness and the need to share lanes. He swam even faster to finish sooner. When observed stimuli are correlated with worsening or improving a stimulus condition, the new stimuli evoke modified responses. These cues threatening aversive or reinforcing conditions are called *reflexive conditioned motivation operations.* Or, should John decide to swim fast given his hunger, the crowded pool, and the time on the clock, he may swim even faster if he sees a food vendor. Sight of the food vendor paired with the myriad of other discriminative stimuli augments his speed to swim fast; or John may even decide *not to swim that day before entering the pool.* The function here of augmenting pre-exiting conditioned motivation operations is called *transitive conditioned motivation operations.* In all, John's daily swim routine undergoes significant changes not just because John is hungry (unconditional), but rather from concurrent conditioned cues equally influencing the valence of motivation operations.

In the case of forensic evaluations of criminal responsibility, conditioned and unconditioned motivation operations play an invaluable role in assessment of causality. Suppose John was not just a routine daily swimmer, but 1 h before he entered the natatorium, while in the locker-room, he allegedly strangled another swimmer. He is arrested for first-degree murder based on investigative police evidence placing John at the scene of the crime, and whose fingerprints encircled the victim's punctured neck. John claims he blacked out and remembers nothing about the crime, raising the legal question of criminal responsibility. Criminal responsibility is a state of mind (*legally insane or insane-like behaviors*) defined slightly differently in each state, although ubiquitously consisting of two criteria (Morse, 2011). The first criterion is intellectual disability. Such a disability manifested before the age of 18 years and is characterized by significantly subaverage intellectual functioning with related limitations in two or more adaptive skills.

Psychometric diagnosis is based on the following assumptions: (a) valid assessment of cultural and linguistic diversity, as well as differences in communication and behavioral factors; (b) the existence of limitations in adaptive skills that occur within the context of community environments typical of the individual's age peers and is indexed to the individual's particular needs for support; (c) specific adaptive skill limitations often coexist with strengths in other adaptive skills or other personal capabilities; and (d) with appropriate supports over a sustained period, the life functioning of the individual with an intellectual disability will generally improve. For example, during recent educational and intellectual testing, if John showed a Full Scale IQ (FSIQ) of 58 (on the WAIS-IV), Cognitive Impairment (CI) from extremely low scores on educational tests (WAIS-III), a history of special education (IEP or 504 plans), poor portfolio academic performance during primary and secondary schools, and a juvenile criminal record or repeated school and home complaints of incorrigibility, his totality of responses (reactionary biography) would constitute valid grounds, *as a predictor,* for intellectual disability.

The second criterion is more diagnostically ambiguous, less immediately measurable, and opens the door to explanatory fictions in traditional (non-behavioral) forensic evaluations. Mental Illness must also demonstrate a *substantial disorder of thought or mood which significantly impairs judgment, behavior, capacity to recognize reality, or ability to cope with the ordinary demands of life*. The impaired judgment means the person *lacks substantial capacity either to appreciate the nature and quality or the wrongfulness of his or her conduct or to conform his or her conduct to the requirements of the law*. In other words, John's sequence of pre-criminal, criminal, and post-criminal acts must depict a pattern where he was so (a) incoherent or delusional, psychotic, or laboring under enough cognitive distortion to preclude (b) awareness and comprehension of his criminal acts, (c) awareness of the culpability or wrongfulness of his acts, or (d) ability to conform to the law. From a behavioral systems standpoint, isolation of the organism's state of awareness or thought disorganization in history is very difficult without corroborative methods of measurement or witness collaboration.

For example, if the locker-room janitor witnessed John's disposition during commission of the crime, that eyewitness testimony may offer reliable (corroborative) response samples of John's criminal behaviors. However, not only is accessibility limited or non-existent to the covert mental state of John during the crime, but that unknown mental state has to address John's degrees of awareness of (a) the crime itself, (b) wrongfulness of the crime, and (c) whether he was lucid enough to comply with lawful behaviors. For this reason, an assumption in traditional forensic analysis concludes that if John had psychotic thoughts (hallucinations, delusions, etc.), he *could not render awareness of the crime, wrongfulness of his actions, or be mindful of legally appropriate action at the time*. Consequently he might be deemed legally insane during the crime or *Not Guilty by Reason of Insanity (NGRI*, cf. Neville, 2010, pp. 1–41; Weiner, 1980).

This implicit tautology that a presumed state of psychosis meets the definition of legal insanity is problematic for behaviorally-analytic evaluators. For behavioral forensic evaluators, the mission is *not to assess and codify non-scientific or hypothetical constructs;* this leads to invention of unverifiable ("mystic") human action and thoughts attributable to flawed, non-existent, or abstract connections between cause and effect (i.e., reification; Ruben, 1986, 1988; Skinner, 1957, 1974). Behavioral forensic evaluators, instead, are translators of vagaries into functional products for observation and measurement; they quantify some previously unquantifiable variables that were invisibly blending into the vague montage of "personality" and "criminal behavior." One way to operationalize vague variables is to focus on physiological behavior changes. Suppose John, the swimmer, claimed the "last thing he recalled" before entering the natatorium, was arguing with another swimmer. Escalated anger allegedly aroused his adrenaline (epinephrine, a hormone secreted by the adrenal gland). Increases in epinephrine frequently associate with high rates of blood circulation, respiration, carbohydrate metabolism, energy, and prepares muscles for exertion. Stimulatory effects of epinephrine also sharpen (cognitive) situational awareness and memory retention of surrounding events (Cadhill & Alkire, 2003; Flint, Bunsey, & Riccio, 2007; Sternberg, 1985). Often referred to colloquially as the "fight or flight" stress reflex, adrenaline produces self-observed increases in perceived strength, anticipatory behaviors, and diminished sense of pain.

Specifically, emotional arousal leads to activation of the locus coeruleus with the subsequent release of norepineprine in the brain, resulting in the enhancement of memory. John's heightened physiological reaction of adrenaline, in other words, probably enhanced attention to the details of his verbal and nonverbal behavior in response to the alleged victim. This psychophysiological fact seemingly contradicts John's claim of blacking out or malingered amnesia of the crime; instead, he possibly "faked" forgetting to avoid culpability (Bradford & Smith, 1979; Cima, Merkelbach, Nijman, Knauer, & Hollnack, 2002; Jeiicic & Merckelbach, 2007). While John's self-report of an adrenaline rush is still an unreliable measure, the neurochemical effects of epinephrine on modulating enhanced memory pose a tenable operational explanation for criminal responsibility during the murder.

This paper explores a case similar to John, of a young male adult suspect reporting (psychogenic) amnesia during violent altercations with a female victim that he subsequently murdered. He reported blacking out while experiencing an adrenaline rush of fear, panic, and anger when the alleged victim provoked him with aggressive verbal insults. His defense of dissociative amnesia, arising from a traumatic or extremely emotional event, was discrepant with the hypervigilance produced from release of epinephrine (adrenaline) and its effects of enhancing his sensory and cognitive awareness of events preceding, during, and after the felony. The case study offers an example of looking inside obvious contingencies (i.e., *intracontingencies)* to discover biophysical functional relationships existing concurrently, sequentially, and contributing to motivational operations underlying the suspect's actions. Analysis of the intracontingencies also illustrates how a behavioral forensic (systems) analysis can dispel fictional or reified explanations used in traditional forensic evaluations and add legitimate empirical support for the opinion of criminal responsibility.

# Case of John Doe Jr

## Education

John Doe Jr represents a fictional suspect charged with Homicide—Open Murder, held at a local country jail for 10 months. He previously fled a neighboring state after learning of an arrest warrant for his sexual assault of a minor female, while he was on parole. Upon entering the arrested state, he stayed at hotels in different cities. Before parole, he spent 8 months in prison in a neighboring state for felony Breaking and Entering. John Doe Jr. Never worked an hourly-wage job. Educationally, John Doe Jr. completed Kindergarten to eighth grade in public school. For ninth and 10th grade, he received his education at a Youth Detention Center, where he largely stayed from ages 14 to 18, with short intervals of time during release to family members until he recommitted juvenile crimes. He never graduated high school. By first grade, he reportedly was diagnosed with Attention Deficit Hyperactivity Disorder (ADHD, combined presentation), and prescribed the psychostimulants Ritalin, later titrated to Adderall. He also apparently qualified for an IEP for Otherwise Health Impaired (OHI) with designation of ADHD, but his mother settled for a 504 plan.

Under this plan, he attended a regular or resource classroom and provided accommodations for test-taking and management of his eruptive angry episodes. He also was assigned one-on-one with a paraprofessional for help with behavior self-control and to complete his homework assignments. His earned grades bottomed at low D's and E's, blamed on (a) lack of parental support, (b) school apathy, (c) poor reading comprehension, (d) poor comprehension of classroom instruction, and (e) non-completion and non-submission of homework assignments. John Doe Jr. also never participated in extracurricular school or community activities.

John Doe Jr. reported being bullied severely in school. He denied interception of bullies perceived as bothering victims. He received suspensions, detentions, but no expulsions. He repeatedly showed authority defiance to adults. He denied gang membership or association with students engaged in violent acts. He denied carrying or use of a firearm or knife. He denied bringing contraband (weapon or drugs) to school. He denied fascination with fire-starting or animal cruelty. Juvenile crimes included assaults and property destruction. He described targets of his angry outbursts, at first, were objects. By early teens, he attacked people perceived as threatening him, physically or verbally, in the same manner as he previously attacked physical objects. When he physically attacked objects or people, *he felt an adrenaline surge arousing intense anger as he explosively "pounced and pulverized" his feared enemy.* Release of adrenaline not only increased his heart rate and strength of physical force, but he also reportedly felt momentarily invincible. He also claimed to "hear voices" before he attacked his victims and then "blackout" during these explosive rages. To his surprise, he did not suffer retrograde amnesia since he always later recalled some if not all of the vivid details precipitating and transacting during the violent altercations. In youth detentions and later prison, he was prescribed the antipsychotics Seroquel and Tegretol, both of which he complained rendered him sluggish and incoherent.

## Substance abuse

John Doe Jr. began abusing substances by age 14. He drank vodka or whisky sparingly on weekends, only around friends, never alone. Ethanol, a depressant, self-medicated his anxiety or anger, and reduced his paranoia. Alcohol use subsided during his recurrent placements in Youth Centers, except on weekends after his release. In prison, he attempted to drink the in-house made ethanol until he got sick. He began using cannabis at ages 12. Use was intermittent and he *insisted he never used it during his incarceration in youth or adult psychiatric or correctional facilities.* Likewise, he briefly tried cocaine and ecstasy. For the most part, he lacked the opportunity for regular drug use during the short windows of non-incarcerated time. He was either on probation in adolescence or in adulthood, requiring him to wear a tether or submit once or twice weekly to random urinalyses. He denied use or abuse of any other licit or illicit (controlled) substances. Medically, John Doe Jr. denied suffering any major vehicular or other accidents causing head trauma. His frequently self-inflicted pain by striking his head against walls or lockers during elementary school, as a visceral (adrenaline) rush when angry. He never suffered any known neuropathology from repeated insults to his skull. He denied suffering CVAs, TIAs, sleep apnea, high fevers, or neurotoxin exposure. He denied any known medical conditions.

*Interpersonally*, John Doe Jr. claimed one or two memories of childhood sexual victimization. He vaguely recalled an adult male performing oral sex on him when John Doe Dr. was 10 or 11 years old. John Doe Jr. denied imitating similar behaviors on same-age or younger male peers. He was first voluntarily sexual at age 19. He conservatively estimated 5 heterosexual partners, none of whom represented meaningful relationships. He only had casual sexual contacts, or relied on cell-phone access to pornography for masturbation. He denied going to adult entertainment clubs or receiving sex from prostitutes until migrating to the state in he was arrested.

*Developmentally,* John Doe Jr. is oldest of three children raised by dually employed and married parents, divorced when John Doe Jr. turned 10 years old. His father absconded the family. His mother apparently suffered depression. She was a nondrinker but struggled to manage John Doe Jr.'s violent tantrums from early childhood, often resorting to escalation of verbal arguments and reciprocal insults. She frequently consulted the police or sought mental health resources, including medication, to combat his oppositional actions. By age 14, exhausted by the futility of trying to control her son's behaviors, she refused to allow her son John Doe Jr. into the house after his discharges from the adolescent psychiatric or youth detention centers.

## The alleged crime of murder

Regarding the sequence of pre-criminal, criminal, and post-criminal events, John Doe Jr. first stole a vehicle in a neighboring state. He then traveled nearly three nights through another state staying in different cities. In one city, he apparently robbed a gas station using a wrench to threaten harm, and left with approximately $300. His length of time in each city was very short. He arrived in the city of the alleged crime early and registered at a motel. According to the motel lock audit times, he arrived at 6:49 p.m. on one day in a specific room. He swiped his card to leave and re-enter the room about eight times, once to visit a strip-club, and subsequently to refill his tank at a gas station. At the strip-club, he vehemently denied receiving a lap dance, due to insufficient money to spend. When John Doe Jr. returned to the motel, he encountered an adult woman locked out of a motel room. She briefly talked with John Doe Jr., who he presumed was a prostitute, although the woman never propositioned him. She claimed she would come back to him at night.

The woman (later, the victim) apparently returned to John Doe's motel room on or about 3:36 a.m., according to surveillance video cameras. The surveillance video series also suggested the entire transaction (including alleged crime) took place between 3:36 a.m. and 4:30 a.m. (or, in 1 h). In that time, John Doe Jr. chronicled the following events of behavior:

1. Woman (victim) came in and they talked briefly about her children.
2. John Doe Jr. shared with her he was on the run (fugitive).
3. Victim began to intravenously self-inject heroin.
4. Victim, likely in post-euphoric effects of warm flushing of skin and dry mouth, kept drinking Mountain Dew soda.
5. Victim offered to perform oral sex on John Doe Jr. while she constantly interrupted his pleasure by taking sips of Mountain Dew.
6. John Doe Jr. lost his erection repeatedly, then aborted the oral sex, and watched pornography on his cell phone to re-stimulate erection.
7. John Doe Jr. tried intromission but again lost his erection. Aggravated by his erectile difficulties, he aborted sex with the victim.
8. Victim, angered by his sex refusal, immediately escalated in anger, sarcasm and called him racial slurs, blaming him for ruining her night. At this point, John Doe Jr. adamantly insisted she never asked for money for sex.
9. Victim began to push (first physical contact) John Doe Jr, calling him a child.

10. John Doe Jr. felt angry, defensive, and wanted to escape the room, but victim blocked the door.
11. John Doe Jr. resisted her block and the two entangled in fighting.
12. John Doe Jr. retrieved a steak knife acquired earlier in his travels, felt an adrenaline surge, and used the knife to stab the victim multiple times around her body.
13. John Doe Jr. covered victim's body and took a shower.
14. John Doe Jr. left the motel room about 4:30 a.m. and head to another city, with the clear goal of purchasing a bus ticket to a neighboring city.

## Results of state forensic psychological evaluation

John Doe Jr. underwent a psychological evaluation for Criminal Responsibility at the State Forensic Center shortly after his arrest and incarceration. The forensic examiner (psychologist) opined the defendant was neither mentally ill nor intellectually disabled during the alleged offense. Conclusions held the defendant did not lack the capacity to appreciate the nature, quality or wrongfulness of his actions or the capacity to conform his conduct to the requirements of the law. Reasons cited for these conclusions included the (a) supposed premeditative purchase of supplies used during the crime, (b) calmness and calculatedness with which John Doe Jr. covered the bloodied body, took a shower, and (c) methodical effort to reach a bus station for transport to another city.

The report also concluded the defendant was not intellectually disabled at the time of the offense, and referred as proof to John Doe Jr.'s (a) presentation during the interview, (b) vocabulary use, (c) verbal comprehension, and (d) past educational level. Omitted from the report were any cognitive or learning assessments verifying the aforementioned conclusions. Similarly, the only psychological testing identified in the report, the Personality Assessment Inventory (PAI), was disqualified due to an invalid profile attributed to the defendant's random and careless answers or from reading difficulties. Absent of any objectively verifiable testing, the conclusions about criminal responsibility entirely predicated on reviews of prior documents and clinical history retrieved from the John Doe Jr.'s case file. The State forensic examiner *surmised from self-reports of John Doe Jr.'s personality or dispositional factors surrounding the crime that he exerted control over his mental faculties.*

## Results of IME, behavioral forensic evaluation

### Cognitive/learning test results

Requested was an Independent Medical (Psychological) Examination to use objective testing, similar document reviews (as available to State forensic examiner), and to question the tenability of the State's opinion on criminal responsibility. The three-part examination entailed (1) clinical intake, (2) administration of intelligence (WAIS-IV) and educational testing (WIAT-III), and (3) self-administration (with examiner present) of personality testing (MMPI-2-RF). Results of testing *demonstrated* intellectual disability from cognitive and learning deficits. Cognitive weakness appeared in Verbal Comprehension and Perceptual Reasoning; learning deficits appeared in Written Language and Oral Language. These deficits were likely consistent with premorbid or baseline measures of his intellectual/educational skills (i.e., before the crime, during his school years). Despite academic and job hardships likely incurred from the deficits, level of intellectual disability did not meet criteria *to prohibit John Doe Jr.'s ability to discern rightness from wrongness.*

## Behavioral assessment results

Two subcomponents comprised the behavioral assessment. First, protocol personality testing identified pervasive patterns in adulthood likely influential (but not necessarily causal) in risk of crime recidivism. Second, a self-reported chronicle of the event-sequence, in corroboration with supportive documents (e.g. motel lock audit report; surveillance time-lapse videotape, police interrogation testimony, reporting during the prior forensic evaluations, etc.), enabled a provisional functional analysis of pre-crime, crime, and post-crime behaviors.

On personality testing, three pervasive behavior patterns identified included (a) obsessive fears of being persecuted by people, (b) always defensive and aggressively reactionary when provoked, and (c) conflict-avoidance or anticipatory aggression. *Anticipatory aggression* is a response pattern consisting of (a) pre-emptive anger in advance of some aversive condition to (b) delay (avoid), (c) attenuate (diminish aversive properties), or (d) terminate (escape from) the aversiveness (Ruben, 2001, 2015). Second, a functional analysis computed from reconstructing the sequence of events precipitating the murder (see above chronicle of events) isolated multiple layers of superimposed contingencies, hypothetically and schematically organized as Contingency$^1$, Contingency$^2$, and Contingency$^3$. Since all three contingencies are mutually interrelative, meaning influence each other, they produce independent as well as interdependent consequences. Conceptually, these integrative (compound) contingencies received extensive discussion and research elsewhere under the rubric of (1) concurrent schedules, (2) mixed schedules, (3) tandem schedules, (4) chained schedules, (5) conjunctive schedules, (6) multiple schedules, and (7) alternative schedules (Lyon, 1982; Saini, Miller, & Fisher, 2016).

For forensic purposes of this case, current and multiple schedules apply to Contingency$^1$, Contingency$^2$, and Contingency$^3$. Below is a functional description of three possible contingencies relative to pre-criminal events:

Contingency$^1$: The victim verbally insults John Doe Jr. for his ineffective sexual performance and calls him a child ($S^D$), interrupting his sexual arousal (unconditioned MO), which *elicits* visceral responses (autonomic effects of muscular contractions, glandular secretions, etc.) of fear and initial escape behavior (negative reinforcement).

Contingency$^2$: Autonomic arousal *also* produces secretion of adrenaline ($S^D$), under a limited hold of 2–5 min before adrenaline fades (unconditioned MO), and limited hold of 1–4 s to race out the hotel room door (conditioned MO); it *evokes* pre-emptive (anticipatory) aggressive behaviors to avoid, diminish, or escape from the onslaught of insults (negative reinforcement).

Contingency$^3$: Victim blocks the door, continues to insult and hit the victim ($S^D$), which *elicits* adrenaline (unconditioned MO), increasing muscular strength; the muscular strength *evokes* a calculated decision to grab the knife and stab the victim (to terminate aversive verbal and physical aversiveness, negative reinforcement).

The above transaction of contingencies occurred sequentially and simultaneously, both independently and interdependently, producing similar consequences, over the span of 10–15 min. Current research paradigms view this compound schedule moving in a linear path along a time continuum (Delprato & Smith, 2009; Inesta, 2018; Kantor, 1976; Skinner, 1969, 1972). On this continuum lay interconnected segments hypothetically consisting of one contingency per segment, each with its own unique or similar setting events. The total segments comprise a trajectory of responses whose probability of occurrence depends on the strength or weakness of each contingency (segment) to produce consequences. However, the concept of behavior linearity also presumes a similar proportionality (contingency effects) among successive segments; that is, where the intensity in one segment predicts equal or similar intensity in subsequent segments. The valence of one contingency weighed against another contingency, could constitute a relationship of *intercontingencies*. But, contingencies are not always monotonic; they are non-monotonic. They are distinct, dynamic, and diverse. Contingencies also are malleable and may be supported by concurrent or sequential contingencies subordinately occurring within the same segment, even intersecting one another. The operation of one contingency intersecting and subordinate to another contingency can be described as *intracontingency*. The progression of Contingency$^1$ to Contingency$^3$, for example, occurs *within or inside the same behavior segment, and it is the cumulative effect (reinforcing or punishing) of all three contingencies (in the same segment) that determines the probability of how the organism (suspect, victim) will respond in subsequent behavior segments.*

A second important finding from computing a provisional functional analysis was the implausibility of dissociative amnesia as the reason for John Doe Jr.'s failure to recall his precise actions during the murder. The intracontingency discussed above hypothesized that exertion of musculo-skeletal and glandular responses activated hormonal release of adrenaline. This adrenaline release boosted energy, enhanced strength, and heightened senses and acuity of awareness. The release of adrenaline (epinephrine) also aroused emotion and prepared muscles for exertion (aggression). John Doe Jr. demonstrated this repeated visceral pattern since early childhood when retaliating against bullies. Onset of adrenaline evoked anticipatory aggression to relieve his visceral effects and to avoid or escape aversive stimulation. The augmented strength also blocked or protected him temporarily from any pain associated with his physical force during anticipatory aggressive outbursts.

However, in a state of adrenaline rush and anticipatory aggression (i.e., multiple stabbing of the victim), he is unlikely to experience blackouts or dissociative states resulting in amnesia. On the contrary, overproduction of adrenaline (fight or flight sensation) can modulate consolidation of events, and ensure short-term memory strength. That is, he is likely to remember more, not less, of what he did during the intense adrenaline rush. His short-term and long-term recall of the events should be more astute, not vague, even after several months following the crime. For this reason, John Doe Jr.'s actions at the time of the crime did not demonstrate *a substantial disorder of thought or mood which significantly impairs judgment, behavior, capacity to recognize reality or ability to cope with the ordinary demands of life.* He did not meet the diagnostic markers for diminished criminal responsibility, or for *legal insanity.*

## Implications for forensic research

Behavioral forensic assessment focused exclusively on personality correlates loses the underlying heuristic value of measurement and prediction when determining the fate of suspect criminal responsibility. The value of investigating contingent relations between psychological events, instead, not only bypasses the guesswork or assumptions likely to miscast the suspect, but it also captures a more realistic snapshot of behavioral interactions likely transacted during the crime. Functional analysis also gives leverage to behavioral forensic examiners' credibility during expert testimony; they describe behavior scenarios and prognosticate the probability of criminal risk behavior predicated on scientific principles—the same principles used to hypothetically validate the likelihood of the suspect's criminal behaviors. While moving in the right scientific direction, the downside of hypothetical functional analyses calculated from retrospective self-reports and corroborative police or school documents is the impurity of indirect observation. Without direct and reliable observation of suspect behavior, unlike in cases of recorded police action on their body cameras, precision of causal connections intracontingently and intracontingently may be weak, subject to alternative interpretations, and may be overturned during cross-examination.

## References

Bradford, J., & Smith, S. (1979). Amnesia and homicide: The Padola case and a study of thirty cases. *American Academy of Psychiatry and Law, 7*(3), 219–231.

Cadhill, L., & Alkire, M. T. (2003). Epinephrine enhancement of human memory consolidation: Interaction at arousal with encoding. *Neurobiology of Learning and Memory, 79*, 194–198.

Cima, M., Merkelbach, H., Nijman, H., Knauer, E., & Hollnack, S. (2002). I can't remember your honor: Offenders who claim amnesia. *German Journal of Psychiatry, 5*, 24–34.

Codd, R. (2018). Pseudoscience in mental health treatments. *The Behavior Therapist, 41*, 1–3.

Delprato, D. J., & Smith, N. W. (2009). Sketch of J.R. Kantor's psychological interbehavioral field theory. *Psychological Record, 59*, 671–678.

Flint, R. W., Bunsey, M. D., & Riccio, D. C. (2007). Epinephrine-induced enhancement of memor retrieval for inhibitory avoidance conditioning in preweanling Sprague-Dawley rats. *Developmental Psychobiology, 49*, 303–311.

Inesta, E. R. (2018). J.R. Kantor. Theory as the basic research instrument. *The Psychological Record, 68*, 267–272.

Jeiicic, M., & Merckelbach, H. (2007). Evaluating the authenticity of crime-related amnesia. In Christianson (Ed.), *Offenders' memories of violent crimes* (pp. 215–234). NY: Wiley.

Kantor, J. R. (1959). *Interbehavioral psychology*. Granville, OH: Principia Press.

Kantor, J. R. (1976). The origin and evolution of interbehavioral psychology. *Revista Mexicana de Analisis de la Conducta, 2*, 120–136.

Laraway, S., Snycerski, S., Michael, J., & Poling, A. (2003). Motivating operations and terms to describe them: Some further refinements. *Journal of Applied Behavior Analysis, 36*, 407–414.

Lillenfeld, S. O., & Landfield, K. (2008). Science and pseudoscience in law enforcement. *Criminal Justice and Behavior, 35*, 1215–1230.

Lyon, D. O. (1982). Concurrent behavior: Are the interpretations mutually exclusive? *The Behavior Analyst, 5*, 175–187.

McGill, P. (1999). Establishing operations: Implications for the assessment, treatment, and prevention of problem behavior. *Journal of Applied Behavior Analysis, 32*, 393–418.

Michael, J. (1982). Distinguishing between discriminative and motivational functions of stimuli. *Journal of the Experimental Analysis of Behavior, 37*, 149–155.

Michael, J. (1988). Establishing operations and the mand. *The Analysis of Verbal Behavior, 6*, 3–9.

Michael, J. (1993). Establishing operations. *The Behavior Analyst, 16*, 191–206.

Morse, S. (2011). Mental Disorder and criminal law. *Journal of Criminal Law and Criminology, 101*, 1013–10885.

Neville, K. (2010). *The insanity defense: A comparative analysis*. Honors College: Digital Commons@EMU.
Ruben, D. H. (1986). The "interbehavioral" approach to treatment. *Journal of Contemporary Psychotherapy, 16*, 62–71.
Ruben, D. H. (1988). Private events revisited: Does unobservable mean private? *Journal of Contemporary Psychotherapy, 18*, 16–27.
Ruben, D. H. (1992). Behavioral systems approach. In C. E. Stout, J. L. Levitt, & D. H. Ruben (Eds.), *Handbook for assessing and treating addictive disorders* (pp. 3–39). Westport, CT: Greenwood Press.
Ruben, D. H. (2001). *Treating adult children of alcoholics: A behavioral approach*. NY: Academic Press.
Ruben, D. H. (2015). *Behavioral guide to personality disorders (DSM-5)*. Springfield, IL: Charles Thomas Publishers.
Ruben, D. H. (2012). *Behavioral forensic assessment: Using applied behavior analysis in forensic psychology*. Presentation at the executive summit, American College of Forensic Examiners International (ACFEI), Las Vegas, NV, October 18.
Saini, V., Miller, S. A., & Fisher, W. W. (2016). Multiple schedules in practical application: Research trends and implications for future investigation. *Journal of Applied Behavior Analysis, 49*, 421–444.
Skinner, B. F. (1957). *Verbal behavior*. Englewood Cliffs, NY: Prentice-Hall.
Skinner, B. F. (1969). *Contingencies of reinforcement*. NJ: Prentice Hall.
Skinner, B. F. (1972). *Cumulative record: Selection of papers*. NY: Appleton Century Crofts.
Skinner, B. F. (1974). *About behaviorism*. NY: Vintage Books.
Steel, C. (2014). Idiographic digital profiling: Behavioral analysis based on digital forensics. *Journal of Digital Forensics, Security, and Law, 9*, 2–18.
Sternberg, D. I. (1985). Age-related deficits in rats and mice: Enhancements with peripheral injections of epinephrine. *Behavioral and Neural Biology, 44*, 213–220.
Turvey, B. E. (2012). *Criminal profiling: An introduction to behavioral evidence analysis*. NY: Academic Press.
Vrij, A., Mann, S., & Fisher, R. (2006). An empirical test of the behavior analysis interview. *Law and Human Behavior, 30*, 329–345.
Weiner, B. A. (1980). Not guilty by reason of insanity; A sane approach. *Chicago Kent Law Review, 56*, 1057–1085.
Youngs, D. (Ed.). (2016). *The behavioural analysis of crime*. NY: Routledge.

CHAPTER

# 6

# Risk of alcohol recidivism in evaluating reinstatement of a Driver's license

Behavior assessment has been widely prolific and recognized as the standard for evaluation of most alcohol and substance abuse disorders (Donovan & Marlatt, 2007; Nathan & Briddell, 1977; Ryan, Popour, Arneson, & Ruben, 1983; Sobell & Sobell, 2003; Vuchinich, Tucker, & Harllee, 1988). Pre-treatment or baseline assessments using self-reports (Alanko, 1984; O'Farrell & Maisto, 1987; Ruben, 1984, 1999b, 2015), analogues (George, Phillips, & Skinner, 1988; Ruben, 1983b; Sutker, Malatesta, Allain, & Randall, 1981) and naturalistic simulations (Ruben, 1987,1989, 2002, 2004) induce realistic behaviors for a more reliable snapshot of actual behavior transaction. These snapshots or response samples provide invaluable data on the chemical use frequency, intensity, duration, latency, inter-time intervals, response patterns and sequences, and progression of psychological events through which abuse behaviors evolve.

Similar protocols for behavior assessment of chemical dependency, particularly for alcoholism, exist for forensic evaluations. Here, the court or agents of the court—prosecutor or defendant attorney—request a pre-sentencing or post-sentencing risk assessment of a recidivistic alcohol user to determine two outcomes. First is whether the individual presents a current proclivity or tendency for relapse following release from jail, probation, or parole. A second question is whether the individual may relapse during probation or parole, despite the controlled environment of twice weekly random drug and alcohol lab screenings, and frequent meetings with probation/parole officers. Evaluations to predict positive or negative risk outcomes depends on both using a behavioral assessment framework for collection of data, and performing a behavior functional analysis to show causal connections between the individual's reactional biography (history of behavior repertoire), current behaviors, and potential behaviors (Ruben, 1983a, 2000).

This case study follows a recidivistic DUIL offender reporting sobriety for three years. He completed a local Sobriety Court after his second DUIL offense despite one probation violation of non-attendance at a therapy session. He also used the breath alcohol ignition interlock device for vehicular travel. Requested was an Independent Medical (Psychological) Examination

*Behavioral Forensics*
https://doi.org/10.1016/B978-0-12-819805-6.00006-3

(IME) to determine his safety and readiness for reinstatement of a full (unrestricted) driver's license given his three years of sobriety and collateral low-risk behaviors engaged in during his job or community activities. In performing *a Behavioral Systems Approach (BSA) in Behavioral Forensic Analysis (BFA)*, care is taken not only to incorporate the principles and laws of behavior directly impacting the micro-contingencies on drinking behavior, but also the molar or integrated-field contingencies co-influencing similar drinking behaviors (Delprato & Smith, 2009; Midgley & Morris, 2006; Ruben, 1990a, 1992a, 1992b, 1999a).

## Case study of Joe

### Background

Joe represents a fictional name of a 30 year old single male Caucasian currently residing 6 months with his 28-year old girlfriend in a Midwestern town. He was a 6-month, full-time employee as Certified Nurse Assistant (C N A) at a local nursing home. There, his duties involve direct patient care and team collaboration with nursing/physician staff. He recently received advanced training and a promotion to Qualified Medication Aide (QMA), legally entitling him to administer medications to the residents. At these jobs, he denied receiving any verbal or written reprimands regarding (a) job performance accuracy or consistency, (b) agency rule compliance, (c) attendance and punctuality, (d) alcohol or drug use on the job, (e) consumer relations, and (f) relations with supervisors and coworkers. He denied being fired from jobs other than layoffs, or his leaving for another job that paid higher wages, or for return to school.

Educationally, Joe attended three different school districts. He attended Kindergarten to the first half of third grade in one state. He completed third grade to fifth grade a second state. He transferred to sixth grade through 12th grade in a third state. He denied undergoing any portfolio assessment or formal school testing to qualify for an IEP (special education). In regular classes, earned grades reportedly clustered around low C's and D's, blamed on (a) distractibility, (b) high absenteeism, bordering on truancy court, and (c) failure to complete or submit his homework. Despite his low grades, he thoroughly enjoyed social science and science classes. He also played league football for two years in high school. In one school term, he helped out with janitorial duties at the high school. Otherwise, he denied participating in any community or volunteer activities. He enrolled in varying business classes for 5 years at a local community college, with similar academic underperformance reported. He did not complete his Associates Degree in Business. He denied being bullied in school. He denied provocation of in-school fights. He denied interception of bullies perceived as bothering victims. He denied gang membership or association with violent friends. He denied bringing contraband (weapons, drugs) to school. He denied packing or carrying any weapons. He denied incurring any suspensions, detentions, or expulsions. He denied fascination with animal cruelty or fire-starting. He admitted to a juvenile arrest for shoplifting that apparently involved a pre-court settlement of restitution. His adult crimes include two DUIL offenses (2016, 2017), the second of which remanded him to Sobriety Court that he completed with one probation violation registered. Outside of mandatory group meetings through Sobriety Court or AA meetings, he denied voluntarily receiving outpatient or residential treatment for his polydrug abuse. At age 14 (in the eighth grade), he suffered "depression," and consulted a psychiatrist, who prescribed the antidepressant Prozac. He continued taking this antidepressant until age 29, when he titrated to the antidepressant Cymbalta (30 mg, once daily), prescribed by his family physician. Joe denied over-or-underusing Cymbalta. He denied admission to any other outpatient or residential mental health treatment centers.

## Alcohol and drug abuse

Joe first experimented recreationally with alcohol at age 18. He drank sporadically on weekends with friends. Alcohol use largely ceased for two years until age 20. From ages 20 to 25, drinking restarted and progressed from one or two glasses of mixed drinks per weekend to three to six vodka-mixed glasses over a 2-h period on Fridays, Saturdays, and occasionally during the week nights; he later shifted from mixed drinks to consumption of 5-beers per night. He denied suffering any major headaches, hangovers, blackouts, or toxicity effects; he attributed this rapid recovery the next day to a natural physiological inoculation to ethanol. He did not see his asymptomatic recovery as increasing evidence of physical tolerance. Ethanol effects also reportedly served to self-medicate anxiety. He experienced a biphasic effect. First, he self-reported high energy and euphoria lasting 1–2 h, followed by, second, a period of sluggish exhaustion. He denied acting violent or socially tenacious while intoxicated. His last drink was reportedly after his last DUIL arrest. Court-ordered steps for relapse-prevention included (a) regular attendance at 1 to 2 AA meetings per week, (b) use of the breath alcohol ignition interlock device for vehicular travel, and (c) outpatient cognitive-behavior therapy. Joe first experimented with cannabis at age 21. He smoked it daily (1–2 g per week), for the self-curative effects to reduce symptoms of depression and anxiety; combined use of marijuana and alcohol dulled the actual self-detected effects of the ethanol (due to its sedative properties), resulting in overdrinking to reach a desired threshold. He discontinued cannabis use when he entered Sobriety Court and reportedly has been abstinent since his last DUIL arrest.

## Joe denied undergoing any surgeries

He possibly sustained a concussion at age 16, playing football, but he denied any post-concussive symptoms and fully recovered to finish playing the football game. He denied any other vehicular or other accidents causing head trauma. He denied having CVAs, TIAs, sleep apnea, seizures, high fevers, or neurotoxin exposure. His only known medical condition includes Type-1 diabetes (insulin dependence); non-routinely used blood glucose meter tests scored between 90 and 200 mg/dL, or slightly higher than normal blood-sugar levels acceptable for before or after meals.

*Interpersonally*, Joe denied any history of sexual victimization. He was first voluntarily sexual at age 18. He conservatively estimated having four heterosexual partners, about two of whom represented meaningful relationships. His longest dating relationship lasted 3 years. Joe described his girlfriend as the principal lifeline of support during his alcohol recovery and process to restore his full driving privileges. He denied any intrapartner domestic violence or relationship tensions compromising his sobriety efforts.

Developmentally, Joe was second oldest of four children raised by dually employed, married parents, who divorced when Joe turned 11 years old. His father, an attorney, was gregarious, assertive, and a frequent cannabis smoker. His mother, currently a paraprofessional in the local school system, was a nondrinker, nonsmoker and more reserved, timid, compassionate, and personable. Contact with his father, now living in another state, grew more distant, after a fallout during the time Joe lived with his father. In childhood, Mr. Joe attended a Catholic church, and later renounced his Catholic faith or any connection to a church. Joe's sister also struggled with alcoholism and incurred at least one DUIL. In retrospect, Joe blamed his father for unabated cannabis-use. He regretted his father's disenfranchisement from the nuclear family, partly due to his geographic distance to find a job. By contrast, Joe praised his mother for her fortitude in keeping the nuclear family intact. He denied either parents mistreated him verbally or nonverbally.

## Behavioral measurement

The clinical assessment utilized self-report, naturalistic, and corroborative behavioral interviewing with other parties to develop a working functional analysis of the drinking response patterns (cf. Delprato & McGlynn, 1988; Ruben, 1990b). Self-reported data included the clinical interview, MMPI-2-RF, SASSI-4, and ACOA-Behavior Profile. Naturalistic measures involved sampled response products of (a) videotaped records of his inebriated social behaviors at parties, (b) store receipts from purchase of beer, (c) verified attendance records from AA or NA meetings, and (d) text messages written or pictures taken before, during, or immediately after inebriated episodes. In addition, corroborative interviews occurred with Joe's girlfriend. Joe's pre-arrest (premorbid) drinking patterns divided into three successive segments of intercontingencies involving field (setting) events, response sequences/patterns, motivation operations, reinforcement and punishment consequences, and maturational or physiological (sensory) changes. Below is a schematic representation of these linked segments:

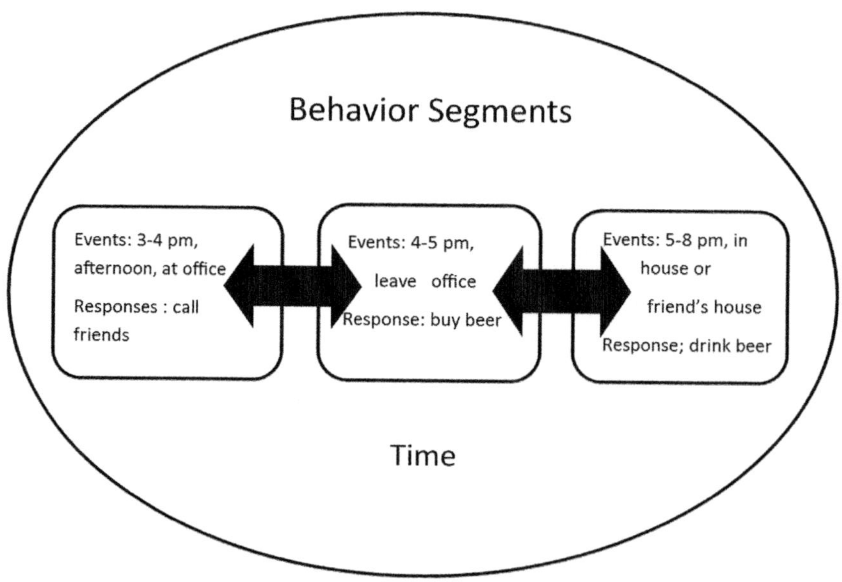

A more thorough forensic behavior analysis of the psychological field events entails subdividing these events into operational component to appreciate the progression of contingencies transacted. First, in Segment 1 between 3 and 5 pm in the afternoon at his office (nursing home), Joe (a) takes multiple breaks, (b) calls his friends to pre-arrange locality of evening drinking and friends who can attend, and (c) receives calls (or texts) from friends confirming the plans. The conditioned motivational operation (MO) established is anticipatory excitement about the party, for which Joe engages in high rates of pre-planning and pre-drinking behaviors. Should that MO be squelched or otherwise interrupted, its dismantling would immediately reduce the probability of transition to sequential segments and prevent inevitable drinking. However, also inside this segment lies concurrent contingencies developed by the same MO that directly affect Joe's job and make him more friendly and productive at work. During segment 1, after he finishes texting plans for drinking hat night, that is, designates a timer periods (schedule of reinforcement) expected to party, his work-response rate increases significantly. He is more attentive to patients, completes nursing notes, avails himself to help coworkers, and outwardly seems gregarious.

This sudden response intensity (burst-pause-burst pattern) by a modified fixed ratio (i.e., number of tasks to do before Joe leaves work) and fixed-interval schedule (he leaves at 5 p.m.) is further strengthened by the MO of his friends showing interest to see him that night (anticipatory arousal of social reinforcement). Moreover, Joe's freedom to contact his friends via cellphone undisturbed would not be possible unless he went into a private room inside the nursing home to make he calls (media of contact). If the media of contact changed, for example, his boss refused Joe privacy to make calls or had him make calls inside the building blocking cellphone service, the absent media of contact might prevent execution of the reinforcement contingency. With multiple or concurrent reinforcement contingencies ("intercontingencies") in maintaining the response strength of Joe's calling his friends, Joe is very likely (probable) to proceed to the next segment.

In Segment 2, events occur after Joe's leaves the office and time ratios between response patterns are increasingly more functionally important to prediction of alcohol recidivism. Time elapsed between two successive responses is called *Inter-response time* or *IRT* (Reynolds & Alastair, 1970; Tanno & Silberberg, 2014). While measurement of IRTs is essential to determine certain behavioral applications such as Differential Reinforcement of Other Behavior (DRO), the forensic purpose of IRTs is slightly different. The shorter the span between two responses, especially on a Variable Ratio Schedule of Reinforcement (i.e., average number of responses produces reinforcer), the more probable the response sequence (chain) will proceed and be maintained. The longer the span between two responses, the higher a risk of response extinction if the next sequential response operated as a reinforcer and thereby produced an abolishing operation. Meaning, one or more of the responses will decrease or terminate. In Joe's case, Joe drives to the grocery store immediately (within 5 min from work). There, he buys a six-case of beer and pays for it all within 10 min. The IRT is very small, and Joe engages in fairly similar (variable) responses to generate each contingency reinforcement outcome.

Should anything obstruct his path along the response continuum, such as traffic delaying him 30 min from the store, or the store being unusually crowded and delaying his purchase of beer, the altered setting events (contingencies) would have a diminishing effect on all of the interdependent responses comprising the segment. Or, for example, suppose Joe was ill at home on a medical leave for 2 weeks, during which time he never engaged in Segment 1 or Segment 2. Upon his return to work, re-instatement of the contingencies *still does not guarantee his response will be equal to its strength before he went on medical leave.* High IRT's, for a prolonged period of time (i.e., prolonged response extinction), limit spontaneous bursts of recovery. Even on his first day back from medical leave, Joe may respond partially or with low energy to antecedent cues in the afternoon and begin to call his friends. But Joe is unlikely to execute the remaining behaviors across all three segments.

In Segment 3, from 5 to 8 p.m., Joe visits a friend's house in which he drinks beer. Subcomponents of the contingencies include unconditioned motivating operations (ethanol effects), conditioned motivating operations (social approval from drinking peers), setting events (his friends, time of day), and positive reinforcers sustaining his verbal or other interactive behaviors. Effects of the contingencies directly predict his physical susceptibility to drinking the same number or greater number of beers. Confounding factors such as the nature and amount of food consumed, remarks his peers make to him, his sleep deprivation, or other thoughts or emotions aroused at work can delude or interfere with how much Joe drinks. If alcohol arouses "liquid courage" or more aggressive verbal behavior (i.e., unconditioned motivating operation), Joe can respond effectively to sarcastic peers and drink more. However, if alcohol does the opposite—is a depressant sedating his anxiety and making him mellow and more vulnerable—Joe will be quieter, withdrawn, and drink less.

The importance of these three-segments is to form a hypothetical functional analysis of the pre-criminal and criminal behaviors as forecasters of future crimes. Procession through each segment unhindered by competing or confounding variables (like longer IRTs, medical leave, no sleep deprivation, etc.), means Joe has a high proclivity (potential behaviors) for a DUIL. Disruption of the intercontingencies in *any of the segments* reduces the response-strengthening MOs or setting events and can mitigate Joe's probability of overdrinking or driving while inebriated. Enhancement of the contingencies does the opposite; it accelerates the propensity for recurrent alcohol use. In the events self-reported by Joe and corroborated by product measurements and interviews, Joe apparently smoked 1−2 joints (1/2 g of) marijuana while also drinking. Mixing cannabis and alcohol not only blinded a realistic awareness of Joe's drinking effects, it also included side-effects of rapid heartbeat (arrhythmia) and anxiety. Joe, who already drank alcohol to self-medicate (remove) his anxiety (negative reinforcement), now was producing *more anxiety from a physiological reaction to cannabis (unconditioned MO) and consequently consumed more alcohol to relieve heightened symptoms.*

## Risk of alcohol (and DUIL) recidivism

Functional analysis within and between each successive psychological segment provides a platform for causal predictions of Joe's risk of alcohol recidivism and recommission of the DUIL offense. After identifying his pre-arrest series of stimulus-response events (baseline), noting that MOs that may vary his behavior slightly, the behavioral forensic examiner asks the question of whether Joe *currently engages in not only baseline behaviors potentiating criminal risk, but also any other behaviors resembling baseline behaviors. "Resemblance"* is operationally defined as (a) substitute responses (that generate similar MOs), (b) exposure to similar antecedents or consequences generating similar MOs, or (c) vicarious exposure to similar contingencies that generate same or similar MOs. In the latter case, vicarious exposure, indirect contact with alcohol-use contingencies by talking about the contingencies (i.e., rule-governed behaviors) away from the tangible contingencies, can evoke same or similar reactions as if Joe directly experienced the contingencies. Current behavioral research on Post-Traumatic Stress Disorder (PTSD), for example showed non-trauma contact victims showed same, similar, or even worse symptoms when learning of the tragedies than their counterparts directing witnessing the trauma (Culver, McKinney, & Paradise, 2011; McCann & Pearlman, 1990). Similarly, Joe's discussion with former drinking friends who extolled their habits of buying beer after work and drinking at night—contingencies replicating Joe's prior functional contingencies—can evoke precurrent behaviors (i.e., curiosity, sensitivity to, longing for, or activation of MO) to engage in some or all of the behaviors generating the contingencies his friends talked about. One of the unusual downsides of attending Alcoholics Anonymous (AA), for example, despite its touted value in alcohol recovery, is that members share stories of personal tragedy involving their drinking, often homogenously similar to each member's life story. These shared rule-governed behaviors may "symbolically" send a warning message to avoid drinking. But empirically speaking, the rule-governed behaviors heard by AA members and recited to themselves can evoke a series of psychological events that historically were preceded by similar verbal self-statements (antecedents) when the AA member used to imbibe in alcohol.

On closer examination, Joe reported his post-arrest behaviors in each Behavior Segment. In Segment 1, around 3–4 pm at work, he calls, texts, instagrams, Facebook chats, or otherwise uses social media to contact a friend to discuss their evening activities. While Joe does not include himself in these activities, and just listens to what the partying pleasures the friend describes, Joe engages in (a) stimulus conditions identical or similar to (i.e. generic or metaphorical extension, Skinner, 1957; Sundberg, 2007) to his precurrents to drinking, and (b) shares the anticipated experiences vicariously with his friends. Both of these response patterns maintain the current *potential* frequency and magnitude of his drinking behavior.

In Segment 2, between 4 and 5 p.m. after leaving the office, Joe habitually stops at either the same grocery store or a party store along the same driving route. He buys a candy bar and soda pop. According to Joe, his choice of soda pop and candy divert purchase of alcohol purchase. Unbeknownst to Joe, his replacement habits are equally *potentiating* alcohol recidivism. First, his driving route engages in the same or similar stimulus conditions (same or similar store, around the exact time). Second, he purchases two sugar products likely metabolized to induce a higher blood sugar level matching level attained when he might drink beer in Segment 3 (i.e., stronger unconditioned MO). Although sugar intake in Segment 2 is *different than his former habit of drinking in Segment 3*, early sugar ingestion triggers the hypothalamus and increases re-ingestion of more sugar within 1–2 h; that second dose of sugar desired in 1–2 h may take the form of beer.

In Segment 3, from 5 to 8 p.m., Joe proudly reported his cessation of daily visits to friends' homes. However, he still enjoyed briefer contacts with friends three-times weekly, including weekends, for 1–2 h instead of for 3 h. While there, he drank club soda or lemonade but refused alcohol beverages. Joe believed his alcohol abstinence reflected his will-power. Joe overlooked how weak his will-power bordered on complete alcohol relapse. First, he again engaged in response patterns directly parallel to his pre-arrest behaviors of attending parties, regardless of reduced frequency of visits. Second, he consumed sugar and carbonated liquids biologically producing similar gustatory (taste) effects as drinking alcohol. Sugar levels and dissolved CO2 gas imitates taste sensations and sugar infusion from drinking one beer (ethanol effects). Unconditioned MOs evoked while drinking the club soda and lemonade can also build physical tolerance to drinking many glasses/cans of these liquids across time, thereby repeating the response sequence (chain) of multiple beers consumed before his arrest (baseline period). In short, re-activation of all three segments, including identical or similar intercontingencies, predisposes Joe to a greater chance of alcohol re-use within 3–6 months.

Joe's unabated social patterns that flirt with drinking contingencies are predictive of alcohol relapse and risk of repeated DUILs. His high risk of repeating social patterns also threatens violation of his probation. Consequently, he does not appear a viable candidate for reinstatement of his driver's license. Under his current court order, Joe must be both alcohol-abstinent and refrain from visiting alcohol-serving restaurants or bar. Judiciary punishment for Joe's violations, the likely outcome, will definitely inconvenience Joe's schedule of work and home life. But it is only a temporary solution. Confinement in jail may interrupt the progressive sequence from Segments 1 to 3 only for 30 days and may permit further biological detoxification if Joe actually drank during his court violations. Jails are holding tanks that put Joe's life in abeyance, not into a trajectory of actual reform. Jail, like any punishment contingency, may stun, momentarily suppress unwanted behaviors, and of course remove bootleg or competing reinforces from exerting control over unwanted behavior. The downside of jail—a coercive punishment contingency in alcohol court cases—is (a) transient response suppression, (b) high risk of spontaneous recovery of alcohol use when punishment is gone, and (c) resentment toward the authorities (judge, probation officers) imposing the sanctions. Joe will now despise the probation system, look for surreptitious ways to undermine or bypass it, and likely be a repeat violator to passively retaliate against the heartless damage the system had on his life. Joe will view himself a victim, a pawn manipulated by unfair court practices, and completely overlook the bigger picture of how his criminal offense meant he disguised a drinking problem.

By operationalizing the functional subcomponents of the Behavior Segments, the forensic examiner puts into perspective a *more believable* cause-and-effect scenario and more solid scientific estimate of Joe's future criminal action. A behavioral forensic analysis also arrives at more definitive reasons why Joe is ineligible for driver license reinstatement in case Joe subsequently appeals the court's decision based on the forensic evaluation. Most importantly, a behavioral forensic analysis augments the credibility of evaluators called to testify in court and who must weather the storm of challenges during examination and cross-examination.

## References

Alanko, T. (1984). An overview of techniques and problems in the measurement of alcohol consumption. In H.CappellF.GlaserY.IsraelH.KalantR.E.Pophamet al. (Series Eds.) & R. G. Smart (Vol. Ed.), *Research advances in alcohol and drug problems* (Vol. 8, pp. 209–226). New York: Plenum Press.

Culver, L., McKinney, B., & Paradise, L. (2011). Mental health professionals' experiences of vicarious traumatization in post-hurricane Katrina New Orleans. *Journal of Loss and Trauma, 16*, 33–42.

Delprato, D. J., & McGlynn, F. D. (1988). Interactions of response patterns and their implications for behavior therapy. *Journal of Behavior Therapy and Experimental Psychiatry, 19*, 199–205.

Delprato, D. J., & Smith, N. W. (2009). Sketch of J.R. Kantor's psychological interbehavioral field theory. *Psychological Record, 59*, 671–678.

Donovan, D. M., & Marlatt, G. A. (2007). *Assessment of addictive behaviors*. NY: Guilford Press.

George, W. H., Phillips, S. M., & Skinner, J. B. (1988). Analogue measurement in alcohol consumption: Effects for task type and correspondence with self-report measurement. *Journal of Studies on Alcohol, 49*, 450–455.

McCann, I. L., & Pearlman, L. A. (1990). Vicarious traumatization: A framework for understanding the psychological effects of working with victims. *Journal of Traumatic Stress, 3*(1), 131–149.

Midgley, B., & Morris, E. (2006). *Modern perspectives on J.R. Kantor and interbehaviorism*. Las Vegas, UT: Context Press.

Nathan, P. E., & Briddell, D. W. (1977). Behavioral assessment and treatment of alcoholism. In B. Kissin, & H. Beglieter (Eds.), *Treatment and rehabilitation of the chronic alcoholic* (pp. 301–346). Boston, MA: Springer-Verlag.

O'Farrell, & Maisto, S. A. (1987). The utility of self-report and biological measures of alcohol consumption in alcoholism treatment outcome studies. *Advances in Behaviour Research and Therapy, 9*, 91–125.

Reynolds, G. S., & Alastair, M. (1970). On the theory of inter-response time reinforcement. In G. H. Bower (Ed.), *Psychology of learning and motivation* (pp. 85–107). NY: Academic Press.

Ruben, D. H. (1983a). Interbehavioral implications for behavior therapy: Clinical perspectives. In N. W. Smith, P. T. Mountjoy, & D. H. Ruben (Eds.), *Reassessment in psychology: The interbehavioral alternative* (pp. 445–469). Washington DC: University Press of America.

Ruben, D. H. (1983b). Analogue assessments in the behavioral treatment of drug addictions. *Catalyst, 2*, 69–77.

Ruben, D. H. (1984). Validity of drug addict population norms for the Rathus Assertiveness Schedule. *Psychological Reports, 55*, 125–126.

Ruben, D. H. (1990b). *The aging and drug effects: A planning manual for medication and alcohol abuse treatment of the elderly*. Jefferson, NC: McFarland Publishers.

Ruben, D. H. (1992a). Behavioral systems approach. In C. E. Stout, J. L. Levitt, & D. H. Ruben (Eds.), *Handbook for assessing and treating addictive disorders* (pp. 3–39). Westport, CT: Greenwood Press.

Ruben, D. H. (1992b). Interbehavioral analysis of adult children of alcoholics: Etiological predictors. *Alcoholism Treatment Quarterly, 9*, 1–21.

Ruben, D. H. (1999a). Behavioral systems approach: Case response. In E. T. Dowd, & T. Rugle (Eds.), *Comparative Treatments of substance abuse* (pp. 79–95). NY: Springer Publishing.

Ruben, D. H. (1999b). Diagnosing alcoholism and its addictive patterns using self-report rating scales. *Alcoholism Treatment Quarterly, 17*, 37–46.

Ruben, D. H. (2000). *Treating adult children of alcoholics: A behavioral approach*. NY: Academic Press.

Ruben, D. H. (2002). *Therapist desk reference of behavioral interventions*. Okemos, MI: Best Impressions International (CD version).

Ruben, D. H. (2004). Drug dependence. In C. Spielberger (Ed.), *Encyclopedia of applied psychology* (pp. 645–653). San Diego, CA: Academic Press.

Ruben, D. H. (2015). *Adult children of alcoholics-revised (ACOA-R) behavior profile*. Okemos: Best Impressions International, Inc.

Ruben, D. H. (1987). Improving communication between the elderly and pharmacies: A self-initiative training program. *Journal of Alcohol & Drug Education, 32*, 7–12.

Ruben, D. H. (1989). Behavioral predictors of alcoholics: A "systems" alternative. *Alcoholism Treatment Quarterly, 5*, 137–162.

Ruben, D. H. (1990a). A "new" systems treatment for alcohol and drug abuse. *Alcoholism Treatment Quarterly, 7*, 47–61.

Ryan, V., Popour, J., Arneson, A., & Ruben, D. H. (Eds.). (1983). *Fundamentals of substance abuse counseling*. Lansing, MI: ARIS.

Skinner, B. F. (1957). *Verbal behavior*. NY: Appleton-Century-Crofts.

Sobell, L. C., & Sobell, M. B. (2003). Alcohol consumption measures. In J. Allen, & V. Wilson (Eds.), *Assessing alcohol problems: A guide for clinicians and researchers* (pp. 75–99). Washington DC: US Department of Health & Human Services.

Sundberg, M. L. (2007). Verbal behavior. In J. O. Cooper, T. E. Heron, & W. L. Heward (Eds.), *Applied behavior analysis* (2nd ed., pp. 526–547). Upper Saddle River, NJ: Merrill/Prentice Hall.

Sutcker, P. B., Malatesta, V. J., Allain, A. N., & Randall, C. L. (1981). Analogue drinking assessment: Sensation seeking and gender. *Journal of Behavioral Assessment, 3*, 167–177.

Tanno, T., & Silberberg, A. (2014). Inter-response time reinforcement and relative reinforcer frequency control choice. *Learning & Behavior, 43*, 14–29.

Vuchinich, R. E., Tucker, J. A., & Harllee, L. M. (1988). Behavioral assessment. In D. Donovan, & G. A. Marlatt (Eds.), *Assessment of addictive behaviors: Behavioral, cognitive, and physiological procedures* (pp. 51–93). New York: Guilford Press.

CHAPTER

# 7

# Behavioral forensic analysis of competency-to-stand trial in the evaluation of an offender accused of car jacking and breaking and entering

Competency to stand trial is an elusive concept of jurisprudence personified over decades as the litmus test of whether a defendant understands the court process and can assist in his or her defense. Evaluations of competency to stand trial occur in civil and criminal cases. The legal concept of trial competency presumes a sufficient present ability to consult with his or her lawyer with a reasonable degree of rational understanding, and similar rationality to discern and weigh the consequences of charges alleged against the defendant. This modern standard for competency definition (Dusky v. United States, 1960; Favole, 1983) not only is ambiguous but results in inconsistent interpretations by forensic psychologists in arriving at conclusions. For example, incompetency often associates with psychosis (Cooke, 1969); or appears different under non-court contexts, such as at home or work (Bonnie, 1992; Grisso, Appelbaum, Mulvey, & Fletcher, 1995). Accuracy of trial competency also depends on the validity and reliability of psychometric instruments used during the assessment (Grisso, 1986; Skeem & Golding, 1998). Between non-empirically validated test instruments, different conceptualizations of the Dusky standard, and enormous heterogeneity in the process of clinical interviewing, outcomes of trial competency vary among each forensic evaluator. Rogers and Johhansson-Love (2009) called for uniformity in test outcome with evidence-based practices in assessment. A milestone in evidence-based, uniform guidelines occurred with the seminal publication of AAPL Practice Guideline (cf. Mossman & Noffsinger, 2007). It provided the legal framework and conceptual basis for the evaluations directing practitioners to ask questions about competency-related abilities, that is, about the defendant's *verbal behavior about functional skills in courtroom situations.*

*Behavioral Forensics*
https://doi.org/10.1016/B978-0-12-819805-6.00007-5

The AAPL guidelines launched a promising solution to conceptual ambiguity and testing-practice inconsistency. It detailed formulation of step-by-step procedures and offered parameters for selection of psychometrics. Proliferation of the AAPL guidelines was slow, but it offered the most systematic protocol for forensic evaluators in the United States. Like any touted innovation, it suffered unforgivable shortcomings. The first was insufficient external validity for applications in Canada and Great Britain due to mental health provisions in the respective country's judiciary (Mackay, 2007'; O'Shaughnessy, 2007). Second, the protocol predicated on mentalistic or pseudo-science concepts not easily amenable to evidence-based practices. For example, in assessing past victimization from trauma, the AAPL warns the subject may be vulnerable to exploitation, is not necessarily blameless, or should not be assumed to have an illegitimate legal case. Language used here intimates some underlying dynamic that all victims are helpless and vulnerable and may be unknowingly contributory to their own fate of traumatization. The accidental and expansive application of such pseudoscience concepts is not new and lately has been the bane of controversy in the arena of cognitive and behavioral treatment interventions (Lilienfeld, 2018; Lilienfeld, Lynn, & Lohr, 2014). By contrast, an evidence-based or *Behavioral Forensic* approach isolates the multiple cause-and-effect variables to create a scientifically plausible explanation (i.e., functional analysis) for criminal behavior occurrence. Even evaluators who use concepts or hypothesize behavior that are not well understood, but premise on *scientifically plausible* explanations, are still respectful of evidence-based practices. The problem arises when nonscientific evaluators opine one conclusion about trial competency and scientific evaluators opine a discrepant conclusion. Disagreement among evaluators, according to one study (Skeem, Golding, Cohn, & Berge, 1998), even showed as high as 75% on assessment of salient deficits.

This disparity of opinions in civil and criminal courts present an enigma for the attorney and judge to sort out. Judges, who rely on the forensic specialist to offer litigation-based science (Dahl, 2008), may be misled by the sheer number of forensic evaluators involved in a case; judges may also erroneously operate on the assumption that all forensic evaluations are uniformly conducted analogous to many surgical procedures. When judges weigh the outcomes, persuaded more by pseudoscience than by science, their decisions my backfire in an out-of-control courtroom. This chapter presents an example of such a situation; it presents multiple forensic examinations done by the State and one by an Independent Medical (psychological) Examiner (IME) of a carjacker who also illegally entered property. Conclusions reached by 75% of the State's forensic evaluators *and the IME* were that the defendant was not competent to stand trial. The one dissenter, a professional not even licensed to conduct psychological evaluations, favored competency after interviewing the defendant on medications and after the defendant underwent "competency" class.

## Case study of Mr. Moe

Mr. Moe is a 20 year old single male currently residing 18 months in a County Jail after arrested for two counts of carjacking. Previously he lived two months with his maternal grandmother. Before that, he lived 3 years with other family members. Mr. Moe's only pre-incarceration job was in a car wash. He worked there for 1 year, although he received verbal and written reprimands for his irregular attendance and tardiness. He denied incurring any reprimands for (a) coworker or supervisor relations, (b) rule compliance with the company, (c) customer service, and (d) performance quality. He denied any history of receiving unemployment compensation or subsidy from social security for developmental or learning disabilities.

*Educationally*, Mr. Moe attended an inner-city Public School. He attended Kindergarten to 12th grade and transferred to an alternative high school before he quit school. He never obtained a GED or high school diploma. He denied undergoing any formal school testing for IEP or 504 eligibility and consequently never received special education services. However, he reported profound difficulties with learning deficits and drug use. Earned grades clustered around low D's and E's, corresponding to a GPA of 1.5. He blamed his academic underachievement on (a) severe absenteeism resulting in multiple truancy warnings, (b) neglected homework completion and non-submission, (c) poor listening comprehension in class, (d) poor reading comprehension, (e) cannabis-induced fatigue interfering with concentration, and (f) frequent suspensions due to in-school fighting. He never received any tutorial or remedial educational services outside of school. He also neither participated in any extracurricular nor community activities.

Mr. Moe reported acting as bully and being bullied. In Elementary through Middle School, he admitted to instigation of aggressive fighting of younger and same-age children for "fun" and "retaliation." He reportedly thrived on the viscerality ("adrenaline rush") of drawing an unsuspecting child into a fight, calling him or her names, and seeing the child helplessly collapse after being struck physically. Anger also was preemptive to perceived assailants. When Mr. Moe suspected attack by other bullies, he intervened in advance, either verbally or physically threatening the anticipated aggressor. Ironically, Mr. Moe also claimed he interceded on behalf of perceived victims of bullies; he often appointed himself as bodyguard or protector against perpetrators of younger victims he either had bullied before or believed were defenseless. He received numerous suspensions and detentions but no expulsions. Physical and verbal attacks at peers generalized to his opposition toward authority (principles, counselors, etc.) and he frequently violated school rules. He admitted to showing "no respect" to authorities. He denied gang membership but did associate with gang members in some violent activities. He denied carrying or use a firearm or knife. He denied bringing contraband (weapon or drugs) to school. He denied fascination with fire-starting or animal cruelty. His denied any juvenile criminal record except truancy. His adult criminal record included a misdemeanor (possession of marijuana), breaking & entering, and carjacking. He denied receiving any pediatric diagnoses of Attention Deficit Hyperactivity Disorder (ADHD) or Oppositional Defiant Disorder (ODD). He denied receiving any residential or outpatient mental health treatment. According to collateral mental health records, Mr. Moe was seen shortly before the crime by a local hospital emergency unit for an apparent overdose of heroin, cocaine, and other substances. He was discharged from the hospital in the custody of law enforcement. To date, Mr. Moe denied taking any prescriptive psychotropic medications.

## Alcohol and drug abuse

Mr. Moe first experimented recreationally with alcohol in fifth grade (12 years old). He drank less than a fifth of whisky or vodka with friends intermittently on weekends. This episodic drinking pattern never increased. He denied using alcohol as a gateway or decelerant drug when later mixing cocaine with heroin. Ethanol reportedly induced a sedate, numb, or relaxed sensation, self-medicating his constant feelings of rage. By age 13 (seventh grade), he began smoking cannabis daily. By ages 15 to 16, he reached 6–8 g per week, risking loss of short-term memory, loss of physical energy, poor psychomotor rate, confusion, severe irritability, and increased susceptibility to paranoid-like reactions. He ingested THC through blunts, joints, and bowls. Thriving on the anesthetic or "numbness" sensation, he began using nonprescriptive Xanax (0.5 mg), mixed with acid, ecstasy, heroin, and cocaine by ages 17 to 19. Co-administration of cocaine (stimulant) and heroin (depressant, opiate synthetic) supposedly created a sudden rush of euphoria without the side-effects of drowsiness or anxiety. Use of heroin also offset the crash, or sudden withdrawal effects after cocaine's short-lived high. Use of ecstasy, cannabis, heroin, and marijuana reportedly accelerated his paranoia (hypervigilance) and spontaneous hyperactivity. He spoke of "panic-like reactions" abruptly "happening for no obvious reason or without reference to some related incident." For example, he might watch a crime-themed television show or movie (while intoxicated) and instantly believe his life was in danger.

*Medically*, Mr. Moe denied suffering any major vehicular or other accidents causing head trauma. He denied undergoing any major surgeries. He denied suffering CVAs, TIAs, sleep apnea, high fevers, or neurotoxin exposure. He denied any currently known medical conditions.

*Interpersonally*, Mr. Moe denied any past history of sexual victimization. He was first voluntarily sexual at age 14. By ages 13 and 14, he also began masturbating to online or other pornography. He conservatively estimated having over 100 heterosexual partners in six years, averaging to 16 casual or "no-strings attached" partners per year. Asked about his promiscuity, he explained he met sexual prospects online in Facebook, Craig's List, or other social media, often for one-time encounters. He denied engaging in paraphilias (gadgets, routines, rituals, sado-masochism, exhibitionism, voyeurism, etc.). However, he did occasionally attend topless or adult clubs and pay for lap-dances. He identified one significant partner dated for a short duration, during which was not monogamous. Asked about his noncommittal relationships, Mr. Moe insightfully observed that most of his nuclear family members abused drugs, were in jail or prison, or abandoned him. He anticipated closeness to any intimate partner might end in the same way of being abandoned.

*Developmentally*, Mr. Moe was the only illegitimate offspring of unmarried parents separated after his birth. His father had been in and out of prison for felony convictions for nearly Mr. Moe's entire life. Mr. Moe's mother previously served a jail sentence for retail fraud, and currently was incarcerated for uttering and publishing. From childhood until age 14, raised exclusively by his mother, Mr. Moe witnessed his mother's polysubstance abuse of marijuana and heroin. He graphically recalled the anxiety of dodging her random explosive outbursts over any household infraction. Mr. Moe rarely understood what he did wrong (capricious) and never precisely predicted the next explosive tirade (arbitrary). Capricious and arbitrary forms of punishment typically induced hypervigilance (chronic awareness, suspicion). Hypervigilance evolved into paranoia (chronic distrust of people's actions, judgments). Moreover, after deluged with a torrent of verbal and physical abuse (yelling, spankings, privilege removal, time-outs, all), Mr. Moe overcame inhibition. He began to argue back at his mother and anticipate her tirades with pre-emptive, violently aggressive reactions. Meaning, at the sight of his mother, before she found fault in him or raised her voice, Mr. Moe exploded with *anticipatory aggression*, or aggression exhibited in advance of and to prevent parental verbal or physical attacks (cf., Ruben, 2014).

By early to mid-teens, Mr. Moe generalized his anticipatory behaviors to the school, both in over-reacting to bullies *before and after they bothered him*, and to adult authorities, perceived with the same threat of attack as Mr. Moe perceived his mother. Consequently he over-reacted to authorities, a behavior the authorities likely deemed as incorrigible or disrespectful. As for his bullying of younger or innocent children, Mr. Moe simply *mimicked or replicated* the antagonistic behaviors his mother did to him. In retrospect, Mr. Moe's only salvation identified in his childhood was his time raised by his maternal grandparents. They provided some semblance of lifestyle and family normalcy, although Mr. Moe at the time, resisted it and regarded their positive habits as strange.

## Criminal incident

In the early afternoon before the incident, Mr. Moe was in the basement of his friend's house watching television. He ingested 3–4 g of marijuana combined with ecstasy and cocaine. He chronicled the events very precisely and articulately. His self-report largely corroborated with police arrest records:

1. He explained he suddenly "freaked out" and felt overwhelming paranoid that his life was in peril.
2. Second, he darted out of the house, through local woods, and into the street to a neighbor's house.
3. Third, he pounded on the neighbor's door, screaming that his life was in imminent danger. The neighbor resisted his access but Mr. Moe shoved the door open pushing neighbor out of the way.
4. Mr. Moe then raced to a closet, pulling out items, trying to hide inside.
5. Within seconds, dismissing the closet as non-protective, Mr. Moe raced out of the house into the street. Asked if he knew the neighbor, Mr. Moe denied prior knowledge of him. Asked about the hallucinatory or otherwise delusionary feeling of danger, Mr. Moe said it reminded him of living with his mother around ages 8 to 14, when he never knew if his mother might explode in a tirade. However, this anticipatory anxiety, he added, was "magnified five-times."
6. He flagged down an oncoming vehicle. The driver stopped and Mr. Moe entered the vehicle by the passenger door. He pleaded with the driver to save him, saying somebody wanted to kill him. He asked her to drive the car fast. When the driver balked, Mr. Moe moved closer to the driver, opened her driver's seat, and pushed her out of the vehicle.
7. Mr. Moe then drove the vehicle recklessly 1 mile until it crashed into a ditch.
8. He escaped the vehicle and repeated the same panic-reactive routine of flagging down a second vehicle. Mr. Moe claimed he entered the passenger door, and immediately shoved the driver out of her side of the door. He drove the vehicle a distance before exiting it on his own volition.

## Behavioral observations and testing

Mr. Moe arrived on the third floor in a County Jail. He met the examiner in a small room with two chairs and a table. He was donned in standard inmate uniform. He greeted the examiner affably and courteously. He agreed with the proposed testing process. He also listened attentively when debriefed about the purpose of testing. Attire was clean and hygienic. He ambulated independently with a normal gait showing no signs of psychomotor disturbance. He sat comfortably in the chair, and made no abrupt gestural or postural movements. Face to face clinical interview and testing lasted 2.5 h. He spent 1 h completing self-testing materials across from the examiner. Attention-span and physical endurance varied. Eye contact was indirect and non-continuous. He smiled, laughed, and interjected questions and statements at inappropriate intervals. Sensorium was intact. Affect showed shifting moods from anger, resistance, opposition, and paranoid statements. He showed confabulation, thought incongruence, hyperbolic statements, and poor delineation between reality and fantasy; he showed poor distinction between truth and falsehood. Speech showed no articulation problems. Vowel and consonant pronunciation (phonetics) was smooth. Speech flowed evenly, rapidly, audibly, and in completed sentences. Prosody was normal and melodic. Speech content consisted of vocabulary and syntax commensurate with his stated educational level. Ideation showed poor coherence, weak rationality, and shifting orientation of person, place, and time.

On objective psychometric testing (Wechsler Adult Intelligence Scale-IV, Test of Memory Malingering, Thematic Apperception Test, Minnesota Multiphasic Personality Inventory-2-Restructured Form, Evaluation of Competency to Stand Trial-Revised), abstractive abilities suggested low skills in visual problem solving and perceptual reasoning. He poorly tracked and discriminated among objects; he reconstructed information slowly from visual memory. He sorted relevant from irrelevant details. He also conceptualized simple but not complex social situations. Analytical reasoning was slow but consistent and accurate; he slowly but effectively used deductive and inductive logic in converting general information into meaningful or symbol order. Likewise, interpretive thinking was slow but accurate; he showed poor insight about past crimes, etiology and treatment progress on alcohol, and her retail fraud case. He showed neither culpability nor remorse about crimes. He did not grasp the larger picture of his crimes. His judgment appeared mildly impulsive. On organizational indices, low scores on content and form suggested inattention to details of object relations. He showed poor adherence to structure suggesting social nonconformity. Visuo-spatial construction and integration of skills were slow but accurate. He poorly grouped objects together by shared properties of angularity, symmetry, and contiguity. He showed the structural abnormality of perseveration: this occur when he repeats the same or similar answer owing to impoverishment of details or obsessive-compulsive thinking. Affective Ratio scores were high; this typifies a person strongly needing affection or intimacy. On the HTP, scores on proportionality, detailing, and locality were unremarkable. On the TAT, a measure of behavioral and emotional patterns, recurrent themes involved detachment, selfishness, self-estrangement, and distrust. Short-term memory showed minor limitations. Immediate recall and long-term memory appeared intact. No evidence seen of impairment to his procedural, episodic, or semantic memory. No impairment found in his executive cognitive (prefrontal dorsolateral cortex) functions. Overall his disposition was variable. He was cooperative during the entire testing protocol.

## Evaluation of Competency to Stand Trial-Revised (ECST-R)

The ECST-R is a step-wise, semi-structured interview instrument generated to measure trial competency. It was carefully constructed and validated using the Dusky standards of criminal defendant's capacities as it relates to courtroom proceedings. Three areas covered by the interview include (a) factual understanding of the proceedings, (b) rational understanding of the proceedings, and (c) rational ability to consult with counsel (Rogers & Johansoon-Love, 2009). Despite its flattering normative data and reliability (Rogers, Tillbrook, & Sewell, 2004), its cut scores were *not* validated for defendants with IQs of less than 60. Mr. Moe's IQ scores were VCI = 70 (second percentile), PRI = 86 (18th percentile), WMI = 66 (first percentile), PSI = 74 (fourth percentile), and FSIQ = 63 (first percentile). Analysis of his ECST-R chart below (Table 7.1) showed clear impairment of his factual understanding. The level of impairment was most prominent in (a) rational ability to consult with counsel, (b) factual understanding of the proceedings, and (c) overall rational ability.

Translating this screening test into behavioral terms, the forensic interview asks direct questions to the defendant about the purpose and process of court and about communication with his attorney. The intraverbal relationship is one where verbal cues from the interviewer may match (i.e., have point-to-point correspondence with) some or none of the corresponding verbal responses of defendant. Defendants struggling to answer questions may unknowingly prompt the interviewer to rephrase, simplify, or re-state the question, providing both more verbal and nonverbal cues (tacts) to facilitate closer approximations to accurate replies. Moreover, the criteria for acceptable defendant answers is generous and requires only one or two word-answers, instead of grammatically correct sentences or elaboration of the questions asked. Hypothetically, a defendant coached in advanced or who memorizes the answers before interviewed could pass the test without having substantive knowledge (competency) of the answers he or she gives.

Further problems, from a behavioral perspective, include psychosis and verbal behavior deficits. First, an interviewee (defendant) outwardly exhibiting disorganized speech patterns (tangential, distortive, and confabulated) and showing poor reality-connection might give inaccurate answers. Even interviewees placed on antipsychotic medication during the interview, while perhaps more coherent in responses, may suffer neuroleptic side effects including drowsiness, confusion, and psychomotor agitation interfering with hearing or comprehension of the questions. Second, receptive and expressive language deficits may be present. Mr. Moe earned Borderline to Extremely low scores on Verbal Comprehension on the WAIS-IV, implicating

**TABLE 7.1** Scores on ECST-R.

| Competency scales | T-score | Impairment | Certitude |
|---|---|---|---|
| Rational ability to consult with counsel | 112 | Very Extreme | Definite |
| Factual understanding of the proceedings | 85 | Extreme | Very Probable |
| Rational understanding of the proceedings | 66 | Moderate | Preponderant |
| Overall rational ability | 94 | Very Extreme | Definite |

weak auditory processing (encoding, decoding, interpreting, and expressing information). Origins of the deficits may be congenital or adventitious. Congenital deficits can be results of possible teratogenic (in vitro) prenatal exposure (e.g., lead, drugs, alcohol), genetic inheritance (e.g., cardiomyopathy), or perinatal trauma (hypoxia, nuchal chord, preterm birth, etc.). Adventitious deficits can range from physiological (e.g., closed head injury, febrile seizures, repeated tubular implant surgeries) to environmental (e.g., multiple school interruptions, impoverished opportunities or verbal thriving, punitive household, peer bullying and intimidation). Impairment scores on the ECST-R, in other words, might be biased (compromised) by known or known origins of verbal comprehension deficits.

On the MMPI-2-RF, another self-report test, Mr. Moe's profile was valid, reliable, and interpretable. Scales on the MMPI-2-RF, behaviorally speaking, can discern macro or larger constellations of behavior interfering with Mr. Moe's' life. Subsequently, a functional analysis can reduce these molar patterns into molecular and sequential patterns connected causally to pre-criminal, criminal, or post-criminal events. On the Higher-Order scale, score elevations in THD BXD profiled a thought-disordered individual who is short-tempered. They externalize or impulsively ventilate their anger with a sense of impunity. They disregard immediate or long-term *bad* consequences, in favor of the immediate *rewards* for discharging their emotions. Externalizers can be callously insensitive, selfishly driven, adventure-seeking, and grandiose about their career dreams and ideals. They set unrealistic short-term and long-term goals, by misjudging their abilities and outright denying limitations. Anger is also a vehicle for self-expression. They rely on anger either for persuasion or in anticipation of impending conflict. Perceived conflict instantly signals to Mr. Moe he may be blamed for some act that he wants to escape or defend himself about. Living with his biological mother, for example, Mr. Moe frequently encountered altercations after being randomly blamed for household infractions. He perceived his mother as unreliable, neglectful, and grossly delinquent of any nurturing qualities he desired. This snapshot into Mr. Moe's world and constellation of behavior may shed light on his truth-telling, his autobiographical history taken during the clinical background, and fact cross-checking when comparing personality results against medical, prison, school, police, or psychological records reviewed as part of report preparation.

## Behavior analysis of competency to stand trial

Self-reported measures of verbal comprehension about competency and about molar patterns of personality are prototypically the yardsticks of whether a defendant meets the Dusky standards. The mandate for expert forensic specialists is to show Mr. Moe does or does not meet adjudicative competence by convincing evidence of impaired intelligence, reasoning, judgment, or other mitigating circumstances that limit appreciation of court proceedings, nature of pending crime, and capacity to assist an attorney or other agent during the trial. More operationally, affirmation of his competency means Mr. Moe:

*Series A*

1. Can verbally state the process of the trial and the roles of judge, jury, prosecutor, and defense attorney
2. Can verbally state some of the facts and procedures pertinent to the legal resolution of the case against him and the process of plea bargaining.

3. Can verbally state verdicts of guilt and not guilt (and no-contest) mean, and the consequences of each.
4. Can verbally state his rights to a jury trial and an appeal, and against self-incrimination.
5. Can verbally state the name of his attorney, reported he had met with the attorney, and said that he does not have any difficulty understanding his attorney's communications regarding the case.
6. Psychometric testing showed low average to average abilities (prerequisite) to listen to the advice of counsel and based on that advice, verbally state (but not necessarily adopt) the fact that one course of action may be more beneficial than another.
7. Verbally state what alleged behaviors led to the charges and verbally explain the possible consequences if he were to be found guilty of the charges.
8. Can explain his plea to a charge.
9. Demonstrated or had medical records attesting to his physical stamina to withstand the stresses of the trial without suffering prolonged or permanent breakdown, and
10. Verbally explained hypothetical defense strategies and verbalized the possible benefits and downfall of each.

Correct *verbal* responses to the above benchmark reflects an exchange of rule-governed instructions about which the defendant either (a) demonstrated actual occasions of engaging in behaviors described by the rules, or (b) only can exchange in intraverbal statements about the rules but never directly engaged in the contingencies of behaviors the rules describe. In the former case, actual performance of behaviors, documented records may or may not exist attesting to mastery of the skills described by the rules. For example, is there a videotape (or some other electronic recording) depicting defendant's proper exchange and understanding during consultation with an attorney? In that record, did the attorney only discus one or *many* scenarios about plea bargaining or punishment for a guilty verdict? Did the video show the attorney explaining the jurisprudence process and Mr. Moe only nodded affirmatively? If some evidence exists on the video or analogue record proving competent exchange, the verbal rules Mr. Moe states during structured interviews promise more veracity. Video capture of attorney-defendant interchanges can be helpful but not always reliable behavior samples of competency. In videotaped or electronic recordings of forensic interviews with children, for example, Cross, Jones, Walsh, Simone, and Kolko (2007) showed uncorrected biases from (a) the repeated times the children told to their stories to interviewers, (b) the interview occurred in stressful or compromising circumstances, and (c) number of interviewers were intimidating. Controlling for these variables, Cross et al. still speculated demand characteristics (what verbal responses the interviewed children expected they must give under scrutiny) would be the Achilles heel undermining a completely objective, prejudice-free interview assessment.

The second case is when defendants exchange in intraverbal statements about the rules of court but never directly engaged in the contingencies of behaviors the rules describe. Sadly, this scenario represents the most common predicament forensic evaluator's face when assailing competency to stands trial. Verbal rules evolve from a multiplicity of behavior experiences, from watching over 60 television episodes of law-drama shows in popular or daytime syndication (e.g., *Law & Order, Superior Court, Swift Court, Judge Judy, etc.),* to reading scholarly journals, trade magazines, or reading social media infused with nationally-headlined court cases, to hearing about a cousin or family member's positive or negative experiences in court. Formation of accurate or inaccurate rules across a continuum of psychological events can build a minimum repertoire of relevant facts to *sound like the defendant is competent of court process.* Precision of details, of accuracy, is less important than a general grasp of abstract information assimilated from the defendant's past history. That past history may or may not pertain, of course, to the defendant's immediate court case on which the competency inquiry is based. Mr. Moe, for example, previously underwent adjudication for possession of marijuana and truancy. His court history, although limited, entailed a stepwise sequence from arraignment, pre-trial to plea bargaining, conferencing regularly with his public defendant attorney. His past cases were significantly different, all in district court and expedited after pre-trial. Now that Mr. Moe's case was in circuit court, he faced felonies, and he faced a "Voir Dire" process. Is Mr. Moe's historical reference from earlier court segments in his life an accurate predictor of his current comprehension and participation in the court process? Possibly not.

The best solution lies with performing a functional analysis. A functional analysis of court trial competency begins, in part, with recognition of some viable or relevant history predisposing the defendant to verbal skills about jurisprudence. The iconic phrase, "start where the behavior is at"—a fundamental principle underlying most elementary behavior-shaping procedures—compels the evaluator to assess baseline or prerequisite skills before teaching or assessing additional skills. Once a pre-potential repertoire is known, the next step is targeting or operationalizing the criteria of skills to observe or measure. Target skills can be one-word or multiple-word answers or represent a lexicon of similar phrases deemed acceptable For example, using Series A shown above (1–10), here are examples of acceptable single word responses, polyword responses, and equivalences from the defendant:

*Series B*

1. Understood the process of the trial and the roles of judge, jury, prosecutor, and defense attorney:
   a. Judge is boss; makes decision; runs the courtroom; is in charge.
   b. Prosecutor represents the people, tries to convict.
   c. Jury is group of people summoned to make decision; are impartial; decide guilty or innocent.
   d. Defense attorney represents defendant; protects rights; is assigned (sometimes) without cost to defendant.
2. Demonstrated understanding of the facts and procedures pertinent to the legal resolution of the case against him and the process of plea bargaining.
   a. Arrested, booked, contact attorney, court hearing, enter plea, jury trial, sentencing.
   b. Offer, agreement between prosecutor and defendant; defendant pleads guilty to lesser charge to avoid trial, avoid some punishment.
3. Knew what the verdicts of guilt and not guilty mean, and the consequences of each.
   a. Guilty means at fault and face jail, probation, placed on register, or record of crime.
   b. Innocent means charges against defendant dropped; not culpable; not on any permanent record.
   c. No contest means concedes to charges without accepting guilt; no defense; faces reduced charges.

4. Understood his rights to a jury trial and an appeal, and against self-incrimination.
   a. Under sixth amendment, defendant has right to jury trial
   b. Right to question judge or jury's decision; need to show a problem with jury, judge, trial.
   c. Fifth Amendment protects against self-incrimination; forced confessions; exposing one's information unwillingly; possibly overturned in appeals.
5. Knew the name of his attorney, reported he had met with the attorney, and said that he does not have any difficulty understanding his attorney's communications regarding the case.
   a. Name of attorney; days of week or actual dates met with attorneys; where meetings took place; discussion had with attorney.
   b. Can summarize or restate one or two recommendations offered by attorney.
6. Had sufficient intelligence and judgment to listen to the advice of counsel and based on that advice, appreciate (but not necessarily adopt) the fact that one course of action may be more beneficial than another.
   a. Scores on cognitive or learning (achievement) tests (i.e., no deficits in listening comprehension or other oral language).
   b. Judgment—defendant explains one good, and one bad outcome of plea decisions
7. Understood what alleged behaviors led to the charges and understood the possible consequences if he or she were to be found guilty of the charges.
   a. Defendant explains in one or many words what the crime was.
   b. Defendant explains one or two words or phrases about guilty verdict: go to jail; pay restitution; on probation; on record; felony limits jobs; etc.
8. Was competent to decide how to plead a charge.
   a. Line of reasoning; defendant explain pros and cons of pleading to offense, or no contest; phrases used include "If I say this, then this happens; if I say this instead, something else happens."
9. Appeared sufficiently stable to withstand the stresses of the trial without suffering prolonged or permanent breakdown.
   a. Defendant explains type of conduct expected in court: Listen and not interrupt; consult with attorney; don't blurt out opinions to judge or witnesses.
   b. Verify medical document showing physical strength or weakness documenting stamina; assess sleep schedule and risk of falling asleep in court
   c. Verify medication schedule to assure proper medicines taken as prescribed before court begins.
   d. Ask defendant to explain a-c above.
10. Engaged in hypothetical defense strategies and verbalize the possible benefits and downfall of each.
   a. Scores on cognitive tests (verbal comprehension).
   b. Defendant uses phrases: "If I follow this strategy, then this occurs"; "if I follow another strategy, this other thing occurs."

Evoking or soliciting defendant target responses shown above gets tricky for two reasons, if the forensic interviewer uses only verbal prompting. First, verbal prompts or cues can be inconsistent and reciprocally shaped by the struggling defendant who waits for the interviewer to supply more verbal clues before answering. Antecedent (discriminative) verbal cues differentially teach the defendant correct responses reinforced by the examiner's revised questions. Second, Mr. Moe's borderline verbal comprehension scores on WAIS-IV (second percentile) suggested oral language deficits that might interfere with exclusively oral (non-visual, non-tactile) questions. One way around these two common errors is using nonverbal or pictorial prompts and primes as stimulus evokers of target responses (tacts). A *tact is a unit of verbal behavior (operants) controlled by a nonverbal stimulus (such as an object, event, or property of an object) and maintained by nonspecific reinforcement*. Under training or assessment, it can be a verbal response or label assigned to an object (picture) systematically presented as one or two pictures, between which a responder must choose and correctly label. This stimulus discrimination training has been widely used in teaching autistic and non-autistic children vocabulary and transfer skills between tacts and mands, another units of verbal behavior involving requests (Arntzen, Halstadro, Bjerke, Wittner, & Kristiansen, 2014; Marchese, Carr, LeBlanc, Rosatii, and Conroy, 2012). Similarly, pictorial stimulus prompts commonly facilitate development of receptive-expressive (tact) learning (Petursdottir & Carr, 2011). That is, children can generate verbal responses without intraverbal (or actual words) prompts, reminders, or cue triggering appropriate answers. Exclusively using pictures in tact training or assessment can identify a valid baseline of skill strength and even increase the reliable utilization of antecedent-based interventions for tact-learning (Cenqher, Jones, & Fienup (2014).

Receptive language development or assessment using pictures can further yield two types of verbal behaviors, categorically called *stimulus selection based* and *topographically-based,* (Michael, 1985; Sundberg & Sundberg, 1990; Wraikat, Sundberg, & Michael, 1991). Selection-based verbal behaviors involve pointing to a verbal stimulus or symbol, such as a child point to a refrigerator manding food. Or, a passenger may point to a street sign indicating which way the driver should turn. Here, the tact (or mind) depends on some antecedent (conditioned or unconditioned) stimulus preceding the tact response and some stimulus (reinforcer) given after the selected response. Topographically-based verbal responses involve production of a unique or different response, also preceded by discriminative cues; but there is no other reinforcing other stimuli present to maintain the behavior. Among common examples with children include sign language, vocal verbal behavior, and extemporaneous writing composition. The implications of these two typologies for forensic assessment of competency-to-stand trial are the following:

1. Adult defendants who are nonverbal or poorly communicative may rely on pointing (selection-based verbal behavior). Adults who are verbally communicative can sign or vocally state verbal answers (topographically based verbal responses).
2. Defendants presented pictures of court-related images can be asked either to point to a picture or explain the picture. Both repertories might assess a repertoire of tacts about the court system matching the operational criteria listed above.

*Assessment of stimulus selection and topographically based verbal behaviors related to competency to stand trial: method and results.* Mr. Moe was seated at a table across from the forensic examiner and engaged in three phases of assessment: Pre-assessment (baseline) and assessment (stimulus selection) and assessment (stimulus selection and topographically based behaviors). Baseline involved open-ended inquiry from Series A (10 questions, see above), without any pictorial cues prompting stimulus selection or topographical based verbal behaviors.

Verbal responses were scored "True or "False" based on Mr. Moe stating at least two key words or phrases accurately answering the inquiry (see chart below) Immediately afterward, initiating assessment, Mr. Moe was presented with a sequence of pictures for which he had to finger-point an answer. For finger-pointing, three pictures were arranged in front of him depicting some properties of the court process. He was asked to point to the picture matching the Examiner's verbal prompts. For example, when asked to point to "the judge in a court room," three pictures were laid side-by-side labeled by the letters "A," "B," and "C" (see Fig. 7.1 below):

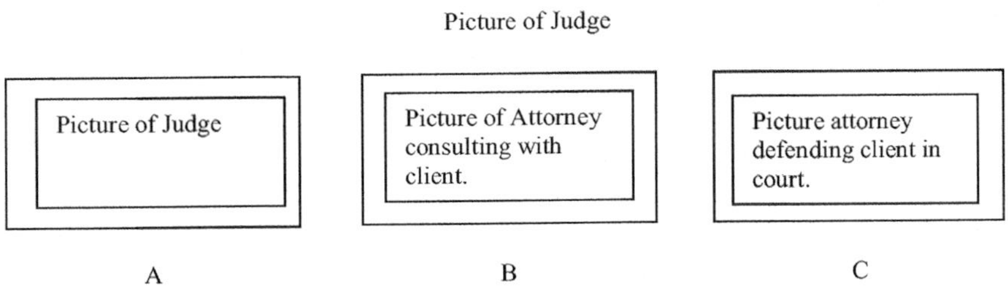


**FIG. 7.1** Description of pictures used with verbal prompts for finger-pointing.

The (pointed) answer "A" was scored as "True" and scored as "False" were pointed answers "B" and "C." A final assessment occurred of ten more successive presentations of three-set pictures. Each presentation allowed for 1 trial of responses versus multiple trials as done in research experiments distinguishing stimulus selection based from topographically based verbal operants (Barlow, Tiger, Slocum & Miller, 2013; Polson & Parsons, 2000). A similar 10-set series of pictures were placed in front of Mr. Moe when assessing topographically-based responses (see Fig. 7.2 below). Here, questions requested both a single finger-point to the picture, followed by a second question prompting a monosyllabic or polysyllabic verbal response. Asked, "Show me which picture is the jury, the responder might point to the jury; the interviewer immediately then asks the question, "What does a jury do?" The schematic illustration below demonstrates a single trial:

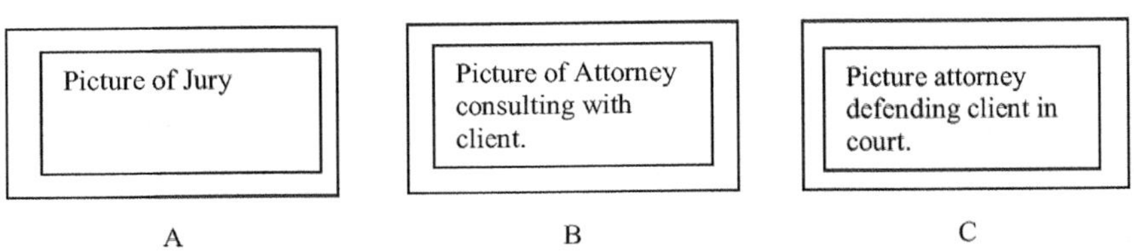


**FIG. 7.2** Description of three pictures used with verbal prompts for finger pointing and verbal responses.

Results of selection based (finger pointing) and topographically-based (finger pointing plus verbal response) proved very significant compared to open-ended inquiries about the same topic during pre-assessment or baseline measures (see Table 7.2 below). Baseline measure showed 10% accuracy of open-ended answers, suggesting either lack of retrievable

TABLE 7.2 Results of baseline, selection based (Assessment 1) and topographically-based (Assessment 2) responses.

| | | | | | | | | | |
|---|---|---|---|---|---|---|---|---|---|
| ***Baseline measure*** | | | | | | | | | |
| False | True | False | False | False | False | False | False | False | False |
| ***Assessment 1*** | | | | | | | | | |
| True | True | True | False | False | False | False | False | False | False |
| ***Assessment 2*** | | | | | | | | | |
| True | True | True | True | False | False | True | False | False | False |

answers (not know answer); poor comprehension (poor understanding of the question), or some other physical state of Mr. Moe preventing coherent and rapid responses (e.g., speech disfluency, traumatic brain injury, on antipsychotic medications, active psychosis). On Assessment 1, 30% true scores suggested finger-pointing revealed more "true" responses via tacting, Assessment 2 showed even higher number of "true" scores (50%), implying Mr. Moe possibly (a) knew more information than evoked during Baseline and Assessment 1, (b) required tact responses to precede intraverbal responses to accurately explain the inquiry, or (c) simply the repetitive exposure to similar pictures over three trials evoked cumulatively more answers. Barring these procedural logistics, assessment employing stimulus selection and topographically based behaviors yielded a more representative sample of Mr. Moe's pool of verbal responses that defined competency to stand trial.

*Repeat evaluations of competency to stand trial and "competency school."* Assessment conclusions that Mr. Moe failed the test of competency to stand trial agreed with three previous psychological evaluations conducted by the state Forensic Center to determine competency. This consensus prompted the judge to order Mr. Moe held over in a prison facility segregated from the general population, and around other detainees of failed competency exams to undergo "competency school." Competency school varies among states and frequently is adjunctive with the defendant placed on a cocktail of psychotropic (frequently antipsychotic) medications. "School" entails systematic and hierarchal exposure to lesson plans teaching different components of court and how to retain and verbalize these components. The Slater method, for example (Wall & Christopher, 2012; Wall, Krupp, & Guilmette, 2003), used mostly with individuals with intellectual disabilities, consists of five modules taught over a span of several weeks either one-on-one or in group settings.

Other competence restoration models (Johnson & Candilis, 2015) incorporate multi-media training in structured group therapies conducted one or twice weekly, using psychologists or paraprofessionals as instructors. Case vignettes drawn from the media are selected for discussion including iconic movies (e.g., *My Cousin Vinnie)* depicting courtroom etiquette or simpler protocols. Multiple episodes of *Law and Order* also are facilitators prompting discussion about relevant courtroom procedure. To help build sustainable repertoires, facilitators (trainers) use word association and acronyms symbolically representing different courtroom components for later retrieval when the defendants are subsequently re-tested. Measured outcomes of these restoration programs, not surprisingly, show impressively high percentages

(32%–60%) of incumbent defendants who regain ample knowledge and verbal articulation about the courtroom process.

While restoration programs appear outwardly effective, and are invaluable as the gateway to a constitutionally fair trial for prisoners, their underlying pedagogy presupposes two mentalistic premises. First is that prisoners deemed incompetent previously had this competence *at some time in their lives* and need a refresher or revitalization course to regenerate the skills. That is, they could be competent once psychotropic medications controlled their manifested psychotic or other psychiatric symptoms preventing accurate "competent" answers. Second, that inculcation of skills from multi-media or from psychoeducational groups can properly develop a conceptual and practical understanding of complex skills that will immediately carry over to the courtroom or other judicially-significant venues. Presumption of these two premises tips raises the legendary debate between *knowing and demonstrating (behaviors)*. Knowing, that is, a state of verbalizing statements about some information, is somehow epistemologically more important than just demonstrating the behavior one talks about. In behavioral terms, debate is less about the elite caliber or dimensions of knowledge as it is about the accuracy of behavior and conditions under which it occurs. Focus is more molecular in breaking down behavior along a continuum from its development (i.e., skill acquisition) to its permanency (mastery); the distinction is between *skill acquisition* and *skill mastery*. This very distinction in learning can be fundamental in appreciating the pitfalls of competence restoration training.

*Skill acquisition* describes a series of steps, often in a controlled environment, of systematically teaching a new or familiar response to a person encouraged by clear contingencies, such as antecedent stimuli cueing the response and then delivery of positive or negative reinforcers once the response (or approximations of it) occur. In competence restoration training, the discrete trials might entail a psychoeducational group exposed to a television court show or power-point discussion. Instructional prompts such as "okay, so who is the judge in this segment?" may engender several correct or near-correct answers for which the instructor either praises responders or grants them permission to return to subsequent classes. With each re-playing of the TV show, responders can refine the precision of their answers until its accuracy meets some criterion. Skill acquisition, in this respect, effectively *teaches a skill*. But the skill is not necessarily "stored" in the repertoire until the next steps of training commence with generalization and maintenance training. These steps build *skill mastery*.

*Skill mastery* requires two types of operant response training: Stimulus generalization and response generalization (Stokes & Baer, 1977). Stimulus generalization generally refers to responding identical or similar across different stimuli having variances of relevant properties as the original training (discriminative) stimulus. Defendants, for example, may point out who the judge is in several different episodes of *Law and Order*, but may describe the judge's role slightly differently in other episodes beyond the first TV episode under which training first occurred. Properties of the judge may vary by a different actor playing the part, or by the plot involving the judge in different roles.

Reponses generalization is usually more complex. Here, responses generated "spontaneously" or "concurrently" with the target response to the some training stimulus produce the same effect of reinforcement as the target response. The defendant who correctly answers the question, "who is the judge here?" not only accurately points out the judge, but might briefly segue to one or two more verbal statements about the judge in this TV episode.

"Yes this is the judge sitting here," begins the defendant who adds, "and he looks just like the judge I had at 45th District Court." The autoclitic verbal response (i.e., responding to his own verbal behavior) may or may not be as relevant as the target response but it *forms a concurrent or sequential (interdependent) strengthening pattern among verbal responses.* Inter-response (verbal) patterns may also be self-reinforcing and not need terminal reinforcers at the end of the response chain to maintain future frequency of the response connection (cf. Delprato, 1986; Delprato & McGlynn, 1988; Ray & Delprato, 1989). Over-statements about the judge, often referred to as *hyperbolic or tangential comments,* may not require or even be resistant to instructors' praise and reprimands. A further step involves increasing response and stimulus generalization under one set of stimulus conditions, or varied across many stimulus conditions, using errorless or "fluency" training (Binder, 1996). Here, instructional programming with multiple trials to boost correct answers can increase the speed and accuracy of target responses. Programming also involves a calculated engineering of the skills in naturalistic settings not only to install wider generalization, but also to install maintenance.

*Maintenance of generalized responses* is a facile process if done correctly. Properly implemented, the five steps nicely summarized by Cooper, Heron, and Heward (2013) include:

**(1)** Minimize the need for generalization as much as possible,
**(2)** Conduct generalization probes before, during, and after instruction,
**(3)** Involve significant others whenever possible,
**(4)** Promote generalized behavior change with the least intrusive, least costly tactics possible, and
**(5)** Contrive intervention tactics as needed to achieve important generalized outcomes.

In other words, skill maintenance involves fading out the anchors, prompts, cues, and other artificial reminders while blending the behavior more naturally into the fabric of social contingencies directly affecting the defendant's expected behavior in court. Remove the TV episodes, the psychoeducational classes, the sterile and methodically implanted discussion groups, and encourage displays of the target behavior more routinely and comfortably around the defendant's attorney or in the courtroom. When these skills mesh with the natural environment under subtle cues, relying more on self-statements (rule-governed behaviors) to evoke occurrence, the outcome effect is called *skill mastery.* For example, the author ran psychoeducational groups of recovering drug dealers in which he taught skills on self-cessation of "hustling" behaviors, or any collateral behaviors associated with the culture of drug dealing even when there was no drug trafficking present (Ruben, 2000). Examples include carrying around large sums of money, over-generosity to buy merchandise for friends, or sexual promiscuity. After several skill acquisition steps, training in response maintenance involved generalization of similar self-restraint behaviors in multiple work settings, rehabilitation agencies, and therapeutic settings outside of training.

However, two additional components added to maintenance management were *neurophysical functionality, and media of contact.* Neurophysical functionality refers to interoceptive, biological conditions within the organism (e.g., nervous system, musculo-skeletal, receptor system, etc.) either increasing or decreasing the conditioned establishing operations or other stimuli that set an occasion for target behaviors. For instance, drug dealers frequently are nocturnal due to their clientele coming at night. For them to realign their sleep-wake cycle to wakefulness during the daytime required adjustment and left them feeling tired, sluggish or even uncomfortable. When they were fatigued, they associated fatigue with weakness or vulnerability and consequently were resistant to implement the target behaviors of impulse control. . For recovering drug dealers who were victims of vehicular head trauma, for example, they may struggle with speech retrieval from left-sided damage to the dorsolateral prefrontal cortex (Broca's area).

For Mr. Moe, neurophysical functions include his adverse side-effects of antipsychotic (neuroleptic) medications, sleep deprivation or malnutrition from self-starvation (in prison), or non-malingering somatic complaints due to other nociceptive (real) underlying organic problems. On Seroquel or Zyprexa, for example, negative side effects of tremors, dry mouth, excessive salivation, and headaches may interfere with physical endurance and attention span in court. Drowsiness, a prominent adverse effect, may retard or distort his retrieval and delivery of coherent responses, mimicking symptoms of inebriety, over-sedation, or even mild catatonia. Further, neuroleptic suppression of amygdala functions within the limbic system may manifest in Mr. Moe as indifference, flattened affect, and depersonalization (e.g., Konradi, 2006). Mr. Moe's response capacity to respond effectively to his attorney, to the judge, or follow proceedings against him in court may be compromised by pharmacotherapy despite earlier evidence showing Mr. Moe mastered the skills of competency restoration training.

*Media of contact* (stimulation) refer to a function connecting a reacting person with stimuli. It is the mediator facilitating activation of behavior around certain cues even when the organism has a conditioned history responding to those cues. Examples include light, sound, touch, or any other communicative agency which permits the organism to interact effectively with surrounding stimuli (cf. Mahan, 1968; Smith, 2006). The media of contact, in the case of drug dealers, was not just darkness or lightness depending on the hour of the day. Temperature also played a significant role. Outside in the cool breeze, as temperatures drop at night, drug dealers could respond faster, more coherently, and practice the generalized skills taught in class. Under the daytime heat, drug dealers felt exhausted, behaviorally anemic, incapacitated, and forgot most of their behaviors.

Media of contact play an essential role in the integrative-field of the courtroom. Mr. Moe's answers to his attorney interdepend, for example, not just on understanding the technical legal language spelled out in the briefs, but also *hearing the legal language without auditory obstruction.* If the courtroom sound-system is broken, and unamplified volume of the defendant attorney's inquiry is hard to hear while Mr. Moe is testifying, his answers may be incorrect, delayed, or Mr. Moe may act odd and confused (superstitious behaviors). Likewise, another side-effect of neuroleptic drugs—photosensitivity—may already limit duration of visual alertness while Mr. Moe reads over notes written to him by his attorney during the trial. Add to his photosensitivity a dimly lit room or shadows cast at the defendant's table, disabling the media of contact (e.g., light), then Mr. Moe's attenuated reading is now made worse. With words on the page imperceptible, Mr. Moe neither can read the words written by his attorney, nor can he consult with his attorney regarding the context of the written words on the paper. Failure to consider the defective media of contact as variables interfering with Mr. Moe's court participation can seriously misrepresent Mr. Moe's competency to stand trial.

While these stages of skill generalization and maintenance seem a natural finale to skill learning, very few if any competency restoration programs include such components as transitional steps to the real world. Defendants indoctrinated with daily instruction on courtroom concepts, vignettes, didactics, and who do generalize responses *within the behavior segments of their confined prison unit or classroom*, may not carry over the repertoire of skills to the courtroom (cf. Morris & DeYoung, 2014; Mumley, Tillbrook, & Grisso, 2003).

## Conclusions about Mr. Moe's competency to stand trial

Mr. Moe was a prototype of a failed competency restoration program. He was evaluated for competency to stand trial over 5 times by the State Forensic Center, and four of the times the conclusions unanimously deemed him incompetent. Inter-reliability agreement was high on test measurements administered, between prison hospital forensic specialists, and even with the independent medical examiner. However, the judge ordered Mr. Moe into 8 months of competent restoration education coupled with his antipsychotic medications. After 8 months, a sixth competency evaluation at the Forensic Center opined the defendant was in excellent shape, had progressed miraculously through the education program, and was now an ideal candidate for adjudication.

On the day of the trial, no more than 10 min after the bailiff called court to order, the judge addressed Mr. Moe and asked if he felt better and was ready to proceed. Mr. Moe leaped out of his chair, jumped over the defendant table, and raced to the judge's podium, screaming hysterically, "I will kill all of you and you're the demon!" Astonished by this violent outburst, the judge immediately yelled to the bailiff to subdue Mr. Moe and without hesitation announced to the court, "This man is obviously incompetent to stand trial!"

## References

Arntzen, E., Halstadro, L. B., Bjerke, E., Wittner, K. J., & Kristiansen, A. (2014). On the sequential and concurrent presentation of trials establishing prerequisites for emergent relations. *The Behavior Analyst, 14*, 1–8.

Barow, K. E., Tiger, J. H., Slocum, S. K., & Miller, S. J. (2013). Comparing acquisition of exchange-based and signed mands with children with autism. *The Analysis of Behavior, 29*, 59–69.

Binder, C. (1996). Behavioral fluency: Evolution of a new paradigm. *The Behavior Analyst, 19*, 163–197.

Bonnie, R. J. (1992). The competence of criminal defendants: A theoretical reformulation. *Behavioral Sciences & the Law, 10*, 291–316.

Cenqher, M., Jones, E. H., & Fineup, D. M. (2014). The effects of presession attention on tacting. *Journal of Applied Behavior Analysis, 47*, 176–180.

Cooke, G. (1969). The court study unit: Patient characteristics and differences between patients judged competent and incompetent. *Journal of Clinical Psychology, 25*, 140–143.

Cooper, J. O., Heron, T. E., & Heward, W. L. (Eds.). (2013). *Applied behavior analysis* (2nd ed.). FL: Pearson.

Cross, T. P., Jones, L. M., Walsh, W. A., Simone, M., & Kolko, D. (2007). Child forensic interviewing in children's advocacy centers: Empirical data on a practice model. *Child Abuse & Neglect, 31*, 1031–1052.

Dahl, R. C. (2008). Science in the courtroom: Examining standards for litigation-based research. *Environmental Health Perspectives, 116*, 116–147.

Delprato, D. J. (1986). Response patterns. In H. W. Reese, & L. J. Parrott (Eds.), *Behavior science: Philosophical, methodological, and empirical advances* (pp. 61–113). Hillsdale, NJ: Lawrence Erlbaum Associates.

Delprato, D. J., & McGlynn, F. D. (1988). Interaction of response patterns and their implications for behavior therapy. *Journal of Behavior Therapy and Experimental Psychiatry, 19*, 199–205.

Dusky v. United States, 362 U.S. 402 (1960).

Favole, R. J. (1983). Mental disability in the American criminal process: A four issue survey. In J. Monahan, & H. J. Steadman (Eds.), *Mentally disordered offenders: Perspectives from law and social science* (pp. 247–295). New York: Plenum.

Grisso, T. (1986). *Evaluating competencies: Forensic assessments and instruments.* New York: Plenum.
Grisso, T., Appelbaum, P., Mulvey, E., & Fletcher, K. (1995). The MacArthur treatment competence study II: Measures of abilities related to competence to consent to treatment. *Law and Human Behavior, 19,* 127–148.
Johnson, N. R., & Candilis, P. J. (2015). Outpatient competence restoration: A model and outcomes. *World Journal of Psychiatry, 5,* 228–233.
Konradi, C. L. (2006). *Antipsychotic drug effects on limbic structures.* Washington, DC: National Institutes of Health. grant 1R01MH074000-01A1.
Lillenfeld, S.0. (2018). Pseudoscience in behavior therapy: Concurrences, confusions, and clarifications—response to Strosahl. *The Behavior Therapist, 41,* 273–280.
Lillenfeld, S. O., Lynn, S. K., & Lohr, J. M. (2014). *Science and pseudoscience in clinical psychology.* NY: Guilford Press.
Mackay, R. D. (2007). AAPL practice guidelines for the forensic psychiatric evaluation of competence to stand trial: An English legal perspective. *Psychiatry and the Law, 35,* 501–504.
Mahan, H. C. (1968). *The interactional psychology of J.R. Kantor: An introduction.* San Marcos, CA: Project Socrates Press.
Marchese, N. V., Carr, J. E., LeBlanc, L. A., Rosati, T. C., & Conroy, S. A. (2012). The effects of the question"What is this?" on tact-training outcomes of children with autism. *Journal of Applied Behavior Analysis, 45,* 539–547.
Michael, J. (1985). Two kinds of verbal behavior plus a possible third. *Annals of Verbal Behavior, 3,* 1–4.
Morris, D. R., & DeYoung, N. J. (2014). Long term competence restoration. *The Journal of the American Academy of Psychiatry and Law, 42,* 81–90.
Mossman, D., Noffsinger, S. G., & Ash, P. (2007). Practice guideline of the forensic psychiatric evaluation of competence to stand trial. *Journal of the American Academy of Psychiatry and Law, 35*(Suppl.). S3–72.
Mumley, D. L., Tillbrook, C. E., & Grisso, T. (2003). Five year research update (1996-2000): Evaluations for competence to stand trial (adjudicative competence). *Behavioral Sciences & the Law, 21,* 329–350.
O'Shaughnessy, R. J. (2007). AAPL practice guideline for the forensic psychiatric evaluation of competence to stand trial: A Canadian legal perspective. *Psychiatry and the Law, 35,* 505–508.
Petursdottir, A., & Carr, J. E. (2011). A review of recommendations for sequencing receptive and expressive language instruction. *Journal of Applied Behavior Analysis, 44,* 859–876.
Polson, A. D., & Parsons, J. A. (2000). Selection based versus topography-based responding: An important distinction for stimulus equivalence? *The Analysis of Verbal Behavior, 17,* 105–128.
Ray, R., & Delprato, D. J. (1989). Behavioral systems analysis: Methodological strategies and tactics. *Behavioral Science, 34,* 81–127.
Rogers, R., & Johansoon-Love, J. (2009). Evaluating competency to stand trial with evidence-based practice. *The Journal of American Academy of Psychiatric and Law, 37,* 450–460.
Rogers, R., Tillbrook, C. E., & Sewell, K. W. (2004). *Evaluation of Competency to stand trial-revised (ECST-R) and professional manual.* Odessa, FL: Psychological Assessment Resources.
Ruben, D. H. (2000). Sensitizing drug dealers to victim impact using mandatory psychoeducation. *Offender Program Reports, 3,* 68.
Ruben, D. H. (2014). *Tantrum Survival Kit: The definitive guide to tantrum management.* Denver, CO: Outskirts Press.
Skeem, J. L., & Golding, S. G. (1998). Community examiners' evaluations of competence to stand trial: Common problems and suggestions for improvement. *Professional Psychology: Research and Practice, 29,* 357–367.
Skeem, J. L., Golding, S. L., Cohn, N. B., & Berge, G. (1998). Logic and reliability of evaluations of competence to stand trial. *Law and Human Behavior, 22,* 519–548.
Smith, N. W. (2006). The interbehavioral field. In B. D. Midgley, & E. K. Morris (Eds.), *Modern Perspective on J.R. Kantor and interbehaviorism* (pp. 87–110). Reno, NV: Context Press.
Stokes, T. F., & Baer, D. M. (1977). The implicit technology of generalization. *Journal of Applied Behavior Analysis, 10,* 349–367.
Sundberg, C. T., & Sundberg, M. L. (1990). Comparing topography-based verbal behavior with stimulus selection based verbal behavior. *Annals of Verbal Behavior, 8,* 31–41.
Wall, B. W., & Christopher, P. P. (2012). A training program for defendants with intellectual disabilities who are found incompetent to stand trials. *The Journal of the American Academy of Psychiatry and the Law, 40,* 366–373.
Wall, B. W., Krupp, B. H., & Guilmette, T. (2003). Restoration of competency to stand trial: A training program for persons with mental retardation. *Journal of the American Academy of Psychiatry and the Law, 31,* 189–201.
Wraikat, R., Sundberg, C. T., & Michael, J. (1991). Topography-based and selection based verbal behavior: A further comparison. *Annals of Verbal Behavior, 9,* 1–7.

CHAPTER

# 8

# Social contingencies potentiating vandalism and violence

Vandalism defined as malicious destruction of property represents a growing threat to schools, municipalities, parks, and neighborhoods. Over the past two decades, concerns about school violence, weapons, drugs, and gangs have eclipsed about diverse vandalism being outcomes of urban decay and unregulated acts of youth misconduct (Cohen, 1973; Goldstein, 1996; Koch, 1975). Of the reported 99,000 separate incidents of school vandalism, in particular, repeated themes or motivators underlying the etiology of such vandalism acts seem assignable into six categories:

1. *Acquisitive Vandalism.* This is property defacement or destruction to obtain property or money.
2. *Tactical Vandalism.* These acts of vandalism are to accomplish goals such as getting school canceled.
3. *Ideological Vandalism.* These acts orient around a social or political purpose or massage, such as protesting school or community rules.
4. *Vindictive Vandalism.* These acts deliberately are retaliatory for prior offensive acts for which civil or policing solutions were ineffective, such as setting fire to the school or building.
5. *Play Vandalism.* This act occurs when youth intentionally damage property during the course of innocent play, such as breaking a school or residential window with a baseball during batting practice during an innocuous baseball game.
6. *Malicious Vandalism.* These acts are intentional to express rage or frustration, mostly with a vicious intent and resemble the category of vindictive vandalism.

In aggregate, vandalism threatens any building or property vulnerably exposed without security monitoring and for which earlier vandalism was successful on the premises. In efforts to prevent school vandalism, in particular, Mayer, Butterworth, Nafpaktitis and Azaraff (1983) implemented a behaviorally-based educational series of in-school talks and organized a school-watch (monitoring team). The staff development model used appeared feasible and economical but lacked the generality of being used in multiple schools or across other types of non-school settings. Following on their coat-tails, a behavioral model goes beyond the

*Behavioral Forensics*
https://doi.org/10.1016/B978-0-12-819805-6.00008-7

establishment and dissemination of vandalism-watch committees. It is also offers an operational redefinition of vandalism under the more descriptive rubric of *property destruction*. Here, vandalism or *property destruction* is explained as:

1. Damaging personal or public property (e.g., breaking an object into two or more pieces, using an object to break other objects, ripping objects or parts of objects from walls, floors or furniture, and denting cars, objects, and walls.
2. Defacement of any object with writing, coloring, indelible ink, chalk, or stain.

This topographical definition of behavior pertains to many circumstances under which property destruction occurs. Iwata, Dorsey, Silfer, Bauman & Richman (1994; Iwata et al., 1994; cf. Fisher, Adelinis, Thompson, Worsdell, & Zarcone, 1998) identified common variables in a functional or causal analysis of property destruction. While their functional description originally pertained to self-reinforcement maintenance of self-injurious behaviors, it also applied to other collateral aberrant behaviors during episodes of self-injurious behaviors. They suggested property destruction was perpetuated or maintained by (a) positive reinforcement in the form of contingent attention, (b) negative reinforcement in the form of avoidance or escape from nonpreferred tasks (homework, chores, etc.), and (c) the sensory stimulation produced by the destructive act. Inherently included in their operational analysis is Michael's (1993) motivating operations, which explains what triggers evoke acts of destruction. In other words, a child deprived of attention or upset by unfulfilled promises constitutes a conditioned motivating operation under which the child is more probable to commit property destruction (vandalism) than if all of his needs are satisfied. By analogy, in performing a behavior forensic analysis of property destruction (vandalism), clinical investigation also examines the propensity of the offender's (a) attention-seeking ratio of reinforcement, (b) manipulation of the negative reinforcement contingencies to avoid or escape adverse consequences, (c) the sensory or other automatic reinforcement generated by frequency or intensity of the destructive act, and (d) motivating operations underlying the high or low probability of vandalism occurrence. In addition, when ecologically considering the wider psychological field, two further variables enter the operational definition: (e) the response-response interactions, and (f) stimulus-stimulus interactions, all part of the interbehavioral mix (or matrices).

Using this operational playbook for analysis of criminal behavior, the following case study describes a first-time offender of vandalism involving spray painting profanities on neighborhood garage doors. A court-ordered psychological evaluation of the offender was to determine his risk of offense recidivism and implications for other violent or aggressive behaviors against people or property.

## Case of Samantha

Samantha is the fictitious name for a 17 year old female Caucasian residing half time at her biological mother's house and half-time at her biological father and stepmother's house. She also works part-time at local restaurants. She denied receiving any written or verbal reprimands for her attendance, quality and rate of performance, customer relations, relations with coworkers and supervisor, violence or anger on the job, positive drug screening, or rule compliance with the restaurant.

## Education

She is a full-time senior at a local high school expecting to graduate with a diploma in June. She denied any history of undergoing multidisciplinary testing to qualify for an IEP or 504 plan. In regular courses, she earned average to low average grades (B's to C's), including routinely completing and submitting her homework, test-studying, and conferences after school with teachers to remedy incorrect school work. Since middle school, extracurricular activities included competitive team softball, basketball, and track. Outside of school, her athletic acumen earned her a ranked position on traveling basketball teams. She also partook in church youth groups, girl-scouts, and 4-H, raising and showing animals. Her aspiration was to advance after high school to community college on a basketball scholarship and major in business. She denied any experiences of being bullied in school. She denied provocation of in-school fights. She denied interception of bullies perceived as bothering victims. She denied gang membership or association with violent friends. She denied bringing contraband (weapons, drugs) to school. She denied packing or carrying any weapons. She denied incurring any suspensions, detentions, or expulsions. She denied fascination in animal cruelty or fire-starting. She denied any prior juvenile or adult criminal offenses beside the current arrest. She denied receiving any outpatient or resident mental health or substance abuse treatment. She denied any history of prescription to psychotropic medications.

## Substance abuse

Samantha first experimented recreationally with alcohol at age 16. She drank occasionally on weekends, lately advancing to three weekends per month. Quantity varies from 6 to 7 beers over a 4 h period of time. With her estimated BMI of 18.4 (normal range), and 7 beers ingested over 4 h, her calculated BAC would approximate 0.12, compared to the Michigan Driving limit of BAC 0.08. In other words, she likely experienced ample impairment in psychomotor ability or judgment impacting her actions or decisions. She also denied post-drinking side effects of headaches, hangovers, blackouts, or any toxicity effects. Absence of these "warning signs" frequently signals the body's higher tolerance (tissue absorption) of alcohol, predictive of rapid development (within 6 months to 1 year) of alcohol (physical) dependence. Moreover, she reported biphasic effects while drinking. Meaning, she first experienced elevation in disinhibition or courage enabling more atypically tenacious, flirtatious, and non-conventional behaviors. By her fifth or sixth beer, energy subsides to a hypnotic-sedative like effect resembling body fatigue (or numbness). For individuals suffering mild social anxiety, this latter change in Biphasic effects is self-medicative to handle stress situations. Her last drink was two weeks ago. Samantha also first experimented with cannabis at age 16. She began to routinely smoke 1–2 g per week (1/2 joint every two days) scattered over two years. She reportedly discontinued smoking cannabis a year ago. Samantha denied use or abuse of any other licit or illicit (controlled) substances. She denied suffering any major vehicular or other accidents causing head injury. She only underwent surgery for wisdom teeth removal, without any post-operative complications with anesthesia or pain medication withdrawal. She denied having CVAs, TIAs, sleep apnea, seizures, high fevers, or neurotoxin exposure. She denied having any known medical conditions.

## Interpersonally

Samantha denied any history of sexual victimization. She was first voluntarily sexual at age 16. She assured she had only one heterosexual partner, about whom she felt romantic interest. She denied fascination or activity with casual sexual relations, or overuse of pornography. She denied any interpersonal difficulties with talking, sharing, or asserting herself around males or females. She perceived herself as popular, likable, and participatory within her peer mainstream, and completely comfortable with any peer rejection. As intimated above, she often rose to sports leadership positions, earning the respect and idolism of other teammates.

## Developmentally

Samantha is the older of two children raised by dually employed parents divorced when Samantha turned 7 years old. Her father remarried to a stepmother. Her father's temper, at times, may flare but Samantha denied he abused her verbally or physically. She denied exposure to any domestic violence or family alcohol or drug abuse; she also denied childhood or adolescent exposure to use of scatological ethnic or racial slurs (or microaggressions). Her mother was more nurturing and sensitive to her emotive issues. Since pre-adolescence, Samantha and her sibling rotated alternating weeks to live at each parents' house under the shared custodial agreement. In retrospect, Samantha denied her parents' action contributed to her exploratory drinking behavior or at-risk actions responsible for the criminal offense.

## The alleged crime of vandalism

The crime in question, occurring over the span of one evening, involved an entourage of four friends, headed by a more precocious friend, fictitiously named "Tara." Tara and her entourage were intoxicated after each consumed 6 to 7 beers for several hours, and were walking aimlessly in a residential subdivision. Tara apparently stole a spray can of red paint from somebody's garage and proceeded to spray racial slurs on random residential household garages. Owners of the household garages were strangers to Tara, not targeted for retribution or in way deserving of the erratic racial graffiti written on their garages. Samantha was a bystander witnessing the spraying of graffiti but never interceded, expressed objection, or left the crime scene in protest of the illegal behaviors. Instead, Samantha retrospectively explained her optics in watching the crime unfold as "surrealistic or unreal, almost movie-like." She felt emotionally disconnected from the ongoing crime, although she fully realized she was present during commission of the crime. She then picked up the spray can and wrote her own racial slurs on garage doors and windows. She even painted an effigy depicting a noose around a human neck, with vitriolic and derogatory language written underneath the sordid picture. Police arrested Samantha with paint on her hands and her aggressively resisting arrest. The next day in jail, Samantha's more sobering account emphasized how incredibly contradictory her written ethnophaulisms were with her "normal" behavior of moral liberalism, respect for people's rights, and the countless marches and rallies she previously volunteered for under the banner of supporting "minority issues."

# Results of the behavioral forensic evaluation

## General observations

Samantha arrived punctually for her appointment accompanied. She greeted the examiner affably and kindly answered pre-interview questions. She consented to the proposed testing process. Attire was clean, hygienic, seasonally appropriate, and properly fitting. She ambulated independently with a normal gait showing no signs of psychomotor disturbance. Sensorium was intact. She sat comfortably in the couch, lying back in the cushions. She made no abrupt gestural or postural movements. Attention span and physical endurance were strong. Eye contact remained direct and continuous. She inserted questions, statements, and humor at appropriate intervals. Affect was energetic, alert, upbeat, elevated, spontaneous, fluid, and dynamic. No anger, resistance, opposition, or psychosis seen. No mood oscillations observed from aggression to anxiety. No indicators of hyperactivity, impulsivity, or distractibility. She showed no signs of overmedication, withdrawal, or intoxication symptoms. She made no statements about suicide or homicide; he denied past suicidal or para-suicidal ideations or plans for self-harm. She delineated right from wrong, reality from fantasy, and truth from falsehood. Speech flowed evenly, audibly, and fluently, in complete sentences. Prosody was rhythmic, melodic. Speech content consisted of vocabulary and syntax commensurate with his stated educational level. Ideation showed coherence, rationality, and orientation x 3.

On projective testing, average abstractive abilities suggested ample facility for problem solving and perceptual reasoning. She tracked and discriminated visual stimuli, and could reconstruct ideas from visual memory. She sorted relevant from irrelevant details. She could conceptualize simple and complex social situations. Analytical reasoning was strong in using deductive and inductive logic to convert general information into meaningful or symbolic order. Likewise, interpretive thinking showed concrete grasp of the bigger picture. She provided a sequential order of facts and commented on the legal, social, moral, ethical, and financial ramifications of her current vandalism offense. Insight was low average. She showed moderate introspection. She showed remorse for his misjudgment and overuse of alcohol; however, she did not acknowledge a possible "drinking problem." Otherwise, judgment appeared prudent, conservative, and judicious.

On organizational indices, scores on content and form suggested average adherence to structure. Such scores frequently correlate with average social conformers (i.e., low chance of rebelliousness, authority defiance). She made common and conventional blot responses. She showed no structural abnormalities: neither perseveration, confabulation nor evasiveness. Visuo-spatial skills appeared strong in grouping objects together by shared properties of symmetry, angularity, and contiguity. Affective Ratio scores were high, suggesting his strong need for physical affection and compliments On the HTP, scores on were unremarkable. On the TAT, a measure of behavioral and emotional patterns, recurrent themes emerged about altruism, trust and compassion. Immediate recall, short-term (working) memory and long-term (implicit, explicit) memory all were intact. Samantha showed no impairment in procedural, semantic, and episodic memory. Further, she showed no impediments in her executive cognitive (prefrontal dorsolateral cortex) functions. Overall her disposition was cheerful, sensitive, talkative, curious, polite, respectful, and fully cooperative during the entire clinical interview and testing protocol.

## Psychopathology

First, her test profile was valid, reliable, and interpretable. Second, on validity scales of the MMPI-2-RF (and ACOA Behavior Profile), low scores depicted a veridical (reliable) reporter. She showed neither tendencies for under-reporting or over-reporting. She presented an objectively balanced version of his positive and negative traits, despite over-moralizing her actions as healthy, functional, and herself as incapable of rebellious, oppositional, or recalcitrant behaviors. She chronicled a sequence of events comporting with the facts outlined in the Police (arresting) report. Overall her testimony appeared acceptable.

Third, on the Higher-Order scales, elevation in THD profiled an internalizer. She withholds her thoughts, opinions, frustrations, and most emotions. She stores it inconspicuously within herself and expects she will work through any difficulties without imposing on other people. She dislikes bothering or upsetting her family or friends with her problems, and consequentially takes pride in managing her own affairs. However, since she lacks the resourcefulness to always solve a problem or confront the right people, Samantha simmers with her frustrations, teetering on explosive anger at any time. On the Restructured Clinical scale, elevated RC6 and RC8 refers to her anticipatory fears of thinking people are negatively judgmental; she may obsess over the image they have of her and relieve anxiety over that negative image by conformist actions. Likewise, on the ANP and ACT codes, higher scores suggested restrained anger over minor problems. However, when inebriated, Samantha gets a furlough from self-restraint. She builds courage, is uninhibited, and may act tenaciously and recklessly in total contradiction with her behavior when sober.

Fourth, on the Psy-5 scale, moderately elevated AGGR-r scales also suggested susceptibility to reactive aggression. She is not outwardly an angry person. She works diligently to portray a happy-go-lucky, people-pleasing, and energetic disposition amiable to most people. She censors her frustration and instead is like a chameleon who blends into most social contexts undetected or without incident. Her flexibility and adaptability in most situations mean she may sheepishly (unconditionally) abide by the group decision. On the evening of the offense, watching the spray-painting of houses, for example, Samantha reported she "sort of knew it was wrong what Tara was doing, but it didn't feel real." That Samantha was intoxicated blunting her perception or judgment was one thing; the more important issue was Samantha's pre-drinking knowledge about Tara's history of rebellious and antisocial behaviors and the dire risks of associating with her (i.e., accused of being an accomplice to a crime).

Fifth, testing and clinical interview data showed a four year progressive use of alcohol. Samantha does not regard her drinking as uncontrollable or contributory to maljudgment; she did not acknowledge her alcohol use rose to a level of public nuisance and police intervention.

## Interbehavioral matrix

Assessment of isolated and cumulative repertories of pre-criminal and criminal behaviors begins with defining behavior by its functional effects. Two responses occurring in sequence may be topographically contiguous but also blend into each other or *morph*. This response morphology has an additive or cumulative effect, so that future occurrences of both response units blended together are larger, more intense, or produce same or different consequences than when the responses are separate units. Hixson (2004) elucidated this complex response morphology in operant conditioning by distinguishing between *cumulative-hierarchical learning* and *behavioral cusps*. Cumulative-hierarchical learning, first conceptually pioneered by Staats (1968) as the *basic behavioral repertoire*, involves higher levels of conditioning. A basic repertoire is a function of many responses aggregated or morphed previously from the continuum of developmental experiences. One skill compiles onto the next, forming more diverse skills enabled by pre-existing skills. A 2-year old stands on his feet after months of trial and error of crawling and lifting himself erect with his hands holding onto a table. The balance gained form standing was dependent on repetitively lifting, falling down, and standing back up again. Standing behavior is the cumulative effect of multilevel skill practice, with each segment of responses producing reinforcement or punishment consequences that shape the skills. Staats' paradigm for this type of learning, *psychological behaviorism* (1975), characterized this morphology of intra-response and inter-response interaction in child and adult behavior segments. In this way, compound behavior in a current situation is a product of previously integrated simpler response and can function in evoking more advanced (multiple) contingencies The standing child—a product of past crawling and self-lifting—can access parental attention faster and reach for his toys more accessibly on the table, thereby abating his motivating operation of wanting the toys. Height of standing also produces new consequences such as tipping over water glasses on the table, or throwing off food dishes onto the floor.

The standing response of a child able to reach taller surfaces *also provides an occasion of bringing this child into contact with new contingencies with which to further augment the behavior repertoire.* This response-enabling function that increases new causal links to consequences was characterized by Rosales-Ruiz and Baer (1997) as a *behavioral cusp*. Behavioral cusps may take several forms as enablers or facilitators of new behavior learning. Imitation, for example, is a behavior cusp because it permits rapid learning of new responses. Reading aloud, for example, is another behavior cusp since allow for decoding (reading) comprehension. Naming repertoires (e.g., "look at that fish!") are behavioral cusps insofar as the child's mand evokes attention (reinforcement) mediated by adults ("yes that is a fish!)? In short, behavior cusps serve a dual purpose. First, they are sub-units of a larger response aggregate formed from previously morphed response experiences. Second, they increase accessibility to contingencies from which new responses and new response cusps develop (cf. Bosch & Fuqua, 2001).

Since behavior cusps reach specific and broad new consequences, they operate on motivation to generate these new contingencies. Cusps function to reduce (or satisfy) drive or motivating variables in producing behavior either that accesses reinforcers or averts punishers. The drive-goal purpose of the cusp lies in its unique response qualities consisting of (a) an excitatory potential, (b) habit strength, (c) high intensity or strength of drive (MO), and (d) media of contact. All four components are codas to Clark Hull's quantifiable formula to explain and predict response proclivity due to *drive-stimulus reduction* (1943). In Clark's theory, the organization of behavior was more about complex associations between stimuli and responses and less about the evocative or causal effects of stimuli on responses, the latter explored more technically by Skinner (1938). Unlike Hull's theory, causal properties of stimuli make the behavior cusp more effective. For example, the child is only likely to stand up from a sitting or crawling position if (a) a stimulus opportunity exists arousing curiosity and exploratory responses (i.e., excitatory potential), (b) the musculo-skeletal strength and prior behavior trials exist for the child to self-propel upward to stand (habit strength), (c) a motivating operation (MO) exists increasing the probability of response activation at that moment versus at another moment, and (d) enough light exists to see the motivator (i.e., cookie on the table).

Framing the act of vandalism (i.e., property destruction) according to conceptualizations of cumulative hierarchal learning and behavior cusps first requires chronicling the psychological events into behavioral segments. In the first behavioral segment (BS1), the entourage including Samantha were in a bar or somebody's house consuming alcohol for 4–5 h. In the second behavior segment (BS2), the entourage ambled onto a neighborhood street and watched Tara spray paint a residential garage. The third behavior segment (BS3) involved spraying the cans of paint on residential garages. Response events interacted with stimulus events during each of the behavior segment as outlined below:

BS1*Stimulus events (S1)*: Two bars, Tara's house.

*Response events (R1):* Drinking in each setting totaling 4–5 h. Motivating operations abated after reaching the satiation threshold from alcohol.

*Stimulus-organism interactions (S ↔ O)*: Reinforcement from peer interaction and flirtation at bar.

BS2 *Stimulus events (S2)*: Neighborhood street at night.

*Response events (R2):* Walk through the neighborhood; observe at close range Tana go into garage, get spray paint, and spray graffiti on the residential garage.

*Stimulus-organism interactions (S ↔ O)* Response disinhibition (due to alcohol) after from watching Tana spray; then Samantha takes spray-can to imitate Tana's behavior.

BS3 Stimulus *events (S3)*: Neighborhood street at night, semi-lit residential homes from street lights.

*Response events (R3):* Samantha (and Tana or others) writing racial slurs and drawing effigies with spray paint on garages.

*Stimulus-organism interactions (S ↔ O):* Reciprocal laughter shared between Tara, Samantha and entourage; visual stimulus (feedback) of graffiti shaping more spray painting; speed of spray painting one house abates one motivational operator and sets an occasion for another motivational operator to spray a second house. This response pattern proceeds across several houses.

The response hierarchy or *cumulatory responses* of Samantha occurring in all three behavior segments consist of (1) drinking at bars or Tara's house, (2) walking into the neighborhood, (3) watching Tara spray paint, (4) imitating Tara's spray painting, and (5) Samantha's self-reinforcement and response generalization of spray painting other garages. Each response builds incrementally from one another in a stair-step order, such that two or more interdependent responses advance upward into a hierarchy of more behavior complexity (see Fig. 8.1 below). Fig. 8.1 depicts two illustrations. The first is a two-step riser labeled "Response Interaction." Each level or riser represents a behavior segment. Three-dimensional panels shown on the riser include the base labeled Stimulus (S1), the side panel labeled Response (R1), and the flat surface of the step labeled (S ↔ O). Seamless progression from one behavior segment to the next behavior segment schematically appears by moving up to the next three-dimensional step. Here, additive responses (R1 + R2) and additive stimuli (S1 + S2), both bilaterally interacting (S ↔ O), suggest the behaver develops more complex repertoires under the control of more complex stimuli. For example, by the third successive segment (R1 + R2+, R3), Samantha was inebriated, already on the neighborhood street watching Tana spray paint, and imitated Tana's spray painting the garages.

Responses in the hierarchal pattern flow in a consistent and predictable sequence, from beginning to end, and the end or terminal response in each behavior segment is likely the *behavior cusp. The last response in any behavior segment potentiates the greatest impact on changing the environment in the next behavior segment.* For example, Samantha's drinking in the bar or at Tara's house produced the first of two biphasic effects, of feeling energy and uninhibited. Her ethanol-induced "liquid courage" generated the behavior cusp; this cusp made Samantha more likely to engage in (had higher motivating operation for) risk behavior (watching and imitating Tara). Samantha's terminal response in segment 2 (BS2), of imitating Tara and spraying graffiti on residential garages, produced another behavior cusp. This cusp enabled access to Tara and the entourage laughing at Samantha (social reinforcement), and for Samantha to laugh at herself (self-reinforcement). The series of responses (and cusps) occurred under a fluid transaction of cumulatory stimulus conditions. Stimuli consisted of alcohol saturation in Samantha's bloodstream (S1), the neighborhood street at night (S2), and watching Tana spray-painting the residential garages (S3). The totality or stimulus aggregate effect (S1 + S2 + S3) proportionally increased Samantha's likelihood or proclivity to engage in criminal spray painting.

The second illustration depicted in Fig. 8.1 is a three-dimensional cube showing the cumulatory function of responses and stimuli. Stimuli and responses not only compound from pre-existing stimuli and responses from earlier behavior segments, these interactions are multilinear and broad. In behavior segment 3 (BS3), Samantha's drinking (R1) interacts both with other responses (R1 + R2 +, R3), and with *any or all of the stimulus combinations* (S1 + S2 +, S3). Her

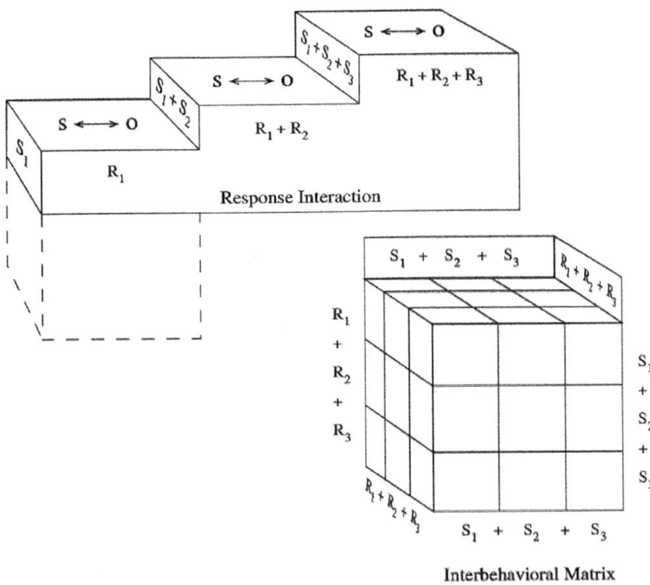


**FIG. 8.1** Cumulatory response and stimulus interactions.

drinking affects how alert or non-alert she is walking in the neighborhood; her drinking, combined with walking in the neighborhood, affects how rapidly or wakeful she is to copy Tana's behavior and spray paint other garages. Under different circumstances, for example, if Samantha's biphasic alcohol effects were drowsiness and lethargy in the first behavior segment, she might be more inclined leave the entourage and go home. Samantha's behavior cusps would have accessed a different set of stimulus conditions and reduced her chances of criminal behavior.

Analysis of Samantha's vandalism behavior through the interbehavioral matrix invites a profoundly different perspective on her criminal intentionality and propensity for future crimes. Traditional analysis of personality typology showed her avoidant personality was a low predictor for crime, but her uncontrolled social drinking was a higher predictor for reckless behaviors. By contrast, a behavior forensic analysis focused on unique response and stimulus conditions influencing Samantha's transaction over a short period of time. The behavioral analysis was less decisive about Samantha's guilt or innocence, unless that is the reason for the psychological evaluation. More frequently the court request is after criminal conviction and concerned with the question, *will she do it again?* By carefully configuring the learning hierarchy and functionality of cusps relevant in her case, conclusions about criminal behavior are more scientifically logical, reliable, socially valid, and offer a better prediction.

## References


Bosch, S., & Fuqua, R. W. (2001). Behavioral cusps: A model for selecting target behavior. *Journal of Applied Behavior Analysis, 34*, 123–125.

Cohen, S. (1973). In C. Ward (Ed.), *Property destruction: Motives and meaning* (pp. 23–53). London: Architectural Press.

Fisher, W. W., Adelinis, J. D., Thompson, R. H., Worsdell, A. S., & Zarcone, J. R. (1998). Functional analysis and treatment of destructive behavior maintained by termination of "don't" (and symmetrical "do") requests. *Journal of Applied Behavior Analysis, 31*, 339–356.

Goldstein, A. (1996). *The psychology of vandalism*. NY: Plenum Press.

Hixson, M. D. (2004). Behavioral cusps, basic behavioral repertoires, and cumulative-hierarchical learning. *The Psychological Record, 54*, 387–403.

Hull, C. L. (1943). *Principles of behavior*. NY: Appleton-Century-Crofts.

Iwata, B. A. (1994). Functional analysis methodology: Some closing comments. *Journal of Applied Behavior Analysis, 27*, 413–418.

Iwata, B. A., Pace, G. M., Dorsey, M. F., Zarcone, J. R., Vollmer, T. R., Smith, R. G., et al. (1994). The functions of self-injurious behavior: An experimental epidemiological analysis. *Journal of Applied Behavior Analysis, 27*, 215–240.

Koch, E. L. (1975). School vandalism and strategies of social control. *Urban Education, 1*, 54–72.

Mayer, G. R., Butterworth, T., Nefpakitis, M., & Sulzer-Azaroff, B. (1983). Preventing school vandalism and improving discipline: A three-year study. *Journal of Applied Behavior Analysis, 16*, 355–369.

Michael, J. (1993). Establishing operations. *The Behavior Analyst, 16*, 191–206.

Rosales-Ruiz, J., & Baer, D. M. (1997). Behavioral cusps: A developmental and behavioral concept for behavior analysis. *Journal of Applied Behavior Analysis, 30*, 533–544.

Skinner, B. F. (1938). *The behavior of organisms: An experimental analysis*. NY: Appleton-Century.

Staats, A. W. (1968). *Learning, language, and cognition*. NY: Holt, Rinehart & Watson.

Staats, A. W. (1975). *Social behaviorism*. Homewood, IL: Dorsey.

CHAPTER

# 9

# Insularity effects of self-reinforcement under concurrent variable interval punishment schedules in the assessment of repeated embezzlement

Identity and money theft top the highest percentage of economic crimes impacting the personal and business communities. In social networking, for instance, identify theft occurs multiple times per day, prompting action by, for example, Mark Zuckerberg–Chief Executive of Facebook, Instagram, WhatsApp, and Messenger—to install private and encrypted communication replacing public posts. Likewise, in private and public sector business, experts called identity-theft detectives are the superheroes hired to patrol illicit activity by staff and to swiftly intervene before cash shortages destroy the business. Awareness they bring to employment settings is to detect red-flags of money theft-or *embezzlement*. Embezzlement it the theft of money or property by a person trusted with those assets. Fraudulent activity can occurs in a number of ways. Deceptive employees can delete ledger entries, endorse cash-payable checks, forge payroll checks, modify payroll, misappropriate credit cards, and use signature stamps without authorization. Crimes aimed to selfishly steal other people's hard-earned money are *white-collar crimes*. Since sociologist Edward Sutherland coined it more than fifty-years ago (Green, 1993; Riemer, 1941; Sutherland, 1949), *white-collar* money theft stereotypically associated with male-dominated perpetrators, although lately crime statistics showed a gender transfer to more women embezzlers (Davies, 2008; FBI, 2009; Zeitz, 1981).

When women represent two-thirds of the offenders charged with embezzlement, questions intuitively arise why they have easier accessibility to treasuries or are overlooked as suspicious. One theory is that women earn trust because of their presumed caretaker qualities. Their sensitivity, compassion, or even "maternal" instincts supposedly are unimpeachable traits admired by employers who reward them with money-access privileges. Feminists may object to this blatant microaggression and claim any person-male or female—can be avaricious (Coleman, 2002; Cressey, 1973). But who the offender is, and how he or she

Behavioral Forensics
https://doi.org/10.1016/B978-0-12-819805-6.00009-9

executes the nearly-perfect crime is less a concern for forensic evaluators as *why the crime occurs and whether reasonable risks exist to repeat the crime elsewhere.*

For starters, embezzlement represents a complex constellation of responses involving *stealing*. Behavioral approaches to assessment and treatment of stealing have been prolific and highly effective (Burth, 1987; Reid & Patterson, 1976). Target responses of boundary violations and removal of unauthorized property received varying applications of time out, overcorrection, response cost, response satiation, or stimulus control interventions (e.g., Azrin & Wesolowski, 1974; Henderson, 1981; Rosen & Rosen, 1983). Procedurally, strategies either served to decrease unwanted behavior (stealing) or increase desirable behavior (maintain one's own belongings). However, a variable rarely modified in the procedure is schedule of punishment delivery. Punishment procedures used to discourage or suppress stealing commonly are administered on a fixed-ratio or contingent basis. That is, time-out begins immediately (contingently) after each occurrence (continuous) of stealing. Staggering the delivery, where the punisher (time-out, response cost, etc.) follows a specific number of thefts (fixed ratio), variable number of theft (variable ration) or fixed or variable amount of time passing after the theft (fixed or variable interval), would seem counterproductive. Delayed consequences (e.g., variable ratio or variable interval schedules), particularly punishers, seem ineffective as deterrents since the response of stealing possibly might receive reinforcement closer in time (proximal) to the stealing behavior. This makes stealing resistant to the punishment.

For example, Jack stole his brother's $20 bill and his parents, learning of the theft 1 week later, fined Jack by taking away his allowance. But in the interim, before his parents discovered the family crime and 1 week before facing his time for the crime, he spent the $20 on buying a new video game. His parents' delayed intervention had marginal or no deceleration effects on Jack's stealing behavior. Consequently, the conventional wisdom derived from the experimental analysis of behavior is that suppressive effects of punishment depend entirely on the density (amount, timing) of the schedule (cf. Bradshaw, Szbadi, & Bevan, 1978; Matthews, Shimoff, Catania, & Sagvolden, 1977).

In a behavioral forensic analysis of stealing, or, in this case, of embezzlement, variable interval schedules of punishment may play a confusing role in deterring expectancy and reactivity responses in the offender. Since embezzlement is rarely a one-time incident, but rather a series of (similar) responses (incidents) transacted over many behavior segments, the displacement of punishment contingencies from earlier to later behavior segments provides a window for more immediate reinforcement contingencies to inadvertently shape bad behavior. The reinforcer most contiguous to stealing behavior is *self-reinforcement*. Self-reinforcers are self-delivered on any schedule desired or engineered by the recipient, although it is typically on a continuous (immediate) basis. For example, the recently sentenced Paul Manafort, former Trump campaign chairman, and perpetrator of decade-long multimillion dollar fraud schemes, convincingly illustrated the power of immediate reinforcement versus delayed or long-term effects of punishment. His wide-reaching lobbying, consulting, bank and tax fraud crimes, lucrative work in the Ukraine and Russia, and lying to federal authorities occurred in his political career that spanned 40 years; during this career, few if any investigations or censorships (i.e., punishment contingencies) imposed sanctions altering his misconduct in organized crime. Earned for his clandestine national and international financial fraudulent schemes were millions in income, extravagantly spent on clothing and property amid his lavish lifestyle. This was Manafort's extensive self-reinforcement.

Manafort's 4-year prison sentence handed down in United States District Court in Alexandria, Virginia, while seen as lenient (Rubin, 2019), was not a crime-deterrent contingency. It was an adjudicative consequence symbolizing the end of his grand lifestyle and power-broker reputation.

The months and years it took for Federal investigators to amass criminal felony charges resembled a variable-interval punishment schedule, which produces unwanted but reliable effects on bad behavior (cf.: Filby & Appel, 1966); These effects include:

1. Behavior becomes resist to extinction
2. Behavior receives continuous, intermittent or "bootleg" reinforcement.
3. Behavior may spike once or twice but otherwise remains steady.
4. After the variable-interval schedule occurs, briefly suppressing behavior, response recovery is fast.

*Behavior becomes resistant to extinction.* Mixed schedules of continuous reinforcement and intermittent punishment schedules produce a disproportional effect on behavior. Rather than decrease or suppress behavior, intermittence may foster a benign, limited, or marginal effect on arousing anticipatory fears (anxiety). Otherwise, the strength of behavior—its frequency and intensity–remains unchanged exposed to continuous reinforcement schedules. Habitual home-invasion offenders, for example, are so successful at pulling their loot from unsuspecting victims and reselling it for a profit, that their awareness of police surveillance barely dents their illegal activity. Once the variable interval schedule catches up with them—arrested after 3 years, imprisoned for two years, and placed on parole for two years—cessation of home invasion may last 1–2 years post-parole. But the high density of self-reinforcement sustaining high rates of robbery behavior before the arrest will be a part of the reactional biography. That repertoire, under certain conducive stimulus conditions, is likely to engender motivating operations in person to repeat the crimes.

*Behavior receives continuous, intermittent, or bootleg reinforcement.* Remote intervention of the variable-interval schedule permits several behavioral segments to occur across time encompassing many intermittent, and bootleg reinforcers. For example, a payroll check reassigned to the offender twice weekly, cashed, and deposited, may add $500 to a personal checking account paying for continuously needed or frivolous purchases. If the deposited laundered money is saved, it may pay for a long-awaited (intermittent) vacation or debt-relief such as a mortgage or student loan. The fact that the deposit is *unearned income* and becomes expendable on self-pleasurable, high-ticket items such as massages, vacations, remodeling a house, or clothing makes its source a "bootleg." It illegally, unethically, immorally, or without authorization occurred in a manner that establishes an opportunity for the individual to behave in ways they otherwise might not behave. Another classic example is when a grandmother pays attention to her 1 year old grandchild's tantrum while the parents withdraw attention from the tantrum, grandmother's unauthorized attention is a *bootleg reinforcer.* Bootleg reinforcers, in a more advanced matrix of behavior, sustain the frequency, intensity, rate, duration, and other properties of responding while inoculating the behaver from the effects of remote punishment.

*Behavior may spike once or twice but otherwise remains steady.* Under variable-interval (VI) "reinforcement schedules," response rates remain constant, with slight variations, and generally may slow down (pause) after random delivery of the reinforcers. Response spikes are atypical unless cues (stimuli) signaling the impending arrival of the reinforcer evoke a motivational operation. This MO increases the responder's tendency to engage more quickly or intensively in some behavior than before the discriminative cue appeared and the responder was relaxed. For example, consider negative reinforcement on a variable interval schedule. When observing the nonprofit agency director leave for 20 min, after waiting patiently for alone time in the office, the removal of the director provides an opportunity for the embezzler to write business checks to herself or even steal cash from the petty cash file. Add to this VI schedule a "limited hold," where the time the director is gone varies from 20 min to 3 h, and is often random. From these conditions emerge a burst of energy or *excitatory response* in the embezzler, who rushes to complete the illegal acts before the director returns and catches the embezzler. Similar response parameters are seen on VR punishment schedules. Here, the random occurrence of aversive stimulation may evoke spikes in *avoidance and escape behaviors.* Avoidance describes the rapid, intense, or high rate of embezzling behaviors performed before the director returns to the agency. Escape implies rapid action after the aversive stimulus returns—the agency director returned earlier than anticipated and any minute will enter the office where unauthorized checks are on the table. Accelerated behaviors may occur to remove the check book from conspicuous view, hide the evidence of a crime, and restore the natural environment to its mundane condition. This accretion of behavior is to escape from or terminate the aversive properties possibly affecting the embezzler after the director is in the building.

*After the variable-interval schedule occurs, briefly suppressing behavior, response recovery is fast.* Under different circumstances, for example, in which the embezzler failed to hide the ledger (did not succeed in escape behaviors) and the agency director observed it laying on the table, the embezzler may receive corrective feedback on using the ledger only when the director is around. That corrective feedback, no matter how polite or saccharine, is likely to suppress or decelerate the embezzler's theft responses not only that day but for 1–2 days afterward. Two days later, theft response rapidly recovers to pre-punishment levels. Two days later, on the cue signaling the agency director leaves the office, the embezzler appears undeterred by the variable-interval punisher, and proceeds to write checks to himself. This amazing resilience and seemingly indifference observed in the embezzler's return to stealing is not some mystical trait of the embezzler's personality. Instead, it is an experimental phenomenon. Recovery from suppression of responses can occur under the following changes in aversive conditions (cf., Appel & Peterson, 1965; Vogel-Sprott & Racinskas, 1969): (a) withdrawal (termination) of punishment, (b) modest punishment still exists, (c) concurrent emotional responses (at high punishment intensities) also are reduced, and (d) reinforcers or motivational operations compete with the punishers.

To appreciate these attenuators of response suppression that contribute to rapid response recovery, below is a table (Table 1.1) that states the principle and gives a corresponding example of embezzler behavior using our current storyline of the embezzler working at a nonprofit agency.

A similar case explored here is of a female adult employed as township clerk in the Midwest, who pilfered over $35,000 over a 1 year period of time. She underwent a post-conviction, court-ordered psychological evaluation to determine her propensity for recurrent economic theft and amenability to offender rehabilitation.

**TABLE 1.1** Effects of attenuators on reversing embezzler behavior from suppression to recovery.

| Attenuators of response suppression | Embezzler behavior segment | Recovery effect on embezzler |
|---|---|---|
| Withdrawal of punishment | Agency director leaves for 3 days affording opportunity to steal money. | Embezzler waits until agency director is absent for any length as discriminative cues for stealing. |
| Modest punishment still exists | Enforced policy of reporting all checks written when agency director is gone for 3 days keeps inadvertent surveillance (punisher) on the embezzler. | Embezzler finds another route of pilfering funds, either from the petty cash drawer or from reallocating agency donations to fraudulent charities. |
| Concurrent emotional responses reduced. | After director accused embezzler of job neglect and weak oversight of funds, he also "felt bad" for the scolding and gave her a salary raise. | Embezzler rebounds from momentary restraint on stealing to the same ritual of stealing money when the director leaves for the day or three days. |
| Reinforcers or motivational operators compete with punishers. | Director accused embezzler of possibly filching money or unauthorized payment of expenses; but embezzler needs money to replace a broken oven and refrigerator in her house, and to pay expenses for a dinner party in two weeks. | Motivational operation of replacing the refrigerator and stove within a limited period of time increases probability of embezzler ignoring the agency director's warning and either repeating the same theft or attempting a less conspicuous theft. |

# Case of Kendra

Kendra is the fictitious name for a 50 year old single female Caucasian re-elected to serve as county clerk for a Midwest township. She is paid a stipend for her township council position, which involves running the entire office as controller for purchases, mail opener, bank deposits, and balancing the financial ledger. She got elected to this job after working a similar job as office manager (on and off) for seven years. At all of her previous jobs, she denied receiving any verbal or written reprimands for (a) performance errors or rate, (b) noncompliance with rules, (c) poor relations with coworker or supervisor, (d) scams, deception, lies, embezzlement or any other economic deviation, (e) poor customer service, or (f) problems with attendance or punctuality. She portrayed herself as the model employee easily entrusted and who quickly advanced up the executive ladder with unlimited and multi-tasking duties.

## Education

Originally from a small town, she attended her primary and secondary education in two public school districts. She denied undergoing any formal school testing or qualification for an IEP. She attended regular classes, earning grades around low B's and C's. She blamed her low grades on "coasting." She easily memorized visual (numerical) text and auditory (oral) information, and rarely opened a book to study. She relied on her visual, auditory, and numerical memory to pass the quizzes and tests. Her academic scores were reportedly higher in mathematics. She also enjoyed extracurricular success for 3 years in cheerleading and 2 years competing on the tennis team. Outside of school, she participated in the church youth group. After high school, she advanced 5 year through a local college to earn a Bachelor's Degree in Business. Not surprisingly, at college, she also "skated through" without reading assigned textbooks or even studying arduously unless it was for math or accounting classes. After college and through her job career, Kendra perceived herself as highly knowledgeable and competent in mathematics calculations, everyday mathematics problem solving, and financial management. She relied little on her parents to earn income and pay for her personal bills.

Kendra claimed she was bullied aggressively in school. He denied provocation of in-school fights and never retaliated by force. She might report the perpetrator to the principal or possibly make discrete rumorous statements about the perpetrator, but never (or rarely) confronted the perpetrator face to face. She denied interception of bullies perceived as bothering victims. Despite her filing complaints and her parents' visits to the principal's office about bullying, the oppressive harassment remain unabated. When her family relocated to another city, Kendra *actually was happy about the transition to a new school where she might be free of bullying*. Asked why she was bullied, Kendra insightfully observed her family was upper middle-class, dressed her in nicer clothing, and in all stirred jealousy among classmates from families of lesser income. She believed her classmates saw her as a rich snob, aloof, uncaring, and ostentatious. She denied gang membership or association with violent friends. She denied bringing contraband (weapons, drugs) to school. She denied packing or carrying any weapons. She denied incurring any suspensions, detentions, or expulsions. She denied fascination with animal cruelty or fire-starting. She denied any prior juvenile or adult criminal offenses. She denied receiving any outpatient or resident mental health or substance abuse treatment. She denied any history of prescription to psychotropic medications until recently. Shortly before her last day of township Clerk employment, her primary physician prescribed her the antidepressant Zoloft (150 mg once daily). Two months later, she titrated to the antidepressant Lexapro (10 mg once daily). She does not currently receive any mental health treatment.

## Substance abuse

Kendra fist experimented recreationally with alcohol at age 16. Curiosity faded until her early twenties. She regularly consumed 6 to 7 beers per weekend, without suffering any post-drinking effects of hangovers, headaches, blackouts, or toxicity. Her weekend intake pattern significantly reduced in the last eleven years (since birth of her first child) to twice monthly bingeing on weekends (instead of every weekend). Asked if she worried about no side-effects of large-quantity drinking, Kendra believed she was fortunate or figured her body absorbed the ethanol between food and activity. *Noteworthy was that binge or other high volume drinking absent of partial withdrawal symptoms indicates rapid physical tolerance to alcohol, predictive of possible overuse or abuse.* Her first use of marijuana was at 19 years old. She denied use or any cannabis for the last 5 years. She denied use or abuse of any other licit or illicit (controlled) substances including cigarettes. She denied suffering any major vehicular or other accidents causing head trauma. She underwent surgery for a right-knee torn meniscus (meniscectomy), and suffered mild post-operative infection (i.e., allergy to latex). She denied any difficulty with eliminating analgesic medications. She denied having

CVAs, TIAs, sleep apnea, seizures, high fevers, or neurotoxin exposure. She denied any known current medical problems.

## Interpersonally

Kendra denied any history of sexual victimization. By age 16, she was first voluntarily sexual. She conservatively estimated having 4 heterosexual partners, all four of whom she regarded as meaningful. She married her husband, a state employee. Married for 13 years, together they produced two children. Kendra denied any co-parenting or communication problems in her marriage, and attested that her children, barring normal mishaps, met normal developmental milestones for their ages. She denied any investigations or interventions by Children's Protective Services (CPS) or any intrafamily domestic violence. She further commented that her husband has been tirelessly supportive of her court ordeal, and remains loyal to their marriage regardless of the court outcome.

## Developmentally

Developmentally, Kendra is the oldest of three children raised by married parents. Her father, a plant manager, was her hero. She admired his command of authority, professionalism, and directness of facts. He showed compassion and praise *in his own way, but Kendra felt deeply loved and appreciated by him.* Kendra's mother, a homemaker, was also direct, somewhat assertive but not as self-disciplined. She showed unconditional love, sensitivity, and always complimented Kendra's high school or college achievements. Neither parent abused alcohol or other drugs. Neither parent mistreated her verbally, physically, or emotionally. She lionized her parents as paragons of moral and ethical values, and insisted they were inculpable for her criminal activity.

## The alleged crime of embezzlement

During her service as township clerk in the midwest, Kendra began writing and endorsing checks or using the business credit card to make unauthorized withdrawals from $300 to $700 about 3–4 times a month. Over a period of 1–2 years, she pilfered about $35,000 for personal use. In August of her second year in office, the new township manager took office and immediately conducted an internal investigation of employees suspected of pilfering funds. Kendra was named in a felony charge for abusing her financial privileges and embezzlement. She resigned from the Township Hall position shortly after accused of the crime. Asked why Kendra wrote the *first check to herself,* she claimed the family recently faced a foreclosure after her husband's construction business failed, and the torrent of bill collectors abound. She always was the financial manager of the household budget, fully entrusted by her husband, with whom she shared some but very little of her personal formulas and strategies to pay off bills. She enjoyed her husband's confidence in her, the same confidence admired by many professionals who she worked for over the years. Kendra could not bear the humiliation of her husband knowing the family exhausted funds or could not pay expenses; she regarded their indebtedness a failure in her financial management ability. Once she wrote one or two township checks or used the township business credit card, she discovered the unmonitored expedience with which she could supplement her own (and the family) income.

## Results of the behavioral forensic evaluation

### General observations

Kendra arrived punctually for her appointment at the examiner's office. She greeted the examiner affably and courteously. She agreed with the proposed testing process. She also listened attentively when debriefed about the purpose of testing. Attire was clean, hygienic, seasonally appropriate, and properly fitting. She ambulated independently with a normal gait showing no signs of psychomotor disturbance. She sat comfortably in the chair, and made no abrupt gestural or postural movements. Testing duration was 1.25 h. She completed the self-testing in 1.0 h. Attention-span and physical endurance were strong. Eye contact remained direct and continuous. She smiled, laughed, and interjected questions and statements at appropriate intervals. She showed appropriate levity in response to some statements. Sensorium was intact. Affect was energetic, alert, happy, elevated, dynamic, spontaneous, and fluid. No anger, resistance, opposition, or psychosis seen. No indicators observed of distractibility, impulsivity, or hyperactivity. No evidence seen of withdrawal or intoxication. No evidence seen of mis-medication. She showed no mood fluctuations from aggression to anxiety to depression. She made no statements about suicide or homicide; she denied past suicidal or para-suicidal ideas and intent for self-harm. She delineated right from wrong, reality from fantasy, and truth from falsehood. She fully accepted culpability for her crime. Speech showed no articulation problems. Vowel and consonant pronunciation (phonetics) was clear. Speech flowed evenly, rapidly, audibly, and in completed sentences. Prosody was normal and melodic. Speech content consisted of vocabulary and syntax commensurate with her stated educational level. Ideation showed coherence, rationality, and orientation x 3.

On projective testing, average abstractive abilities suggested ample proficiency in visual problem solving and perceptual reasoning. She accurately tracked and discriminated among objects; she reconstructed information from visual memory. She rapidly and accurately sorted relevant from irrelevant details. She also conceptualized simple and complex social situations. Analytical reasoning was consistent and accurate; she used deductive and inductive logic in converting general information into meaningful or symbol order. Likewise, interpretive thinking occurred at high rates; she showed impressive insight about her perceived problems with distractibility. She also grasped the larger picture of her career goals. Her judgment appeared prudent, conservative, and judicious.

On organizational indices, high scores on content and form suggested alertness to details of object relations. She showed strong adherence to structure suggesting social conformity. Visuo-spatial construction and integration of skills was *rapid but inaccurate*. She grouped objects together by shared properties of angularity, symmetry, and contiguity. She showed no structural abnormalities: neither confabulation nor perseveration. Affective Ratio scores were high; this typifies a person strongly needing affection or intimacy. On the HTP, scores on proportionality, detailing, and locality were unremarkable. On the TAT, a measure of behavioral and emotional patterns, recurrent themes involved hyper-altruism, hypersensitivity, overtrust, self-motivation, and stability. Short-term memory showed no limitations. Immediate recall and long-term memory appeared intact. No evidence seen of impairment to her procedural, episodic, or semantic memory. No impediments found in her executive cognitive (prefrontal dorsolateral cortex) functions. Overall her disposition was amiable and cooperative during the entire testing protocol.

## Psychopathology

First, her test profile was reliable, consistent, and interpretable. On validity scales, no elevations appeared in indices of over-reporting or under-reporting. She presented a balanced version of positive and negative traits. She showed no indicators of fabrication, deception, evasiveness, or omission. Overall, her scales suggested a reliable and credible historian.

Second, on the MMPI-2-RF, Higher-Order scale, elevated EID scores suggests a stoically rigid, internalizer of emotions. She can appear cold, aloof, serious-minded, mechanical, and calculated in her logical approach to problem solving. This does not mean she is insensitive, unemotional, or is self-driven. Just the opposite. She is highly (almost excessively) altruistic, in that she places her husband or family's priorities exceedingly higher than her own priorities. She can forgo personal needs, defer to somebody else's preferences, and is highly amenable to the majority rule among family or friends. However, she is secretive. She *does not share her feelings, opinions, fears, or failures.* Her analytical or calculated side is when it comes to business. She can be a work-horse, deeply enmeshed in solving the riddles of any Rubik-cube-like financial puzzles. She *must get it right or she feels unforgivably stupid, wrong, and imperfect.* This need for correctness and following universal principles or right-wrong, and good-bad, and doing things *the appropriate* way is very characteristic of a person with Obsessive-Compulsive Personality Disorder. Different from Obsessive-Compulsive Disorder (OCD), Obsessive-Compulsive *Personality* Disorder does not deal with compulsive rituals, routines, or superstitious patterns a person follows. Instead, it connotes a way of life where people seek perfectionism. They usually gain control over life by painstaking attention to rules, procedures, lists, schedules, and check for mistakes. This is done to the expense of flexibility, openness, and efficiency. Kendra demonstrated these traits while working for her father's business, and other similar jobs, and at the township clerk position. The *traits of perfectionism and rule-obedience were compromised only when she faced the inevitable exposure of looking incompetent about her home finances.* That is, Kendra did not know how to communicate her vulnerability to her husband that she lacked income to pay bills. This admission would have destroyed her persona of appearing invincible in solving all of the financial enigmas she faced in life.

Third, on the Internalizing and Interpersonal scales, elevations in NFC, IPP, SAV, and SHY profiled a quiet, unassertive, passive, self-doubting, and people-pleasing person. Her outward sociability or gregariousness at jobs were a decoy to hide underlying anxiety and constant feelings of being judged negatively. She *can be* strong, proactive, and even adversarial on behalf of *other people* (her family, children, friends), but not on behalf of herself. She is very meek, uncertain, and inside feels like an impostor, or someone whose faults are seen transparently. She disguises this anxiety by immersion into concrete fact-based activities such as, in the past, handling family budgets, or planning trips, or being the family entertainment coordinator. She feels energized, invaluable, and a healthy dose of control when she masterfully completes specific tasks, with specific timelines, for specific outcomes.

## Behavioral analysis

Kendra's wizardry with numbers, finesse with mathematics, conflict-avoidance history, and role as consummate family organizer and budget manager presents an interesting reactional biography. Her history and current behavioral events provide the groundwork to operationalize her stealing behaviors. Earlier we saw the conditioning outcome of people exposed to variable interval schedules of (reinforcement and) punishment. Similar schedules operated in Kendra's life concurrent with mixed and chained schedules predating her township position and onset of family financial problems. On her job itself, the following relevant schedules in relationship to her theft behavior (contingencies) were in effect shortly into her first term in office. These contingencies persisted through time (multiple behavior segments) unabated and created a false impression that Kendra could solve her financial deficits at home by repeating theft behaviors. Consider her progression of theft behavior in two behavior segments (BS1 and BS2). The behavior segments below represent a snap-shot of two segments likely drawn from different time sequences, otherwise flowing continuously and seamlessly across hours and days at her township job; each segment captures measurably discrete units of behavior interacting with specific setting events. Many of these segments were repetitive or habitual, with moderate variation, except the temporal dimension of moving Kendra forward in time to new setting events in which showed response and stimulus generalization.

### *Behavior segment 1 (BS1)*

*Setting events:* Absent of township manager, alone in office, during day.

*Motivational operations:* Family budget deficit, accessibility to township check book or credit cards, limited time before husband learns of unpaid bills.

*Target Responses:* Write unauthorized checks or make withdrawals from credit card per month to pay household expenses (bills, foreclosure, help subside husband's failing business).

*Concurrent emotional responses:* Anxiety from imperfection of money management; fears of exposure of financial incompetence; excitation from stealing the money and re-distributing it into personal account.

*Reactional Biography:* High performance competence in mathematics problem solving and numerical calculations. History of effective short-term and long-term fiscal planning. History of being entrusted by employers and family. History of self-initiative/leadership in organizing and paying bills.

*Schedules of Consequences:* First, self-reinforcement (positive reinforcement) involved a continuous schedule of self-praise and self-verification for any financial-decision she made. Second, a fixed-ratio schedule of negative reinforcement involved her stealing money to eliminate each occurrence of anxiety responses about exposing the family debt. Third, a variable-interval schedule of punishment and reinforcement involved biding her time to steal only when the township manager was gone, despite some budgetary surveillance in place.

### *Behavior segment 2 (BS2)*

*Setting events:* New township manager in place; audits are performed on accounting; unspecific accusations of Kendra rumored in the township office.

*Motivational operations:* Limited time to hide or falsify ledger, efforts scurried to repay money stolen; Kendra weighs the risks and benefits of disclosing unpaid family bills to husband.

*Target Responses:* First, selective and temporary suppression of money-stealing behaviors. Second, increased lying (deceptive behaviors) to invent reasons why credit card and check-writing distributions mad. Third, Kendra engages in high intensity of compensatory behaviors to organize or show leadership (competence) in other job tasks or sub-tasks to deflect attention away from accusations of her stealing.

*Concurrent emotional responses:* Anxiety from anticipatory fears of the audit, fraud exposure, and incompetence exposure in her family.

*Reactional Biography:* History of (a) deceptively disguising manipulation of numbers, (b) passive-aggressive decisions, (c) self-relying on fixing fiscally damaged situations, and (d) rationalizing (falsifying reasons) to herself that embezzlement is a legitimate and responsible solution to be an effective household money manager.

*Schedules of Consequences:* First, variable-ratio negative reinforcement involves being investigated randomly for any number of tasks done. Effects of schedule increase avoidance/escape by her doctoring or fudging the data, delaying data presentations to staff, and increasing absenteeism. Second, fixed-interval punishment schedule consists of every 3 days after audit performed, debriefing follows about the reasons for financial shortages and possible embezzlement. Third, variable-interval punishment schedule occurs in Kendra awaiting the uncertainty of time before an indictment is issued.

Fluctuations occurred in Kendra's money theft behaviors, from high to low frequency, passing from Behavior Segment 1 to Behavior Segment 2 (presuming several behavior segments occurred in between). Lower frequencies likely occurred in behavioral segments in which the new township manager conducted internal audits and provisionally accused Kendra of illegally managing the treasury. Inside these segments, contingencies occurred irregularly that threatened suppression or cessation of stealing behavior, while other contingencies flourished that reinforced response recovery of embezzlement. Below is Table 1.2 explaining this variability of contingencies. It describes attenuators and competing effects of variable interval schedules and self-reinforcement schedules in preserving a steady state of Kendra's embezzlement.

Kendra's downfall after 1–2 years of embezzling money from the township was the product of several co-occurring contingencies. Contingencies consisted of (a) variable interval reinforcement and punishment schedules, (b) self-reinforcement (continuous) schedules, (c) motivational operations reducing or reversing any response suppression, and (d) a complex reactional biography of mathematical proficiency helping her to creatively manufacture reasons to mask her fraudulence. While the forensic personality testing also illuminated traits about Kendra's passivity, conflict-avoidance, and hyper-benevolent behaviors, these traits alone lacked the operationalism and predictability for assessment of criminal recidivism. Instead, presented here was an application of a natural science of behavior—its laws, principles, and spatial-temporal transaction across behavioral segments—all serving to elucidate her white-collar economic crime.

TABLE 1.2 Effects of attenuators and effects of variable interval schedule and self-reinforcement in maintenance of embezzlement behavior.

| Attenuators of response suppression | Effects of variable interval schedule | Effects of self-reinforcement |
|---|---|---|
| Withdrawal of punishment | Randomly intermittent audits across two months initially created anticipatory fears and then anxiety diminished after the audits were finished. Kendra returned to writing illegal checks and making withdrawals from the credit card. | She shaped her own efforts to cover her tracks, doctor the ledger, and alter documents to show pre-authorized signatures. Her craftsmanship in forgery and manufacturing threads of correspondence were visual reinforcers shaping her increased production of more cover-ups. |
| Modest punishment still exists | Auditors came on the premises at different times during the month to work with Kendra. Together they went through questionable documents. Fearing some detection of her theft, she shifted from writing checks to withdrawing larger amounts on the credit card during planned township activities, legitimizing use of credit card. | Fraud cover with the auditors (at first), overpaying herself on the credit card during endorsed township activities, and higher response efforts to appear invaluable (by her impressive efficiency in coordination of activities), all served as self-reinforcers magnifying her confidence. |
| Concurrent emotional responses reduced. | Random compliments to Kendra by the township manager for expertly explaining the bookkeeping to auditors alleviated her fears of fraud exposure and job termination. | Feeling re-inspired and less anxious, money-stealing behaviors generalized to buying personal groceries and restaurant meals with the township credit card, both of which she regarded as "gifts" or "perks" (self-reinforcers) for her impeccable budgetary oversight. |
| Reinforcers or motivational operators compete with punishers. | Despite the looming audits at work, payoffs of family debt and foreclosure relief occurred variably over time (VI reinforcement), as well as Kendra's husband lavishly praising her on average three times per month for her genius in budgeting. | Kendra's self-discipline of only spending her stolen money on household debt, or her husband's business, or for simple remodeling increased her self-assessment of being altruistic, more hard-working than other people, and more mathematically clever than her peers. |

# References

Appel, J. B., & Peterson, N. J. (1965). Punishment: Effects of shock intensity on response suppression. *Psychological Reports, 16*, 721–730.

Azrin, N. H., & Wesolowski, M. D. (1974). Theft reversal: An overcorrection procedure for eliminating stealing by retarded persons. *Journal of the Applied Behavior Analysis, 7*, 577–581.

Barth, R. P. (1987). Assessment and treatment of stealing. In B. Lahey, & A. E. Kazdin (Eds.), *Advances in clinical child psychology* (Vol. 10, pp. 137–170). Boston, MA: Springer.

Bradshaw, C. M., Szabadi, E., & Bevan, P. (1978). Effect of variable-interval punishment on the behavior of humans in variable-interval schedules of monetary reinforcement. *Journal of the Experimental Analysis of Behavior, 29*, 161-160.

Coleman, J. W. (2002). *The criminal elite: Understanding white collar crime.* NY: Worth Publishers.

Cressey, D. (1973). *Other people's money: A study in the social psychology of embezzlement*. NJ: Patterson Smith Publishing Corporation.

Davies, P. (2008). Is economic crime a man's game? *Feminist Theory, 4*, 283–303.

Federal Bureau of Investigation. (2009). *Uniform crime report: Crime in the United States*. Washington DC: U.S. Government Printing Office.

Filby, Y., & Appel, J. B. (1966). Variable-interval punishment during variable-interval reinforcement. *Journal of the Experimental Analysis of Behavior, 9*, 521–527.

Green, G. (1993). White-collar rime and the study of embezzlement. *The Annals of the American Academy of Political and Social Science, 525*, 95–106.

Henderson, J. Q. (1981). A behavioral approach to stealing. A proposal for treatment based on ten cases. *Journal of Behavior Therapy and Experimental Psychiatry, 12*, 231–236.

Matthews, B. A., Shimoff, E., Catania, A. C., & Sagvolden, T. (1977). Uninstructed human responding: Sensitivity ratio and interval contingencies. *Journal of the Experimental Analysis of Behavior, 27*, 453–467.

Reid, J. B., & Patterson, G. R. (1976). The modification of aggression and stealing behavior of boys in the home settings. In A. Bandura, & E. Ribes (Eds.), *Behavioral modification: Experimental analyses of aggression and delinquency* (pp. 123–145). Hillsdale, NJ: Erlbaum.

Riemer, S. (1941). Embezzlement: Pathological basis. *Journal of Criminal Law and Criminology, 32*, 411–423.

Rosen, H., & Rosen, L. A. (1983). Eliminating stealing: Use of stimulus control with an elementary student. *Behavior Modification, 7*, 56–63.

Ruben, J. (2019). Americans have every right to be furious over Manafort's sentence. *The Washington Post*. March 8. Opinion.

Sutherland, E. H. (1949). *White-collar crime*. NY: Holt, Rinehart & Winston.

Vogel-Sprott, M., & Racinskas, J. (1969). Suppression and recovery of a response in humans as a function of reward and punishment. *Behaviour Research and Therapy, 7*, 223–231.

Zietz, D. (1981). *Women who embezzle or defraud: A study of convicted felons*. NY: Praeger Publishers.

CHAPTER

# 10

# Cultural contingencies of survival intermingled with domestic violence: A case of evocative effects of metaphorical extension

Avid followers of the news keep track of the scandals *de jour* surrounding the White House, Hollywood, or celebrity CEOs accused of sexual a domestic abuse. Often, the two abuses overlap. Panthers owner Jerry Richardson was accused of sexually harassing a NFL wardrobe stylist. New England Patriots owner Robert Kraft was caught in a sex trafficking sting. Rapper Kaalan Walker was charged with nine counts of sexual of felony sexual assault. R & B legend R Kelly currently faces charges of aggravated criminal sexual abuse. Making matters worse, a grift so heinous and under-reported were immigrant women physically coerced to work in massage parlors and perform sexual favors to male patrons. In strip malls across the country, neon signs and brightly colored placards promising relaxing shoulder rubs, hot stones, and acupuncture instead were hubs for prostitution. An estimated 9,000 illicit massage parlors, mostly Asian-run, were viable sex-trafficking venues. The epicenter of this national illicit activity—in Chinatown in Flushing, New York—recruits innocent female immigrants paying off debts to loan sharks (back home in China) or to their smugglers who secured safe passage to the United States (Bouche & Crotty, 2017; Huff, Wallace, Riggs, Katz, & Choate, 2018). Ironically, owner of similar Asian day spas nationwide, Cindy Yang, also suspected of selling sexual slavery, boasts her insider-connection with President Donald J. Trump at his West Palm Beach fortress Mar-a-Lago; her webpage, until recently, offered a consultant fee to arrange a meeting between high-paying customers and the president (Wade, 2019).

The list abounds of public figures embroiled in physical and sexual violence kept hushed to maintain the status quo and minimize publicity disaster. According to Evans, Davies, and DiLillo (2008), estimates show 1.5 million women are raped or physically assaulted by intimate partners. In families where violence prevails, exposure to the domestic violence makes children seven times more likely to grow up repeating similar behaviors on adults.

*Behavioral Forensics*
https://doi.org/10.1016/B978-0-12-819805-6.00010-5

Intergenerational transmission of violence becomes the dark family secret, a tradition implicitly interwoven into the fabric of the household and viewed as normal. Bonem, Kime, and Corbin's (2008) formulation of this vicious aggressive family cycle into operational terms found salient antecedent, behaviors, and consequences defining the tripartite contingency. Similarly, Hamberger and Lohr (1989; Cohen & Mannarino, 2008) specifically pinpointed the warning signs and unintended reinforcement mediated between spouses or family members in the acquisition and maintenance of violent behaviors.

Research on the ubiquity of domestic violence is unequivocal; maltreatment occurs in a heterosexual or homosexual romantic or family relationships between adults or adolescents, regardless of gender. While domestic abuse strikes all races, religions, social economic status, and sexual orientations, risk factors for men and women belong victims or abusers frequently include (a) poverty, (b) lack of high school education, (c) witnessing family violence in childhood, (d) low sense of self-worth, (e) substance abuse, and (f) cultural norms. The latter variable, *cultural norms,* raises most eyebrows. Emotional experiences naturally differ across cultures. In some cultures inundated with urban oppression and minority discrimination, underlying fury persists not just in one or two members of the culture, but in aggregates of the culture. The larger the size of shared or group ferocity the tougher it is for individual's in the group to regulate their own angry emotions. Poor cultural emotional regulation, in other words, is congruent with poor individual emotional regulation (Leersnyder, Boiger, & Mesquita, 2013; cf.; Mesquita, Frijda, & Scherer, 1977; Mesquita & Leu, 2007).

Their argument, that intense emotional experiences are congruent with culturally central values, ideals, goals and concerns, raises the problem of whether violence indigenous to some cultures may generalize to cultures in which violence is atypical or abhorrent. Cross-cultural similarities, for example may exist in two metropolitan urban family households using corporal punishment as standard discipline for child misbehaver. The one family, African-American, and second family, Anglo-Saxon Caucasian, shared exposure to martial law enforcement of verbal and physical abuse. Their values, beliefs, ideas, and rules governing child behavior management entirely revolve around expectations and endorsement of these interventions. Comparing these family norms to a suburban neighborhood family norm, regardless of race, creed, religion, or gender orientation, the differences may be more dynamic. Cultural differences, in viewing corporal punishment, not only vary across socioeconomic factors, but also between urbanity and rurality, between western and eastern civilization, and between the geography of East coast states, Midwest, Northern and Southern states, and west-coast states. Cultural emotional regulation may be endemic to unique structural conditions and traditions of one community. But it is not fixed. It is mutable, transient, fluid, and subjected to the contingencies shaping the community (Kantor, 1982; Roseman, Dhawan, Rettek, & Naidu, 1995; Shwder & Haidt, 2000).

Cross-cultural discrepancies in emotional regulation are common when individuals transfer volatile behaviors from one (home) environment to another (non-home) environment as if both environments were the same. The phenomenon of response transferability around like stimuli is called *stimulus generalization.* From its early foundations in experimental research (Guttman & Kalish, 1956; Sidman, 1961) and expanded study in applied research (Fields, Reeve, Adams, & Verhave, 1991; Wilson & Pearce, 1989), the concept of stimulus generalization has been the scientific answer to the question, "Why do people respond similar in (structurally) similar circumstances?" Stimulus generalization conveniently and empirically explains how a response may begin to occur in a variety of contexts without being directly reinforced or taught to occur in those contexts. Jonathan, for example, is hot-tempered at home during the day isolated in his room playing online multiplayer video games. His frustration is when he cannot advance up levels of player challenge and takes too long on simple, mundane, routine moves in lower levels. He takes a break and goes to Target (retail store) to buy some socks. While there, he cannot find the socks he wants to buy and immediately gets frustrated. He yells profanity aloud just as he does to the computer video screen at home when he fails level challenges.

Does Jonathan have a personality problem? That is one way transcendental or traditional psychologist might characterize his "pervasive" behaviors occurring in many settings. Inside him, in other words, must lay the homunculus of some personality manifesting volatility whenever he cannot satisfy his urges. It may be true, Jonathan is under urges, that is, has motivational operations; it also may be true, Jonathan "carries over" angry behaviors (obliviously) form one setting to another setting. However, reasons for this generalization go beyond the mysticism of personality. In both environments, Jonathan responded to *stimulus properties. Some properties were identical or very similar in both settings, and were considered relevant properties. Some properties were significantly dissimilar and considered irrelevant properties.* Skinner's analysis of verbal behavior (1957; see Michael, 1984) offered a taxonomy of stimulus generalization distinguishing between stimuli with relevant and irrelevant properties. New stimuli that have identical (relevant properties) to the training (original) stimuli, to which an organism responds, are called *generic stimuli and responding to them is called generic extension.* When Jonathan plays the same multiplayer game at his friend Herald's house, Jonathan explodes in rage exactly the same way he does at home. A second type of extension is *metaphorical extension.* Here, the new stimuli bear some but not all of the relevant properties found in the original (training) stimuli. More commonly, Jonathan loses his temper when he plays any multiplayer game resembling the ones he plays at home. They all share similar properties or qualities evoking his identical repertoire of responses: Character names are similar, level challenges to reach each tier are similar, and high rate or pace of responding is similar. In experimental controlled conditions, evidence of using generic and metaphorical extension in educational applications to teach object concepts have been widespread (Alessi, 1987; DeSouza, Akers, & Fisher, 2017; Sautter & LeBlanc, 2002; Sundberg & Michael, 2001).

Metaphorical extension is similar conceptually to Kantor's (1922) interpretation of memory subtypes (see Chapter 1) of *collective memory acts.* He classified collective memory acts under three subtypes, *casual remembering of reminiscence, direct recollection, and memorial recovery.* Casual remembering of reminiscence is when the organisms recalls some unimportant or obscure stimulus, but it is tied to consummation (interaction with) stimulus-response connections. Direct recollection is more intentional and allows retrieval of archival facts needed at the moment or to achieve a practical result. The third subtype, memorial recovery, operates to affect some change in the person, whether a thought or feeling. All three typologies depend on interbehavior (or prior interactions) with clear stimulus properties (references).

That is, *at one time the individual responded effectively to relevant properties of these stimuli.* When responders react to *remote verbal* (relevant) properties not present in the current stimulus but are representations of other properties, Kantor called these remote verbal properties *symbols* (Kantor, 1977). Linguistic symbolism pertained mostly to verbal versus nonverbal properties in stimuli, although the vagueness of these cues varied enormously. Six types of symbol (vagueness) cues included (1) existent-existent, (2) existent-nonexistent symbols, (3) representant-existent symbols, (4) representant nonexistent symbols, (5) sign-significant symbols, and (6) indicator-denotant. First, existent-existent symbols are objects, events, and action producing a previously conditioned response. John says "Hello," and Sally responds "Oh, hi John" (also called intraverbal behavior by Skinner, 1957). Representant nonexistent symbols are when cues trigger responses not directly related to the actual stimuli present. John just waves to Sally, saying nothing, but Sally responds "Oh, Hi John," as if John verbally greeted her. Representant existent symbols are when substitute objects or properties represent past relevant cues. John just looks over to Sally, saying nothing and does not wave over to her. However, since his eye glance historically accompanied verbally greeting Sally, she responds to his nodding in the same way, "Oh, Hi John." Representant nonexistent symbols are abstractive or vaguer properties in the stimuli having peripheral features. These properties of stimuli are sufficient for the responder to interbehave with. John does not even glance at Sally—he glances at somebody else entirely and walks into the building ignoring Sally. However, since Sally is accustomed (from prior behavior segments) to observe John greet her, even though he does not, she responds *as if he did perform the evocative cues* and she still says, "Oh, Hi John." Sign-Significant symbols are contrived and not representative per se of their significant stimuli. They are arbitrarily made to represent or symbolize something toward which the responder possibly never interacted. John's employee # is 4567. Sally does not see or hear Join in the morning. John is nowhere in the stimulus configuration of her behavior segment. However, she notices an incoming text whose last four digits are 4567. She sputters aloud, "Oh, Hi John." Finally, indicator-denotant symbols are when other verbal properties, such as a written sentences, references or describes John's behavior. Sally reads a note her friend sent on Facebook saying John usually comes to work between 7:45 and 8:00 a.m. She mumbles to herself subvocally, "Oh, Hi John." In sum, Kantor's theoretical formulation of symbol and referential behavior occurring under one or many stimuli, is an attempt to explain the elusiveness of how remote, non-relevant properties of stimuli can evoke behavior. The same behavior seen before around very relevant properties of stimuli.

Under the headings of metaphorical extension or symbolism, depending on one's preferential taxonomy, the responder—in this case an angry responder—discriminates some but not all of the relevant properties of stimulus conditions. He may even respond to irrelevant properties combined with relevant properties. To return to our example of Jonathan's temper, his anger may explode at the "drop of a hat," when any delay of immediate gratification occurs regardless of whether it deals with playing a video game. In line at the grocery store, for example, he impatiently utters rude comments to patrons ahead of him to speed up their transaction. Stimulus cues, here, are physiological (autonomic arousal creating a motivational operation) and visual cue of waiting in line. On the surface, these cues seem irrelevant to the onset of his temper during the original training stimuli of playing online video games. However, that is not true. Jonathan must wait for software programs to start-up, depending on the speed of his computer operating system (or cellphone, if played online there). He gets annoyed at slow activation durations, delaying (depriving) his time to commence the game. If speed of his cellphone or computer is slow (e.g., Windows 98) and inferior to the expected processor speed of Windows 10, Jonathan becomes over-excitable. The processing speed of the computer is not a relevant property of the game that he learned to respond to. But he learned same or similar responses to same, similar, or even some dissimilar properties of stimuli, all proximal to the game-playing stimuli.

The case reviewed here is like Jonathan's generality of angry behavior from playing video games to non-game playing stimulus conditions. Instead, it is about a recidivistic juvenile and adult offender of domestic violence. She was convicted of assault and battery against another adult during a heated altercation. She had a reactional biography fraught with fighting behavior endemic to her culture; her excessive temper, polysubstance abuse were survival strategies in her cultural matrix. She even survived two traumatic brain injuries affecting her right-sided frontotemporal region and subsequently to her occipital and hindbrain (cerebellum) region. A court-ordered psychological evaluation was to determine her risk of repeating assaultive crimes, and whether she might complete probation.

## Case of Gwen

Gwen is a fictitious name (and gender) for a 28 year-old single (never married) female currently residing 1 year with her biological mother and mother's female friend in a Midwestern city. She is 1-month unemployed since released from two incarcerated in county jail. She reportedly will start a part-time temp-job and work part-time in housekeeping at two local hotels. Before placed in jail, she worked 6 months at a local grocery store as produce food clerk, after a slew of motel housekeeping jobs lasting 3–4 months. She admitted being terminated at jobs due to tardiness and excessive unexcused absences, and coworker altercations. She regarded her work performance as industrious, diligent, generally cooperative and conscientious, focused, respectful of authority, and reliable. Despite her moderate job transience, she denied receiving any verbal or written reprimands for (a) performance rate and quality, (b) rule conformity on the job, (c) positive drug or alcohol screening results, (d) customer service, and (e) relations with supervisors.

### Education

Educationally, Gwen attended public school. She reached the ninth grade before transferring to adult education. There, she lasted a semester before expelled for in-school fighting. She denied previously undergoing any multidisciplinary testing or qualification for an IEP or 504 plan certified under Specific Learning Disability or Emotional Impairment. Instead, in regular courses, she underachieved with borderline failing grades of C's and D's, attributed to (a) non-completion and non-submission of homework, (b) school apathy, (c) school absenteeism (skipping, without truancy charges), and (c) preoccupation with social groups (gangs). She denied difficulty with comprehension of class lectures, reading assignments, or homework, despite her non-participation in the curricula. She denied partaking in any extracurricular, extracurricular, or community activities. She aspired to complete her GED.

Gwen claimed she was mercilessly bullied, aggressively retaliated at her enemies, and always protected classmates perceived as victimized. She frequently "went off" violently on males or females taunting her or threatening to hurt other people. Once her temper ignited, she was unstoppably brutal in assaulting the classmate until she "blacked out" from her overexertion of anger. She even struck classmates pre-emptively, or when she anticipated the aggressor might harass her. Gwen incurred several detentions and suspensions, and one expulsion. She joined the Blackstone gang, frequently partaking in physically violent activities. She carried a knife to school and on the street. She denied fascination with fire-starting or animal cruelty. She incurred multiple juvenile offenses for UDA, malicious destruction of property, minor in possession (of alcohol), and assault. She twice was remanded to juvenile detention for 1–2 weeks and returned to her nuclear family household. Adult crimes included two assault and batteries and one domestic violence, multiply incarcerated for 1–2 days until she met bail. Gwen's recent charge of assault and battery resulted in approximately a 2-month duration of jail. After each offense, probation required her submission to outpatient therapy for varying durations, none of which she continued after probation ended. She also participated in psychoeducational groups on domestic violence and relapse prevention. She denied voluntary or involuntary admission to psychiatric or substance abuse facilities. She denied taking any psychotropic medications. She also denied receiving any pediatric diagnoses of Attention Deficit Hyperactivity Disorder (ADHD) or Oppositional Defiance Disorder (ODD).

## Substance abuse

Gwen first experimented recreationally with alcohol at age 15. From ages 15 to 23, she drank a fifth of cognac daily over a 5–6 h period of time. Her biphasic effect included initially feeling euphoric, energetic, hyperverbal, flirtatious, and "silly." However, if confronted verbally or physically, or *if she thought she was threatened,* retribution was swift. She exploded spontaneously and viciously with a propulsion of unrestrained physical aggression until the challenger was subdued or hurt. During these eruptive episodes, often associated with drinking, Gwen insisted she would blackout or be amnestic (not remember) her fighting. The second half of her biphasic effect was to feel withdrawn and sleepy. Alcohol use ceased for short durations during her placement in youth detention and incarceration as an adult. Even when sober, she believed her impulsive temper escalated so quickly and furiously that she poorly recalled details of the altercation. However, she relapsed to equivalent drinking levels from ages 26 to until her recent arrest. She first smoked marijuana at age 14. From ages 14 to 23, she regularly consumed 2–3 joints or blunts per day equaling 14–15 g per week. At that near-lethal dose sustained in her bloodstream, three effects would occur. First, mixed with alcohol, ethanol intake levels skyrocketed without her accurately gauging the amount of alcohol consumed. Second, her outward demeanor would appear listless, sluggish, despondent, indifferent, and disconnected, probably the reason for her school apathy and underproduction of school work. Third, and most significantly, excessively smoking marijuana likely impaired immediate and short-term memory, impaired decision making, slowed her visual-motor coordination, and likely contributed to amnestic effects after fighting.

She also briefly experimented with cocaine when dating a drug-dealer. She denied use or abuse of any other licit or illicit (controlled) drugs except cigarettes. She began smoking cigarettes at age 14, plateauing t 1 pack every two days. After her recent jail release, she apparently smoked cannabis once or twice until her probationary drug testing began. She vehemently claimed abstinence from alcohol and cannabis for the last month. She explained two possible incidents of Traumatic Brain Injury (TBI). The first occurred at 15 years old during a reciprocal domestically abusive episode with her mother's boyfriend. He apparently threw Gwen, then inebriated, against the wall striking her right-sided front-temporal region. She denied a concussion or intracranial damage but thereafter had headaches frequently lodged in that region. A second incident at age 22 was being "pistol whipped" at the back of her head (occipital-hindbrain) by her physically abusive boyfriend. Residual effects of the latter TBI include visual field distortions and current need for bilateral corrective lenses for near-sightedness. She denied undergoing any major surgeries. She denied having CVAs, TIAs, sleep apnea, seizures, high fevers, or neurotoxin exposure. She denied any known medical conditions.

## Interpersonally

Gwen vaguely recalled an incident of sexual molestation at 1 year old. Unclear impressions consisted of a teenager of 14 or 15 years old digitally penetrating her vagina. After-effects were few. She denied any precocious exploratory presexual or sexual behaviors with same-age peers during preschool or elementary age. She was first voluntarily sexual at age 14. She conservatively estimated having over 60 heterosexual partners, most of whom were casual while inebriated. Her affinity for partners was to be "loved and given affection," although she partly hated loneliness and took brief comfort during sexual acts. However, idealizing the casual encounters backfired frequently, with her being devastated emotionally each time the partner rejected her after a no-strings attached encounter. On reflection, she claimed to only "love" two men. Her first and longest relationship of 5 years was with a professed drug dealer. She felt subordinate to her boyfriend's vitriol temper and scapegoating Gwen for his own problems. She claimed victimization of frequent physical battery and fully admitted she likely stoked the fire with her own angry provocation. A second relationship she cared for was short-lived when she aborted the relationship. His kindness, softness, doting tendency, and tolerance annoyed her to the point of faulting him for being spineless. She repeated this same sordid display of hypercriticism with her current boyfriend, also described as sensitive, supportive, nonconflictual and affectionate. Gwen recognized her paradoxical reactions of starving for a male to treat her nicely and now verbally abusing this kindness when she received it. She understood she unknowingly expected and knew how to navigate around abusive men but new nothing about appreciating or responding to kind-hearted men.

## Developmentally

Gwen is the only offspring of unmarried parents separated shortly after her birth. She still met with her father until age 11 and then saw him intermittently during her teen years. Her father, often unemployed, was a polydrug abuser with a reportedly furious temper. He died recently, leaving an emotional vacancy in Gwen, not because she misses him, but because she never developed a healthy father-daughter relationship. Gwen's mother, also inconsistently employed, also was a polydrug abuser of cocaine, marijuana, and opiate synthetics. Her mother's boyfriend entered the family picture when Gwen turned 5 or 6 years old. For approximately 23 years, she witnessed her mother's boyfriend's explosively random temper, particularly when he was "high" from polysubstances. His anger reigned the household causing constant chaos, sleepless nights filled with anxiety, and anticipatory fears of being in danger. By late childhood, Gwen defended herself with both pre-emptive and reactive aggression to insulate against threats of her mother or mother's boyfriend's uncontrolled outbursts. Gwen grew accustomed to stressful ("war-zone") family households and particularly of men mistreating her physically, calling her derogatory and obscene names, and expecting her to viciously retaliate toward them as a sign of fortitude, competence, and respect. In retrospect, Gwen was ambivalent about her childhood and parents' tirades. She resented their maltreatment but also felt an odd gratefulness to them for teaching her survival skills.

### The alleged crime of domestic violence

The arresting incident apparently stemmed from resentment at the landlord of a house that Gwen and her mother lived in. Persistent disrepairs bordering on the house being red-tagged (for eviction) nearly required her family to leave the house. On or about a Tuesday, after consuming 4–5 glasses of cognac over 3–4 h, Gwen walked home from a local bar during early evening and spotted the landlord working on another tagged house. She charged at him with verbal obscenities and accusations for his house neglect, moving closely into his physical boundary. The (approximately) 50 year old male landlord remained slightly stoic but escalated verbally when affronted. He insisted Gwen leave the premises. Instead, Gwen propelled closer to his body and punched him in the face, knocking him off balance. She left the premises cursing under her breath but was arrested shortly afterward for assault and battery. Asked if Gwen recalled her visceral effect of anger *before or after she confronted the landlord,* she humbly admitted her fury started the moment she spotted the landlord after leaving the bar.

## Results of the behavioral forensic evaluation

### General observations

Gwen arrived early for her scheduled appointment. Gwen greeted the examiner affably. She cordially answered brief pre-interview questions. She agreed with the proposed testing process. Attire was clean, hygienic, seasonally appropriate, and properly fitting. She ambulated independently with a normal gait showing no signs of psychomotor disturbance. She sat comfortably in the couch lying against the back cushions. She made no abrupt gestural or postural movements. Attention span and physical endurance were strong. Eye contact remained direct and continuous. She showed no distractibility, impulsivity, or hyperactivity. Sensorium was intact. Affect was upbeat, energetic, talkative, fluid, dynamic, and spontaneous. No evidence seen of resistance, opposition, or defensiveness. No indicators observed of positive or negative signs of psychosis. No evidence seen of withdrawal or intoxication symptoms. She interjected questions, laughter, and statements at appropriate intervals. She showed no odd, eccentric, stereotypy, or ritualistic behaviors. She distinguished reality from fantasy, truth from falsehood and right from wrong. She made no statements about suicide or homicide. She denied prior suicidal ideas or plans for self-harm (including parasuicidal). She showed no mood fluctuations from aggression to anxiety to depression. Prosody was appropriate, audible, fluent, and in complete sentences. Speech content consisted of vocabulary and syntax commensurate with her stated educational level. Ideation showed coherence, rationality, and orientation ×3.

On projective testing, borderline abilities suggested poor problem solving ability and perceptual reasoning. She tracked and discriminated among objects, and could reconstruct information from visual memory. She sorted relevant from irrelevant details. She conceptualized simple and complex information. She showed no tangentiality or circumlocution. Analytical reasoning showed borderline use of deductive and inductive logic in converting general information into meaningful and symbolic order. Likewise, interpretive thinking showed sequentiality in chronicling events. She poorly described the social, legal, ethical and moral consequences of her action. Insight was very weak about her temper. On organizational indices, she saw and could respond to the larger visual perspective of geometric shapes.

Borderline scores on content and form suggested noncompliance with structure. Such scores typically correlate with *non-conformity*. She showed analogical and categorical thinking; she grouped objects together by shared properties of angularity, symmetry, and contiguity. Visuo-spatial integration of skills was intact. No structural abnormalities seen; neither confabulation nor perseveration. Affective index ratio was average; this suggests receptiveness to physical affection and social attention (compared to indifference, isolationism, or disregard for people—misanthropy). On the HTP, scores on proportionality, locality, and detailing were unremarkable. On the TAT, recurrent themes emerged about distrust, paranoia, and over-reactivity. Recall, short-term (working) memory, and long-term (implicit, explicit) memory all were intact. No evidence seen of impairment to her semantic, episodic, or procedural memory. No impediments observed in her executive cognitive (prefrontal dorsolateral cortex) functions. Overall her disposition was pleasant, talkative, responsive, respectful, and cooperative during the entire clinical interview and testing protocol.

## Psychopathology

First, her test profile was valid, reliable, and interpretable. Second, on validity scales of the MMPI-2-RF, high scores on F-r, Fp-r, and Fs signify deflators, self-deprecators, and individuals who over-humble their circumstances with an underlying victimization theme. They feel inferior, useless, and internally defective. They are anxious, self-devalued and perceive self as undeserving and peripheral to mainstream life. Over-reporters frequently will overstate their negative features while downplay or completely omit any positive features. They are bad fakers about happiness, energy, intelligence, optimism, and ambition. They make hollow promises to appease their listeners whereas their actions show profound alacrity (lack of follow through). Third, high scores on Fs (somatic responses) suggest preoccupation with body sensations absent of any underlying organic or medical causes. Introceptive hypersensitivity frequently associates with recent drug or alcoholic recoverees accustomed to altering their body chemistry through addiction. During abstinence, the sudden absence of physical or sensory changes creates an odd, strange, or "dull-like" effect in the body misinterpreted as depressed or "something is wrong." Since she presents an elaborate version of bad events, and overlooks any redemptive features, Gwen may be a poor and unreliable historian. Fourth, high RBS scores implicate her withholding truthful information about which she denied occurred. For this reason, caution is strongly advised against accepting her reporting without corroboration with supportive documentation.

Fifth, score elevations on the THD, BXD, and Psy-5 scales profile a highly impulsive, cyclically mood disturbed externalizer. She has weak or poor filters to differentiate appropriate from inappropriate opinions to anger. She overpersonalizes most social situations and automatically blames other people for negative judgments about her. She thinks like a victim, obsessed with paranoia of people mistreating or deceiving her, to the point where she may distort, inflate, or alter a sequence of events to prove there was suspicious activity. For this reason, Ms. Gwen is constantly anxious, on guard, foreboding, and expects hatred among her peers. She misattributes wrong reasons to people's motives and behaviors without later doubting her action or offering remorse. She is both pre-emptive and defensive in her reactions. Pre-emptive anger or *anticipatory aggression,* occurs from feeling cornered or randomly accused of (perceived) lies when she expects an impending conflict; reactive anger is directly in response to offensive action toward her. If verbally responsive, she quickly is caustic, abrasive, and maligns the person with a torrent of unfounded accusations. If physically responsive, she spirals rapidly into a firestorm of volatile action until her perceived opponent is subdued or surrenders. Fig. 10.1 below showed collaborative scores on the ACOA Behavior Profile (cf. Ruben, 2015). High percentage scores distributed across domains of Feelings, Control, and Relations signify Gwen is (a) hypersensitive, over-reads into people's verbal and nonverbal behavior, making unfounded inferences, (b) desperately seeks empowerment or control over any urge or threatening situation, impulsively reacting with a sense of impunity or disregard for immediate and remote adverse consequences, and (c) frequently gravitates to

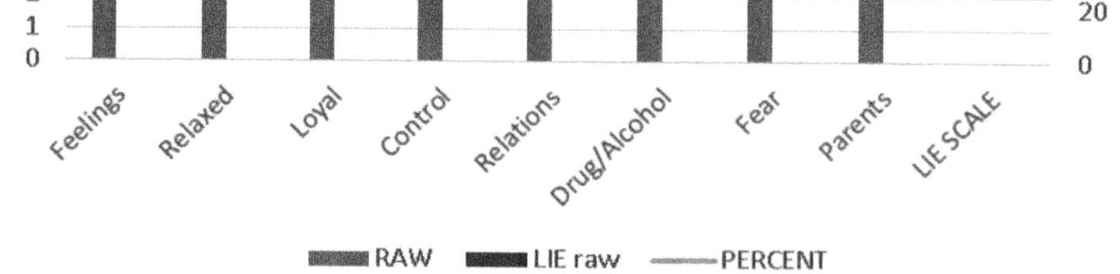


FIG. 10.1 ACOA behavior profile-revised results on Gwen.

intimate partner relationships for sexuality and falsely expects unconditional loyalty from her partner after debasing him for inferred (non-substantiated) reasons.

Sixth, on the Internalizing, Externalizing, Interpersonal, and Interest scales of the MMPI-2-RF, score elevations showed her moods shift unpredictably from overexcitable and verbally belligerent to withdrawn–abruptly quiet, and passively inhibited, especially after she exploded with anger. Mood swings are rapid, without clear precipitants, and largely relate to her inner obsessions about what she thinks people did to mistreat her. When inebriated, over-reactive hostility is faster, more intense, and may be propelled more by her own misperception of what people do than of what they actually do. For example, her crescendo of aggression at the landlord *just from visually spotting him, without any immediate provocation on his part,* was more from ruminating over his alleged negligence of her domicile than what the landlord did at the moment to provoke her. She lunged physically at him after the landlord apparently made one or two remarks to diffuse the situation. Similar scenarios of unprovoked explosive behavior recurred in her late childhood, adolescence, and adulthood.

Overuse of hostility appeared an implicit behavior (Kantor, 1958; Morris, Higgins, & Bickel, 1982; Parrot, 1983). Implicit responses, theoretically, are made to objects not present in the immediate environment; either there are substitute stimuli or vagaries of previous stimuli evoking past behaviors in earlier behavior segments (cf. Dixon & Hayes, 1999). Measurable correlations of implicit responses occurred with three types of hostility—Cynicism, Anger, and Aggression. These dimensions appeared across percentage scores on the Hostility Index (Fig. 10.2). This scale is derived from the Cook-Medley Hostility Scale (1954; Contrada & Jussim, 1992), using subtypes from the MMPI-2. Higher percentage scores on aggression (100%) and Anger (100%) predict both anticipatory and impulsive anger in ambiguously anxious situations in which Gwen felt threatened, defensive, or over-responded to avoid or escape inevitable confrontation. The Hostility Index is also a predictor of *rate and intensity of subjective or perceived anger.* Gwen described her anger escalations as rapid, very loud, and fierce (possibly accompanied by her fingers or fists clenched, and waving at the enemy).

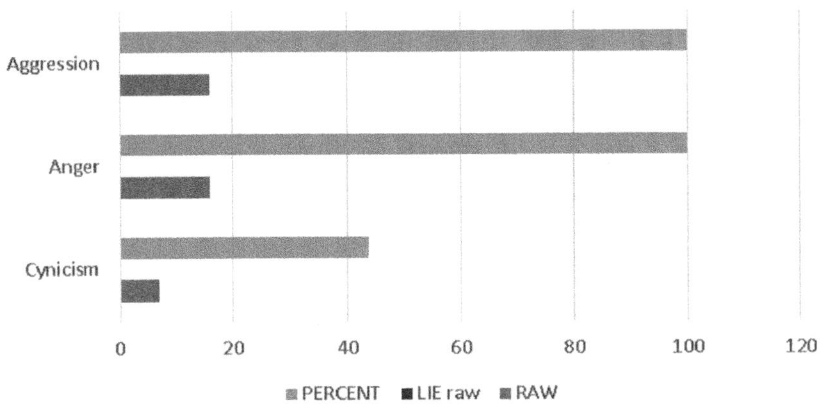


**FIG. 10.2** Hostility index scores for Gwen.

## Behavioral analysis

Gwen's reactional biography of assault behaviors ostensibly shows indiscriminable responses made to her stimulus environment containing some but not all of the relevant properties of the original anger-training environment. The original anger-training environment was her childhood family household raised by verbally and physically abusive biological mother and stepfather. Their confluence of polychemical abuse and aggression produced a random schedule of punishment. Randomness involved capricious and arbitrary contingencies such that Gwen never exactly knew when punishment might occur, or for what specific behavior she received it for. Under arbitrariness and capriciousness, side-effects of punishment exposure on offspring are predictable and typically include many of the conditions outlined in Chapter 1. In addition, adverse effects of random punishment also include (cf. Azrin & Holz, 1966; Axelrod & Apsche, 1983; Mayhew & Harris, 1978; Risley, 1968).

1. Rapid, intense punishment effectively suppresses behavior.
2. Variability of punisher (i.e., changing it) effectively suppresses behavior and maintains suppression.
3. Superimposing one punisher upon another punisher or upon a reinforcer causes conditioned suppression of the reinforced response.
4. Entire situations or the transitions between different situations come to be perceived as entirely aversive.
5. Pain produced by aversive stimuli induces aggressive and defensive (escape/avoidance) responding.
6. The probability of escape behavior under pain is greater when the person has opportunity to physically or emotionally attack.
7. Punished behaviors acting concurrently or sequentially to other behaviors may have specific or general effects upon those concurrent or sequential behaviors. This is also true for identical behaviors under two different schedules of punishment.
8. People exposed to multiple schedules of punishment develop distinctly different patterns of anxiety or fear-behaviors associated with each schedule despite how similar the behaviors are.
9. Elimination a responses with punishment can cause the individual who is being punished to attack nearby individuals or persons delivering the punisher.
10. Punishment can disrupt social relationships as the subject grows to dislike those who punish him almost as much as he dislikes being punished.
11. The development of a dislike for an entire domain can develop.

Effects of childhood exposure to punishment partly was operationally responsible for Gwen's poor emotional regulation and weak stimulus control. She lived in an inner city surrounded by street and gang violence, surviving by loyalty to gang members by demonstrating fighting. Ritualistic "beat-ins" as the ceremonial initiation taught Gwen to act and talks tough, flex muscles of physical aggression, and be appositionally defiant. Gwen transferred her learned skill s of violence around her family to violence around her classmates, instructors, and the school administration. After she left high school, she transferred (generalized) anticipatory and reactive aggression to adult employment and social situations.

Verbal and nonverbal cues in the adult situations having direct (relevant) or indirect (irrelevant) properties equally evoked her spiral of behavior progressing through multiple behavior segments; these cues represented *metaphorical properties of the stimuli*. Behavior segments consisting of vaguely familiar metaphorical stimulus properties, were not identical to past situations under which she inferred (anticipated) conflict, became verbally defensive, or robustly exploded. Nevertheless, she paid little attention to other non-evocative cues or obvious differences in the behavior segments, and focused exclusively on memorable discriminative cues signaling occasions for aggression. Increasing her response susceptibility to the metaphorical stimulus properties were two other functional variables: Motivating operator (MO) and *estimations of variable ratio and interval punishment schedules (PE)* The motivating operation pertains to an established urge aroused at the time (temporally) for which she is more likely to engage in some (angry) responses currently, rather than later, to satisfy the urge. But she also needs to survey the feasibility of consequences for acting on her motivation operation. *Estimations* are subjective assumptions regarding the probability of punishment delivery after an average number of emitted responses or an average time elapsed after any number of responses have occurred. She estimates, in other words, the gains and losses of concurrent reinforcement and punishment contingencies, mostly the latter, to predict consequences for her angry behavior. This application of symmetrical law of effect (e.g., Critchfield, Paletz, MacAleese, & Newland, 2003; Farley & Fantino, 1978) enables awareness of how differential-impact between desirable (appetitive) and undesirable (aversive) consequences exert differing degrees of control over behavior. These assumptions or "educated guesses" underscore a calculus of weighing the odds that verbal or nonverbal punishers have higher or lower rates and magnitudes given the synchronicity and contiguity of relevant and irrelevant stimulus cues interacting together at the moment (cf. Magoon & Chritchfield, 2008).

For example, past behavior segments in Gwen's reactional biography of anger taught her to escalate rapidly when adult men (1) are preoccupied with a task (Stimulus irrelevant, SI1), (2) visibly present with nobody around (Stimulus relevant, SR1), (3) wearing loose fitting clothing (Stimulus irrelevant, SI2), (4) resist or ignore her comments (Stimulus relevant, SR2), (5) are ready to walk away (Stimulus relevant, SR3), and (6) clear their throats before talking (Stimulus irrelevant, SI3. All six of these stimulus properties, for instance, may comprise the original training environment of her parents or friends with whom violent altercations occurred frequently over her childhood, adolescence, and early adulthood. If only two of these relevant (SR1, SR2) and two irrelevant (SI1, SI2) stimulus properties reappear in subsequent stimulus conditions of behavior segments, the probability of Gwen's anger reactivity to these metaphorical cues lies with the hypothetical formula of:

$$ME = f\,(SR1 + SR2 + SI1 + SI2 + MO + PE),$$

where:

ME = Evocative effects of the metaphorical stimuli
*F* = is a function of (the additive effects of)
SR1 = relevant stimulus-1
SR2 = relevant stimulus-2
SI1 = irrelevant stimulus 1

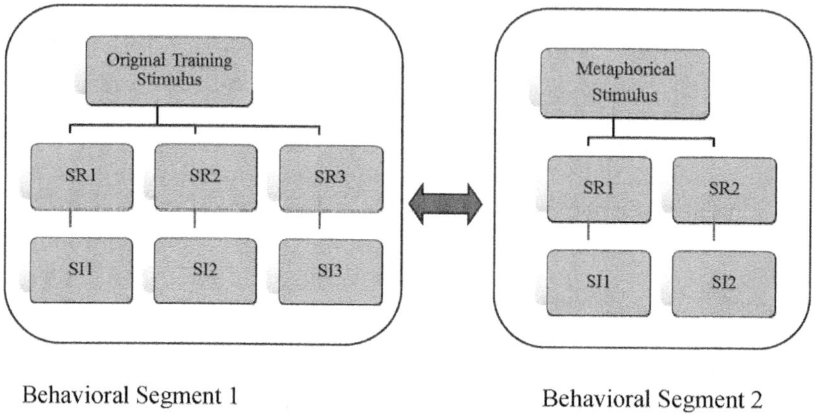


**FIG. 10.3** Transfers of stimuli from original training stimulus to metaphorical stimulus.

SI2 = irrelevant stimulus 2
MO = motivating operation
PE = estimated punishment schedules

A schematic presentation of these stimulus conditions appears in Fig. 10.3. Illustrated is the reciprocal and transactional flow of one behavior segment into another segment, from the original training stimuli to metaphorical extension. In this depiction of events, Gwen's learning curve predicts her anger is more prone to occur when (1) the landlord was preoccupied with a task (SI1), (2) was visibly present with nobody around (SR1), (3) he wore loose fitting clothing (SI2), and (4) he resisted and ignored her comments (SR2). Onset of the motivating operation was instant, potentiating her angry response that she estimated would produce mild to benign effects from variable or ratio punishment schedules.

Analysis of metaphorical extension in this case followed a behavioral forensic approach to isolate and predict Gwen's anger propensity in a risk assessment. Among many conclusions possibly drawn, one empirically-based recommendation is that she may repeat assaultive behavior in future situations in which (metaphorical) cues exist and her estimation is a low rate of retribution (punishment) from the victim/enemy. Her generalizability of poor emotional regulation (explosive anger) encounters a further problem. The evocative (metaphorical) cues may be indigenous to her family and urban lifestyle, both condoned and promoted by a cultural matrix of violence. This makes her contingencies for aggression and survival reinforcing no matter what the adverse effects may be of the social and legal consequences of punishment.

## References

Alessi, G. (1987). Generative strategies and teaching for generalization. *Analysis of Verbal Behavior, 5*, 15–27.
Axelrod, S., & Apsche, J. (1983). *The effects of punishment on human behavior*. NY: Academic Press.
Azrin, N. H., & Holz, W. C. (1966). Punishment. In W. K. Honig (Ed.), *Operant behavior: Areas of research and application* (pp. 213–270). NY: Appleton-Century-Crofts.

Bonem, M., Stanley-Kime, K. L., & Corbin, M. (2008). A behavioral approach to understanding domestic violence: A functional assessment based on batter-identified contingencies. *The Journal of Behavior Analysis of Offender and Victim Treatment and Prevention, 1*, 209–221.

Bouche, V., & Crotty, S. M. (2017). Estimating demand for illicit massage businesses in Houston, Texas. *Journal of Human Trafficking, 4*, 279–297.

Cohen, J. A., & Mannarino, A. P. (2008). Trauma-focused cognitive behavioral therapy for children and parents. *Child and Adolescent Mental Health, 13*, 158–162.

Contrada, R. J., & Jussim, L. (1992). What does the Cook-Medley hostility scale measure? In search of an adequate measurement model. *Journal of Applied Social Psychology, 22*, 615–627.

Cook, W. W., & Medley, D. M. (1954). Proposed hostility and pharisaic-virtue scales for MMPI. *Journal of Applied Psychology, 38*, 414–418.

Critchfield, T. S., Paletz, E. M., MacAleese, K. R., & Newland, M. C. (2003). Punishment in human choice: Direct or competitive suppression? *Journal of the Experimental Analysis of Behavior, 80*, 1–27.

DeSouza, A. A., Akers, J. S., & Fisher, W. W. (2017). Empirical application of Skinner's verbal behavior to interventions or children with autism: A review. *The Analysis of Verbal Behavior, 33*, 229–259.

Dixon, M. R., & Hayes, L. J. (1999). A behavioral analysis of dreaming. *The Psychological Record, 49*, 613–627.

Evans, S. E., Davies, C., & DiLillo, D. (2008). Exposure to domestic violence: A meta-analysis of child and adolescent outcomes. *Aggression and Violent Behavior, 13*, 131–140.

Farley, J., & Fantino, E. (1978). The symmetrical law of effect and the matching relation in choice behavior. *Journal of the Experimental Analysis of Behavior, 29*, 37–47.

Fields, L, Reeve, K. F, Adams, B. J, & Verhave, T (1991). Stimulus generalization and equivalence classes: A model for natural categories. *Journal of the Experimental Analysis of Behavior, 55*, 305–312.

Guttman, N., & Kalish, H. I. (1956). Discriminability and stimulus generalization. *Journal of Experimental Psychology, 51*, 79–88.

Hamberger, L. K., & Lohr, J. M. (1989). Proximal causes of spouse abuse: A theoretical analysis for cognitive-behavioral interventions. In P. L. Caesar, & L. K. Hamberger (Eds.), *Treating men who batter: Theory, practice, and programs* (pp. 53–76). NY: Springer Publishing.

Huff, J., Wallace, D., Riggs, C., Katz, C. M., & Choate, D. (2018). Examining the association between massage parlors and neighborhood crime. *Crime & Delinquency, 10*, 1–33.

Kantor, J. R. (1922). An analysis of language data. *Psychological Review, 29*, 267–309.

Kantor, J. R. (1958). *Interbehavioral psychology*. Chicago, IL: The Principia Press.

Kantor, J. R. (1977). *Psychological linguistics*. Chicago, IL: Principia Press.

Kantor, J. R. (1982). *Cultural psychology*. Chicago, IL: Principia Press.

Leersnynder, J. D., Boiger, M., & Mesquita. (2013). Cultural regulation of emotion: Individual, relational, and structural sources. *Frontiers in Psychology, 44*, 55–80.

Magoon, M. A., & Chritchfield, T. S. (2008). Concurrent schedules of positive and negative reinforcement: Differential impact and differential outcomes hypotheses. *Journal of the Experimental Analysis of Behavior, 90*, 1–22.

Mayhew, G. L., & Harris, F. C. (1978). Some negative side effects of a punishment procedure for stereotyped behavior. *Journal of Behavior Therapy and Experimental Psychiatry, 9*, 245–251.

Mesquita, B., Frijda, N. H., & Scherer, K. R. (1977). Culture and emotion. In P. Dasen, & T. S. Sarawathi (Eds.), *Handbook of cross-cultural psychology* (pp. 255–297). Boston, MA: Allyn & Bacon.

Mesquita, B., & Leu, J. (2007). The cultural psychology of emotions. In S. Kitrayama, & D. Cohen (Eds.), *Handbook of cultural psychology* (pp. 734–759). NY: Guilford Press.

Michael, J. (1984). Verbal behavior. *Journal of the Experimental Analysis of Behavior, 42*, 363–375.

Morris, E. K., Higgins, S. T., & Bickel, W. K. (1982). The influence of Kantor's interbehavioral psychology on behavior analysis. *The Behavior Analyst, 5*, 159–173.

Parrott, L. J. (1983). Similarities and differences between Skinner's radical behaviorism and Kantor's interbehaviorism. *Mexican Journal of Behavior Analysis, 9*, 95–115.

Risley, T. R. (1968). The effects and side-effects of punishing the autistic behaviors of a deviant child. *Journal of the Applied Behavior Analysis, 1*, 21–34.

Roseman, Z. L., Dhawan, N., Rettek, S., & Naidu, R. K. (1995). Cultural differences and cross-cultural similarities in appraisals and emotional response. *Journal of Cross-Cultural Psychology, 26*, 23–48.

Ruben, D. H. (2015). *Adult children of alcoholics-revised (ACOA-R) behavior profile*. Okemos: Best Impressions International, Inc.

Sautter, R. A., & LeBlanc, L. A. (2002). Empirical applications of Skinner's analysis of verbal behavior with humans. *The Analysis of Verbal Behavior, 22*, 35–48.

Shwder, R. A., & Haidt, J. (2000). The cultural psychology of the emotions: Ancient and new. In M. Lewis, & J. Haviland (Eds.), *Handbook of emotions* (pp. 397–414). NY: Guilford Press.

Sidman, M. (1961). Stimulus generalization in an avoidance situation. *Journal of the Experimental Analysis of Behavior, 4*, 157–169.

Skinner, B. F. (1957). *Verbal behavior*. Cambridge, MA: Prentice-Hall.

Sundberg, M. J., & Michael, J. (2001). The benefits of Skinner's analysis of verbal behavior for children with autism. *Behavior Modification, 25*, 698–724.

Wade, P. (March 9, 2019). Asian Spa founder has been selling access to Trump and family. *Rolling Stone*.

Wilson, P. N., & Pearce, J. M. (1989). A role for stimulus generalization in conditioned discrimination. *Quarterly Journal of Experimental Psychology B, 41*, 243–273.

# CHAPTER 11

# Contingencies of vicarious conditioning resembling Munchausen by proxy in the assessment of parental competence

The scheme unveiled recently of rich parents buying college admission for their children is the latest scandal to hit academia. A high school boy eager to enroll at the University of Southern California was falsely deemed to have a learning disability so he could take his standardized test with a complicit proctor who would make sure he got the right scores. Cost to his parents: $50,000. A student with no experience rowing won a spot on the University of Southern California crew team after a photograph of another person in a boat was submitted as evidence of her sportsmanship. Cost to the parents: $200,000. A teenage girl who did not play soccer magically becomes a fantastic soccer recruit at Yale. Cost to the parents: $1.2 million. In total, fifty over-ambitious parents were charged by Federal prosecutors of buying college spots for their children (Coaston, 2019; Levitz & Korn, 2019). Charges ranged from mail fraud to honest services fraud and indictments ricocheted to multiple college sports coaches and administrators, recently fired or put on paid suspension. Code named, "Operations Varsity Blues," the Feds undercover operations since 2011 implicated some of the nation's preeminent universities in the scandal including Yale, Stanford, Georgetown, Boston University, Northeastern, UCLA, USC, University of Texas at Austin and Wake Forrest. The fallout? No matter what charges stick or penalty fines imposed, the bottom line is this: It is another example of how far desperate parents will go to get their children into American universities.

Bribery and conspiracy charges aside, has the X-generation's helicopter parent hovering over their child's affairs created a marionette scenario? This is where the parent is the puppet-master dangling the strings of their sweet child's futures without the children having control? Ask Actress Felicity Huffman, married to actor William H. Macy, an unindicted but investigated parent in the scam. Or John Wilson, founder and CEO of a private equity firm, who allegedly bribed a college to admit his son on a water polo scholarship. The list of


https://doi.org/10.1016/B978-0-12-819805-6.00011-7

suspects abounds of celebrities and economically advantaged parents who advanced their personal agenda on their children without considering the long-term effects it may have on the child's or parent's world. Actress Lori Loughlin, *Full House's "Aunt Becky,"* among the defendants, possibly was removed from her leading role in Hallmark Channel's show "When Calls the Heart," due to her complicity. That Loughlin and others donate money to colleges to secure matriculation of their children is only partly the issue under scrutiny. The bigger picture here is deception, bribery, and fraud. Inventing falsehoods about a child's or adult's behaviors under the guise of heroic honesty is hoped other people may accept the falsehood as truth.

A similar act of deceptive reporting is misrepresentation of self or children as having medical or psychiatric symptoms. In 1951, Dr. Richard Asher introduce the term *Munchausen Syndrome* to describe adults who fabricated illness of their children to get medical attention, with no secondary gain except to serve as caretaker for the ill child (Asher, 1951). Extending his definition, Meadow (1977) coined the term *Munchausen Syndrome by proxy* to describe parents lying about fake symptoms and inducing symptoms in their children. For example, a parent who methodically feeds a child poison causing unusual irritable bowel syndrome and insists on painfully arduous and extensive lab diagnostic tests or biopsy of the intestinal tract *might be seen as* proof of the parents' unmistakable loyalty to cure the child (cf. Schreir & Libow, 1993; Sheridan, 2003). They do not leave the child's bedside and are parent experts on medical knowledge. Their knowledge feeds from the zealous efforts of the medical community to solve the child's organic mystery. Parent expertise is different from the parent, for example, who is traumatically drawn into the perils of some medical emergency such as post-natal heart surgery due to cardiomyopathy; these parents learn technical language and knowledge about the infant's serious medical condition *along the journey of saving the child; they do not already present with encyclopedic medical jargon and expertise before the trauma occurs.*

In 1994 and 2000, the Diagnostic and Statistical Manual of Mental Disorders (DSM-IV) and DSM-IV TR, respectively (American Psychiatric Association, 1994, 2000), used the term *factitious disorder by proxy (FDP)* to describe a psychiatric illness of the perpetrator who fabricates or inflicts illness on self or victims. In 2013, DSM 5 used the term *factitious disorder imposed by another (FDIA)* to expand perpetrator's incentives of building a rapport with the medical community (APA, 2013). Distinctions were clearer between disorders imposed on self or disorders imposed on other people. In both cases, perpetrators simulate, intentionally produce, or grossly exaggerate symptoms in the absence of apparent external incentives (Zaky, 2015).

Symptom exaggeration for parental heroics or to gain favor in the medical community has been the conventional etiology of FDIA. But, in legal jurisdictions, there may be another reason for FDIA or equivalent behaviors. Overprotective parents who are territorial of their children may be unwilling to relinquish custody to another party during a divorce or other legal proceeding. When mediation, hearings, and direct petitions to the judge supporting their reasons for *sole custody* pale in comparison to arguments in favor of *joint custody*, the desperate parent may resort to fraud. Parents may feign symptoms in their children or coach the child to unwittingly echo the same fabrication of symptoms as the parent, as proof of why the parent *must remain exclusive guardian of the child.* For example, suppose a mother files an injunctive order to alter visitation based on the petitioner parent's observations that her child Kara started to masturbate and touch the pet dog's genitals immediately after returning from the visitation with her biological father. Suspicion arises that the noncustodial father may be unsafe with the daughter. The court, in its duty for *parens patriae*, may order an investigation of the putative father purely on unfounded speculation, including his submission to psychological evaluations, police forensic interviewing, or a polygraph test. This manufacturing of false allegations can distance or *alienate* the child from the noncustodial father. Richard Gardner (1985) described this phenomenon as *Parental Alienation Syndrome (PAS)* (cf. Bruch, 2001; Gardner, 2001). Underlying the deceptive practice of PAS is the motivating operation of destroying the parental bond between a child and parent to prevent joint custody. Interestingly, despite its ubiquity from hundreds of case records of family law cases (Cartwright, 1993; Clawar & Rivlin, 1991; Dunne & Hedrick, 1994), the American Psychological Association's Presidential Task Force on Violence and the Family took the unpopular position of dismissing parental alienation syndrome as invalid due to lack of supportive research data (APA, 1996).

Controversy aside, acts of parental manipulation are frequent occurrences and need a more scientific assessment to determine causes and the harmful effects invariably impacting a family system. A behavioral perspective of symptom fabrication (malingering, FDIA, or PAS) considers other setting events or variables in the perpetrator parent's life that sequesters personality traits or psychiatric illnesses from naturalistic behaviors. Less focus is on parental alienation syndrome or factitious disorders than on the integrative-field of contingencies enabling a parent to coach her child into believing fabrications about another parent. This chapter reviews a case of a father falsely accusing his ex-girlfriend of inappropriately touching their mutual 6 year old son. The case prompted instigation by a local Children's Protective Services, not about whether the complainant's allegations were valid and warranted inquiry, but about the complainant himself. Concerns arose about his manufacturing lies (false allegations) and using the child as conduit or surrogate to mislead the court into terminating parental contact between the biological mother (accused) and her child.

## Case of Marcus

Marcus is a fictitious name for a 24 year-old (pending divorce) male currently residing 1 year with his biological mother in a house in a Midwestern city. He is 1-month unemployed since released from two grocery jobs in which he fail to punch out before leaving early on his shift. Retail grocery stocking of products was his favorite jobs since he worked alone on the night shift. In former grocery jobs, he boastfully described his performance on job tasks as cooperative, conscientious, agreeable, respectful, and highly flexible. He vehemently denied receiving any verbal or written reprimands for (a) performance rate and quality, (b) rule conformity on the job, (c) positive drug or alcohol screening results, (d) customer service, and (e) relations with supervisors.

### Education

Marcus attended a Midwest Public School System. He denied undergoing multidisciplinary school testing to qualify for an IEP or 504 plan, although he struggled continuously with mathematics problem solving (everyday math), mathematics calculation (written math equations), and listening comprehension (oral learning). Earned grades reportedly clustered around low C's and D's, blamed on irregularity of homework completion and submission, (b) poorly understanding the assignment and class lecture, and (c) embarrassment to ask for help. He enjoyed art and choir classes, but he learned his tenor part from memorizing the melody, and not by sight-reading musical notation. His auditory memory of music was strong, whereas his recall of verbal statements (instructions, words) was very poor. After high school, he advanced three years to a community college. He passed the English proficiency but not the Math proficiency test, requiring remedial classwork in mathematics. He barely completed his Associates Degree majoring in business and marketing.

Marcus reported severe bullying from classmates about his obesity. He absorbed their insults with docility and shame, never retaliating or assertively complaining to the principal or teachers. Low self-esteem contributed to his hypersensitivity to people's criticism and disapproval, automatically assuming he was internally defective or unlikable. He denied instigation of in-school fights. He denied protecting other students perceived as bullied. He received one suspension for fighting but denied any detentions, or expulsions. He denied gang membership or association with violent friends. He denied bringing in contraband (drugs, weapons). He denied fascination with fire-starting or animal cruelty. He denied receiving any juvenile convictions. His one adult conviction was for filing a false police report. He denied receiving any past outpatient therapy. He denied voluntary or involuntary admissions to psychiatric or substance abuse facilities. He denied taking any psychotropic medications.

## Substance abuse

Marcus first experimented recreationally with alcohol at 15 years old. He drank irregularly on weekends and denied progression to any weekday or weekend habits. He currently is an occasional social drinker and never received any arrests or convictions regarding drinking. Likewise, Marcus smoked cannabis once and found it repugnant, never repeating use again. He denied use of any other licit or illicit (controlled) substances. He denied suffering any major vehicular or other accident causing head trauma. He underwent a tonsillectomy and two colonoscopies without post-operative complications with anesthesia or analgesic drugs. He denied CVAs, TIAs sleep apnea, seizures, high fevers, or neurotoxin exposure. He denied any other known medical conditions.

## Interpersonally

Interpersonally, Marcus claimed a stranger assaulted him sexually in his early teens but was never prosecuted. He explained the female stranger lured him into working side-jobs located at the adult female stranger's house. There, the adult female persuaded Marcus to perform oral sex, vaginal sex, anal sex, and be the recipient of oral sex. Despite odious memories of the incident, Marcus explained there were multiple incidents repeated over a 1-year period during which he experienced ambivalence. He enjoyed the sensory and physical stimulation of sexuality but realized the oddity of their age difference and moral wrongness; six months into the molestation period, Marcus viewed sex acts less about erotica and more about having a "girlfriend" who he trusted and listened to him. Her sexual diversity and sophistication also educated Marcus in female anatomy and advanced his knowledge of sexually satisfying female partners. By his mid-teens, as contact faded with the perpetrator, Marcus performed similar sophisticated sexual acts on female and male peers. He regarded himself as bisexual, indiscriminately enjoying erotic pleasure from either gender. By his late teens, he amassed over 40 bisexual partners, few of whom represented meaningful relationships. Casual encounters ensured his uncomplicated transition among different partners without monogamous commitment. He explained he enjoyed replicating the same no-strings attached euphoria he first experienced with the perpetrator and it minimized stressors in his life.

By age 20, he had unprotected intercourse with a girlfriend impregnating her with a daughter, Tonya (now 4 years old). He contemplated living with the biological mother (Maria) but was anxious about her cyclical mood swings, from highs in anger to lows in depression, including her overuse of opiate synthetic medications. Marcus remained her boyfriend during her pregnancy with Tonya and ended their relationship after Tonya's birth. For the last four years, both Marcus and Maria agreed on a joint legal and physical custody arrangement including liberal visitation schedules and first right of refusal opportunities for babysitting. In the meantime, Marcus began a "serious" partner relationship with a woman with whom he considered having children. His new girlfriend, Kara, questioned his unrestricted latitude granted to ex-girlfriend Maria and constantly complained to Marcus that he deserved full custody to prevent Maria's psychological problems from ruining Tonya's life.

## Developmentally

Developmentally, Marcus is the offspring of dually employed, married parents divorced when Marcus turned 15 years old. His father absconded the family and only re-appeared once Marcus was in his mid-twenties. Reasons for his parents' divorce apparently revolved around her father's polysubstance abuse and domestic violence. Marcus' mother, a factory worker, married a stepfather with whom they produced two-half siblings. Marcus described his mother as affable and affectionate but prone to a ferocious temper. His mother "was a yeller," lambasting Marcus for minor infelicities. Fearing her mother's negative comments, Marcus was highly obedient, over-responsive to family needs, and a "good kid." He rarely displayed any rebellious behaviors and instead appeared gracious and flexible. Similarly around his peers, then morbidly overweight at 250 lbs., Marcus offset peer teasing by being a people-pleaser; he altruistically conceded to his friends' priorities while self-sacrificed personal needs. Marcus' stepfather, employed at the same factory as his Marcus' mother, apparently was a nondrinker and very serene, conservative, sensitive, and supportive of Marcus. His pious Catholic upbringing and regular attendance at Sunday School inundated him with moralistic beliefs, values, and rules regarding the propriety of social behaviors.

## The alleged crime of sexual assault

Regarding the incident in question, Marcus explained a series of fluid events leading to his filing a complaint with Children Protective Services. First, his daughter Tonya returned home after a 1week rotation at her mother Maria's house. Unprompted, Tonya "anxiously" told him "Mommy" touched my private parts." Asked to show on her body where touching occurred, Tonya allegedly pointed to her upper and lower torso, and said touching occurred while she slept naked in bed with her nude mother. Subsequent inquiry also revealed (a) "Mom touched my private a lot," (b) "mom touched me in the bathtub," and (c) "mom had me touch her private parts." Taken at face value, Tonya's impromptu remarks reportedly resonated to Marcus' memories of being molested in his teens by an adult woman who also touched (fondled) his upper and lower torso and encouraged an exchange of sexual acts. He remembered his odd ambivalence of feeling moral wrongness about the sexual acts while seeking more pleasure from the genital stimulation. Fearing Tonya may fall prey to similar victimization, he progressively asked more questions on the assumption that Maria acted exactly like or similar to the adult molester who inflicted sexual behaviors on Marcus. His skewed questions and answers given by Tonya appear below:

| Question | Answer |
|---|---|
| "Did mommy put her finger inside your front area (called "Ginny")?" | Yes |
| "Did mommy put your finger inside your back area (called "butt")?" | Yes |
| "Did mommy put your fingers inside her Ginny?" | Yes |
| "Did mommy put your fingers inside her butt?" | Yes |
| "Did mommy put her mouth or other objects in your Ginny?" | Yes |
| "Did mommy make you do any of these things when you did not want to? | Yes |

After Marcus recorded his daughter's answers, he consulted his girlfriend Kara for her opinion. Kara was reportedly vehement about wasting no time to file a complaint alleging sexual abuse with Children's Protective Services and the local police department. Kara reminded Marcus, after filing this complaint, he could contact his attorney or the Friend of the Court directly and file an ex parte motion to immediately prohibiting visitation/custodial rights of Maria until the matter properly undergoes investigation. Acting on her advice, Marcus swiftly filed the petition within two days of his discussion with Kara and agreed Maria should not get away with molesting his daughter like the adult female got away with molesting him years ago.

Within one week, CPS began its first of several home visits at both Maria's and Marcus' households and twice interviewed Tonya. Tonya also underwent a separate police forensic interview in a different location, followed by similar police forensic interviews of both Marcus and Maria. After 1 month of collecting preliminary investigative data, Children's Protective Services dismissed the allegations of sexual abuse against the biological mother Maria. They found flagrant and repeated discrepancies send contradictions in Tonya's testimony both reported to the same and different interviewers. Moreover, Maria furnished medical documentation of Tonya's vaginal yeast infection and prescriptive treatment of topical ointment to be spread around her "private areas." The local police, agreeing with Children's Protective Services, dismissed charges pending against the biological mother. Police were more curious about the sudden synchronicity between Marcus' complaint to Children's Protective Services, and his ex parte motion to halt parenting time with Maria. The police conducted a second forensic interview with Marcus regarding his own history of sexual molestation, resentment toward Maria, and exactly how he generated his daughter's verbal history about

Maria's abuses. One week after completion of the police interview, Marcus was arrested for false accusations of a crime and lying to the Friend of the Court.

## Results of the behavioral forensic evaluation

### General observations

Marcus arrived late for his evaluation. He greeted the examiner affably and sat down in the lobby. He patiently listened while debriefed about the purpose of testing. He agreed with the proposed testing process. He also answered pre-interview questions. Marcus' attire was clean, hygienic, seasonally appropriate, and properly fitting. He ambulated independently with a normal gait showing no signs of psychomotor disturbance. He sat comfortably in the middle of the couch, laying against the back cushions. He made no abrupt gestural or postural movements. Sensorium was intact. He laughed, answer questions, and interjected statements at proper intervals. Eye contact remained direct and continuous. Attention span and physical endurance were strong. Affect was happy, cheerful, energetic, upbeat, fluid, dynamic, and spontaneous. He showed no signs of anger, resistance, opposition, or psychosis. He showed no mood oscillation from aggression to anxiety to depression. He displayed no indicators of hyperactivity, distractibility, or impulsivity. He showed no signs of alcohol, drug, or medication withdrawal or intoxication. He made no statements about suicide or homicide. He denied any past suicidal ideas in the past. He delineated right from wrong, reality from fantasy, and truth from falsehood. Speech flowed evenly, audibly, fluently, and in complete sentences. Prosody was rhythmic, melodic. Speech content consisted of vocabulary and syntax commensurate with her stated educational level. Ideation showed coherence, rationality, and orientation x 3.

On projective testing, low average abstractive abilities suggested moderate deficits in problem solving and perceptual reasoning. He visually tracked and discriminated objects, and could reconstruct information from visual memory. He poorly sorted relevant from irrelevant details. She conceptualized simple and complex social situations akin to her age norms. Analytical reasoning was weak, in his use of inductive and deductive logic to convert general information into meaningful or symbolic order. Interpretive reasoning was slow and lacked description of meaningful facts given in chronological sequence. He poorly conceptualized ideas about the ethical, social and moral ramifications of false accusations of sexual abuse. He showed low introspection.

On organizational indices, his high rate of responding on content and form suggested adherence to structure. He provided common blot or conventional responses. She showed no structural abnormalities; neither perseveration nor confabulation. Visuo-spatial skills were strong in grouping objects together by shared properties of angularity, symmetry, and contiguity. She showed categorical and analogical thinking. High Affective Ratio scores indicated strong need for physical affection and reassurance. On the HTP, scores on proportionality, detailing, and locality showed mildly inflative egocentricity. That is, larger or overdrawn pictures commonly associate with dreamers, idealists, or exaggerators of self-worth and skills beyond the actual level of these skills. On the TAT, a measure of behavioral and emotional patterns, recurrent themes emerged about hyper-altruism (over-helping, people-pleasing), overtrust, vicarious empathy, and strong needs for affection. Immediate recall, short-term (working) memory, and long-term (implicit, explicit) memory all were intact. No evidence appeared of impairment to her semantic, procedural, or episodic memory. No impediments appeared in her executive cognitive (prefrontal dorsolateral cortex) functions. Overall her disposition was talkative, animative, inquisitive, amiable, and cooperative during all phases of the clinical interview and testing protocol.

On the MMPI-2-RF, several markers appeared. First, his test profile was valid, reliable, and interpretable. Third, on validity scales, high scores on F-r, Fp-r, and Fs signify deflators, self-deprecators, and individuals who over-humble their circumstances with an underlying victimization theme. They feel inferior, useless, and internally defective. They are anxious, self-devalued and perceive self as undeserving and peripheral to mainstream life. Over-reporters frequently will overstate their negative features while downplay or completely omit any positive features. They are bad fakers about happiness, energy, intelligence, optimism, and ambition. They make hollow promises to appease their listeners whereas their actions show profound alacrity (lack of follow through). Third, high RBS scores implicate his withholding truthful information about which he denied occurred. For this reason, caution is strongly advised against accepting his reporting without corroboration with supportive documentation.

Fourth, on the MMPI-2-RF, score elevations on the Higher-Order, Restructured Clinical, Internalizing, Externalizing, Interpersonal, and Psy-5 scales profile an endogenously depressed, introversive individual who easily gets disillusioned, deflated, demoralized, and feels ostracized from people. He abhors the feelings of rejection and robustly rebounds from such defeat by over helping. He may drift quickly into an unhealthy partner relationship, digging his heels into the project of fixing the person from dysfunctions (e.g., disloyalty, drug abuse, etc.). Or, he may immerse himself in a job with overeagerness to appease his employer. When he feel betrayed or critically assailed by the people he helps, Marcus mercilessly blames himself for acting inappropriately and seeks other people's affirmations for his misdeeds.

Fifth, on the Parenting Stress Index, Ms. Marcus' stressors fall into a normal range in overall management of his children's behaviors. He appears relatively confident in his use of positive discipline and suppression of yelling. More importantly, Marcus regards his reinforcing relationship with Tonya as reciprocal. That said, his recurrent complaint is lack of external support and poor control over stressors outside of the child rearing domains. That is, when Marcus feels lonely, helpless, not valued, or isolated, he may quickly doubt himself, he spirals downward into the morass of worthlessness, self-effacement, or isolationism. Rebound from his depression depends on clinging onto some opportunity to regain purpose and value. For this reason, Marcus is very susceptible to the persuasion of other authorities or significant partners whose opinions seem venerable and unimpeachable.

## Behavioral analysis

Assessment of false allegations of child or sexual abuse affected by adult influence presents a complex challenge for the forensic evaluator (Cyr & Bruneau, 2008; Lyon, Malloy, Quas &

Talward, 2008; Ney, 1995). Several important factors evaluated in influencing or *coaching child dishonesty* include the (a) parent coaches' motivating operation MO), (b) malleability of the recipient child to understand the *rule governed behavior taught to them,* (c) repetitive rehearsing of dishonesty, (d) reinforcement or punishment contingencies governing the child's conformity with lies, and (e) whether feasible or underlying portions of truth are at the core of hyperbolic or false allegations. The motivating operation plays a crucial role whether as vengeance or a calculated navigation around the court stalemate. Parents under a time constraint within limited access to setting conditions and urgently wanting their child available to them, may fake stories to satisfy this establishing operation. For example, under a court order granting primary custody to the her ex-husband, and facing limited visitation time with her daughter before military deployment to Afghanistan, the ex-wife army sergeant may fabricate allegations of sexual abuse by the ex-husband, urgently reversing the court order and allowing more time with her daughter. Instigation of the lie not only started with the MO, but it also grew into a convincing story inculcated in the child. Her mother persuades her child that unexplained bruises and her stomach ache reported from the last visit with her father were actually signs of sexual abuse. This verbal explanation is more than just a mand or enjoiner for the daughter to agree with the mother. It also sets up a series of false cause and effect circumstances or *rules* under which the daughter now views her behavior relative to her father. For instance, "When daddy hugs me, he really is trying to touch my private parts." The mother may repeat or embellish through multiple examples the invented series of false events through which her daughter was molested by the father. With each new repetitive explanation, the mother may pause and ask her daughter, "Do you remember when he did this and how it felt?" Her mother adds, "Just tell mommy and I will support you." The mand of enlisting her daughter's verbal confirmation of made-up events also prompts the daughter to invent an emotion associated with made-up events. This rehearsal of providing rule-governed labels or behavior about a non-existent event, and reinforcing a fake memory of it by association with emotions meets another goal. The daughter observes her mother's happiness, pleasure, and generous physical affection given to her for every approximation of repeating or echoing the made-up statements her mother told her. Reinforcement for the child repeating the lies exactly as the mother stated the lies is on a fixed-ratio schedule and may be more dense or extensive than any other reinforcers the mother gives to her daughter. Finally, believability of made-up allegations also depends on the clever parent tapping some suspicious background ambiguity of the father about improper sexual behaviors. A nebulous mand such as, "You know, your dad has done this before," lacks any factual or referential foundation. However, it evokes the listener-daughter to ask questions, or distrust her father, or to even generate examples from her recent experiences with him confirming the mothers' mand. Distortions result in the child's immediate memory of events with her father that blur truth from falsehood, and it may be very difficult for traditional mental health assessment batteries to discern the lies (Faller, 2007; Poole & Lamb, 1998; Trocme & Bala, 2005).

Let us look closer at the contextual factors and functional role of mands. Mands can help explain the parent and child's motivation to tell a fabricated story. The section afterward offers an operational analysis of how the parent "vicariously identifies" with a child taught false sexual-abuse allegations.

## The role of mands

Memory contamination induced by parental coaching is thus largely a function of the instigator (parent's) environment. Parents use mands to establish, persuade, or arouse certain behaviors in the learner-child to better achieve a surreptitious goal that the parent, alone, appears unable to achieve alone. The mand, by definition, is a verbal operant reinforced in response to relevant conditions of deprivation, satiation, or aversive stimulation (Skinner, 1957, pp. 35–36). Functional outcomes of parental mands on children are manifold but generally include the following (cf. Hall & Sundberg, 1987; Hernandez, Hanley, Ingvarsson, & Tiger, 2007; Lamarre & Holland, 1985; Michael, 1988; Wallace, 2007):

1. Manding brings about desired changes or conditions.
2. Manding provide specific information (about contingencies) to a child to control his or her environment.
3. Manding is the only verbal operant that directly benefits the speaker.
4. Mand training (coaching a child to lie) can establish the parent as valid (convincing).
5. Mand training can increase both parent and child's access to certain reinforcers and deferment or elimination of punishers.
6. Manding become an essential bond-builder between parent and child.
7. Manding allows for *extensions.*

The word *extensions* refer to subtypes of mands that accelerate the generalization and promulgation of lies about some allegation of sexual or physical abuse. The most common subtypes of mands include *superstitious mands, and magical mands* (cf. Miguel, 2017; Stafford, Sundberg, & Braam, 1988; Stewart, McElwee, & Ming, 2013). Superstitious mands are frequently directed to inanimate objects, such as begging the frozen vehicle in the middle of a Midwest winter to start in the morning, "Please, car, have pity on me, please start." Superstitious mands get their name by the fortuitous association of continuity between the mand and outcomes in the environment seemingly caused by the mand. When the car starts miraculously, it reinforces the magical mand to recur in similar situations in the future. When the car fails to start, the superstitious mand is not necessarily ineffective or diminished if it occasions another superstitious mand whose outcomes are more probable (e.g., "My car is a dud, but bet my wife's car wills start", and it does). Contiguity of events are usually accidental or spurious, which is why the term "superstitious" is used. Verbal mands used in baseball, for example, before the batter enters the batter's box usually accompany an entire "superstitious" ritual historically paired with hitting homeruns. In coaching children, superstitious mands attribute some stimulus control to inanimate, non-corporeal, or abstract events about which the child cannot see and hear but come to believe are real. In the case of Marcus, superstitious manding occurred when asking Tonya where her mother supposedly touched her, and referencing her mother as doing bad behaviors.

A second extension is called *magical mands.* Magical mands are verbal operants for which the reinforcers never occurred. For example, "I can really use a vacation now," may not generate vacation or holiday plans instantly or remotely. However, the speaker as listener may be more inclined to cruise online websites for all-inclusive hotels in the Bahamas for a later date. This *autoclitic mand* enjoins or encourages the speaker to behave (even emote or think) as his or her own listener, *wishing for an idealistic, or unattainable goal.* In coaching children to lie, magical mands (not autoclitic mands) are like religious prayers that propose a belief elusively related to some contrived or non-existent stimulus events. For example, if a pious parent asks of his child, "Did you remember to say your prayers at night before you go to bed so that God can hear you?," the magical mand evokes the child to believe God or some entity will hear her and she must respond in certain ways for God to listen. There are no immediate consequences directly experienced from the God; but there are consequences incurred directly from the parent for the child *not saying prayers before bed.* When Marcus asked Tonya, "Did mommy make you do any of these things when you did not want to?, he magically manded Tonya to expect aversive contingencies from her mother. Tonya's answering "yes" to her father's questions is not to avoid any remote or abstract aversive consequences from the mother; her answer of "yes"was avoid her father's persistent inquiries (punishment) if she said "no."

A third subtype of mand proposed here may be more functionally explanatory of how Marcus mobilized his daughter Tonya to lie about the sexual assault. It also might explain operationally the phenomenon of how the child becomes the mail carrier of the parent's agenda to fabricate allegations. A parent does more than mand a child to listen to, imitate, or talk about made-up stories about another parent. Mands—superstitious or magical—simply explain the abstract, intangible, or remote stimulus conditions to which the mand refers. Manding also has the function of motivating a child to recite the lies in subsequent behavioral segments exactly as the parents rehearsed the child. The transmission or generality of manded behaviors across different psychological fields to extend the parent's motivating operation by the child might be called a *surrogate mand.* A surrogate mand is when the listener is engaged by the speaker to reproduce verbal behavior (for the speaker) that has point to point correspondence (in the same mode or identical) with the speaker's verbal behavior. When Marcus coached the series of questions for Tonya to answer about sexual abuse, she repeated the questions and answers nearly verbatim (close to echoic, but not exactly) during the police forensic interviewing. She was under a motivating operation to generalize or repeat the questions prompted by the mand (the speaker or her father gave her). Her delivery of the speaker's (her father's) verbal behavior to the forensic police interviewer was an act of mediation or transfer using the listener as *surrogate* for the speaker-parent. A more colloquially way of explaining a surrogate mand is that the *child does the bidding for the parent.* Here, Tanya learned a lie from the speaker and served as surrogate to mediate or convey the lie to another listener.

## Vicarious (observational) learning and role of the tact

As pointed out in other chapters, there is a plethora of confusing and misleading publications of books on forensic psychology entitled "behavioral analysis" that promise evidence-based conceptual and applied research in behavioral sciences. However, for some bizarre reason, their contents have nothing to do with applied behavior analysis, experimental analysis of behavior, or principles of natural science advanced by learning theorists (e.g., Houck, 2018). Earlier chapters of this book exposed these frauds and even questioned why they hijacked the name, *behavior analysis*. Deceptively promoted is that police and psychological evaluations automatically look at natural science behavior as central in assessing death, violence, and abuse. A similar misrepresentation of terms occurred with the concepts of *vicarious learning*. Vicarious learning or *vicarious reinforcement* conventionally means a person can learn attitudes, feelings, beliefs, and emotions, not through direct exposure to a stimulus, but through observing how others react to the stimulus. For example, a young teen watches his older brother sell drugs to neighborhood buyers and subsequently imitates the behavior of selling drugs to another group of buyers without ever directly *being taught the trafficking trade step by step or with the same stimulus events observed interacting with his brother*. Observational learning research did refine operational definitions of initiative responses, inspired by the pioneering work of Albert Bandura (1962, 1965, 1973; Bandura, Grusec, & Menlove, 1966). Frlyng, Bandura's *social learning theory* (Bandura & Walters, 1963) essentially claimed human beings can learn without directly experiencing the consequences of their own actions. The model hypothesizes how learning actually occurs; either it is transmitted by three types of models (live model, instructional model, symbolic model) or skill acquisition occurs from *intrinsic* (not extrinsic) reinforcement. Such intrinsic reinforcement included pride, satisfaction, and sense of accomplishment. Further bridging the gap between observation and skill learning is the role of cognition. Internal thoughts act as attentional mediators processing the information.

Following this theory, a four-step sequence of learning proceeds from observation to imitation of the behavior absent of consequences (see Fig. 11.1).

Bandura's ingenious attempts to eschew protocols of operant conditioning by explaining learning without associations or the three-tier contingencies earned extensive praise and sparked extensive research innovations (Anderson & Bushman, 2001; Devi, Khandelwal, & Das, 2017; Paik & Comstock, 1994). His theory explained a medium for alternative learning in schools and in criminal justice, where students, offenders and victims exposed to influential models (e.g., watching aggression on television or through multiplayer, online video games) could replicate these observed behaviors with varying precision. Observational

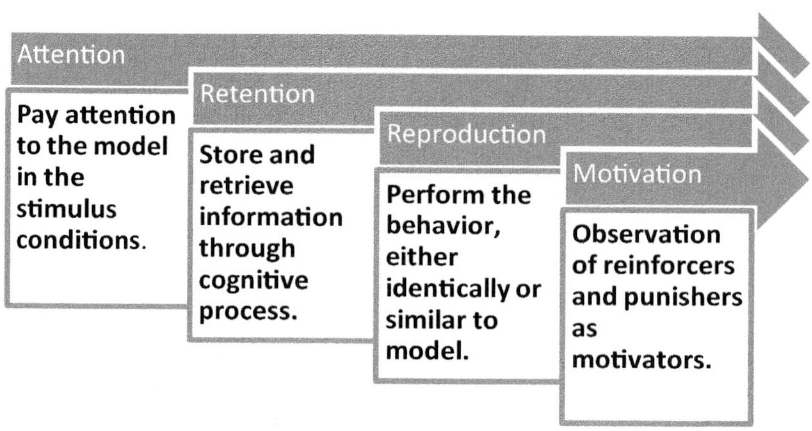


FIG. 11.1 Bandura's four step observational learning process.

learning might also explain the rash of copy-cat murders and terrorist bombings, engineered to repeat the devastating trauma and carnage produced by the modeler's initial heinous crimes (Huesmann, 1986; Hurley & Chater, 2005; Surette. 2016). As elucidatory as Bandura's theory has been for criminal analysis, his model still relies on the existence of hypothetical constructs that do not exist in the psychological field defining the natural world (Fryling, Johnston, & Hayes, 2011). Fryling et al., questioned the intangible entities of mediating cognitions in Bandura's retention phase of his theory. They proposed a viable alternative explanation for observational learning borrowing form Kantor's (interbehavioral) concept of *stimulus substitution* (cf. Kantor, 1957, 1958). Stimulus substitution occurs when the stimulus conditions evokes a memory or response from an earlier behavior segment involving contact with these stimuli.

For example, suppose a 60 year old individual revisits his elementary school. Entry into the foyer confronts visual and olfactory stimuli cuing responses. One response, when smelling the hallway scent and reading the signs is to walk to the office and report being a guest in the building. But simultaneously evoked are responses of wanting to run out of the building from recalling the principal chasing you down the hall after you broke the school trophies over 56 years ago. This secondary memory or response (of wanting to leave the building) comes from the school cues serving a substitute stimulus function. Kantor further distinguished between both responses generated by the substitute stimulus. The visceral arousal of panic compelling you to leave the building was an *endogenous response.* The realization that this fear is 56 years old, is obsolete, but still creates guilt, defines the *exogenous response* (cf. Pronko, 1980, p. 22).

Kantor's conceptualization of endogenous and exogenous responding perhaps moves closer to a more complete behavior analysis of observational learning, especially as it relates to the crime of coaching false allegations in a child. The model, in this case the father Marcus, is a product of two types of conditioning co-existing simultaneously when he learns the news from his daughter Tonya about being touched sexually by the mother. The two types of conditioning are *respondent and operant.* First, words his daughter says about being touched are *conditioned stimuli (CS) eliciting* an unconditioned response (UR) or Marcus' visceral arousal (fear). In Marcus' reactional biography, neutral stimuli paired repeatedly with unconditioned stimuli (US), precipitating and during the molestation, becoming conditioned stimuli (CS); these conditioned stimuli (CS) acquired elicitive properties after so many pairings to equally produce fear or physical arousal in Marcus. . Unconditioned stimuli (US) on Marcus, for example, consisted of genital stimulation, paired continuously with such neutral stimuli as the perpetrator's words, face, perfume, and her taking off her clothes. Marcus' unconditioned responses (UR) possibly consisted of tactile stimulation, erection, and fear. Second, when unconditioned responses (UR) (fear) occurred frequently, not just around unconditioned (training) stimuli (US), but also around conditioned stimuli (CS), the term changes to describe Marcus' behavior, from unconditioned response (UR) to *conditioned response* (CR) (see Fig. 11.2 below), Inside Behavior Segment 1, during Marcus' episodes of being molested, recurrent associations occurred between the US and UR, between US and CS, between CS and UR, and between CS and CR. First-level respondents, where one US elicits one UR, or one CS elicits one UR and CR, are only hypothetical since psychological fields consist of multiply concurring behavior segments engendering a vast constellation of other neutral or conditioned responses.

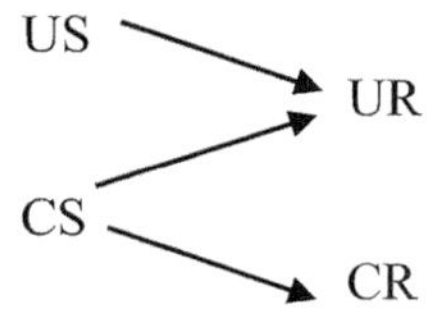


FIG. 11.2 Behavior segment 1.

Concurrent or sequential conditioned responses equally elicited by the unconditioned or conditioned stimuli develop in subsequent behavior segments (see Fig. 11.3). Here, UR1 is an adrenaline rush (anticipatory arousal), UR2 is tactile (genital) stimulation (including penile erection), and UR3 is an arrhythmia (rapid heartbeat) associated with fear. Conditioned responses (1, 2, and 3) are the same response forms (e.g., topography, magnitude) as the unconditioned responses, except the functionality is different. They are elicited by the Conditioned Stimulus (CS) instead of the Unconditioned Stimulus (US).

Tonya's description of her mother touching her, in other words, were conditioned stimuli eliciting visceral (involuntary) physiological changes in Marcus, from his rapid heartbeat to perspiration, to possibly early hyperventilation. Elicitive responses conditioned years earlier in behavior segments associated with his own sexual molestation made the sensations cued from Tonya's words seem vivid, real, and concrete. Tonya's words were conditioned stimuli inducing anxiety the way Marcus experienced these physical reactions in the past. Marcus' biophysical arousal was his way to *empathize with Tonya's allegedly similar ordeal. Empathy, in other words, is an aggregate of sensations generated from several receptors lodged subcutaneously in the body elicited from the conditioned or unconditioned stimuli of another person.* Sensory receptors cover sight, smell, taste, touch, hearing, vestibular, and proprioception. Any convergence of these receptors triggered by Tonya's statements makes Marcus identify with what Tonya must have felt. (Olsson et al., 2016). He does not *feel her emotions.* His *vicarious empathy is an impact reaction of biophysical receptors (unconditioned responses) triggered by what somebody (Tonya) told him and that hypothetically match the biophysical sensations described by the speaker.*

Here, Marcus traced onset of his autonomic arousal (emotions) to his daughter's words. But what if the origins of elicitation are not conspicuous? When respondent effects are more spurious, unpredictable, or not easily attributable to discernible conditioned or

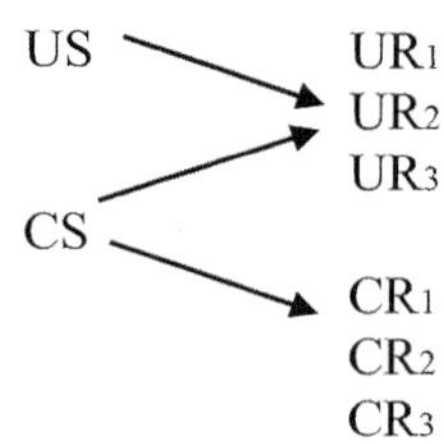


FIG. 11.3 Behavior segment 2.

unconditioned stimuli, the tendency is for people to invent explanations for the unexplained or mysterious onset. For example, postpartum mothers undergoing natural hormonal changes, lactation production, breast enlargement, and uterus contractions may experience accompanying proprioception that seem ominous. They may label or tact these sensations as strange, atypical, or even eliciting Deja-vu-like recollections incongruent with the current setting events. Spontaneous crying, rage, or irritability may seem inconsistent with the person's general moods or even the neutrality of ambient events. On behavioral explanation offered for this unusual respondent phenomenon is that introceptive or proprioceptive stimuli elicit responses historically learned around certain unconditioned and conditioned stimuli that do not exist in the current context (Ruben & Ruben, 1985). A mother may abruptly cry sitting outside on a sunny warm day. Her crying *is not elicited or induced by current stimulus conditions of nice weather or from any other social or psychological events in her life. Instead, proprioceptive stimuli generated arbitrarily by biophysical postpartum permutations resemble the elicitive cues arousing crying.* The sudden jolt of pain or skin tightness historically associated with people yelling at her or making her "feel guilty" for making a mistake. Now only the proprioceptive stimuli of pain or skin tightness occur, without people yelling at her or people making her "feel guilty." However, she still cries. Her crying results from a mis-application of an autoclitic tact to label or interpret the proprioceptive sensations as responses to the original elicitive (or evocative) stimuli occurring long before her pregnancy. None of these stimulus conditions (motivational operations) exist at the moment she cries. That is what confuses the behaver. *The postpartum biophysical sensations are unconditioned stimuli triggering behavior usually associated with very specific setting events that are absent and even antithetical to her current setting events.*

Empathy is similar. It is mislabeling (falsely tacting) one's biophysical sensations as if it were the same biophysical sensation another person experiences. But this mislabeling is not a product of respondent conditioning alone. Autoclitic tacts or tacts that describe another person's nonverbal behavior are multiply controlled by several operant effects as well (Bondy, Tincani, & Frost, 2004; Greer, Dudek-Singer, & Gautreaux, 2000). Acquisition of both operant and respondent repertoires makes it possible not only for Marcus to vicariously identify with his daughter's trauma, but to become the believable model for her subsequent recitation of false allegations. The idea that both operant and respondent conditioning co-exist is not new and has been the subject of intense debate and experimental research (cf., Estes, 1948; Pear & Eldridge, 1984; Rehfeldt & Hayes, 1998). In his *festschrift* to Ivan Pavlov, Rescorla (1998) reveals the ubiquity of mixing operant (instrumental) and classical (respondent) conditioning under controlled or basic experimental lab conditions. His elucidation of the Two-Process Learning Theory (Rescorla & Solomon, 1967) settles the historical dichotomy that learning is discretely operant or respondent and overlap is coincidental (cf. Mowrer, 1951). For example, in Marcus' empathy to Tonya, his response is an amalgam of previous conditioning around US and CS, and also the direct operant consequences immediately impacting the outcome of his empathic response. Consequences depend on the contingencies in a behavioral segment. In Chapter 1, four common contingency relationships defined included positive reinforcement, negative reinforcing, positive punishment, and negative punishment (see Fig. 11.4 below). Positive reinforcement describes Tonya's echoic or positive

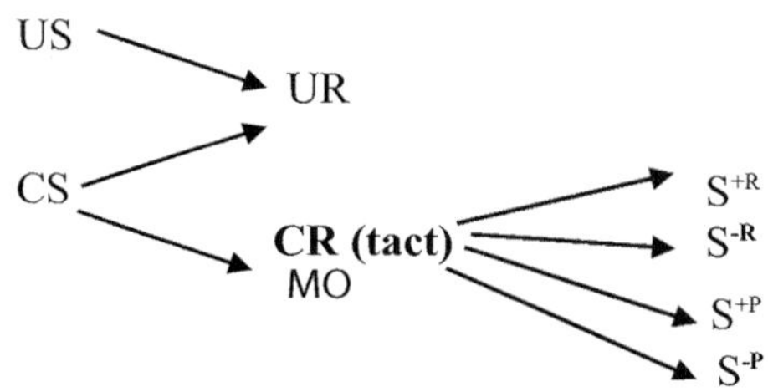


FIG. 11.4 Behavior segment 2.

intraverbal responses back to her father, repeating back what her father said to her or elaborating on the mother's alleged sexual touching. Negative reinforcement describes Marcus selectively withholding or avoiding any pleasant topics about Tonya's mother, the removal of which increases his unpleasant (deprecatory) talk or accusations about Tonya's mother. Positive punishment describes any verbal resistance Tonya exhibits during coaching sessions. Tonya may disagree with her father or reverse blame on him for allowing her to visit her mother. Aversive behavior can also include Tonya's nonverbal rantings, tantrums, crying, property destruction, running away, harm to others, or self-injury. Effects of positive punishment decelerate or discourage Marcus' coaching, at least for that behavior segment. Negative punishment also reduces his coaching efforts, but this time due to Tonya threatening to stop (remove) visitation with her father if he continues bad-talking her mother. Sizing up the contingencies, Marcus may carefully weigh the time, schedule, and expected outcome of reinforcement against the spatio-temporality and expectancy effects of punishment to decide the best moment to empathize with Tonya (cf. Herrnstein, 1970).

Fig. 11.4 schematically outlines the two-factor learning components of operant and respondent conditioning on Marcus. Exposure to US and CS elicit introceptive or proprioceptive stimuli labeled with pure autoclitic tacts as *the way he used to feel when he was sexually molested.* Marcus is the speaker (a) who becomes his own listener of self-verbal behavior (autoclitic tacts), (b) who is under the motivating operation (MO) of his daughter Tonya's sadness, and (c) who fabricates false allegations about the mother producing an equally probable effect from Tonya of positive of negative reinforcers, or positive or negative punishers.

This lateral sequence of two-types of conditioning represents only one, among infinitely many contingencies concurrently impinging on Marcus' decision to coach his daughter. It illustrates how a natural science approach relies on the facts instead of hypothetical fictions about personality types, traits, or imagined constructs. . Marcus' commission of false allegations and misleading his daughter to lie under oath is not about his narcissistic personality or trait equivalence to Munchausen by Proxy. Reifications of personality drift from the corporeal facts and invent reasons and assumptions floating outside the stratosphere of psychological fields. Inside the psychological fields, the realm permitting a more measurable and predictable account of Marcus' behavior, the question asked of the psychological examiner is not "What is wrong with Marcus to make him do this?" but instead, "what is wrong with the contingencies under which he behaves to produce these criminal acts?"

# References


American Psychiatric Association. (1994). *Diagnostic and statistical manual of mental disorders* (4th ed.). Washington DC: American Psychiatric Association.

American Psychiatric Association. (2000). *Diagnostic and statistical manual of mental disorders IV TR*. Washington DC: American Psychiatric Association.

American Psychiatric Association. (2013). *Diagnostic and statistical manual of mental disorders* (5th ed.). Washington DC: American Psychiatric Association.

American Psychological Association. (1996). *APA statement on parental alienation syndrome*. Washington, DC: American Psychological Association.

Anderson, C. A., & Bushman, B. J. (2001). Effects of violent video games on aggressive behavior, aggressive cognition, aggressive affect, physiological arousal, and pro-social behavior: A meta-analytic review of the scientific literature. *Psychological Science, 12*, 353–359.

Asher, R. (1951). Munchausen's syndrome. *Lancet, 1*, 339–388.

Bandura, A. (1962). Social learning through imitation. In M. R. Jones (Ed.), *Nebraska symposium on motivation* (pp. 211–269). Lincoln, NE: University of Nebraska Press.

Bandura, A. (1965). Influence of model's reinforcement contingencies on the acquisition of imitative responses. *Journal of Personality and Social Psychology, 1*, 589–595.

Bandura, A. (1973). *Aggression: A social learning analysis*. Oxford, England: Prentice-Hall.

Bandura, A., Grusec, J. E., & Menlove, F. L. (1966). Observational learning as a function of symbolization and incentive set. *Child Development, 37*, 499–506.

Bandura, A., & Walters, R. H. (1963). *Social learning theory and personality development*. NY: Holt, Rinehart and Winston.

Bondy, A., Tincani, M., & Frost, L. (2004). Multiply controlled verbal operants: An analysis and extension to the picture exchange communication system. *The Behavior Analyst, 27*, 247–261.

Bruch, C. S. (2001). Parental alienation syndrome and parental alienation: Getting it wrong in child custody cases. *Family Law Quarterly, 35*, 527–552.

Cartwright, G. F. (1993). Expanding the parameters of parental alienation syndrome. *The American Journal of Family Therapy, 21*, 205–215.

Clawar, S. S., & Rivlin, B. V. (1991). *Children held hostage: Dealing with programmed and brainwashed children*. Chicago, IL, USA: American Bar Association Press.

Coaston, J. (2019). *The FBIs college admissions fraud case against Felicity Huffman and many more, explained*. Vox. March 12.

Cyr, M., & Bruneau, G. (2008). Assessing false allegations of child sexual abuse. In M. St-Yves, & M. Tanguay (Eds.), *The psychology of criminal investigation: The search for the truth* (pp. 199–228). Toronto: Carswell.

Devi, B., Khandelwal, B., & Das, M. (2017). Application of Bandura's social cognitive theory in the technology enhanced, blended learning environment. *International Journal of Applied Research, 3*, 721–724.

Dunne, J., & Hedrick, M. (1994). The parental alienation syndrome: An analysis of sixteen selected cases. *Journal of Divorce & Remarriage, 21*, 21–37.

Estes, W. K. (1948). Discriminative conditioning II. Effects of Pavlovian conditioned stimulus upon a subsequently established operant response. *Journal of Experimental Psychiatry, 38*, 173–177.

Faller, K. C. (2007). Coaching children about sexual abuse: A pilot study of professional's perceptions. *Child Abuse & Neglect, 31*, 947–959.

Fryling, M. J., Johnston, C., & Hayes, L. J. (2011). Understanding observational learning: An interbehavioral approach. *The Analysis of Verbal Behavior, 27*, 191–203.

Gardner, R. (1985). Recent trends in divorce and custody litigation. *Academy Forum, 29*, 3–7.

Gardner, R. (2001). Parental alienation syndrome (PAS): Sixteen years later. *Academy Forum, 45*, 10–12.

Greer, R. D., Dudek-Singer, J., & Gautreaux, G. (2000). Observational learning. *International Journal of Psychology, 41*, 486–499.

Hall, G., & Sundberg, M. L. (1987). Teaching mands by manipulating conditioned establishing operations. *The Analysis of Verbal Behavior, 5*, 41–53.

Hernandez, E., Hanley, G. P., Ingvarsson, E. T., & Tiger, J. (2007). A preliminary evaluation of the emergence of novel mand forms. *Journal of Applied Behavior Analysis, 40*, 137–156.

Herrnstein, R. J. (1970). On the law of effect. *Journal of the Experimental Analysis of Behavior, 13*, 243–266.

Houck, M. (Ed.). (2018). *Behavioral analysis*. NY: Academic Press.

Huesmann, L. R. (1986). Psychological process promoting the relation between exposure to media violence and aggressive behavior by the viewer. *Journal of Social Issues, 42*, 125–139.

Hurley, S., & Chater, N. (2005). Introduction: The importance of imitation. In S. Hurley, & N. Chater (Eds.), *Perspectives on imitation: From neuroscience to social science* (Vol. 1, pp. 1–52). Cambridge, MA: MIT Press.

Kantor, J. R. (1957). Constructs and events in psychology: Philosophy, banished and recalled. *The Psychological Record, 6*, 55–60.

Kantor, J. R. (1958). *Interbehavioral psychology*. Chicago, IL: The Principia Press.

Lamarre, J., & Holland, J. G. (1985). The functional independence of mands and tacts. *Journal of the Experimental Analysis of Behavior, 43*, 5–19.

Levitz, J., & Korn, M. (2019). The Yale Dad who set off the college admissions scandal. *Wall Street Journal*.

Lyon, T. D., Malloy, L. C., Quas, K. A., & Talwar, V. A. (2008). Coaching, truth induction, and young maltreated children's false allegations and false denials. *Child Development, 79*, 914–929.

Meadow, R. (1977). Munchausen syndrome by proxy—the hinterland of child abuse. *Lancelet, 11*, 343–345.

Michael, J. (1988). Establishing operations and the mand. *The Analysis of Verbal Behavior, 6*, 3–9.

Miguel, C. F. (2017). The generalization of mands. *The Analysis of Verbal Behavior, 33*, 191–204.

Mowrer, O. H. (1951). Two-factor learning theory: Summary and comment. *Psychological Review, 58*, 350–354.

Ney, T. (1995). *True and false allegations of child sexual abuse: Assessment and case management*. NY: Psychology Press.

Olsson, A., McMahon, K., Papenberg, G., Zaki, J., Bolger, N., & Ochsner, K. N. (2016). Vicarious fear learning depends on empathic appraisals and trait empathy. *Psychological Science, 27*, 25–33.

Paik, H., & Comstock, G. (1994). The effects of television violence on antisocial behavior: A meta-analysis. *Communication Research, 21*, 516–546.

Pear, J. J., & Eldridge, G. D. (1984). The operant-respondent distinction: Future directions. *Journal of the Experimental Analysis of Behavior, 42*, 453–467.

Poole, D. A., & Lamb, M. E. (1998). *Investigative interviews of children: A guide for helping professionals*. Washington DC: American Psychological Association.

Pronko, N. H. (1980). *Psychology from the standpoint of an interbehaviorist*. Monterey, CA: Brooks/Cole Publishing.

Rehfeldt, R. A., & Hayes, L. J. (1998). The operant-respondent distinction revisited: Toward an understanding of stimulus equivalence. *The Psychological Record, 48*, 187–210.

Rescorla, R. A. (1988). Pavlovian conditioning: It's not what you think it is. *American Psychologist, 43*, 151–160.

Rescorla, R. A., & Solomon, R. L. (1967). Two-process learning theory: Relationships between Pavlovian condition and instrumental learning. *Psychological Review, 74*, 151–182.

Ruben, D. H., & Ruben, M. J. (1985). Behavioral implications of the postpartum blues (depression). *Birth Psychology Bulletin, 6*, 1–9.

Schreir, H. A., & Libow, J. A. (1993). *Hurting for love. Munchausen by proxy syndrome*. NY: Guilford Press.

Sheridan, M. S. (2003). The deceit continues: An updated literature review of Munchausen Syndrome by proxy. *Child Abuse & Neglect, 27*, 431–451.

Skinner, B. F. (1957). *Verbal behavior*. NY: Appleton Century-Crofts.

Stafford, M. W., Sundberg, M. J., & Braam, S. J. (1988). A preliminary investigation of the consequences that define the mand and the tact. *The Analysis of Verbal Behavior, 6*, 61–71.

Stewart, I., McElwee, J., & Ming, S. (2013). Language generativity, response generalization, and derived relational responding. *The Analysis of Verbal Behavior, 29*, 137–155.

Surette, R. (2016). Copycat crime and copycat criminals: Concepts and research questions. *Journal of Criminal Justice and Popular Culture, 18*, 49–78.

Trocme, N., & Bala, N. (2005). False allegations of abuse and neglect when parents separate. *Child Abuse & Neglect, 29*, 1333–1367.

Wallace, M. D. (2007). A comprehensive analysis of mand training. *The Journal of Speech and Language Pathology, 2*, 278–286.

Zaky, E. A. (2015). Factitious disorder imposed on another (Munchausen syndrome by proxy): A potentially lethal form of child abuse. *Journal of Child and Adolescent Behavior, 3*, 1–3.

CHAPTER

# 12

# Intrafamily contingencies exposing contradictory testimony and parental incompetence in two parents vying for child custody

Historians of the Watergate scandal were mesmerized by the apostate president Richard M. Nixon obstructing justice in the cover up of wiretapping crimes. Forty-five years later, historians see parallels in the Robert S. Mueller investigation of present Donald J. Trump's obstruction of justice to cover up a Russian collusion in the 2016 campaign interference. When attorney general William P. Barr's 4-page summary of Mueller's 400-page completed report showed no Trump-Russia conspiracy, congress Democrats, and anti-Trump supporters objected to the premature exoneration of president Trump. They felt the Barr findings were wrong and wanted release of the full Mueller document before conceding defeat; or they lauded another investigation by the House Intelligence Committee, who might unveil missing facts indicting the President. Ironically, feeding the frenzy of Democrat and anti-trump paranoia, members of the Mueller team leaked that Robert Muller's confidential report may indeed contain damaging information about the president. This ignited a fresh round of political fighting, ushering in a new phase of the nearly two-year old battle over the Russia probe. Notwithstanding the House Committee's eventual findings, or how much of the Mueller confidential report finally sees daylight, underlying this seesaw battle is *legal discordance and the right for recourse.*

Similar civil discordance and recourse occurs in the family court system when two opposing parties, usually the biological parents, fight over custody of their children. Custody disputes represent one of the most arduous, costly, and unpleasant sub-disciplines in law because of being endlessly contentious when agreements mutually or unilaterally break down (Fidler, Bala, Birnbaum, & Kavassalis, 2008; Gould & Martindale, 2009; Rohrbaugh, 2008; Stahl, 2010). When acrimonious custody disputes go unmediated or parents (or guardians) return repeatedly in front of court referees or judged, one precedent followed is to order psychological evaluations of all parties concerned in the case. Courts use child custody evaluations as an aid to judicial fact-finding and decision making.

*Behavioral Forensics*
https://doi.org/10.1016/B978-0-12-819805-6.00012-9

The appointment of psychologists or other mental health specialists to evaluate family members and determine which parent deserves physical or legal custody (or both) is often a thankless and legally risky task for both the expert evaluator and parents subjected to the evaluation. The mental health expert, looking at the best interests of the child, may disqualify one or both parents due to risk of abuse, neglect, parental incompetence, or other mental health or practical reasons (drug abuse, felony record, geographical distance, disrupting happiness of child, etc.). The parent, on the other hand, unwillingly opens Pandora's Box of their lives, exposing previously hidden character flaws, personality disorders, wrong choices, and reasons why the biological parents' relationship dissolved. While parents eventually recover from embarrassing disclosure, the court-appointed mental health expert may be in for a rude awakening. Experts face a perilous journey into unsafe legal waters that may directly jeopardize their license or cause unsalvageable damage to their professional reputation. One reason for this peril is the parents' right to contest the completed evaluation not only by filing a petition in family court, but by filing a formal complaint against the evaluator with a particular state board of licensure. Formal complaints result from parents unhappy about outcome decisions of the evaluation report and who want recourse. Once the Board receives this formal complaint, no matter how frivolous or feasible, legal protocol requires the board to notify the expert of this complaint and the steps of a preliminary instigation undertaken to explore the merits of the case. Formal communication also returns to the complainant updating the progress on the complaint process. The moment the complainant receives official confirmation that the evaluator or evaluation is under review, the complainant (parent) can submit this notification to the Friend of the Court as leverage to disqualify the *evaluation report or evaluator* and request that the court appoint another evaluator (Bow, Gottlieb, Siegel, & Noble, 2010; Glassman, 1998; Kirkland & Kirkland, 2001).

Laws passed in some states to protect court-appointed mental health evaluators from incriminations are starting but the movement is slow and dispute over this immunity is controversial (Emery, Otto, & O'Donohue, 2005). One approach to risk management of custody evaluation liability is when the procedures and orientation of testing are evidence-based. A scientifically-crafted evaluation, using behavioral assessment recording of data and fact-based analyses, can reduce the guess-work and subjectivity biasing evaluation outcomes (cf. Gould, 1998). This chapter demonstrates the practice of a forensic behavior analysis in a custody evaluation involving two parents and two children. First explored are risk management issues affecting the evaluator. Second, discussion introduces some uniform guidelines for procedures to conduct custody evaluation. Third, a case study presents the Jacob family undergoing a series of different assessments through behavior analytic optics to reach conclusions regarding the best interests of the children.

## Liability and risk management

The exigency of parents to retaliate against forensic evaluators who deny their bid for child custody has grown exponentially in the last 10 years and become an abuse of judicial rights. Disgruntled parents who disagree with content or recommendations of the court-appointed evaluation report enjoy a legal right to appeal the report findings through definable channels in the family court system. Often this system is cumbersome, time-consuming, possibly expensive if navigated by hired attorneys, and delays reversal of custody denial that can interfere with family dynamics. One expedient route around the maze of family court is to file a complaint against the mental health expert with the proper licensure board. Receipt of the complaint immediately ignites a cascade of investigatory steps from gathering more facts on the subject, to board hearings, to eventually sanctions against the expert affecting his or her clinical practice. Along the course of investigation, notifications of progress are sent to the complainant affirming the action taken and responsible protection of their consumer rights. With one notification received, the complainant can attach the Board letter to a petition filed with the Friend of the Court to disqualify the forensic expert and request the court to re-assign another evaluator. For parent-complainants, this strategy reverses a bad decision of one evaluation report and provides another opportunity to positively influence an evaluator to win custody. But for the forensic evaluator notified of a licensing complaint, the headaches and costs associated with a licensing board's ethics review has just begun (cf., Piker, 2007).

Licensing boards in most states, consisting of gubernatorial appointed mental health experts, attempt to represent a cross section of the specialty (psychologist, licensed counselors, social workers, etc.). Cross-sections in psychology, for example, may cover clinical psychologists, academic psychologists, hospital psychologists, prison psychologists, and child psychologists. Within these broad disciplines, coverage is less comprehensive but still diverse among schools of orientation, such as psychoanalysis, behaviorism, humanism, and more contemporary approaches. One conspicuously omitted or rarely included subspecialty found on licensing boards is forensic psychology. A dearth of practicing forensic experts sit on the board who can help screen incoming complaints and lend critical insight on court processes or legal vulnerability of court-appointed forensic evaluators. Without these oversights specialists, the unrestricted autonomy of licensing boards during investigations can easily go beyond the initial complaints and include other infelicities discovered in the expert's practice. Unlike a criminal case in civil or district court, rules governing licensing board discovery of facts associated with the original complaint are boundless in evidentiary inquires; in addition, damaging data collected on *another matter unrelated to the initial complaint* may even supersede the original complaint.

For example, a court-appointed psychologist who performed a custody evaluation of multiple family parties and assembled her results in a report submitted to the court received a licensing complaint questioning the validity of tests used and results generated in the report. After 7 years of protracted letter exchanges with the Board, two hearings defending the science of tests used and reasons for results, and costs exceeding $30,000 for legal representation concerning transactions with the Board, the Board concluded the forensic expert *did not engage in unethical conduct, did follow protocols for testing and conclusions, and did follow the court's order to properly assess custody behavior*. That is, the Board dismissed the original charges filed against the psychologist by the parent. However, the Board also fined the psychologist for allegedly misleading the consumer to believe she had an association membership credential that had expired one month prior to the evaluation date. The misrepresentation of the membership, while unethical in its own right and likely due to a clerical oversight, was the only punitive action taken by the Board in seven years.

The unintentional lesson learned from this example—which is more common than uncommon—is for mental health practitioners aspiring to enter forensic arenas to shy away from conducting family custody evaluations (Bow & Quinnell, 2002). But there appears relief for this trend on the horizon. Decline in professionals risking malpractice from custody evaluation has been offset slightly by promising laws passed in many states to protect court-appointed specialist with *immunity clauses.* Immunity clauses are not purely iron-clad shields against irresponsible or frivolous board complaints seeking disqualification of the expert. States give *limited immunity from complaints, assuming the evaluator is acting in good faith and conducts the evaluation pursuant to standards that a reasonable forensic expert would have used as recommended by some uniform standards* (e.g., *from the American Psychological Association)* (Georgia Psychological Association, 1990; Greer, 2004). Immunity does not mean complete protection from ethic charges for violating the standards of ethical evaluation procedures. Instead, the limited protection means proper board consideration for extenuating circumstances of the high-risk activity. It also hopes to re-motivate reticent and highly trained forensic specialists to continue contracting with family courts. Proactive States proposing or ratifying limited immunity polices into Board rules include Florida, Georgia, Illinois, Metropolitan Denver, Colorado, Nebraska, New Jersey, North Carolina, and Oklahoma. Dismissal of bogus complaints is part of the rules protection clause. Protection safeguards also attempt reduction of rising costs of attorney fees, malpractice insurance, and repeated sanctions against legitimate mental health evaluators who later are rejected on HMO, PPO or other third-party-payer insurance panels due to history of board reprimands.

However, any law aimed at protecting forensic evaluators from frivolous complaints does not preclude consumers from filing complaints for legitimate reasons. Even good-faith evaluators may overlook proper protocol or overstep the evidence in adducing conclusions about custodial assignment to parents. For example, a plaintiff parent fighting for sole physical and legal custody, who alleges physical or drug abuse of the defendant parent hires a psychologist to evaluate *only the plaintiff mother and her children.* While lopsided or unilateral evaluations are not entirely unethical, the problem is limitations in conclusions about the non-interviewed parties. During the interview, plaintiff mother and the children paint an abysmal picture of the father as dangerous, physically abusive, and recklessly alcoholic. The psychologists performs separate interviews with each child and parent and even performs observational sessions between the mother and children to determine the mother's parental competence. Conclusions in the report favor the mother's exclusive (sole) physical and legal custody in view the father's abuse.

Ethically, two problems inherently discredited the veracity of this psychologist's one-sided report (cf., Martindale, 2003). First, forensic interviewing and testing only occurred with plaintiff mother and children and excluded the father. Data regarding the father is hearsay, second-hand, and subject to distortion, misinformation, fabrication, or coaching by the mother. Without direct forensic interview of all parties concerned, no conclusion can be reasonably made about the weight of either parents' positive or negative attributes on the best interest of the children. Even if the mother furnishes e-mails, text or audio, or video recorded messages or stolen diaries or hospital documents from the defendant exhibiting his physical abuse, polymorbid diagnoses, or previous substance abuse hospitalization, the discovery evidence is only circumstantial, tenuous, and both susceptible to being "doctored" or incorrectly represented without direct one-on-one contact with the father to clarify and attest to the reliability and validity of evidentiary documents. Second, on the current joint legal and physical custody, most states mandate both parents mutually consent to any professional provider (psychologist, dentists, physician, etc.) to the children. Here, the mother unilaterally hired the psychologist without prior knowledge of or consent of the co-custodian father. Despite the often inconvenience of acrimonious parents coordinating schedules to meet with a court-appointed or non-court appointed evaluator, the consent and presentation of both parties and their children provides the fairest and most objective opportunity for assessment accuracy.

## Procedure of custody evaluations

Despite broad agreement about needed components in forensic custody evaluations, there is little agreement about how to assess them (Baerger, Galatzer-Levy, Gould, & Nye, 2002). For example, guidelines issued by the American Psychological Association (APA, 1994) and Association of Family and Conciliation Courts (AFCC, 2006) provide a generic blueprint for multi-method approaches combining clinical interviews, direct observation, archival document review, and psychological testing. Domains of parents recommended for assessment, while also general, include (a) parenting ability, (b) capacity to provide a stable loving home, (c) inappropriate behaviors negatively influencing the child (e.g., substance abuse), (d) parental psychopathology and its impact on parenting ability, and (e) the child's own wishes for custody placement. Research on practices of custody evaluators confirm this ubiquity of assessment domains and frequent protocols followed (Ackerman & Pritzi, 2011, 1997; Bow & Quinnell, 2002; Grisso, 1990, 2003; Heilbrun, 2001). Evaluations typically proceed through a series of orderly steps with each party court-ordered for inspection. Steps include:

1. Separate one-on-one meetings with each parent (or other guardians)
2. Separate one-on-one meetings with each child (unless too young, < age 4).
3. Parent-child observations consisting of one parent and one child at a time. For example, with two children, observations occur with each child separately.
4. Testing of the parents and children (if applicable, depending on age and abilities)
5. Collateral contacts or access to archival collaborative documents (e.g., past psychological evaluations, IEP or 504 plans, medical and hospital records, police reports, etc.).

Family court evaluators working in culturally diverse counties face even more complex challenges to assure principles underlying interview assessment and psychological testing are ethnically sensitive (Chiu, 2014), Use of nonverbal tests or tests not relying on English or any indigenous language (e.g., Comprehensive Test of Nonverbal Intelligence, Leiter-3) replace standard instruments standardized almost exclusively on populations in the United States (McCallum, 2017). Priorities of ethical testing and assessment focus on test fairness, protection against sample bias, and interpretations endemically including heritage, rituals, customs, or other promulgated cultural norms representing the social matrix of the particular subject under inquiry.

Since many courts accord significant weight to the option of child custody evaluators, practice of custody evaluations depends on uniform ethical guidelines on conceptual and some procedural matters. The APA guidelines for child custody evaluations in divorce proceedings (1994) offers a playbook of aspirational, not mandatory standards expected of competent professionals engaged in custody evaluations for family litigation. Conceptual directives range from focus on the best interests of the child to detection of parenting attributes and how it fits psychological needs of the child; Procedural guidelines are very general and give extensive latitude to practitioners on implementing interviews and diagnostic testing providing the methods comport with approximately 14 priorities ranging from (a) evaluations being timely and consistent with the referral questions, (b) commenced with appropriate informed consent, (c) evaluations using multiple methods of data gathering,. And (d) maintenance of professional records in accordance with ethical and legal obligations (cf. American Law Institute, 2002; APA, 2002, 2007; Melton, Petrila, Poythress, & Slobogin, 2007). Parting the seas of this ambiguity, innovative research and test constructors moved to a more evidence-based or scientific foundation for custody evaluations (Gould, 1998; Grisso, 2005).

In Gould's Chapter 7 on "psychological variables to consider in custody determination," he surveys holistic or wide-spectrum factors within the child integrative-fields preceding, concurrent with, and likely following the formidable evaluations. Problems identified such as (a) children's reactions to separation and divorce, (b) age interactions with developmental level, (c) attachment behavior in children, (d) need for continuity and stability, and (e) primary versus secondary caregiver roles. Emotional and behavioral sequela associated with pre-divorce and post-divorce, in other words, are paramount in assessment beyond answering the judicial questions of custody assignment. Gould drew attention, not just to the humanism of custody disputes, but to the reactional biographies and setting events implicitly enmeshed in the child and parents' behavior segments in need of closer measurement.

In the case study presented here, the Jacob family undergoes a routine court order for psychological evaluations to determine a custody recommendation. The difference between the Jacob family's evaluation and traditional custody evaluations akin to the APA, AFCC or other uniform guidelines, is employment of behavioral assessment methods and operationalism of parent-child interactions from a behavioral-analytic and interbehavioral perspective. Data collection uses time-sampling recording methods and quantification of response and stimulus functions comported better with a natural science. Likewise, enlisting (Kantor's 1963, pp. 5–9) concept of investigator in psychological levels of interactions adds objectivism to the role of mental health evaluator. It further shows both weakness and strengths of observing and assessing parent-child transactions.

## The Jacob family

The Jacob parents are fictitious name for litigants in a Midwest country court ordered to undergo psychological evaluations after protracted unresolved custody disputes. Failed attempts at mediation and referee hearings, in addition to endless troves of retaliatory petitions protesting divorce decree violations prompted the judge to seek judicial advice from an independent forensic evaluator. Plaintiff mother alleges the Defendant father is a polydrug abuser dealer and prone to violent rages. Defendant father's rebuttal marginalized his substance abuse and criminal history and accused Plaintiff mother of deception and prevarication. He also accused Plaintiff mother of having aggression problems and being the perpetrator of their marital dissolution.

## Procedure

Interviewed separately were Ms. Jacob and Mr. Jacob. Child Ralph (fictitious name) was 2 years old, below the qualifiable age for reasonable individual interviewing or submission to psychodiagnostics. Instead, four observational recording sessions occurred between both parents. Mr. Jacob met with Ralph for 1 h, divided into "structured" and "play" interactions Ms. Jacob separately met with Ralph for 1 h under identical stimulus conditions. Parents submitted to a conventional diagnostic battery of the MMPI-2-RF, Substance Abuse Subtle Screening Inventory, Test of Memory Malingering, and Parenting Stress Index. Examiner data collection during interview sessions supplementally incorporated the Uniform Child Custody Evaluation System (UCCES) (Munsinger & Karlson, 1994; Otto, Edens, & Barkus, 2000). This tool offer a process for structuring data gathering and organizing information during custody interviews to minimize observer drift or examine tangentiality. Like any information retrieval systems, its advantages for navigating through the bumpy terrain of parenting interviews weighs against distinct disadvantages of (a) allowing the Examiner subjective latitude to bypass or ignore a specific line of inquiry, or (b) only measuring verbal behaviors descriptive of the parents' contingencies with their children. It lacks the measurement precision to record and code actual instances of observed parent-child behavior interactions. Replacing the UCCES during observational sessions was a variation of the Planned Activity Check time-sampling procedure (PLA-CHECK) (cf. Hall, 1971; Ruben, 1983).

## Mr. Jacob

Mr. Jacob is a 31-year-old twice married male Caucasian currently residing with his sibling at a residence owned by his parents. Previously he lived with his wife and two children. Employed 1-year at an auto-repair shop, he touted a 15-year history in the auto-mechanic business. He reached the 11$^{the}$ grade in High School barely passing classes with low "D's" and "E's" blamed on incompletion of homework, weak comprehension, and school apathy. He decided to switch to the Adult Education program where he lifted his grades and found solace in caring teachers; he quit school in 12th grade ... He later achieved his GED two years ago. Disillusioned by education, he drifted in his adolescence toward a drug-peer group experimenting with cannabis and alcohol. Weekend party binges progressed rapidly by age 18 to daily consumption of 5–10 beers per day and smoking 2–3 joints per day; drug use eclipsed when arrested for a Minor in Possession. Other juvenile crimes included breaking and entering, drug possession with intent to deliver, joy riding, larceny, and domestic violence. In adulthood, he incurred three DUILs in a matter of two consecutive years, serving time in county jail time and mandated by court into a 30 day residential alcoholism treatment hospital. After a two-year post-hospital abstinence from drinking, he reportedly relapsed before marrying his first wife Ms. Jacob. Short of cash, he resorted to weekend drug sales of cannabis and cocaine to local friends under the guise of playing fantasy football (or some sports) with his buyers. He hid his drug-trafficking from his wife until his debt increased to the intermediary drug distributor, who "blew up his cell phone" (made several calls to he and his wife) demanding instant payment or be subjected to retribution. His wife bailed him out of debt, withdrawing from their limited 401 plan and paid hefty penalties for their early fund withdrawal. On the obverse side, the couple enjoyed drinking together as their primary compatibility until Ms. Jacob became pregnant with her first child. Together they produced one child, Ralph (2 years old).

While caretaking their children, Mr. Jacob reported he and his wife frequently drank alcohol, smoked marijuana, and used meta-amphetamines. Drug use (mostly the meta-amphetamine) boosted their libido for frequently mutual sexual fulfillment. Ritually combing drug use and sex rapidly built an erotic tolerance where they sought more adventurously risk-taking sexual activities such as inviting in other partners or attending Swinger-parties. On the downside, post-sex intoxication frequently occasioned arguments. The couple fiercely escalated into acrimony over minor disagreements when both mis-interpreted each person's comments as defensive or "hiding something." Mr. Jacob's loud voice usually accompanied throwing objects at his wife, whereas his wife reportedly charged at Mr. Jacob and slugged his shoulder. On two occasions, neighbors hearing loudness permeate from their household contacted the police and Mr. Jacob was arrested on first degree Domestic Violence. His arrest (and subsequent conviction) also triggered a referral and immediate investigation by the local Children's Protective Services (CPS) who, after fact-checking, substantiated allegations of improper supervision and failure to protect the children. Fearing threats of physical violence against the children, CPS removed the children and temporary placement them in foster care homes. A long and drawn-out trial lasting 1 year resulted in reunification with their children providing the couple abide by court-mandated requirements of parent training and outpatient therapy in relapse prevention and maintenance. A two-year honeymoon period elapsed of relational happiness between the couple until Mr. Jacob relapsed into drink and marijuana use.

Developmentally, Mr. Jacob is oldest of two children raised by married parents who divorced when Mr. Jacob turned 12 years old. His father vanished to Europe, estranging himself nearly permanently from the family nucleus. His mother, a solidly assertive and resourceful person, remained gainfully employed and later remarried when Mr. Jacob turned 18 years old. For 6 years, however, under his mother's tutelage, Mr. Jacob felt affection, nurtured, and retrospectively believes he had privileges equal to his cohorts whose parents were intact. But his mothers' work schedule made her unavailable and oblivious to Mr. Jacob's adolescent indiscretion of exploring drug and alcohol use.

## Ms. Jacob

Ms. Jacob is a 29-year-old twice married female Caucasian currently residing 2 years in a rented house in the same city as Mr. Jacob. She pays approximately $700/monthly for rent. Previously she lived in her own apartment after moving out of her grandmother's domicile. She is a 1-year supervisor in a local bank and denied any performance quality problems warranting verbal or written reprimands. Past jobs entailed minimum wage and self-employment ranging from housekeeping to stuffing inserts into local newspapers. Her longest job, apart from current employment, involved domestic housekeeping. Born locally, he parents' divorce sent to live in San Diego, California until age 10, after which her single parent moved to Phoenix, Arizona. There, she spent adolescence ages 11 to 20. She graduated high school with failing grades ascribed to chaotic family problems impairing her concentration. Neglected homework, absenteeism, and generally falling behind in academics hemorrhaged by the 11th and 12th grade years, when she experimented using alcohol, acid, and cannabis. Through last-minute diligence of summer and night school courses, she met her high school requirements for graduation. She never underwent multidisciplinary testing for an IEP or 504 plan. Drug use flourished after high school including her foray into methamphetamines. Daily polysubstance rituals reportedly pervaded her life until 2 years ago. Three years ago, she began selling crystal (methamphetamines) and cannabis to pay high expenses incurred from two medically uninsured surgeries.

Ms. Jacob regretted her promiscuity during her post-adolescence and early adulthood immersed in crystal-meta-amphetamine use. Disinhibitive properties of alcohol (combined with crystal) lowered her resistance to multiple male sexual partners, totaling over 20 encounters by age 19. Many of these partners were one-night stands aggressively pursued and subverted for sexual gratification without her using contraception. By age 19, focused on monogamous relationships, she married her first husband with whom she produced two offspring. Distrust damaged the already frail partnership sparked by mutual infidelity and their shared drinking episodes. Mutual drinking further instigated frequent verbal arguments. While married but emotionally disconnected, she rebounded with infatuation in an intense romance with Mr. Jacob. She aggressively pursued him. His quiet, placid, and shy style reportedly excited her challenge to entice his physical affection. Once she prevailed, the couple married for 5 years producing one child (Ralph). Reinforcing the couple's compatibility was their shared polysubstance abuse of nearly 6-beers daily cross-addicted to crystal. However, intoxicated states often were counterproductive for the couple. Ms. Jacob freely expressed cynical remarks that ignited Mr. Jacob into a tirade of domestic violence. After brushes with Child protective Services and court system for her husband's assaults, Ms. Jacob reportedly filed for divorce in 2000 but rescinded the process when Mr. Jacob quit drinking. Ms. Jacob also quit drinking and using crystal Meta-amphetamine.

Two years later, convinced that her own drug abstinence was strong, she witnessed her husband fall off the wagon. His alcohol recidivism quickly reprised the entire ritual sequence of their reciprocal arguments and Mr. Jacob resorting to physical violence. Ms. Jacob again filed for divorce citing her husband for physically and emotionally threatening her safety and that of the minor child. While separated pending divorce litigation, the couple shared legal custody whereas primary physical custody was awarded to Ms. Jacob due to her proximity to the school district and accessibility to her child. She told the court that (a) when her son returned home from weekend visitations, he explodes in destructive tantrums, (b) unsupervised weekend visitations fail to monitor Mr. Jacob's polychemical use, and (c) Mr. Jacob's explosive temper poses immediate danger to the child. As support for her declaration of Mr. Jacob's violence, she provided the exhibit of the PPO recently filed against Mr. Jacob for his aggressive actions during their weekend exchange of Ralph at MacDonald's. In the brief she explains Mr. Jacob opened the car door to talk with Ralph when "I asked him not to talk to the children and not to open or touch my car." Ms. Jacob proceeds to say Mr. Jacob used profanity in response to her request in front of Ralph. Finally, her brief ends by reminding the court of Mr. Jacob's past domestic assault conviction involving malicious property damage.

Developmentally, Ms. Jacob is the only legitimate offspring of married parents divorced when Ms. Jacob turned 2 years old. This divorce, prompting migration to California and then Arizona, distanced her from contact with her father until one her early adulthood. Torn from family, she survived with her daily drinking, alcoholic mother. Her mother's rapidly cyclical moods ran the gamut from suicidal-episodes of depression to hypermania. In both extremes, her mother either was neglectful of Ms. Jacob or viciously cruel to her. Hypercritical remarks were arbitrary and capricious. Arbitrary, in that Ms. Jacob never knew how to predict the deluge of insults. Capricious meant the insults or other faults never fit with any specific wrongdoing of Ms. Jacob. She never could match exactly what she did with what her mother chastised her for. Such a random schedule induced hypervigilance. Ms. Jacob walked on egg-shells or was anticipatory of any montage of sounds, words, or actions likely associated with her mother's ferocity. Into her mid or late adolescence, Ms. Jacob's cowering passivity evolved into a gutsy tenacious and oppositional child, blasting her anger and defensiveness against her mother any time Ms. Jacob anticipated some impending confrontation. Surviving her mother's tirades achieved one milestone. By ages 12 to 13, Ms. Jacob vividly recalled her mother's drunk boyfriend repeatedly sneaking into her bed with her and performing oral sex on her. At first surprised and even disgusted by the intruder's actions, she grew accustomed to his late night rendezvous and erotic stimulation. She remained quiet and let him complete his ritual. She held her breath, bit her tongue, and moaned softly from the strange tingling sensations. Mid age 13, after her mother broke up with the boyfriend and her sex phantom was gone, Ms. Jacob replaced him by enlisting male friends to perform oral sex on her. As tolerance grew for stronger stimulation, Ms. Jacob used stimulant drugs (meta-amphetamine) that boosted her arousal either to masturbate or recruit male partners to "finish her off."

## Analysis and assessment

### Mr. Jacob

Psychological testing and clinical data reveal an introversively, psychosocially deficient adult exhibiting traits of avoidant personality. His strengths abound in employment stability, in benevolence to peers, and in forming a palpable rapport with his daughter. He also shows decision-making qualities capable of living an organized, responsible, and routine lifestyle, but may derail from the structure when abusing drugs and alcohol. His outward signs of kindness and patience are unfortunately diametrical to his hostile actions when inebriated. In light of these positive points, four preponderant pathologies factor into his overall parenting. First, elevated repression and introversive scales suggest he is largely docile, placid, and submissive. He avoids conflict, is phobic about rejection and abandonment, and works feverishly to placate his intimate partner either sexually or through self-sacrificial means beholden to the partner's needs. Rarely does he display outward anger, unless disinhibited by alcohol or cannabis. Then, episodic angry outbursts may explode verbally, not physically, unless the arguer initiates physical attacks.

Second, although not an instigator, he nonetheless may be deceptive, surreptitious, and passive-aggressive, insofar as hiding his anger from his adversaries until it is safe to show it elsewhere. Elevated repressive scales also suggest internalization of feeling and opinions as a safe haven from the risk of social rejection and criticism. Third, elevated imperturbability scales suggest he is dubious about authority and may be derelict in following orders or rules. Misanthropic resentment may emerge from, in his perception, being falsely accused of domestic violence and charged with crimes perpetrated by his wife. Fourth, although he espouses current sobriety, addiction scales affirm unaltered changes in his lifestyle predictive of polydrug recidivism.

## Ms. Jacob

Results of psychological testing and clinical data profile a histrionically aggressive, cyclical mood disordered young adult post-traumatically damaged by her highly punitive childhood years. Among her personal strengths include employment stability, interpersonal assertiveness, and capability of following through with promises. She also can be excruciatingly loyal and benevolent to people submissive to her dominance. They in return receive her unconditional protection, love, and fastidious care. Her deep affection for people often fastens a relationship, although she and her partner can become codependent. Against these redemptive qualities, serious pathology revealed in testing raises questions about her complicity in past failed marriages. The fear of aggression she claims undermines safety for herself and the minor child, actually, may be her own temper. Three major conditions figure prominently. First, elevated impulsive and hostility scales suggest an inflammatory-reactive adult who is preemptively aggressive in situations she perceives as adversarial. Her anticipatory aggression builds on misinferences about her partner's motivations and actions, none of which she diplomatically questions ahead of time. Escalation of anger is rapid, furious, and viciously driven to squelch the perceived aggressor. Although this defensive anger may stop an upset husband when he is sober, it unequivocally catapults the ferocity of an intoxicated, angry person. Likewise, when her daughter grows into adolescence and challenges her mother, the probability of a showdown resembling the arguments between Mr. and Mr. Jacob appears inevitable.

Second, elevated impulsivity is counter-balanced by moderately low depression scales. She may spiral upward into a frenzy of distortive, paranoid, and vindictive thinking, propelling exaggerated reactions. Or, she may appear despondent, anhedonic, withdrawn, and feel helpless, powerless, and deeply out of control. Her interepisodic recovery is fast, and thus shifting phases of moods are ephemeral. However, her daughter may find these mood swings a hard benchmark to understand; her daughter, like Ms. Jacob felt during childhood, may not know exactly when or why her mother gets upset. Third, elevated addictive scales suggest not only admission of past polydrug abuse, but high proclivity for relapse. The main reason for her high risk of polydrug relapse is to self-medicate her hyperarousal state of feeling nervous, for which she used cannabis and alcohol as sedatives in the past. Although she appears reliably abstinent, unchanged behavior patterns either will compel drug re-use, or she will quickly gravitate to another emotionally susceptible male using sex as her self-medicated relief for anxiety.

## Behavioral assessment of parent-child interactions

Samples of parent-child interactions in naturalistic settings are always, in varying degrees, defective by unfiltered variables controlling the response and stimulus conditions (Johnston & Pennypacker, 1980; Sidman, 1960). Behavioral records of children, in particular, can be more difficult by the plasticity and fluidity of their responses changing discretely and broadly across sequential behavior segments (Gelfand & Hartmann, 1975). At best, captured are *representative and anecdotal behaviors associated with similar and different circumstances.* Representative data are the exact or similar response forms targeted for measurement seen in each observational interval recorded Anecdotal data are collateral or secondary responses remotely associated the target response that are informative and predictive about the target behavior, but with less precision. Anecdotal behaviors compete with or occur simultaneously with the target behavior and can interfere with the pristine quality of the target behavior. In the first case, a child saying "no" or refusing to respond to instructional prompts are representative samples of the target behavior for oppositional behavior (i.e., noncompliance to instructions). In the second case, a child given an instruction may quietly start playing with a puzzle or even talking excessively about some topic. While the child is not outwardly defiant, behaviors incompatible with compliance fill the observational interval to record. Innovative measurement systems to record representative and anecdotal behavior during parent-child interactions in custody psychological have been scarce; the evaluations previously focused on attachment responses (e.g., Solomon & George, 2008), and conflict responses (e.g., Bennett, Sullivan & Lewis, 2006). Observations resembled diaries in recording continuous dialogue or exchanges between parties.

Behavioral assessments of parent-child interactions also use continuous recording formats but have categorized the data collected to make the process simpler and more scientifically meaningful (Gardner, 2000; Hughes & Haynes, 1978). The methodology of classifying behaviors reduces time, energy, and mistakes in reliably observing behaviors and its relations to setting events. For example, one continuous recording system is to watch events just preceding behavior (antecedents), followed by specific behavior, and the events after the behavior (consequence). Continuous recording is convenient for slower, less frequent, and shorter behaviors, like a child completing math equations. High frequency behaviors are more difficult to record continuously and best sampled using time-interval procedures (Harrop & Daniels, 1986; Lane & Ledford, 2014). One type of time-interval sample system to measure child behavior is the Planned Activity Check. This approach designates a recurrent interval, say, after 5 min, during which observers watch a child or parent-child interaction for a limited time (10 s) to see if specific behaviors were present. Observed occurrence of responses, not the frequency or duration of responses, is entered as a word ("yes") or number ("1") on a record sheet. Total occurrences are counted at the end of the recording session and divided by the number of recording intervals to compute percentage of occurrences for that observational period.

A similar Planned Activity Check (PLA-CHECK) procedure was used in assessing specific target behaviors during observations of interactions between Mr. Jacob and Ralph, and Ms. Jacob and Ralph. Observational periods divided equally into 30 min under conditions of either structure or play. Measurement divided into spot-checks every 5 min over a 30-min period (or 6 observational intervals, for structure and play, respectively). Each observation lasted 10 s, during which to determine if the specific behaviors occurred or did not occur. If behaviors occurred, scored inside the interval box were codes assigned to specific behaviors. Inserted codes meant the behaviors occurred for more than 5 s. Assignment of codes to specific behaviors appears below in Table 12.1.

Table 12.1 presents a taxonomy of codes corresponding to child and parent behaviors observed for only 10 s for 6 intervals during PLAY and 6 intervals during STRUCTURE. While hardly an exhaustive list of behaviors inherently transactional during the interchange, the attempt was to sample critical predictors of parental tolerance, frustration, and ability to establish productive interactions. Selection of the child responses, while more prototypical in assessment procedures (cf. Fiske & Delmolino, 2012), also allowed a natural reaction to the parents' behaviors. Interactions discerned from parent and child provided a baseline to hypothesize functional analyses in the cause-effect relationships analogous to relationships likely occurring in the household. Codes scored in these observational data sessions appear in Tables 12.2 and 12.3.

Results of the Pla check (time sampling) procedure revealed important data possibly contradictory to each parents' testimony that children are fearful of time spent with their parents.

**TABLE 12.1** Behavior codes for observations of parent-child interaction.

| | | | | |
|---|---|---|---|---|
| ***Play*** | | | | |
| Physical proximity | Close (c) | Far (f) | Contiguous (CT) | Affection (a) |
| Child avoidance | Avoidance (avoid) | Escape (esc) | Resistance (R) | Anger (ang) |
| Instructional compliance | Compliance (comp) | Delay (d) | Tantrum (tan) | Argue (arg) |
| Child activity | Playing (play) | Walking around (walk) | Change activities (ca) | Sitting still (ss) |
| Child/parent eye contact | Child eye-contact (ce) | Parent eye-contact (pe) | Fixed on task (fot) | Distracted or looking away (d) |
| Parent tone | Loud (l) | Soft (s) | Fast (f) | Slow (sl) |
| Child tone | Loud (l) | Soft (s) | Fast (f) | Slow (sl) |
| ***Structured*** | | | | |
| Instructional compliance | Compliance (comp) | Delay (d) | Tantrum (tan) | Argue (arg) |
| Parent describes task | Describe (de) | Repeats (r) | States differently (s) | New task (nt) |
| Child on task | On task (ot) | Off-task (oft) | Argue about task (at) | Parent does task for child (pt) |
| Parent response | Praise (p) | Criticize (cr) | Ignore (i) | Anger (ang) |
| Child response | Defensive (de) | Manding parent (mp) | Cry (c) | Laugh (la) |

TABLE 12.2 Observational codes recorded during play and structured conditions between Mr. Jacob & Ralph.

| Play | 1 | 2 | 3 | 4 | 5 | 6 |
|---|---|---|---|---|---|---|
| Physical proximity | C | C | CT, A | CT | A | CT, A |
| Child avoidance | 0 | 0 | 0 | 0 | 0 | 0 |
| Instructional compliance | D, COMP | D COMP | COMP | COMP | COMP | COMP |
| Child activity | PLAY, W | SS, PLAY | PLAY | PLAY | CA | PLAY |
| Child/parent eye contact | CE, PE | CE, PE | D | FOT | CE, PE | CE, PE |
| Parent tone | S, SL | S, SL | S, SL | S, SL | S, SL | S, SL |
| Child tone | S, F | S, F | S, SL | S, SL | S, SL | S, SL |
| ***Structured*** | | | | | | |
| Instructional compliance | D, COMP | D, COMP | COMP | COMP | COMP | COMP |
| Parent describes task | DE | DE, R | R | DE | NT | NT |
| Child on task | OT | OT, PT | OT, PT | OFT | PT | OT |
| Parent response | P | P | P | P | P, CR | P |
| Child response | MP, LA | MP | MP | MP | LA | MP |

Figs. 12.1–12.4 present percentage distributions of response frequency sampled during observational intervals under Play and Structured conditions for both Mr. Jacob and Ralph, and Ms. Jacob and Ralph. Role of independent observer (Examiner) was unobtrusive or inaccessible to the parents' and child's sight and unlikely a cause of demand characteristics influencing parental behavior (cf. McCambridge, Bruin & Witton, 2012; McCambridge, Wittin, & Elbourne, 2014). For the Play conditions, Mr. Jacob and Ralph scored 80–100% of intervals demonstrating physical proximity, instructional compliance, child-parent eye contact, and both soft and slow parent and child tones. Observational intervals did not show significant or spike scores in child avoidance, tantrums, and arguments. Similar data trends under Play conditions appeared for observed interactions between Ms. Jacob and Ralph. Under Structured conditions, Mr. Jacob and Ralph again showed consistent scores of 80–100% of intervals depicting instructional compliance, parent describing a task, parental praise, and a child manding a parent. No evidence appeared of off-task or arguing about tasks. Similar percentage distributions appeared under Structure between Ms. Jacob and Ralph. While some variations in Ms. Jacob's scores appeared for how much she did the task for Ralph, these permutations were minor compared to her overall scores homogenous with Mr. Jacob.

Interval behavior sampling procedures, inasmuch as they expedite capturing a slice of naturalistic behaviors, are also susceptible to bias interference from previous and current behavior segments impacting the parents' and child's behavior. For example, shortly before observational periods commenced, Ms. Jacob possibly spoke to her attorney who reminded

**TABLE 12.3** Observational codes recorded during play and structured conditions between. Ms. Jacob & Ralph.

| **Play** | **1** | **2** | **3** | **4** | **5** | **6** |
|---|---|---|---|---|---|---|
| Physical proximity | CT, A | C, A | CT | CT, A | CT, A | CT, A |
| Child avoidance | 0 | 0 | 0 | 0 | 0 | 0 |
| Instructional compliance | COMP | COMP | D, COMP | COMP | COMP | COMP |
| Child activity | PLAY | PLAY | PLAY | CA | CA | SS |
| Child/parent eye contact | CE, PE | CE, PE | CE, PE | FOT | CE, PE | D, PE |
| Parent tone | S, SL | S, SL | S, SL | S, SL | S, SL | S, SL |
| Child tone | L, F | S, F | S, F | S, SL | S, SL | S, SL |
| ***Structured*** | | | | | | |
| Instructional compliance | D, ARG, COMP | D, COMP | COMP | COMP | COMP | COMP |
| Parent describes task | DE | DE, R | DE, S, | DE | DE | DE |
| Child on task | OT | PT | PT | PT | OT | PT |
| Parent response | P, CR | I | P | P | P | P |
| Child response | MP | C, D | MP, LA | MP | MP, LA | MP |

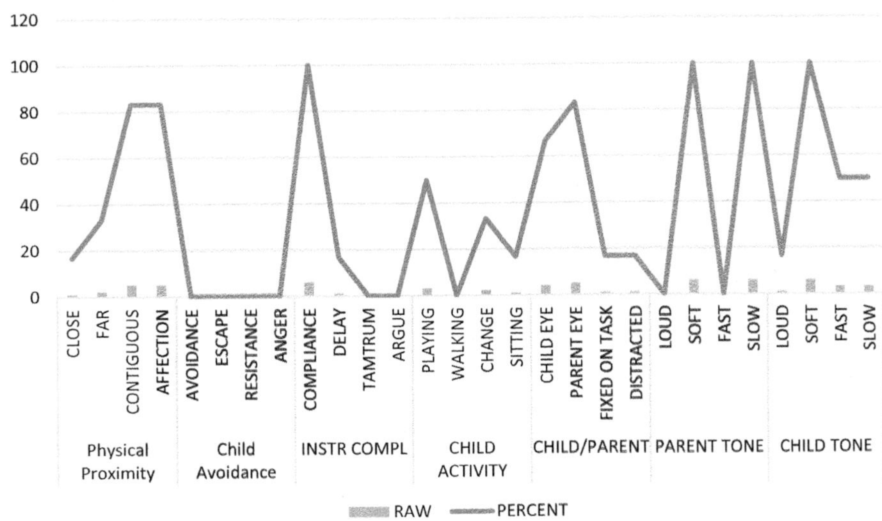


**FIG. 12.1** Percentage of coded behavior recorded during play conditions between Mr. Jacob & Ralph.

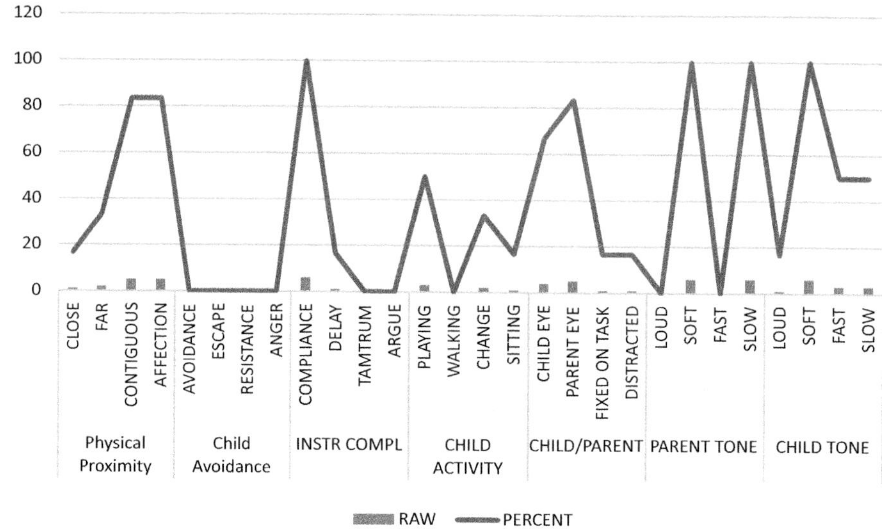


FIG. 12.2 Percentage of coded behavior recorded during play conditions between Ms. Jacob & Ralph.

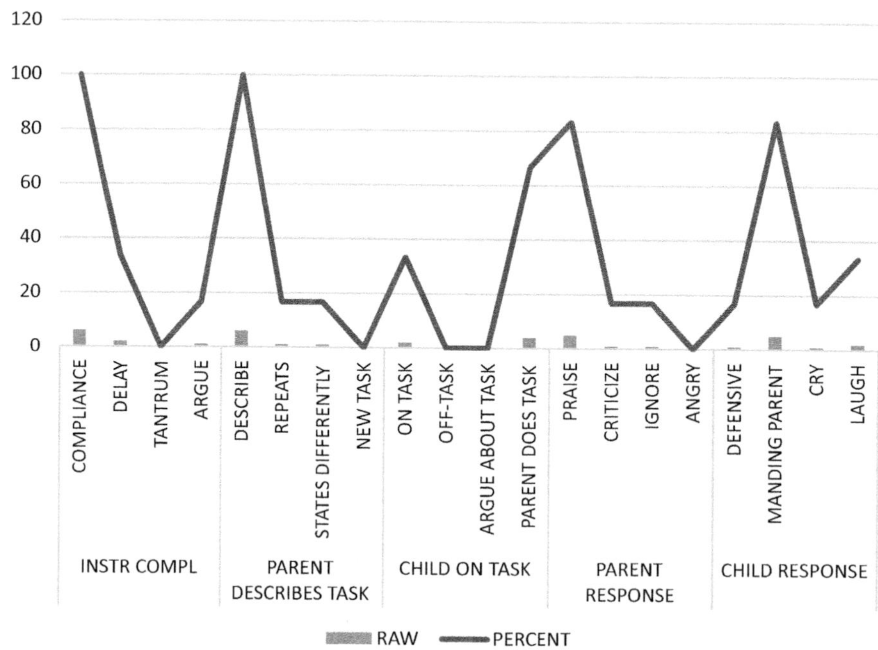


FIG. 12.3 Percentage of coded behavior recorded during structured conditions between Mr. Jacob & Ralph.

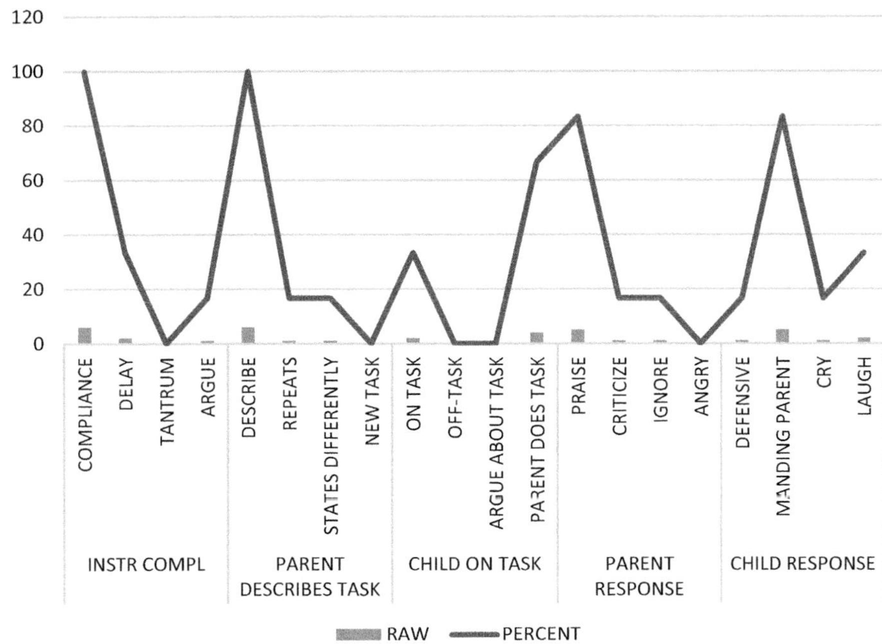


**FIG. 12.4** Percentage of coded behavior recorded during structured conditions between Ms. Jacob & Ralph.

her to "be on her best behavior." Or, Ralph possibly had lunch 30 min before the observational periods, satiating him and making him more pliable to parental requests. By comparison, if unfed for 2 h before observational periods commenced, food deprivation might cause a motivational operation increasing his low frustration tolerance, tantrums, and proneness to noncompliance. While conditions for observation are never ideal, the goal is to extract some biopsy of behavioral interactions sufficiently connected to a sample of response and stimulus conditions resembling homelife. Accepting this limitation of the observational method, conclusions from the data raise important forensic implications from the standpoint of independent observer or investigator in determining the best interest of the child.

## Behavior analysis of the "observer"

A field systems analysis of parent-child observations not only uses investigative procedures (Delprato, 1992), the investigative procedures consider the unique position of the Investigator or Forensic Evaluator. In primary scientific levels of psychology, the field under observation is the organism reciprocally interfaced with stimulus conditions while the investigator stands back, objectively assessing the field (Kantor, 1963, pp. 5–9) regarded this sequential order of boundaries as contrived and acknowledged some inevitable interaction the investigator has with the experimental boundary, thereby using the term *inter* (as in *inter*-behaviorism) to refer to "across the fields." Fig. 12.5 is a schematic illustration depicting the linearity of field-events boundaries artificially separating the primary observer (forensic

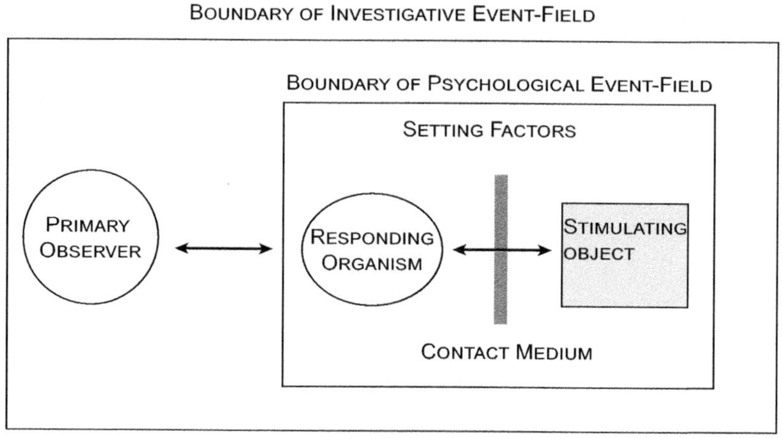


**FIG. 12.5** Boundary of investigative event-field of forensic evaluator observing the boundary of psychological event-field of parent/child interactions and stimulating objects.

evaluator) from the boundary of psychological events. In the psychological events are (a) responding organisms (parent or child), (b) stimulating objects (another parent or child, or objects they interact with), (c) setting events (location of interaction, motivating operations, etc.), and (d) contact medium (how much light, odors, or other stimuli in the room affect receptor capacity for responses to occur. On the latter, for example, Ralph may cry more in a dark room, with the blinds shut than in a brighter room with the blinds open. Similarly, if the custodians washed the floors with chlorine 1 h before the observational period began in the same room, residual inhalant odors may evoke both parental and child tearfulness or aggression than under non-pollutant environments.

The primary observer has the unique opportunity to watch both ongoing behaviors and discern historical contingencies from these interactions. Dual role as objective investigator of current and past events derives from interbehavioral applications of an investigator observing naturalistic historical events (cf. Cone, 1983; Mountjoy, 1972; Mountjoy & Ruben, 1984a, 1984b, 1985; Mountjoy & Sundberg, 1981). Here, Kantor's boundaries extended to a second scientific level of event-fields to include the *Historian. The Historian* as primary investigator observes the interacting boundary of primary observer, who is interbehaving with the psychological event field involving some organism and stimulus conditions. The purpose of this horizontal sequence of boundaries was to show that, with each successive boundary added, perspectives of analysis grow larger, consist of more variables assailed, and encompassed interactions not just inside the boundaries but between the boundaries as well (i.e., interdependence). In recorded observations of the Jacob Family, for example, primary observer (Forensic Examiner) also serves as Historian. First, primary observer recorded time-sampling data of the interbehavioral field segments of Mr. Jacob and Ralph and Ms. Jacob and Ralph. Second, primary observer, as archivist (historian) pre-read previous court, medical, educational, and psychological documents collaterally contributing to the current parent-child observation. These documents provided measurable (and non-measurable) products of family interactions and interventions, ranging from reinforcing to aversive contingencies. The documents also provided quasi-baseline data with which to compare to more pristine or naturalistic data culled from the actual or formal observation of parent and child.

Discrepancies detected between archival data (records) and current psychological events (parent-child observations) occur for many reasons. One reason is intermediary changes impacting both parent and child that can be positive or negative. These intermediary changes are like nylon threads reaching across behavior segments that occurred before the primary observer took data. Examples of intermediary events include weekly parenting classes, both parents already 3-months into individual therapy mandated by Children's Protective Service, or continuous parent-coaching received from onsite (home) parent trainers. All three changes transacted in previous or preceding behavior segments before the day of recording parent-child observations. The primary observer-historian can weigh these three (or more) behavior changes against the parents' past psychiatric diagnoses of personality, addiction, or record of crimes. Previous disqualifiers of competent parenting from, for example, police records of drug trafficking, drug possession, and resisting arrest, are given clemency or reconsidered as less predictors of parent behavior than current predictors recorded in the parent-child session. By looking at the bigger picture of changes, the investigator-historian sees the *entire* system of things and conditions operating in preceding and current behavioral events (cf. Kantor, 1969; Kantor & Smith, 1975).

## Behavior analysis of the best interest of children

Both litigant parents alleged abusive or neglectful actions affecting the minor child in hopes of assuaging the court to settle the custody dispute in their favor. During separate interviews, they claimed marginal responsibility for their past alcohol and drug abuse and mutually instigative domestic violence. They also trivialized repeated investigations by Children's Protective Services documenting correlations between their polysubstance abuse and unrestrained volatility. Each parent glorified their own addiction recovery progress, their redemptive qualities as parent, and insisted their child's loyalty or attachment inherently was stronger with them. In self-extolling their virtues, the litigants overlook the fundamental principle guiding family law. It is not about the parent, it is about the child's *best interests* (Elrod, 2006; Kelly, 1977). Conceptualization of *child's best interest* can be ethically controversial and even compromise a rational custody dispute resolution (e.g., Miller, 2002). One possible redefinition of the best interest standard is to assess the contingencies of child adjustment. These contingencies enable the child's *adaptability, functionality, healthy balance of reinforcers and punishers, and generality of behavior within their cultural matrix.* Second to these factors is the efficacy, reliability, reciprocity, and continuity of parental communication.

*Contingencies of child adjustment.* In the Jacob family case, 2 year old Ralph fell below qualifiable age for meaningful diagnostic interviewing. He instead becomes profiled (positively or negatively) by his parents, and from documented collaborative evidence from Children's Protective Services, the daycare, or other resources offering naturalistic descriptions of his behavior. His young age, in other words, prevents a forensic evaluator from getting a logical and reliable answer to the question, "So, how do you cope with life around either parent?" Alternatively, supplemental documents are rich sources of behavioral products that can challenge or comport with the parents' opinions and possible spin on their child's behavior. For example, under his mother custody, Ralph attends a state-of-the art Montessori daycare educational program advancing his pre-primary academic skills in math, reading, and written expression. He is already toilet-trained, established routines socially seeking and playing evenly with friends, and generally is compliant. Few if any incidents appear of Ralph acting oppositional or angry, unless due to his sleepless naps followed by robust athletic activities. Daycare records attest to Ralph's (a) ability to adapt to new or changing circumstances in school, (b) mands for assistance or self-care for daily living skills, (c) recovers quickly from any peer harassment or disappointments during the day, and (d) maintains and transfers his politeness, respectfulness, and compliance during field trips and across several different daycare care substitute or regular teachers. Ralph also is observed soliciting appropriate attention for healthy or prosocial behaviors and not soliciting attention for disruptive, aggressive, or destructive behaviors. He operates within a (loosely defined) classroom structure defining his accessibility to reinforcers, which he learned to optimize and even carry over into his mother's primary custodial household. Both parents reported Jacob is "well-behaved" around his cousins or extended family and even can wait patiently in stores and restaurants. Moreover, direct observation during parent-child exchange under play and structured conditions showed similar generality of adaptive, flexible, and patient behaviors.

*Parental communication (coparenting).* Preservation of the child's cultural matrix—the environment they live and thrive in—is paramount in weighing the pros and cons of custody assignment. This is especially important if awarding custody means uprooting a child from stable anchors. Behavioral evidence of Ralph's accelerated learning and installation of resilience skills in his community are reasons for retention of the current custody arrangement, providing Ms. Jacob can continue affording Ralph these reinforcing contingencies. On the other hand, if Ms. Jacob was physically or psychiatrically incapacitated or her job loss threatened suspension or termination of Ralph's contingencies, the question for the Forensic evaluator is *will the other party maintain Ralph's contingencies enabling his healthy lifestyle and best interests?* Custody transfer or even assignment of joint custody by default when the primary custodian loses the opportunity and ability to maintain positive contingencies is only one behavioral logarithm for decision making. The tougher, and more crucial variables to isolate, measure, and use as predictors include efficacy, reliability, reciprocity and continuity of co-parenting communication. In most family courts, communication between litigant parents is a priority to the judgment of custody (Kamp-Dush, Kotila, & Schoppe-Sullivan, 2011). Post-dissolution co-parenting involves a reliable and consistent mechanism though which non-married couples can ask questions, fact-check on information, coordinate schedules, and share concerns civilly without retribution. Shared dialogue via texting, talking on the phone, Email, or social media (e.g., snapchat, Instagram, Facebook) facilitates relatively rapid transmission of contact and can alleviate speedbumps of acrimony. When these protocols of social exchange break down due to abuse (e.g., argument while texting, bad-mouthing a parent on Facebook) or neglect (failure to respond), one option adopted by the courts is a monitored email system on which parties can post their exchanges safely and knowing any bullying can trigger a court violation. *Our Family Wizard,* for example, is an online calendar (and email platform) allowing management of reciprocal parent interactions. Copies of email transactions between co-parents deliver to the referee or friend of court case worker as backup evidence of the couple's viability of working together.

Overcoming parenting conflicts and ambiguity of visitation schedules are strong reasons for using *Our Family Wizard*, or any equivalent online sharing database (e.g., Google calendar). The downside is that it provides the exclusive means of communication for highly charged, acrimonious parents. It also *does not guarantee co-parenting continuity and conflict-resolutions in the best interests of the child.* Angry parents may never talk anywhere in the community with the Co-parents unless they first reach amiable agreement via the email server. For example, if Ralph's parents were both invited to the daycare's fall open house and never communicated beyond the walls of *My Family Wizard*, meeting together on behalf of Ralph in open public risks rapid deterioration into verbal arguments and may make a spectacle of their disruption. A precondition exists, then, for amicable co-parenting to occur across many different situations and via many different communication media. The use of *Our Family Wizard* is better as a practice simulator of communication; here, correspondence about parenting styles, visitations, and activity schedules can be developed routinely and diplomatically on a weekly basis. The online analogue can remain in effect but be a stepping stone to both parents sharing identical information face-to-face. Post-divorced or non-married couples who trust face-to-face meetings and even eventually interlope their lives can substantially increase generalization of the child's reinforcement contingencies across both parents' families.

For Mr. and Mrs. Jacob, co-parenting was nonexistent. The couple lacked any effective reciprocal interchanges and the rare occasions they spoke rapidly escalated into verbal altercations. The forensic evaluator considered the promises each parent idealized about drug recovery, anger control, and going though metamorphoses in their lives. Both parents had equal opportunity to pitch their planned enrichment opportunities for their son and compare their own plans to the pre-existing success of Ralph's current daycare and social contingencies. Most importantly, they had the opportunity to propose methods or goals on building a more communicative co-parenting relationship. But they did not propose any such viable medium for better parenting interaction. Without evidence to warrant altering Ralph's life or interrupt his healthy pace of meeting developmental milestones; without demonstration that Ralph's positive contingencies were equally accessible in the defendant father's world and could produce identical or same positive behavior changes; and without secure and effective co-parenting communication either using the email technology of *Our Family Wizard* or a social media equivalent, the defendant's counter-suit for custody change was denied. Instead, in keeping with the safety and welfare of the minor child Ralph, conditions for the plaintiff's retention of custody and defendant father's visitation required:

**a.** Both parties attend outpatient therapy focused on impulse control, relapse prevention, anger control, and interpersonal communication.
**b.** Both parties submit to random Breathalyzer and urinalysis for 3–6 months as deemed necessary by the Friend of the Court or Judge.
**c.** Both parties enter in an assault-reduction psychoeducational group of their choice.
**d.** Both parties identify a single exchange location wherein the child can walk freely from one party to the other without parties in physical or verbal contact. All correspondence between parties for the first 3 months be documented in writing and sent by snail or email or using *Our Family Wizard*.

**e.** The rotation of child visits occur biweekly (every two weeks) using Sunday as the pivotal day. For example, Ralph leaves on Sunday night, returns on Sunday morning.
**f.** Both parties remain abstinent of drugs and alcohol during contact with the minor child.

Even in the snake-infested waters of custody litigation, a mental health evaluator who employs behavioral assessment methods and behavioral systems analysis in decision-making can get though unscathed. Lowering the risk of professional liability is a twofold process. Either, in a perfect world, forensic experts refuse to perform custody evaluations and steer clear of any ethically or legally dangerous traps. Or, experts realize the traps are due to neglecting precautions in risk management. With the right precautions, such as following uniform protocols of custody evaluation, and using an empirical approach to formulation of hypotheses and conclusions about the parents, forensic experts will not be just experts. They will be *smart experts*.

## References

Ackerman, M. J., & Pritzi, T. B. (2011). Child custody evaluation practices: A 20 year follow-up. *Family Court Review, 49*, 618–628.

American Law Institute. (2002). *Principles of the law of family dissolution: Analysis and recommendations*. Newark, NJ: Bender.

American Psychological Association. (1994). Guidelines for child custody evaluations in divorce proceedings. *American Psychologist, 49*, 677–680.

American Psychological Association. (2002). Ethical principles of psychologists and code of conduct. *American Psychologist, 57*, 1060–1073.

American Psychological Association. (2007). Record keeping guidelines. *American Psychologist, 62*, 993–1004.

Association of Family and Conciliation Courts. (2006). *Model standards of practice for child custody evaluations*. Madison, WI: AFCC.

Baerger, D. R., Galatzer-Levy, R., Gould, J. W., & Nye, S. G. (2002). A methodology for reviewing the reliability and relevance of child custody evaluations. *Child Custody Evaluations, 18*, 35–73.

Bennett, D. S., Solomon, M. W., & Lewis, M. (2006). Relations of parental report and observation of parenting to maltreatment history. *Child Maltreatment, 11*, 63–75.

Bow, J. N., Gottlieb, M., Siegel, J., & Noble, G. (2010). Licensing board complaints in child custody practice. *Journal of Forensic Psychology Practice, 10*, 403–418.

Bow, J. N., & Quinnell, F. A. (2002). A critical review of child custody evaluation reports. *Family Court Review, 40*, 140–176.

Chiu, E. (2014). Psychological testing in child custody evaluations with ethnically diverse families: Ethical concerns and practice recommendations. *Journal of Child Custody, 11*, 107–127.

Cone, D. M. (1983). The historical development of scientific psychology. In N. W. Smith, P. T. Mountjoy, & D. H. Ruben (Eds.), *Reassessment in psychology: The interbehavioral alternative* (pp. 347–360). Washington DC: University Press of American.

Delprato, D. J. (1992). Behavioral field systems analysis: History and scientific relatives. *Journal of Teaching in Physical Education, 12*, 3–8.

Elrod, L. D. (2006). A move in the right direction? Best interests of the child emerging as the standard for relocation cases. *Journal of Child Custody, 3*, 29–61.

Emery, R. E., Otto, R. K., & O'Donohue, W. T. (2005). A critical assessment of child custody evaluations: Limited science and a flawed system. *Psychological Science, 6*, 1–29.

Fidler, J. F., Bala, N., Birnbaum, R., & Kavassalis, K. (2008). *Challenging issues in child custody disputes: A Guide for Legal and mental health professionals*. Canada: Thomson Reuters.

Fiske, K., & Delmolino, L. (2012). Use of discontinuous methods of data collection in behavioral intervention: Guidelines for practitioners. *Behavior Analyst in Practice, 5*, 77–81.

Gardner, F. (2000). Methodological issues in the direct observation of parent-child interaction: Do observational findings reflect the natural behavior of participants? *Clinical Child and Family Psychology Review, 3*, 185–198.

Gelfand, D., & Hartmann, D. P. (1975). *Child behavior: Analysis and therapy*. NY: Pergamon Press.

Georgia Psychological Association. (1990). *Recommendations for psychologists involvement in child custody cases*. Atlanta, GA: Georgia Psychological Association.

Glassman, J. B. (1998). Preventing and managing board complaints: The downside risk of custody evaluation. *Professional Psychology: Research and Practice, 29*, 1210124.

Gould, J. W. (1998). *Conducting scientifically crafted child custody evaluations*. CA: Sage Publications.

Gould, J. W., & Martindale, D. A. (2009). *The art and science of child custody evaluations*. NY: Guilford Press.

Greer, M. (2004). Ensuring that "good-faith" evaluations are safe. *APA Online, 36*(June).

Grisso, T. (1990). Evolving guidelines for divorce/custody evaluations. *Family & Conciliation Courts Review, 28*, 35–41.

Grisso, T. (2003). *Evaluating competencies: Forensic assessments and instruments* (2nd ed.). NY: Kluwer Academic/ Plenum.

Grisso, T. (2005). Commentary on "Empirical and ethical problems with custody recommendations": What now? *Family Court Review, 43*, 223–228.

Hall, R. V. (1971). *Managing behavior (Part I). Behavior modification: The measurement of behavior*. Lawrence, KS: H & H Enterprises.

Harrop, A., & Daniels, M. (1986). Method of time-sampling: A reappraisal of momentary time sampling and partial interval recording. *Journal of Applied Behavior Analysis, 19*, 73–77.

Heilbrum, K. (2001). *Principles of forensic mental health assessment*. NY: Kluwer Academic/Plenum.

Hughes, H. M., & Haynes, S. N. (1978). Structured laboratory observation in the behavioral assessment of parent-child interactions: A methodological critique. *Behavior Therapy, 9*, 428–447.

Johnston, J. M., & Pennypacker, H. S. (1980). *Strategies and tactics of human behavioral research*. NJ: Lawrence Erlbaum Associates.

Kamp-Dush, C. M., Kotila, L. E., & Schoppe-Sullivan, S. J. (2011). Predictors of supportive coparenting after relationship dissolution among at-risk parents. *Journal of Family Psychology, 25*, 356–365.

Kantor, J. R. (1963). *The scientific evolution of psychology* (Vol. I). Chicago, IL: Principia Press.

Kantor, J. R. (1969). *The scientific evolution of psychology* (Vol. 2). Chicago, IL: Principia Press.

Kantor, J. R., & Smith, N. W. (1975). *The science of psychology: An interbehavioral survey*. Chicago, IL: Principia Press.

Kelly, J. B. (1997). The best interests of the child: A concept in search of meaning. *Family and Conciliation Courts Review, 35*, 377–387.

Kirkland, K., & Kirkland, K. (2001). Frequency of child custody evaluation complaints and related disciplinary action: A survey of the association of state and provincial psychology boards. *Professional Psychology: Research and Practice, 32*, 171–174.

Lane, J. D., & Ledford, J. R. (2014). Using interval-based systems to measure behavior in early childhood special education and early intervention. *Topics in Early Childhood Special Education, 34*, 83–93.

Martindale, D. A. (2003). *Family evaluation in custody litigation: Reducing risks of ethical infractions and malpractice*. NY: John Wiley & Sons.

McCallum, R. S. (2017). *Handbook of nonverbal assessment*. NY: Springer Books.

McCambridge, J., Bruin, M. D., & Wittin, J. (2012). The effects of demand characteristics on research participant behaviors in non-laboratory settings: A systematic review. *PLoS One, 7*, e39116.

McCambridge, J., Wittin, J., & Elbourne, D. R. (2014). Systematic review of the Hawthorne effect: New concepts are needed to study research participation effects. *Journal of Clinical Epidemiology, 67*, 267–277.

Melton, G., Petrila, J., Poythress, N., & Slobogin, C. (2007). *Psychological evaluations for the courts: A handbook for mental health professionals and lawyers* (3rd ed.). NY: Guilford Press.

Miller, G. H. (2002). The psychological best interests of the child is not the legal best interest. *Journal of the American Academy of Psychiatry and Law, 30*, 196–200.

Mountjoy, P. T. (1972). Jean Henri Masers de Latude (1725 – 1805): An unappreciated practical psychologist. *The Psychological Record, 22*, 145–149.

Mountjoy, P. T., & Ruben, D. H. (1984a). A science of history (in response). *The Behavior Analyst, 7*, 75–76.

Mountjoy, P. T., & Ruben, D. H. (1984b). Extinction and resurgence of scientific history: An interbehavioral analysis. *The Psychological Record, 34*, 553–566.

Mountjoy, P. T., & Ruben, D. H. (1985). Historical note: On validity measurement of Hannibal's crossing of the alps. *The Psychological Record, 35*, 77–80.

Mountjoy, P. T., & Sundberg, M. L. (1981). Ben Franklin the protobehaviorist I: Self-management of behavior. *The Psychological Record, 31*, 13–24.

Munsinger, H. L., & Karlson, K. W. (1994). *Uniform child custody evaluation system*. Odessa, FL: Psychological Assessment Resources.

Otto, R. K., Edens, J. F., & Barcus, E. H. (2000). The use of psychological testing in child custody evaluations. *Family and Conciliation Courts Review, 38*, 312–340.

Pikar, D. B. (2007). On being a child custody evaluator: Professional and personal challenges, risks, and rewards. *Family Court Review, 45*, 103–115.

Rohrbaugh, J. B. (2008). *A comprehensive guide to child custody evaluations: Mental health and legal perspectives*. Boston: Springer Books.

Ruben, D. H. (1983). The effects of praise and ignoring on relevant and irrelevant verbalizations by preschool children within a classroom. In P. T. Mountjoy, & D. H. Ruben (Eds.), *Behavioral genesis: Readings in the science of child psychology* (pp. 169–181). Lexington, MA: Ginn Publishing.

Sidman, M. (1960). *Scientific research: Evaluating experimental data in psychology*. NY: Basic Books.

Solomon, J., & George, C. (2008). The measurement of attachment security in infancy and childhood. In J. Cassidy, & P. R. Shaver (Eds.), *Handbook of attachment: Theory, research, and clinical applications* (2nd ed., pp. 383–416). New York: Guilford Press.

Stahl, P. M. (2010). *Conducting child custody evaluations: From basic to complete issues*. CA: Sage Publications.

CHAPTER

# 13

# Avoidance/escape (operant) conditioning and respondent biophysical arousal in the behavioral forensic assessment of an adolescent arsonist

In a digital informational world, bombardment of social media is everywhere. It dominates communication. Multiplayer online games absorb children's attention span, and robocalls threaten the privacy of households. Two decades ago, in an era before smartphones, before apps, and before all manner of devices that monitor everything from a person's use of Lift and Uber to dating preferences, people were more patient. Digital technology now makes us the most data-generating, data-chomped, and definitely the most exposed nation. But in our insatiable hunger for online life, one underlying theme is expediency and impulsiveness. Human beings are notorious creatures homologous to their phylogenetic cousins in poorly controlling impulses. Impulses are immediate urges or motivating operations (MOs), triggered by biophysical or environmental cues that seek to obtain gratifying conditions, or to avoid and escape aversive conditions. The ubiquity of uncontrolled urges (MOs) among adults and adolescents has been the bane of human survival because it compels irrational or counterproductive actions. These actions accompany urge-fulfillment and produce irreversible physical and interpersonal damage (Ruben, 1993a, 2018). Poor urge control ranges from the slip of scatological language when tripping over one's shoelaces to the apocalyptic and homicidal bloodsheds of terrorist attacks on civilians in Sri Lanka and in synagogues in Pittsburgh and Poway, California. For this reason, immediate gratification is an individualistic or social behavior condition spanning the globe in its colossal impact on economic and political arenas.

Since taming compulsory internet use is hard in Democratic public-access countries (e.g., United States compared to China), poor impulse control thrives among dystopian countries as well as it does among troubled children with chaotic lives. For example, increasingly high

*Behavioral Forensics*
https://doi.org/10.1016/B978-0-12-819805-6.00013-0

cases of children diagnosed with Attention Deficit Hyperactivity Disorder (ADHD, combined presentation; NSCH, 2017), implicate a disturbing trend in the millennia and post-millennia parents who are both under-attentive and verbally punitive. These parents expect immediate child obedience and become outraged when the children talk back. (cf. Smith, Dishion, Wilson, Winter, & Patterson, 2014). Ruben (1993b) further showed the systematically progressive development of how "disobedient" youngsters, misappropriated negative attention, form symptoms of attention deficits and hyperactivity. Similar applied and experimental analyses of impulsiveness etiology (Ainslie, 1974; Neef, Bicard & Endo, 2001; Rachlin, 1974; Schweitzer & Sulzer-Azaroff, 1988; Vollmer, Borrero & Daniel, 1999; Williams & Potenza, 2008) showed impulsive behavior quickly generalizing to topographically and functionally complex forms of social deviance. One area of complex deviance was fire-starting.

Fire-starting is usually divided into three categories—*Fire-setting, pyromania, and arson.* Fire-setters are children, adolescents (or adults) who sets fires for various reasons. Fire onset may start from curious or accidental fire-setting from unsupervised access to matches or lighters. Curious ignitors of fire may be safety-conscience, fearful of its dangerous impact, and non-enticed from the self-stimulatory effects of fire temperature or visual effects. By contrast, pyromania goes beyond a simple fire-setter to include repetitive impulses to explore, ignite, and thrive on the stimulatory properties of fire dissemination and destruction (Fineman, 1980; Lambie & Randell, 2011; Mehregany, 1993; Merrick, Bowling & Omar, 2013). The *sadism of imparting injury or damage on objects* combines with sensory and autonomic (biophysical) arousal. The arousal, an intermingling of operant and respondent conditioning, develops from (a) repeated pairings between Unconditioned stimuli (the fire) and unconditioned stimuli (abrupt rise in body temperature or thermal receptor arousal and watering eyes) and neutral responses (lighting matches, setting the fires), and (b) direct positive reinforcement from the response sequence of fire-setting behaviors that produce flame permutations, heat effects, and varying property destruction. Opdyke and Rothbaum (1998; cf. Kolko, 2002; Kolko & Kazdin, 1986) further reported on behavioral underpinnings of pyromania. Reinforcers rarely were social (peer attention, profit, or escape from criticism), and often the fire setters had unusual role models also setting fires or who acted enviably tenacious. The severe or "pathological" fire-setter (pyromaniac) inevitably violated social norms and rules and amassed a juvenile arrest record. These fire-setters often shared diagnostic characteristics of conduct disorder and subsequently antisocial personality. Meaning, repeaters of fire-setters lacked remorse, felt invincible, discarded immediate social consequences, and selfishly garnished the pleasure from permanent destruction of other people's property.

Arsonists, a more complex hierarchy of adolescent fire-burners, engaged in deliberate, methodical, and pre-planned manipulation of fire, historically called *impulsive incendiarism* (cf. Andrews, 2010; Meckel, 1820). This maladaptive behavior, supposedly spawned by profound criminal motivations, seemingly recurs despite legal consequences of arrest, conviction, or even prolonged juvenile incarceration (Berkey & Wooden, 2012; Davis & Lauber, 1999; Klein, Mondozzi, & Andrews, 2008; Vaughm et al., 2010). Intentional fire-setters ranged in age from 12 to 18 years old, users and non-users of drugs, and from varying socioeconomic classes. The one common characteristic shared is disturbance of family origin and bullying. The child directly experienced oppressive effects of randomly distributed punishment either from parents or cohorts. Aggressive parenting consisted of verbal and nonverbal (physical) discipline given arbitrarily and capriciously, in both cases where aversive stimuli were unpredictable and thereby unavoidable and inescapable. Similarly, ruthlessly malevolent peer harassment occurred for seemingly untraceable or non-identifiable antecedents to behavior and for different behaviors. Ambiguity of punishment not only made it uncontrollable, it developed hypervigilance in the child. Such hyperalertness is to relevant and irrelevant minutia (stimulus properties) in the environment about which the child always anticipates some impending doom (i.e., foreboding). Victimized by control-paralysis, children "displace" or take out their retaliation against parents or peers in passive-aggressive actions intended to mitigate or terminate future occurrences of the parents or peers bullying them. One actualization of retaliatory behavior is by setting fires.

The following case of an adolescent arsonists illustrates the behavioral paradigm of convergent operant and respondent conditioning in both the avoidance (escape) behavior (from bullies) and biophysical (self-stimulation) effects of fire-starting. The repeated fire-starter burned down the family pole barn that culminated from a serial pattern of arson over several years. Adjudication of his conviction required the juvenile offender undergo a psychological evaluation to determine proclivity or risk potential for re-engaging in arson, and to rule out any other psychopathology likely co-influencing his maladaptive actions.

## Case of Phillip

Phillip is a fictitious name of a 16 year old adolescent convicted for one count of arson related to lighting fire to the family pole barn, registered as a historical monument for the county. Similar unconvicted fires by this "serial arsonist" included demolition of the family household bathroom, three field fires, and three vehicular incinerations using inflammable liquids (gasoline). After detention in a youth facility and subsequent conviction, the court requested a forensic evaluation of his proclivity for fire-behavior recidivism and related psychopathology possibly interfering with offender rehabilitation outcomes.

### Education

Born in a small town in the Midwest, Phillip attended a parochial Baptist school from Kindergarten to fifth grade. Classroom sizes were small, consisting of 5–10 students combining 2 or 3 grades co-taught by several teachers. In other words, in third grade, he shared the same classroom with fourth and fifth graders, except he followed a different educational curriculum. Under close surveillance of teachers, his grades steadied at low B's and C's. In sixth grade, he transferred to local public schools in larger classrooms without a generously high teacher-student ratio. Now on his own, his grades plummeted instantly to low D's and E's, blamed on (a) forgetfulness to complete or submit homework, (b) poor listening comprehension in class, and (c) weak reading comprehension. He underwent multidisciplinary evaluations qualifying him for an IEP certified in Specific Language Disability (SLD) for Basic Reading, Reading Comprehension, and Mathematics Calculation. He primarily attended a resource room with limited mainstreaming to one or two regular courses other than to gym or art class. Teacher itinerant support slightly rose and stabilized his grades to C's, unless he missed school. By seventh and eighth grade, absences topped 70% of the school year for unauthorized or nonmedical reasons and the principal referred him to truancy court. Truancy investigators found Phillip unsupervised in mornings before school and early afternoons after school. The court ordered parental or parentally-assigned monitoring of Phillip during both periods and mandated a 90% attendance record for 6 months. By ninth grade, Phillip dropped out of school and twice failed to pass the GED. He made feeble attempts at online high school diploma completion programs, each lasting 2–3 months before he terminated enrollment. Online programs frustrated him due to poor self-discipline in semi-structured virtual classrooms run independently at one's own pace. Phillip lacked the self-discipline to routinely prioritize online study time and instead he gave up on education. He did not participate in any extracurricular activities. He also never participated in any community activities. He also denied working any hourly-wage job or for extra money baby-sitting, pet-sitting, landscaping, or in any other capacity.

Philip claimed he was bullied aggressively when he entered the public school. He denied in-school fights. Ridicule was for his small size, shyness, interpersonal awkwardness, and passivity. He cowered when verbally harassed, often crying inside. Anger at his perpetrators would simmer for days until Phillip either reported their mistreatment of him to school authorities, or Phillip *passive-aggressively retaliated*. Phillip was secretive in his methodical vengeance. For example, once he forged notes using the hand-written styles or pen ink used by one male perpetrator. These notes were "love notes" discretely given to popular females who read them aloud and embarrassed the perpetrators, who had no idea how the fake note got passed. Another time Phillip called the perpetrator's parents, imitating the principal's voice, and announced their son (perpetrator) was suspended for cheating on tests. Believability of Phillip's phone calls triggered a cascade of self-pleasing events. Phillip learned the perpetrator was reprimand mercilessly from his parents for academic dishonesty and was forced to apologize to the school. When the bully initially plead innocent, saying the accusations were a hoax, his defensiveness sounded suspicious and his peers attributed it to the bully's unethical behavior being exposed. Phillip also vicariously empathized with other students seen as victimized by similar bullying. He played the same "methodical" prank on other perpetrators of victims. Over months, his brilliant clandestine strategies earned the notorious reputation in school as the "Equalizer," borrowed from the 1980's television show (starring Robert McCall) and two motion pictures of the same name starring actor Denzel Washington. Phillip felt empowered like a superhero by his covert operative schemes of seeking redemption against bullies. His pride derived from the observed punishing consequences impacted on the perpetrators, and from the stream of gratefulness expressed by the victims. Philip became cleverer in his vendettas and began damaging the property of his enemies. On two occasions, Philip set fire to backpacks and clothing inside the lockers of each enemy. He set a slow fuse to burn and ignite combustible gas both for the rapid explosive noise and flames shooting from the seams of the locker. Detonation of his gas-fire bomb worked more superbly than he anticipated. The force of the fire blast torpedoed the locker door off of its hinges and shot flames horizontally from the locker at least 4 feet into the air. The immense fire power and spectacular spray of multi-colored lights projected into the school hallway were euphoric. Phillip clamored inside with unbridled excitement and felt an adrenaline rush to return to his home lab and concoct another fire-link ignition device.

Phillip denied any other "bad behaviors." He denied packing or carrying any weapons. He denied receiving past suspensions, detentions, or expulsions. He denied fascination with animal cruelty. His only current juvenile conviction was for setting fire to a family pole barn. Phillip also denied receiving any outpatient or resident mental health or substance abuse treatment. He denied any history of prescription to psychotropic medications.

## Substance abuse

Phillip denied ever drinking alcohol or use or abuse of any licit or illicit (controlled) substances. He denied suffering any vehicular-related or major head trauma. He denied undergoing any surgery. He denied having CVAs, TIAs, sleep apnea, seizures, high fevers, or neurotoxin exposure. He denied any known current medical problems.

## Interpersonally

Phillip denied any history of sexual victimization. He felt indifferent and asexual toward females, blamed on his social inexperience and embarrassment talking to females. He once looked at internet pornography and felt penile arousal but worried the viewed webpages might spread Trojan viruses, and he subsequently quit visits to the webpage or using any alternative erotic stimuli. In school, he was shy, reserved, unassertive, solitary, and rarely spoke out unless engaged by a selectively small cadre of intimate friends. He distrusted motives and behaviors of most people, both from his history of being maligned by peers and from fearing the unhelpfulness of adult authorities. Underlying his distrust was a pulsating fear or anxiety of horrible things people may say to him about his perceived internal or external defects. He felt like an impostor, a freak, and terribly ostracized by enviably superior people to him, who he admired secretively from a distance. He lost this adoration for somebody once the person verbally or physically badgered him for seemingly no apparent reason. Idolism would turn into antipathy, with a relentlessly aggressive vendetta to hurt the enemy through annihilation of their property by fire-bombing it.

## Developmentally

Developmentally, Phillip is youngest of two children raised by dually employed, married parents who were affectionately neglectful and ran very busy lives. His father, a pipefitter for a large auto industry, often traveled cross country for special job repairs, lasting one to two weeks with rare communication with the family. Phillip's mother, a nurse, worked 12-h pm shifts in surgery and often stayed overtime, leaving home before school let out and returning home mid-morning after Phillip left for school. Her high-demanding job removed her surveillance of Phillip, who she entrusted to independently care for himself. Older 18 year old brother Max (fictitious) was a useless caretaker, since he commuted to community college and hung out with his cannabis-smoking friends after classes. Phillip learned basics of home young-adult daily living survival, from cooking for himself, washing his clothes, and following a routine self-hygiene schedule, to housekeeping. He grew accustomed to his Cinderella-like loneliness in the house and expectations of keeping the house tidy. He denied either parent mistreated him verbally or physically. He also denied he held any grudges against his parents. He did hold grudges against his brother.

## The alleged crime of arson

During mid-summer months, amid a dry spell where the underbrush was prone to spontaneous wildfires, Phillip spent his late mornings and afternoons in the family pole barn. His brother, a woodcrafter, set up his small shop there, doing woodworking jobs for pay and slowly built a respectable reputation in town for oak-quality furniture. On a Wednesday, his brother was busy on the machinery in the pole barn and could not find certain tools. Knowing his younger brother frequently "snooped around" the pole barn in his equipment cases, Phillip's brother turned his frustration against Phillip. He accused him of deliberately "monkeying" around with his expensive equipment and losing important tools. His fury escalated into other, unrelated topics of berating his brother for being socially odd, strange, unlikeable, and a pregnancy mistake of his parents who originally wanted to abort him when their mother was pregnant with Phillip. A passively timid Phillip was meek, silent, and absorbed the deluge of sordid insults beating him into the ground. Phillip never bothered his brother's tools, and even previously had admired his brothers' workmanship. His hours spent in the pole barn were reading *Harry Potter* books in a place he felt comfortable—a place the only other family member of the household occupied and made the space feel like *home*. Phillip was so dumbfounded and upset by his brothers' rage that he ran back to the house into his bedroom. There, he assembled simple ingredients to make a low-combustible firebomb. He mixed vinegar and baking soda together for an incendiary effect and wrapped it in burlap. He waited for his brother to visit with friends later in the afternoon. When his brother left he pole barn, Phillip lit a small fuse attached to the burlap bag and placed the bag underneath a gasoline-generated heater inside the pole barn. With 10 min of clearing a safe distance from the barn, Phillip witnessed a fireball blast explode through the sidewall and roof of the pole barn, as it engulfed in raging flames. Phillip watched with salivary delight at the fast-burning inferno ripped through the entire structure, decimating it within 30 min.

# Results of the forensic evaluation

## General observations

Phillip arrived punctually for his appointment at the examiner's office. He greeted the examiner affably and courteously. He agreed with the proposed testing process. He also listened attentively when debriefed about the purpose of testing. Attire was clean, hygienic, seasonally appropriate, and properly fitting. He ambulated independently with a normal gait showing no signs of psychomotor disturbance. He sat comfortably in the chair, and made no abrupt gestural or postural movements. Testing duration was 1.25 h. He completed the self-testing in 1.0 h. Attention-span and physical endurance were strong. Eye contact remained direct and continuous. He smiled, laughed, and interjected questions and statements at appropriate intervals. He showed appropriate levity in response to some statements. Sensorium was intact. Affect was energetic, alert, happy, elevated, dynamic, spontaneous, and fluid. No anger, resistance, opposition, or psychosis seen. No indicators observed of distractibility, impulsivity, or hyperactivity. No evidence seen of withdrawal or intoxication. No evidence seen of mis-medication. He showed no mood fluctuations from aggression to anxiety to depression. He made no statements about suicide or homicide; he denied past suicidal or para-suicidal ideas and intent for self-harm. He delineated right from wrong, reality from fantasy, and truth from falsehood. He fully accepted culpability for his crime. Speech showed no articulation problems. Vowel and consonant pronunciation (phonetics) was clear. Speech flowed evenly, rapidly, audibly, and in completed sentences. Prosody was normal and melodic. Speech content consisted of vocabulary and syntax commensurate with his stated educational level. Ideation showed coherence, rationality, and orientation x 3. Overall his disposition was amiable and cooperative during the entire testing protocol.

### Psychopathology

First, his test profile was reliable, consistent, and interpretable. On validity scales, no elevations appeared in indices of over-reporting or under-reporting. He presented a balanced version of positive and negative traits. Second, on MACI personality test, score elevations appeared for scales on Inhibited, Doleful, Submissive, Anxiety, and Depressive Affect. Inhibited describes a generally quiet, shy, or ill at ease person who prefers closeness to people but is guarded, reserved, and doubtful of self. For example, in school, Phillip hesitantly talks to female peers fearing his social skills are poor. Consequently he avoids intimacies, sharing vulnerability, and appears self-conscious of his flaws. Likewise, a doleful individual simmers with dejected and gloomy mood, always feeling victimized by helpless situations. Phillip can be pessimistic, prone to guilt feelings, and views self as worthless. Part of his self-invalidation comes from lack of any close friends. High raters of submissiveness means he is generally socially compliant. He is soft-hearted, sentimental and kindly in relationships with others, always yearning to help them. Outwardly he is pleasing, catering and selfless, whereas indirectly or unobtrusively he may engage in passive-aggressive behaviors as part of a quiet protest. His seamless thread of arsons in retribution for bullying attacks demonstrated this prototypical passive-aggressive pattern.

Anxious feelings describes a teen with a constant sense of foreboding or anticipation about chaos and conflict. He is accustomed to a busy schedule of stressful expectations and receiving verbal reprimands for arbitrary or idiosyncratic behaviors in school. Bullies preyed on him vulturously for unexpected reasons no matter how much he appeased his bully, reported him or her to the principal, or even enlisted more oppositional friends coming to his rescue. He always is on guard, fears the worst scenarios, and believes people are negatively judgmental of him. Depressive affect describes a person reducing his activity level, clearly distinct from his energy or rate of performance in the recent past. He feels ineffective, valueless, unattractive, and struggles to see redemptive qualities in his life. The one motivator that rebounds Phillip from despair and resembles hope is the empowerment from setting fires.

## Behavior analysis

In a behavioral forensic analysis of crimes against persons and property, observations show how the adverse impact affects family victims in the most personal ways. Domestic violence, for example, is an underlying factor in murder, rapes, and assaults, which destroys family connections and sets off a domino chain of intergenerationally transmitted aggressive behavior patterns through a lifetime of behavior segments. Likewise, child arsonists tear apart the family fabric by unraveling threads of trust invested in that child, as both of Phillip's parents had invested in him. No matter, in hindsight, how obvious the family dysfunction appeared insofar as the mother and father neglecting supervision of Phillip and Phillip's brother acting irresponsibly, the fact remains that Phillip still developed his own habits or patterns of fire-starting behavior. Moreover, Phillip's evolution of fire-setting behavior is not entirely the fault of his neglected family nor of his underdeveloped social skills. Nor does his personality traits of inhibition, dolefulness, submissiveness, anxiety, and depression fully complete the etiology underlying Phillip's recidivistic fire-setting, pyromaniac, or arsonist behaviors. The evidence in Phillip's case implicate a matrix of polycontingencies transacted over a large psychological field, involving very specific, isolated, predictable, and potentially measurable behavior segments precipitating Phillip's *pre-fire* setting and *actual fire-setting* behaviors. Among the diversely complex contingencies present, the primary one identified for forensic analysis here is the cyclical pattern of motivating operations in respondent and operant conditioning.

## Cyclical pattern of motivating operation in respondent conditioning

Analysis of Motivating Operations (MOs) already received much discussion in Chapter 1 and cameoed in almost every chapter of this book. MOs, technically replacing the legendary terms *establishing operation*, are a fundamental function that describes behavior propensity. A person is more prone to higher rates, intensity, magnitude, or extensive topography of behavior given a limited time under which a favorable condition exists. That favorable condition is (limited) accessibility to reinforcement or punishment, depending on whether the response function is to increase or decrease closeness to reinforcement or distance (avoid, escape from) punishment. MOs, while principally classified under operant conditioning (Laraway, Snycerski, Michael, & Poling, 2003; McGill, 1999; Michael, 1993), can equally apply to respondent conditioning (Hayes & Rehfeldt, 1998). For example, latency from onset of Unconditioned Stimulus (US) to onset of Unconditioned Response (UR) depends on many parameters of the behavior segment. These parameters include timing, temporality, contiguity, speed of pairings, plasticity of the reflex (involuntary response), and effectiveness of receptors (e.g., mechanical, gustatory, etc.). Enabling these parameters are the media of contact and motivating operators. For example, the vaporous fumes from burning fires must reach a threshold to permeate onto the human body. If the fire is too far away, fumes disintegrate after so many feet and never reach a person's body. But closer proximity to the vapor emissions (contact media) can elicit tear duct secretions. Moreover, tear duct secretions will be faster in a healthy eye and slower in a person who just underwent retinal surgery. Even with a healthy eye, smog, fog, or other environmental pollutants blurring, deluding, or even preventing optical contact with the fire's vapors (i.e., media of contact) can delay, if only by seconds, the reflex behavior. Media of contact, in this respect, are the essential conduits providing a bridge between US and UR, or later, between Conditioned Stimuli (CS) and

Conditioned Responses (CRs). When the media of contact offer a generous or unlimited exposure time for the US to trigger the UR, there is no pressing motivating operation. But when the media of contact are sparse, occur for short durations, or do not exist, thereby limiting exposure time for the US to elicit the UR, that short window establishes a motivating operation. The media of contact set an occasion for a US-UR connection; the MO increases the probability of the UR or CR occurring during that connection.

Conceptualization of motivating operations within classical conditioning derives, in part, from the Rescorla-Wagner model (1972; cf. Pearce & Hall, 1980). This mathematical model describes the associative process of respondent conditioning, including progressive phases from acquisition to extinction. Reponses *extinction*, to be exact, is when CS-US pairings cease or are followed by presentations of the CS alone; this weakens the UR. The response hierarchy of first or second level conditioned responses also undergo changes. One effect is that CR1 decreases, followed by any second- or third-order of conditioned responses associated with it (e.g., CR2, CR3). Another possibility is that, as CR1 decreases, paradoxical (opposite or different) changes occur in the other sequential conditioned responses. This is because responses are in patterns consisting of simultaneous or sequential responses. Decreases in one response, the CR1 concurrently and reciprocally affects specific and broad changes in other temporally contiguous responses. For example, crying (CR1) may be accompanied by negative stomach aches (CR2) and escape behavior (CR3). As pairings between the visible presence of a parent (CS) and yelling (US) cease, reduced rates of crying (CR1) may result in *proportionally or disproportional changes in stomach aches (CR2) or escape behavior (CR3). The responses may increase or decrease depending on other setting events establishing motivating operations*. Although crying is less, responses involving stomach aches may still trigger or evoke accelerated rates of escape behavior when, for example, a child anticipates the parents' return (fear of impending pairings of CS and US), due to the child disobeying some family rule—a rule likely to produce pairings of CS and US In other words, response extinction effects—the CR losing strength when pairings cease between US and CS—may not be so simple or entail of myriad of confounding contingencies.

Kehoe (1988) tried to make sense of this multiplex contingency system. He offered a layered network model of associative learning in which the CS interacts with hidden units of US, UR, and CRs. Much like original works of Pavlov (1927) and years later replicated in the research by Buhusi and Schmajuk (1996, 1999), response conditioning and extinction effects vary by modulations in (a) timing of US-CS parings (Interstimulus Interval, ISI), and (b) timing between one pairing segment and another pairing segment called Intertrial Intervals (ITI's). Using the example above of crying, short ISI's between the parent being visible and parent yelling (US-CS) are negligible upon all three CRs (crying, stomach aches, and escape behavior) But, when this interval is longer, that is, more time passes from offset of the parent's visibility to onset of yelling, that longer latency profoundly increases rates of crying, stomach aches, and escape behaviors. Similarly, the longer time passes between two successive behavior segments of pairings between the parent's visibility and yelling (US-CS), or longer ITI's, the greater the likelihood of all the CRs (crying, stomach aches, escape behavior) decreasing.

ITI's and ISI's interact with media of contact to produce *opportunities for responsivity. These opportunities* are both an operant and respondent event. For example, just before a theatrical play begins, an adult male taking diuretics for hypertension may use the restroom. After voiding to satisfaction, he sits down in the third row to watch the play. Close to intermission, nerves in the bladder send physiological messages of a full bladder and need for urination. Despite sphincter muscles wanting to release the urethra (unconditioned response), the adult male *voluntarily tightens the muscles like a rubber band around the opening of the bladder to prevent leakage*. When the curtain falls for intermission, the window of opportunity exists for a series of operant responses to leave the auditorium and hastily find the restroom under a limited 15 min time interval before the second act begins. The media of contact (and discriminative cues) were the lights coming up in the auditorium, signaling the etiquette to stand up and leave. If the first act goes longer than expected, delaying intermission (and onset of the media of contact), constriction of the sphincter muscles is tighter, more difficult to sustain, and pressure increases physical and emotional stress on the human organism. Likewise, when Phillip sets up an ignition device of an incendiary fire, packed with accelerants and trailers, he expects a jolt of very hot heat impacting his body (thermal receptors) and bolts of fire ravishing the oxygen seen by his photoreceptors. Sensations produced by each sensory receptor (among other receptors) elicit an excitatory response (adrenaline). However, if he sets the fire on a rainy cold day in March or April (in the Midwest, United States), lower temperatures may insulate against or block the rapid transmission of heat; rain drops also may suppress the height or velocity of fire bursts. Media of contact, in this case, are the weather. By stalling or preventing the US-CS pairing expected by Phillip, that longer ISI may actually *increase* adrenaline arousal (UR) and positive self-statements (CR) about the fire. On the obverse, when longer ITI's of US-CS pairings occur (i.e., more time separating behavior segments of the pairings), Phillip does not feel the rush of adrenaline (UR) and positive self-statements about fire burning (CR), both CRs lose strengths and Phillip *has less interest in fire setting (i.e., response extinction)*.

Another way of schematically presenting the progression of response extinction on behavior decrements under both evocative (operant) and elective (respondent) conditions is by the predictable phases of an establishing operation (see Fig. 13.1 below). Fig. 13.1 depicts the two phases a behavior under a motivating operation that pass from a point of excitation to extinction (operant or respondent). On the vertical scale appears the variable intensity, whereas on the horizontal scales is a measure of time elapse. As US-CS pairings co-mingled with operant cues, a motivating operation begins. Either it is an unconditioned motivating operation (UMO) triggering Phillip's tear duct secretions from the heat of the fire and autonomic arousal from its booming burst of flames, or it is a conditioned motivating operation (CMO); the CMO sets the occasion for Phillip wanting to take pictures on his cellphone of his feat. However, as the UMO or CMO proceeds from onset to approximately 15 min, and there are obstacles in the way preventing Phillip from execution of his responses (CRs or

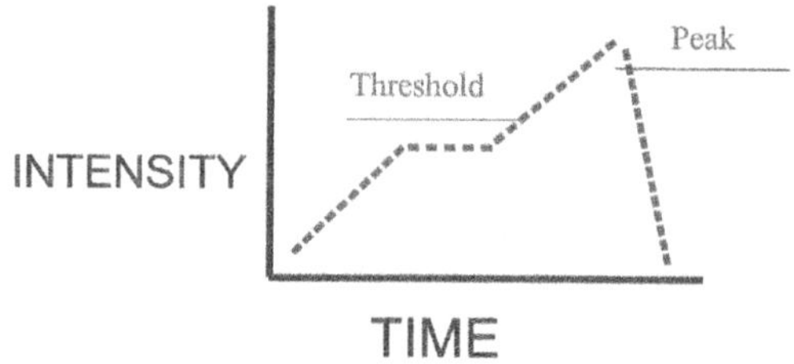


**FIG. 13.1** Two phases of the motivating operation. Before the "urge" deteriorates ("fades").

operant behavior), effects of response delays may include increases in (a) musculoskeletal constriction, (b) glandular secretions, and (c) self-statements labeling his biophysical sensations. Responses at first occur *under the skin* and are inconspicuous from observation of people around Phillip. Phillip may feel "tension," and get angry at himself (negative self-statements) for his failure set the fire accelerants correctly. This is called the *threshold phase*. After 15 min elapses in the threshold phase, without any US-CS pairings or evocative stimuli, Phillip's behavior evolves to the *peak phase*. Here, rapid changes appear in outward or more conspicuous exhibitions of frustrations. Philip is self-scolding aloud or throws objects around him, stomps his feet, or demonstrates an ostensible "tantrum" from evolving extinction effects. However, after 30 min pass with no reinstatement of US-CS pairings or operant antecedents, the motivating operation ("urge") subsides significantly and correspondingly reduces Phillip's response intensity. He *no longer cares about the fire, walks away, and indifferently resigns from the situation*.

Sensory stimulation generated from a burning fire via visual, auditory, tactile vestibular, gustatory, and olfactory receptors dually serve as respondent and operant (reinforcement) effects in the acquisition, perpetuation, and maintenance of fire starting behavior. Forensic awareness of these unique conditions provide a different type of blueprint in the behavioral assessment and prediction of Phillip's risk of criminal recidivism. First, isolation of the scientific contingencies eliminates reliance on personality factors, like *conduct disorder*, underlying some mythical core inside of Phillip that has to be changed through medication. It also prevents a jury of 6–12 people from deliberating on abstract and stereotypical inferences about Phillip's behavior indirectly related to the naturalistic behaviors of fire-starting. Second, operationalizing the exact contingencies of respondent and operant conditioning shows functionally (cause-effect) why Phillip started fires, what sustained his interest in fire-starting, and what needs to occur to ameliorate his fire-starting behavior. Cessation of fire-starting behavior, for example, involves removal of US-CS pairings as part of respondant or operant extinction.

Third, and most importantly, the process of jurisprudence proceeds with a more pristine standard of objectivity in arson investigation. Facts examined are across a continuum of psychological fields in which behavior and setting events are accorded the same evidentiary status as incinerated debris, ignition starters, shoe prints, trace samples, and other artifacts collected in a fire scene for subsequent laboratory testing. In this way, behavioral forensic assessment is not just a side-show at the carnival tempting curious gawkers; instead, it becomes the essential process that facilitates and promises a more logical criminal investigation of highly complex human psychopathology.

## References

Ainslie, G. W. (1974). Impulse control in pigeons. *Journal of the Experimental Analysis of Behavior, 21*, 485–489.

Andrews, J. (2010). From stack-firing to pyromania: Medico-legal concepts of insane arson in British, US, and European contexts, c. 1800-1913, part 1. *History of Psychiatry, 21*, 243–260.

Berkey, M. L., & Wooden, W. S. (2012). *Children and arson: American's middle class nightmare*. New York: Springer.

Buhusi, C. V., & Schmajuk, N. A. (1996). Attention, configuration, and hippocampal function. *Hippocampus, 6*, 621–642.

Buhusi, C. V., & Schmajuk, N. A. (1999). Timing in simple conditioning and occasion setting: A configuration. *Behavioural Processes, 45*, 33–57.

Davis, J. A., & Lauber, K. M. (1999). Criminal behavioral assessment of arsonists, pyromaniacs, and multiple firesetters. *Journal of Contemporary Criminal Justice, 15*, 273–290.

Fineman, K. R. (1980). Firesetting in childhood and adolescence. *Psychiatric Clinics of North America, 3*, 485–500.

Hayes, L. J., & Rehfeldt, R. A. (1998). The operant-respondent distinction revisited: Toward an understanding of stimulus equivalence. *The Psychological Record, 48*(2), 187–210.

Kehoe, E. J. (1988). A layered network model of associative learning: Learning to learn and configuration. *Psychological Review, 95*, 411–433.

Klein, J. J., Mondozzi, M. A., & Andrews, D. A. (2008). The need for a juvenile fire setting database. *Journal of Burn Care and Research, 29*, 810–955.

Kolko, D. (Ed.). (2002). *Handbook on firesetting in children and youth*. Boston, MA: Academic Press.

Kolko, D., & Kazdin, A. (1986). A conceptualization of firesetting in children and adolescents. *Journal of Abnormal Child Psychology, 14*, 49–61.

Lambie, I., & Randell, I. (2011). Creating a firestorm: A review of children who deliberately light fires. *Clinical Psychology Review, 31*, 307–327.

Laraway, S., Snycerski, S., Michael, J., & Poling, A. (2003). Motivating operations and terms to describe them: Some further refinements. *Journal of Applied Behavior Analysis, 36*, 407–414.

McGill, P. (1999). Establishing operations: Implications for the assessment, treatment, and prevention of problem behavior. *Journal of Applied Behavior Analysis, 32*, 393–418.

Meckel, A. A. (1820). *Beiträge zur gerichtlichen Psychologie*. Halle: Carl Friedrich Schimmelpfennig.

Mehregany, D. V. (1993). Firesetting in children. *Jefferson Journal of Psychiatry, 11*, 18–28.

Merrick, J., Bowling, C. H., & Omar, H. A. (2013). Firesetting in childhood and adolescence. *Front Public Health, 1*, 40–50.

Michael, J. (1993). Establishing operations. *The Behavior Analyst, 16*, 191–206.

Neef, N. A., Bicard, D. F., & Endo, S. (2001). Assessment of impulsivity and the development of self-control by students with attention deficit hyperactivity disorder. *Journal of the Applied Behavior Analysis, 34*, 397–408.

NSCH. (2017). *National survey of children's health*. Washington DC: United States Census Bureau.

Opdyke, D., & Rothbaum, B. O. (1998). Cognitive-behavioral treatment of impulse control disorder. In V. E. Caballo (Ed.), *International handbook of cognitive and behavioural treatments for psychological disorders* (pp. 417–440). NY: Elsevier Press.

Pavlov, I. P. (1927). *Conditioned reflexes*. London: Oxford University Press.

Pearce, J. M., & Hall, G. (1980). A model for Pavlovian learning: Variations in the effectiveness of conditioned but not of unconditioned stimuli. *Psychological Review, 87*, 532–552.

Rachlin, H. (1974). Self-control. *Behaviorism, 2*, 94–107.

Rescorla, R. A., & Wagner, A. R. (1972). A theory of Pavlovian conditioning: Variation in the effectiveness of reinforcement and nonreinforcement. In A. H. Black, & W. F. Prokasy (Eds.), *Classical conditioning II: Theory and research* (pp. 64–99). NY: Appleton-Century-Crofts.

Ruben, D. H. (1993a). *The avoidance syndrome: Doing things out of fear*. St Louis, MO: Warren Green.

Ruben, D. H. (1993b). A behavior analysis of impulsive child behavior. In L. F. Koziol, C. E. Stout, & D. H. Ruben (Eds.), *Handbook on child impulse disorders and ADHD: Theory and practice* (pp. 78–107). Springfield, IL: Charles C. Thomas.

Ruben, D. H. (2018). *Evil inside us: Dangers of no impulse control*. Okemos, MI: Best Impressions International Inc.

Schweitzer, J. B., & Sulzer-Azaroff, B. (1988). Self-control: Teaching tolerance for delay in impulsive children. *Journal of the Experimental Analysis of Behavior, 50*, 173–186.

Smith, J. D., Dishion, T. J., Wilson, M. N., Winter, C., & Patterson, G. R. (2014). Cocercive family process and early onset conduct problems from age 2 to school entry. *Development and Psychopathology, 26*, 917–932.

Vaughn, M. G., Qiang, F., DeLisi, M., Wright, J. P., Beaver, K. M., Perron, B. E., et al. (2010). Prevalence and correlates of fire-setting in the United States: Results from the national epidemiologic survey on alcohol and related conditions. *Comprehensive Psychiatry, 51*, 217–233.

Vollmer, T. R., Borrero, J. C., & Daniel, D. (1999). Evaluating self-control and impulsivity in children with severe behavior disorders. *Journal of Applied Behavior Analysis, 32*, 451–466.

Williams, W. A., & Potenza, M. N. (2008). The neurobiology of impulse control disorders. *Brazilian Journal of Psychiatry, 30*, 524–530.

CHAPTER

# 14

# Effective communication of psychological evaluation findings for the court

Right on west 44th street, in the Broadway district, around the corner from Roxy Delicatessen and inches from the Theater Circle Gift Shop, sits the St James Theater. It is home to Disney's second year running show *Frozen*. Underneath the marquee reads the bold words, "The message is clear: LOVE WINS!" Likewise, inside the *Playbill* theater magazine, about pages 30 or 31, is a market page alphabetizing current shows on Broadway. Above each show name is a catchy phrase or *slogan* reprinted from the critic's rave reviews. "Fabulous & Extravagant!" says the *New York Times* of Disney's *Aladdin*. "An Explosion of Fabulous Excess!" praises *Rolling Stones* of jukebox bioplay *The Cher Show*. "Instantly Joins the Ranks of the Irresistible," boasts the *Huffington Post* of *Beautiful: The Carol King Musical*. These are illuminous words captivating the reader's eyes and within seconds conveying a precise and unanimous message: *Go see it!* The artistic linguistics of Broadway, in its creative distillation of words into elegant product marketing, is an example of translating complex ideas into simple and digestible phrases. The advertising industry, for years, has been at the forefront of conversion from hard to easy concepts. Reader-friendly language acts as powerful mands to persuade a person to think favorably about and eventually to buy enticing products. When applying principles of advertising, even difficult-to-read vernacular in the social sciences can be trimmed, manicured, and polished. Complex ideas can translate into sensible sentences to reach a wider consumer audience (Ruben, 1995). Communication begins and ends, then, with whom the message is intended for. So, who is the audience?

When the *New York Times* prints a headline like "Trump Squeezes China with a Set of Fresh Tariffs," the expected audience or reader is presumed to understand basic economics, world affairs, or has been a follower of social and other media coverage of news. When Peter Travers, columnist for *Rolling Stones*, writes "All Rise for the Miracle That is 'Mockingbird,' "referring to actor Jeff Daniels' unmissable ad unforgettable Broadway performance as Atticus Finch, he is galvanizing theater lovers, English majors, fans of Pulitzer Prize writer Harper Lee, and movie buffs of Jeff Daniels. Audience identification is the proverbial goal


https://doi.org/10.1016/B978-0-12-819805-6.00014-2

of any successful communication, whether the objective is selling theater tickets or testifying in court regarding the complex findings of a forensic psychological evaluation. The effectiveness of reporting scientific facts in plain language, without risking loss of its integrity, has alluded professionals who frequently shift from talking to colleagues to talking to *everybody else*. Skeptics, for example, of Cochrane's collaboration plan to simply science (e.g., Pushparajah, Manning, & Michels, 2018), resist that lay summaries will clarify hard concepts and help researchers widen their reach of unlimited audiences. Systematic reviews in everyday or simplified language, they fear, basterdizes pristine science and opens Pandora's Box for gross misconceptions that will over-generalize into rumorous gossip. For example, in the early 1960s, when leaping outside the lab into real life, researchers granted interviews with newspapers and published articles in lay magazines to discuss everyday implications of behavior modification. While publicity of behavior modification" reached its marketing goal of becoming a household word, it also suffered irrevocable damage in its public image as an ethically evil manipulation of scientific principles (e.g., Boivin, Sewell & Scott, 1986; Carey, Carey, & Turkat, 1983; Leslie, 1997; Todd & Morris, 1983; Turkat & Feurstein, 1978). Controversies swirled over the reification of "b-mod" as some sinister behemoth threating the safety of families with its mind-control. Director Stanley Kubrick's dystopian crime film *A Clockwork Orange* (1971) further accelerated the misrepresentation of behavior modification, with its unabashed message of cruelty using aversion therapy.

Social validation of behavioral psychology has improved since its beating in the 1960s and 1970s, owed in part to strategic changes in the proliferation of case studies of highly effective treatments of behavior therapy and life-saving interventions of applied behavior analysis for autism populations (e.g., Garfield, 1983; O'Leary, 1984; Schreibman, Koegel, Mills, & Burke, 1981). Crucial information born in sophisticated applied and experimental research can be told in simpler terms. One avenue reflecting this successful language transition has been the dissemination of self-help books with a behavioral orientation (e.g., Pantalon, Lubetkin, & Fishman, 1995; Redding, Herbert, Foreman, & Guadiano, 2008; Ruben, 1997). While many self-help guidebooks are smartly congruous with actual principles of conditioning, other books may depart too profoundly from the herd and be seen as eclectic spinoffs lacking any relevance to the science of behavior (cf. Glasgow & Rosen, 1979; Pehrsson & McMillen, 2007). Still, the mass self-help books for therapy—or *bibliotherapy*—is a viable vehicle for transportation of trade secrets and methods into the households of families who never sought professional therapy or never thought therapy might work (Ruben, 1989).

This chapter begins with the same goal of self-help books to reach wider audiences with a clearer presentation of the facts. The target audience in this case are jurors, attorneys, judges, and other multidisciplinary professionals unfamiliar with the technical jargon endemic to a behavioral forensic analysis. A plain-language translation and summary provides a more meaningful picture of the assessment. It lifts the interpretation of data beyond the scope of science and renders the message intelligible and insightful for non-scientific audiences. First considered are the do's and don'ts of expert testimony in court when presenting findings from the psychological report. Second, briefly reviewed are guidelines concerning consolidated but effective communication of psychological findings when interviewed by the news or other media.

## The do's and don'ts of expert testimony

*The Daubert rule.* Expert testimony, for starters, must pass the *D. rule*. This is a standard of evidence regarding the admissibility of the expert witness's credentials and anticipated presentation of facts to the jury relevant to the case (Groscup, 2004). The scientific expert should proceed from the presumption that testimony derives from scientific knowledge or incorporated scientific methods (accepted practices), consistent with the expert's scientific education, publications, or other representative sources showing he or she is an authority (and competent) in the field (cf. Dixon & Gill,. 2002). Court approval of the expert paves the way for prosecution, defense, and the judge to examine and cross-examine the expert, either to present fact-based information or to interpret hypothetical examples gleaned from the facts given. During this testimony, experts in mental health bear the unique task of educating the court of test data, observations, or other empirical artifacts on which decisions partly or entirely will later depend. Psychologists and other evaluators reporting findings also are aware their lexicon of psychometric and diagnostic technical language is likely to be misunderstood or not understood, in both cases distracting the court from central points about the offender. One error frequently made, even before experts launch into a monologue of test data, is disposition. Or, how the expert presents himself or herself.

*Emotional disposition.* Behaviorally-trained practitioners, more than any other mental health professional, are notorious for lacking the tact, empathy, and affable interpersonal skills putting the court at ease. They can sound stoically rigid, mechanistic, and even condescending from their exclusive focus on data collection, precision of interventions, and intolerance to (human) subjects who drift from these idealistic expectations for behavior change. Corrective efforts were strongly advised to soften, humanize, and "tone-down" the perfectionism in talking to clients and the public (e.g., Iwata, Wong, Riordan, Dorsey, & Lau, 1982; Keane, Black, Collins, & Vinson, 1982; Ruben, 1986). The purpose of these training safeguards was to reduce the harsh wave of coldness and impersonalization. Interpersonal skills training aimed to soften behaviorists' misconception of human being as simply *organisms who operate on schedules of contingencies of reinforcement*. Human beings are not lab rats—not in the courtroom—no matter how analogous rat behavior is to human behavior or served as the scientific foundation for operant and respondent conditioning. When addressing the court, both in stating one's name and credentials or when first responding to inquiries, the expert's emotional disposition is vital. Among favorable behaviors to display include:

1. Smile, especially if it is a jury trial. Jurors watch every nonverbal and verbal nuance of the experts.
2. Speak slowly, articulately, and moderately softly (but audible for the court stenographer).
3. Thank the court for opportunities to explain by saying "thank you, your honor," or if examined or defense,

   "Thank you, I will be happy to explain." The "thank you" is a mand enjoining the listening audience (jurors, judge, attorneys, etc.) to respond with interest (motivating operation) to the expert's next statement. Listeners will also "tact" the expert's nonverbal qualities of speaking in a calm, reassuring voice, historically associated with clergy, close friends, or other people unconditionally entrusted when they speak. The "trust" resonating from the trusted sound of the expert's voice is an important step to a believable or credible testimony.

Expert testimony by mental health and allied health professionals in a deposition, courtroom, or tribunal can be an ominous and often aversive experience. It is frequently avoided due to anxiety over the formality and unpredictable course of direct and cross examination (cf. Allan, 2010; Neill, 2015; Otto, 1989). Opinions offered undergo the terrifying ordeal of interrogation, refutation, and repudiation of the expert's credentials. Painfully hearing a prosecutor or defendant in open court question the expert's credentials weighs against the expert's ethical duty of aiding the legal process. Even with the best of intentions, the specialist's information for legal decisions can get turned around where the expert feels he or she is on trial in an adversarial system. (Newman, 1992). Adversary persists when the trier of facts, either the judge or jury, considers both sides to every argument. No matter how convincing both sides may be, only on side can prevail. This unexpected acrimony and debasement of the expert are the pivotal reasons why many professionals refuse to testify in court (unless subpoenaed) or stay clear of a forensic practice. In the author's (D. Ruben's) metropolitan Midwest City, for example, of an estimated 150 psychologists and another 200 social workers and licensed counselors, only two mental health professionals (psychologists) actively engage in forensic evaluations. Representative samples statewide and nationwide reflect similar trends in shying away from the forensic arena despite an infusion of college graduate programs offering Masters and Doctorates in forensic psychology. A first step to defuse this pervasive epidemic of court-fears and support a new breed of court-savvy experts is to provide guidelines on the Do's and Don'ts when testifying about results of psychological evaluations (cf. Ruben, 1994, 2002). First reviewed are *Do's* or advisable strategies for better self-control on the witness stand. This follows with caveats or *Don'ts* for over-eager testifiers to remain calm, collected, and speak only within the bounds of one's specialization.

## Do's

1. Semantic equivalence.
2. Speaking in "sound bytes."
3. Use everyday examples.
4. Data-based points.
5. Groups of three.
6. Exclude or define technical jargon.
7. Be truthful.
8. Speak directly to jury or judge.

*Semantic equivalence.* Semantic equivalence is replacing technical words or "obfuscated" phrases with plain language conveying the same meaning. Descriptions of clinical history, purpose of tests used, outcome results, diagnoses, and implications for criminal risk behavior are jargon-free, unless it is defined (see below), and consistent with high-school level verbal comprehension. Take a technical word and divide it into two or three words, and present the words instead of the technical term. Instead of saying, "Jack showed antisocial personality disorder," replace it with, "Jack was unremorseful, selfish, and disregarded rules." On explaining Sally's reinforcement contingencies for embezzlement, say, "Sally took the money to pay for her debts; *or* debt relief made her take more money."

*Speaking in "sound bytes."* Sound bytes in commercial adverting means one or two words summarizing an entire idea. Political and sports pundits crowding the airways on MSNBC, CNN, FOX, ESPN, SPORTSCENTER, and the like are linguistic experts at consolidating pregnant ideas into brevity. They state one or two phrases capturing the essence of an idea to help viewers track and better understand their position. In court testimony, discussion of behavioral forensic assessments is particularly tricky since the taxonomy of technical scientific words is unfamiliar to the lay public. Unlike traditional psychology terms, such as "obsessive-compulsive disorder, which became popular household nicknames, "Oh, honey, you are so OCD"—behavioral terms are less affectionately integrated into mainstream conversation. One is unlikely to hear a spouse saying to another, "Bruce, now just tame the motivating operation before you spiral into a response ratio strain." In court, esoteric language is a distraction unless it is properly defined relative to some pertinent case illustration (see below). When describing a homicide offender's repeated stabbings of a victim to avoid a continuous punishment schedule of verbal reprimands (harassment) from the murderer accomplice, a sound byte might be: "Fear of aggression can increase more aggression." On explaining a perpetrator's forced sexual intercourse on a woman fighting back, when his actions were responding to compound contingencies (variable ratio schedule of reinforcement, respondent arousal, motivating operation), say, for example, "Sexual impulses can intensity with partner resistance."

Sound bytes are not substitutes for natural science explanations. They do not dumb-down or marginalize causal relationships investigated and detailed in the psychological report. Instead, they are laying the foundation for defense and prosecution to follow up with more detailed questions.

*Use everyday examples.* Use of excessive jargon, or *jargon overload* risks miscommunication. It alienates listeners lacking the advanced education to know these words are makes the people feel inferior. Jurors, especially, are a hybrid of socioeconomic, educational, racial, and cultural backgrounds; they are most susceptible to adverse impact effects of jargon overload. Intentionally or unintentionally insulting jurors by over-speaking in technical words not only discredits the expert, it also builds lingering resentment toward the expert and undercuts the merits of a case. One way around jargon overload in discussing results of a psychological evaluation is to normalize or speak in everyday language about the diagnoses, prognoses, or behavior explanations. Examples likely befitting the jury, judge, tribunal, friend of the court referee, magistrate, or any trier of judgment pertain to daily routines, habits, parenting, common hobbies or activities, sports or theater (depending on one's location and current events), and normal transitions in life. Everyday examples portray a humbling, sweet-tempered, and vicariously identifiable slice of life instantly drawing the attention of listeners. For example, here is a way to convert a complex behavioral explanation into common language: Instead of saying, "retail fraud involves initial visceral arousal before entering the store and stealing merchandise," say this: "Remember the excitement you felt before watching Michigan State University's basketball team play in the final four? And that was even before the game started. That is how the thief felt even before he stole from the store." The analogy draws comparisons between a local sport riveting the city (here in East Lansing,

Michigan), and the adrenaline rush motivating the thief. It concisely conveys the *essence* of a functional analysis of (some) economic crimes.

*Data-based points.* Reference to statistics or *numbers supporting a test result* are ethical and prudent sources of evidence in discussing a psychological evaluation. Scores on IQ tests, learning/achievement tests, personality tests, vocational tests, and even from supplemental surveys and scales completed by secondary parties (parents, teachers, etc.) all remarkably fortify the power or significance of psychometric data relative to some population. To say, for example, in reporting intellectual deficits in a criminal responsibility evaluation, that "Jack scored at the second percentile on the Verbal Comprehension Index "means Jack scored equal or greater than a distribution of scores derived from some test norm of other people sharing Jack's same age and demography. It is an "inferential" statistic describing several chunks of data (from subtests) compressed together to form an index score. The inferential or descriptive statistic does not characterize specific functional effects of behavior on the environment and therefore lacks precision in variables which controlled the offender's behavior (cf. Michael, 1974). The index scores, for example, does not operationally define which of Jack's verbal skills are deficient or fall below standards earning him the low score. The static also is inexplicit about setting events (antecedents, consequences, and previous behavior segments), reactional biography, or motivating operations equally responsible for Jack's underdeveloped verbal responses in certain contexts.

Lacking this specificity may deflect attention away from a behavioral forensic analysis and seemingly impregnate the results with confusing or abstract information. But there is one saving grace. Statistics are benign and abstract if used as the sole explanation of behavior, but not if they are data supporting certain contingencies and response forms (topography, duration, intensity, magnitude, etc.). Jack's extremely low score on the Verbal Comprehension Index (VCI), for example, explains why he qualified for an IEP and was placed in resource classes. While there, he associated with brutally aggressive bullies who stifled his social skills and developed social phobias. These are the contingencies produced through multiple behavior segments triggered by his low test score. The low test scores also translate into concrete behavior deficits. Jack poorly answers questions, is always quiet, feels nervous, speaks in one or two-word phrases, and frequently apologizes when talking. Response properties reflected by the low VCI are now more meaningful to a jury who now understands *what impact the scores had on Jack's education and trajectory of underdevelopment of social behaviors.*

Often data describe predictive or social trends based on survey samples drawn from mass populations. Such sociologic or epidemiologic (if related to medical information) data serve as guidelines compared with the defendant's behaviors to explain a likely course of criminal action. Chapter 2 discussed the pros and cons of actuarial data. Use of risk probability charts, geographic risk charts, demographic crime charts are all among hundreds of numerical prognosticators used to explain criminal psychopathology. The advantage of this data was having prior research that showed preponderance or high tendencies of behavior under certain parameters. The disadvantage was crunching numbers to a point of obviating specific instances of cause-effect interactions in one or multiple behavioral segments of the suspect. In courtroom testimony, under time pressures and need for succinct answers, data should closely match the behaviors in question. For example, IQ scores may be relevant to establishing intellectual deficits regarding extenuating factors in criminal responsibility. Other quantitative descriptors of response and stimuli are equally important. For instance, in a bar-robbery scenario, important quantitative facts might include "the suspect's mother said he went to the bar 10 times per week after work, from 6 p.m. to 11 p.m.," "the suspect followed the same ritual of ordering two drinks, going to the bathroom twice, and playing two games of darts before returning to his barstool, closet to the cash register." On quantitative properties of the reactional biography, or about his history, similar numerical profiling of home invasion might include "he broke into five homes within a radius of 1 mile during a two-month period last year; two were his homes of his cousins, and one of his girlfriend." Recorded measurements of current (within the last month) behavior are even more valuable as representative snapshots of the offender's cumulative patterns. For example, on testifying about a post-conviction psychological evaluation on sex-risk behaviors, data include "in the last two weeks, using his sex tracker app on his phone, we found he visited 6 pornographic sites, and twice went on Tinder."

*Groups of three.* Improvisational responses on the witness stand, whether guided by oral examination questions or from referencing a "cheat sheet" in the expert's hands, depend on an articulate command of language and relaxation. A carefully-crafted answer is not only semantically correct, and relevantly corresponds to the questions, but it is also succinct, complete, and objectively grounded. A common semantic device used in public speaking in political or social arenas for sharpening improvisation and testimonial credibility is classifying behaviors or situations in groups of three. This rhetorical rule of three engages listeners by unique pattern recognitions (Holbrook & Howard, 1999). For example, in history and social media, examples abound of stating the 3-sequence rule: "Faith, Hope and Charity," "Mind, Body, Spirit," "Blood, Sweat, and Tears," "Location, location, location," "Stop, look, and listen," and "I came, I saw, I conquered." More than superstition to name three over four in a list, the rhythmic triad sounds more believable and may even become a catchy phrase (for example, the "tripartite motto").

One reason this Hendiatris device works so effectively at conveying a central theme pertains to the function of mands and tacts. The listener, for example, hears a preamble from the expert who professes a domestic violent offender escalates into three forms of anger. This statement mands the listener to prepare for or listen three upcoming forms (word phrases) occurring within a short latency. After the first phrase (form of anger) is given, "verbal abuse," listeners may anticipate several corollaries associated with verbal abuse as the second item in the sequence. This anticipatory arousal, a type of motivating operation, generates multiple autoclitic mands or self-statements uttered silently (sub-audibly to oneself), rehearsing possible word choices that might come next. "Is it physical abuse?" "Is it property destruction?" When the speaker continues the list, "Second one is physical abuse," it reinforces the listener's preceding self-talk behavior of prospecting word choices. "See, I knew that was the right answer." A similar motivating operation for the listener occurs between the speaker's verbalizing the second and third forms of anger in the sequence. The only difference, for the listener, is that hearing the final form of anger (word phrase) reinforces both a similar motivating operation as before, and it also the terminal reinforcer shaping the listener's entire chain of responses from anticipatory arousal and self-generating word options to attentiveness to the speaker.

Jurors, attorneys, judge, and spectators in court will likely focus on the expert's testimony in the same way. They will await for the second and third set of words in the tripartite to see if the words match their expectations. A similar example is when home viewers of the TV game show *Jeopardy* watch contestants unscramble long phrases based on alphabet letter cues. While contestants sound out phrasing on TV, home viewers verbalize aloud or subaudibly their guesses of what the contestant may say (tacts, autoclitic tacts). When game host Alex Trebek declares, "That's right!" for the contestant's answer, it reinforces the television viewer's entire chain of autoclitic behaviors.

*Exclude or define technical jargon.* Pedantics is the habit of describing obscure facts, using archaic language, and imitating an accent to sound more "intellectual." Exaggeration is intentional to bolster one's competency. In a malicious examination and cross-examination, experts may act pedantically to offset anxiety; they may overstate encyclopedic facts beyond the scope of answering questions. Exponentially expounding on one or two or ideas, or on technical jargon, may sound impressive to the expert self-listener, but not to anybody else in the courtroom. In the NBC drama *Quincy ME,* airing between 1976 and 1983, actor Jack Klugman played a tenacious county medical examiner frequently subpoenaed to testify on murder cases. His signature style was relentless, open-ended hyperbolic monologues about his forensic findings on the stand. Quincy's ebullient delivery was highly theatrical and probably inadvisable in a real court of law. By contrast, an example of realistic testimony appears when Dr. George Huang (played by actor B.D. Wong) speaks on the witness stand, in the long-running crime drama *Law and Order: SVU.* His answers are brief, parsimonious, and more congruent with prosecutorial questions. Each of these TV shows mimicked real-life courtroom testimony as lessons for future mental health experts. The lessons gleaned are fourfold.

*First,* selective, careful, and minimal use of technical jargon should reflect an analysis of operational definitions or conclusions about prognosis, not buttress the credibility of the expert witness. For example, if no other words can describe the inadvertent rewards of homicide suspect Melinda's multiple infidelities other than "reinforce," use the term with precision. Cause and effect for specific behaviors should be clear. Use the denotation not connotation of the word. Say, for example, "Her promiscuity was reinforced by (i.e., increase the future probability of) finding more sexually-willing men on Facebook." A wrong use of the technical term, for example, might be "Melinda's overuse of men for sex reinforced her addictive personality." While the latter *sounds* correct, after all, *sex did increase something,* the exact response it reinforced may be ambiguous and is probably one of many behaviors inside the patterns reified as *addictive personality.*

Second, use a technical term immediately followed by a real-life example even if the example goes outside the crime under question. For example, "Maurice was under severe motivating operations (MO) to sell his drugs within 2 h before the drug middle-man demanded payment for upfront costs." Follow this statement with, "He was desperate like a thirsty person asking for water in a desert." While uninformed listeners may still be confused by the MO term, they get a picture of its meaning by identifying with thirsty travelers in the desert. Technical jargon used, re-used, or layered with more technical vocabulary quickly loses the listener's attention span and, from the listener's perspective, diminishes overall meaning of the testimony.

Third, define the technical words with a brief qualifier. Characterizing "Battered Woman's Syndrome" as *stimulus generalization,* explain, "This occurs when we respond similar to similar situations. The offender-victim got anxious every time a man looked at her funny or talked in a deep tone-voice, just like her abusive husband did to her." When given permission by the prosecutor or defense to explain a concept further, be careful with traveling fast through this green light. Temptation is to embellish one explanation with a trove of experimental or applied research underlying the principles or concepts discussed. Such elaboration is too academic and diverts attention from facts. Instead, it may be prudent to offer one or two analogues from basic science for clarification. For example, start with the facts and segue into the analogue. "The offender reported helplessness after being physically beaten for no obvious reason. Physical abuse was random. Similarly, experimental studies of dogs' feet electrically shocked both continuously and randomly showed the dogs just stopped responding and sat motionless on the ground; this was basic evidence showing how depression starts" (e.g., Learned helplessness, also known as conditioned suppression, Seligman, 1972). Over-detailing Seligman's experimental research is redundant and goes beyond the scope of keeping it simple and relevant to the case.

Fourth, when asked a question, confine the answer to the question. Anxious witnesses may see a trajectory or line of inquiry likely followed by the attorney. The witness may think to stay ahead of the inquiries by adding more details to avert the direction of questions. Inferences about the prosecutor or defense attorney's line of questions not only are wrong or misleading, but may trigger a litany of exhaustively excessive details in the expert's testimony. A remedy for raising the periscope nervously to see beyond the immediate horizon is to restrict answers to just the facts presented. For example, asked if the clergy offender who embezzled money from a parish could discern right from wrong, truth from falsehood, or conform to the conduct and requirement of law, for example, say "Yes, he could; testing evidence showed he acted judicially, prudently, and with calculated decisions regarding all authorized expenditures he made on behalf of the church." Even if, in answering this question, the expert intuits the prosecutor may next ask about the same conduct for "all unauthorized expenses," resist the urgency (motivating operator) to volunteer answers to the inferred question.

*Be truthful.* Under the momentary duress of answering questions, experts can summon their immediate and intermediate memory of information given ample verbal cues prompting those memories. Without adequate verbal (evocative or elicitive) cues, answer flagrantly are vague, abstract, evasive, and risk inflation of details. This phenomena of distant cues causing unreliable or invalid testimony underlies the notorious problem of eyewitness memory distortion (Ross, Read, & Toglia, 1994; Wells, 1995). From early scientific research on memory (Ebbinghaus, 1913), the principle investigated has been *associations and conditioning.* Memory of objects, events, and people depend on repeated connections to preserve vivid stimulus recognition. Vividness or accuracy is especially important in reconstructing criminal scenes from bystander witnesses. The mental health expert also has to reconstruct information from the memory of a psychological report. Reminders of verbal cues often are part of the attorney questions, such as "if you will turn to page 45, please read the passage you wrote on ..." Other verbal or nonverbal cues come from the cheat sheet or file accompanying the expert witness to the witness stand. Cues can be facilitators of memory accuracy or truth regarding exact test data, observations of the offender during the evaluation, and even diagnostic and prognostic implications for risk behavior. In accord with the principles of any forensic practice, truthful recall plays an essential role in (a) advancing the line of examination, (b) forming a realistic behavior analysis, and (c) validating the credibility of the expert. "Veracity," among the premiere principles of forensic practice, however, goes beyond testimonial accuracy. It includes control over bias, prejudice, or philosophical stoicism—the tendency to conceptualize events differently than reporting the events themselves (cf. Robertson & Codd, 2019).

Accurately reporting results of forensic evaluations, without risk of contamination, depends on multiple calculated and protective steps taken in advance and during the actual delivery of courtroom answers. First, prepare cheat-sheet notes consistent with the case file. Second, always report on data generated exclusively from the case file or through clinical and psychometric assessments during the evaluation. Third, admit openly to not knowing an answer or lacking data from the case file or report to support the hypothetical example asked in the question. Fourth, offer a clear boundary around the specialization of the expert testimony and particularly when questions ask for speculation or for facts outside that boundary.

*Show court etiquette and agree on general matters, if possible.* In Emily Post's *Etiquette* guidelines (Post, 1937), she ingeniously and creatively operationalizes the reason for polish in a business person, stating,

> ... One advantage of polish is that one's opponent can never tell what is going on under the glazed surface of highly finished manners, whereas an unfinished surface is all too easily penetrated. And since business encounters are often played like poker hands, the unpolished man is sure to be at a disadvantage in playing with a mind-reader who can divine his opponent's cards while his own are unrevealed ... (p. 656)

Mrs. Price Post foreshadowed the insidious jockeying between expert witness and prosecutor or defendant attorney during examination and cross-examination. A smartly dressed witness sitting poised in the chair awaiting questions, with eyes focused on the inquisitor, is a less vulnerable target for intimidation, since the witness exudes confidence, patience, and calmness. While these inferences of nonverbal behavior may seem non-scientific or even trivial idiosyncrasies of pseudo-science, much research on nonverbal behaviors of jurors and witnesses (Dunault & Dunbar, 2017; LeVan, 1984) line the bookshelves of consultants hired to interpret these behaviors in strategizing for tort case victories. Reading the correct verbal or nonverbal cues in demeanor can set the tone and line of inquiry pursued. Extrapolated from this research are idealized behavior protocols expected of professional experts. Experts should:

1. *Always Be On Time.* Subpoenas to appear in court usually specify the date and time the expert must appear. It is essential the expert signs in or appears in the courthouse and ready to go at the designated time. Ideally the best estimate is 30–45 min in advance of the designated time, allowing attorneys to meet, consult, and review content of the testimony in private with the expert. Since pre-trial negotiations between prosecution and defense are inevitable and delay the court session, let alone postpone being called to testify, experts allow flexibility in their time allotment in the court house and are not pressing the court to abide by a schedule.
2. *Dress Appropriately.* Experts should treat any courtroom appearance like a day at the office and dress in business-appropriate attire. Shorts, T-shirts, tank tops, baseball caps, or casual attire are not acceptable. Dressing professionally not only shows respect to the court and its proceedings, it also makes the expert testimony appear more credible. While degree of formality vary among different court locations, and the prevailing climate, neatness and dressed in one's "Sunday's best," guarantees admission into the judge's graces.

3. *Respect the Court and Its Officers.* The judge not only presides over the courtroom, he or she represents the court itself and the law. When a judge enters the room, everybody rises. One must also show respect to the attorneys for both sides, as they are all considered officers of the court. Conformity to courtroom customs are non-negotiable. In an age of patriotic protests by kneeling during the national anthem, such public displays of dissent are not only unacceptable, violating court protocol, but may move the judge to find the expert in contempt of court.
4. *Speak Clearly.* When asked a question by an attorney, experts should answer "yes" or "no." A nonverbal nod or shaking the head provides an unclear indication to the jury or the expert's response made. Clearly enunciated verbal responses are even more essential during telephonic court testimony. Here, due to geographic distance or other reasons waived by the court, experts' responses are live-streamed by video or telephone, and their testimony treated identically as if given orally inside the courtroom.
5. *Answer Directly.* While experts always should testify truthfully, answers should pertain specifically to the stated question. If experts do not know the answer to a specific question, the polite response, "I don't know the answer" is appropriate. Guesses, estimates, or speculations on hypothetical case illustrations or questions are acceptable but should be so described. Such prefatory remarks include, "If it pleases the court, I can offer an estimate but it is not conclusive."
6. *Wait for ruling on Objections.* If an attorney asks a question and the opposing attorney objects, do *not* answer until the judge has ruled on the objection. Do not, as improperly depicted in TV courtroom shows, offer to answer the question in spite of the objection. An objection indicates the question may not be permissible under the rules governing court proceedings, and speaking before the judge makes a determination may compromise the trial itself.
7. *Be Prepared.* Even routine trials can take a great deal of time. Experts may be at the courtroom for several hours on the day before called to testify. Make sure all business and personal affairs for the day are in order before arriving in court. Preparation also means reviewing the case file or details in the psychological report with anticipated "response sets" or word bytes to use in response to inquiries. In most court trials, attorneys, paralegals or other office personnel may send pre-trial questions or offer guidelines concerning the scope of testimony expected. Pre-trial interviews by telephone, Email, texting, or in person with the prosecution or defense team also provide questions and objectives with which to rehearse answers. The time allotted to preplanning, from familiarity with case documents, to the content of an evidentiary psychological report, will increase the expert's sharpness of articulation, seamless fluidity of coherent responses, and enhance an image of impeccable credibility.
8. Address *the court formally.* Verbal responses directed to the judge precede with, "Yes, your honor." Responses given to defense or prosecution may precede by stating the attorney's name, "Yes, Mr. Smith," or one can omit saying the attorney's name and begin an acknowledgment or praise for asking the question, particularly if it enables clarification of test findings, "Thank you for asking," or "I appreciate the opportunity to expound."

*Speak directly to jury or judge.* In Judge-only trials, jurisdiction for authority rests with the judge who listens to and will form an opinion on the case. In jury trials, while judges are still officers of jurisprudence and give instructions to the jury, focus for the expert shifts from directing eye contact exclusively to the judge to the jury and judge. In a jury trial, experts look at the jury while answering questions to build a rapport. Eye contact spread across the jurors diminishes the formidability and detachment of expert as cold, uncaring, and peripheral to the emotionality of the crime. Continuous eye contact sends a clear message of compassion for the facts, not for the offender's welfare, and awareness of the juror's equivocal position of sorting through objective data without prejudice (Cooper, Bennett, & Sukel, 1996; Cupon & Jahn, 2002).

## Don'ts

A miscarriage of justice occurs when the judicial system fails to reach justice as in the conviction of an innocent person. Infiltrators to a miscarriage can be technical or procedural protocols omitted or incorrectly followed during a trial. An equal cause of justice impediment are the errors expert witnesses make in reporting findings from psychological or mental health evaluations (cf. Greene, 1988; Wise, Sartori, Magnussen, & Safer, 2014). Reviewed in this section are the common mistakes to avoid in expert testimony. More importantly is the caveat of suppressing the therapist-healer role. This is very difficult at first. Mental health providers, normally speaking, are behavior observers and educators in primary and secondary interventions. They astutely diagnose and treat people showing problematic or abnormal behaviors, and teach families prevention and maintenance techniques to preserve therapy outcome success. Behaviorally-trained providers are even more obsessive about detection, intervention, and education of behavior problems. They observe, record, measure, and operationalize microscopic behavioral units across a wide field of events. They assemble a series of systematic and sequential interventions designed to change, not just the person, but the person's surrounding environment. They focus on several variables affected in altering unwanted behavior. Once implementation of multi-contingencies achieves the goal of equilibrium, it means the problem behavior is corrected and the community around the target person is now stable.

Behavior therapists often go one more step unlike their non-behaviorally trained clinician cohorts. They document behavior changes from Baseline and treatment phases and eventually share these results among colleagues. Behavioral psychology, as a disciplinary science, prospers from its clinical and field applications progressing from anecdotal case studies to single subject and group studies; research results graduate to the next step of being presented at conferences and conventions. Once collegial feedback at professional meetings helps to refine conceptualization of the data, behaviorists are encouraged to publish their findings in referred journals or books.

This evolution of data dissemination, from treatment to publication—a signature of a true *scientist-practitioner* (Barlow, Hayes, & Nelson, 1984) – advances behavioral psychology and provides guidelines for new behaviorists to repeat the data reporting cycle ad infinitum. The problem with this natural evolutionary cycle is that it does not fit in a courtroom. Courtrooms are neither clinics to treat nor classrooms to teach. Behavioral experts do not have a duty to expound on research, instruct on principles of applied behavior analysis, publish their data there, or give advice to the tiers of law regarding recommendations of behavior change. Their role is limited to the scope and purpose of the trial, *only.*

That is why many mistakes occur in the execution of expert testimony. As a primer to understand these mistakes, below are the "Don'ts" when providing expertise about some report, review, or assessment performed in the course of pretrial discovery.

1. Don't use humor or sarcasm.
2. Don't berate other mental health professionals.
3. Don't overstate one's credentials as proof of points.
4. Don't get angry or defensive.
5. Resist invention of words or using colloquial expressions.
6. Never advocate a cause.

*Use humor or sarcasm.* Tensions simmering before or during expert examination are uncomfortable for most witnesses. Witnesses lay their reputations on the line when offering opinions in a disputed case, and each side attempts to carve minor lesions in the credibility of the expert. Inexperienced testifiers impacted by this unorthodox forum that encourages open criticism and even bullying of witnesses may revert to familiar responses engaged in under similar, non-legal circumstances of daily life. They may use sarcasm, humor, cynicism, poke fun at the attorney, or lighten tensions with general court levity. Humor outwardly may dismantle a line of antagonistic questions or even offset the witnesses' momentary paralysis from intimidation. Jokes and parodies can arouse courtroom laughter, relieve jurors of anxiety from the dramatic testimonies or graphically sordid elaborations by defense and prosecution, particularly in murder cases. But the downside of humor is obvious. The courtroom is not *Comedy Central.* The expert witness is neither the warm-up nor headliner, nor is he or she Falstaff in a Shakespearian tragedy of Henry do the fourth parts one or two.

Experts owe a duty to the court of self-disciplined objectivity in refraining from de-stressing the court or making fun of its actors. While experts are human, and think it is appropriate to make light of provocative questions, masking the courtroom pathos with jocularity undermines the *value of seeing emotions in an expert.* For example, in reporting a chronic history of repeated animal torturing, fire-setting, and aggressive bullying in school—all in laying the foundation to predict the offender's high propensity for serial murders—the expert may sputter, get "choked up" and reluctantly state the offender is a threat to society. Jurors observing this shift in vocal tone in the expert from a rhythmically fluid cadence to difficulty in expressing words of a phrase (i.e., anacrusis) may react to the nonverbal properties (tact) by interpreting it as "this is very serious." This nonverbal properties of speech–the tact—may be a deciding factor in the juror's agreement of a guilty verdict. This pivotal nonverbal cue would have been lost had the expert witness disguised his or her vulnerability with gratuitous and facetious humor.

*Berate other mental health professionals.* Attacks on an expert's credentials, particularly when it explodes unexpectedly and drills deeply into embarrassing past legal or ethical sanctions, raises a bane of contempt and desire to be defensive. A witness under scrutiny for past State Board complaints about unethical conduct in performing custody evaluations, for example, may feel the walls collapsing around him or her. Rather than to calmly explain the Board inquiries and resolutions thereof, the expert panics in defensiveness and spirals into blaming other forensic specialists of professional jealousy, lacking a certain caliber of education, and barely escaping Board reviews of their own flawed reports. Berating other mental health professionals is a cheap and weak strategy to bolster the expert's credibility; it foils the expert's supposed impeccability against the fallibilities of other experts, especially ones who previously testified or whose opinions the expert is asked to comment on.

In behavioral forensics, experts trained in applied behavior analysis come from a radically different educational pedigree than their cohort forensic examiners. Many examiners trained in eclectic psychology, counseling, social work, or rehabilitation departments, for example, learn psychoanalytic or humanistic theory and principles. They see behavior as gestalts of personality instead of as molecular units of cause-effect contingencies transacted across behavioral fields. Even in forensics science programs emphasizing empirical or evidence-based approaches, training is a smattering of cognitive-behavioral concepts and principles with a clear dualism between thought and action, instead of seeing them as integrative patterns. These discrepancies in training orientation frequently come up when a behavioral forensic examiner is asked to critique a nonbehavioral psychological report for its veracity of prediction. An arrogantly-driven critic may seize the spotlight not only to systematically discredit the report but also to decry the underlying psychological model of the examiner writing the report. Part of promulgating the behavioral movement, in the minds of some experts, may involve trashing the opposition and extolling the virtues of one's own forensic model. But be aware of the *Ides of March.* The proselytizer gunning for this attack is on the wrong track. Debasement of any expert or professional at equal, higher, or lower educational ranking as the expert witness is an attack on the expert himself or herself. Condemnation of bad report writing, bad administration or scoring of test batteries, and faulty score interpretations backfire as negative statements said about the internal defects of one's larger spectrum of profession. The debunker is unknowingly alerting the jurors, judge, tribunal, or attorneys to beware of any mental health professional prone to make similar errors and thus the group as a whole are suspicious reporters of truth. *Et tu, Brute?*

*Overstate one's credentials as proof of points.* At the beginning of any testimony, prosecution or defense asks to *qualify the professional as an expert*. Unless the expert previously testified in a particular courtroom or enjoys a stellar reputation among officers of the court, obviating the qualification process, he or she must undergo some inquiry for both parties to stipulate (agree) to the expert. Inquiries are generally perfunctory by asking the expert about past education, specialty certifications, years of practice, past testimonies for both sides (prosecution, defense), books or articles authored relevant to the case, and professional memberships. Under Daubert standards, surveys of expert credentials is to establish the witnesses' likely scientific testimony and scientific reasoning applied to the facts of the current issue. Experts fearful that their credentials may lack face validity or be challenged due to ambiguity of their degree title, training, or practice may be prone to orally inflate or "doctor" their credentials. For example, a social worker (MSW) asked to administer a personality and aptitude test battery to an offender feared the voire dire process, the process used to establish an expert's qualifications. She already knew her administration and interpretation of psychometric testing were outside of her professional training realm, despite her employer mandating her role as tester. She worried about exposure of her license violation and disqualification from the case, both humiliating and even threatening the security of her job. When asked the very question she dreaded under cross examination, she lied and inflated her credentials.

She explained her original graduate program was in clinical psychology and she transferred to social work. She also explained gaining post-graduate specialty training in psychometrics working under licensed psychologists. The court not only disqualified her, but also censored her for padding information beyond what her updated curricula vita showed.

Honesty is always the best practice in defining the limits or boundaries around which an expert's specialization fits. Had the social worker confessed the testing was outside of her trained expertise and she preferred not to testify on that matter, the court might still regard other parts of her forensic analysis valid such as the clinical interview and document review, both of which fell perfectly within her purview. Her credibility upheld, the social worker expert might qualify as a fact-witness or purveyor of other specific information in the case. Inflation of credentials either as a decoy deflecting attention away from the expert or to over-glamorize the expert's knowledge and training, both run the precarious risk of compromising personal integrity and dignity.

*Get angry or defensive.* At the peak of a courtroom battleground, when experts see the cross examination turning from civility to outright incivility, autonomic instincts are to fight or flight. That is, both seasoned and unseasoned experts fall prey to the luring temptation of getting angry and defensive, or detaching with an emotionless analytical expression or stoicism, suppressing any volatile rumblings from surface observation. Anger on the witness stand is, to use a sports analogy, at the point of *game over.* On the racquetball court playing an opponent who is ahead by 10 points and inside feeling the game is a bust, players may get angry, revengeful, and acts recklessly aggressive. Misuse of anger completely ruins the game, increases errors in judgment, and the game in effect is over. A similar case exists during examination and cross-examination when prosecution or defense grills the expert on untenable hypotheses or conclusions reached in the report, or belittles the expert for failing to reach scientifically valid outcomes. For behavioral forensic examiners, who pride themselves on the strictest of empirical practices including data-generated, operational analyses, rejection of their conclusions is not just a slap in the face. It feels like an assassination attempt.

Inducement of expert witness anger partly is methodical and partly is an inferential reaction of the witness. In jury and judge-only trials, under limited opportunities to discredit witnesses, getting the ire of a witness dismantles the poise, objectivity, and detachment first presented when the witness swears in and sits on the witness stands. Observers detect a "breaking point" or hypersensitivity from personalizing some incriminating question, thereby humanizing the expert; he or she falls from grace, loses venerability, and is no longer the mythical gods commanding the universe. Humanization of an expert levels the playing field to make the expert as vulnerable and suspicious of hiding truth as the criminal on trial. On the other hand, experts over-react with anticipation of where the examination or cross-examination is going. Anticipatory anxiety over questions, for example, that stir up painful memories of taking and re-taking the national licensing boards, might unseat a calm expert. Other accusations such as previous evaluation reports biasedly favoring only the prosecution or that always diagnose sexual offenders as untreatable, will also feel like bullets fired in rapid succession. Experts suddenly feel assaulted, and think they are the character of Joseph K in Franz Kafka's existential novel, *The Trial (1946)*, arrested and prosecuted by a remote, inaccessible authority for reasons never disclosed. The unspecified crime for unspecified reasons builds unending panic in Joseph K until he dies at the end obligated to perish for unspecified causes. This surrealistic enigma of punishment is analogous to experts seemingly scapegoated for "no apparent reason" inside the dome of criminal activities.

Effectively overcoming a "Kafka" moment requires patience and looking at examiners' questions as grandstanding and not premeditative ambush. Grandstanding is an action strategically intended to make judge, jurors or other deciders notice the examiner in an animated performance of persuasion. The intent is less about the nullification of the expert, and that moment, and more about the awe-striking magnificence of the attorney spinning an argument eloquently and convincingly. When the mental health expert realizes they are a pawns in this theatrical performance—a mere trick in the Houdini's arsenal of smoke and mirrors—the new perspective lowers resentment, depersonalizes the moment, and allows the expert to remain composed.

*Resist invention of words or using colloquial expressions.* The late comedian actor Tim Conway, a virtuoso of ineptitude, had a brilliant sense of humor. He often invented words accompanying his trove of pratfalls, double-takes, facial tics, and other hyperboles of physical and emotional distress. His devotion to foolishness made his neophilic characters on TV shows like "McHale's Navy" and "The Carol Burnett Show" a Petri dish for classic scenes. Like other popular TV and stage stars, his word salads were marks of talented showmanship. In the court room, Tim Conway's shenanigans would be a distraction and undermine the scientific integrity expected of expert witnesses. A Conway-like problem plaguing mental health experts is their liberty to use terms in psychology, psychiatry, and allied fields that are inaccurate, misleading, or colloquial expressions. They are ambiguous, oxymorons, pleonasms, and lead to misconceptions of cognitive and behavioral phenomena (cf. Lillenfeld, Sauvigne, Lynn, Cautin, Latzman & Waldman, 2015). Problems of esoteric scientific technology, as suggested above, can be minimized by scarce and selective use with simplified explanations. For example, explain *reinforcement* as "Some event that occurs after a behavior and increases that behavior in the future, like a parent smiling at her child and the child smiles back."

Sub-distinctions such as between *positive and negative reinforcement* get trickery but can be just as easy. For example, "Positive means give and negative means take away, but both outcomes increase the child's behavior." Clarification hinges on accuracy of the technical term and using it appropriately in examples a jury or judge can identify with. By contrast, experts often invent their own technical library of words or use common phrases mean to abbreviate an idea. To say, "Jack yelled at her to short-circuit her response" meaning to quickly evoke her behavior, loses the functional value of what took place. Likewise, vernacular expressions such as *brainwashing, bystander apathy, chemical imbalance, hard-wired, and hypnotic trance* all purport a highly sagacious explanation of some phenomenon. But the terms are empty, lacking any scientific meaning, and entirely depend on the fervor embellishing the words as the expert says them. The safe alternative is to stay within the comfort of professional nomenclature using real-life examples.

*Never advocate a cause.* Expert testimony is not the professional's spotlight to rant on a philosophical, political, social, or political points. Court experts are not TV and radio pundits, whose job is commentator and speculator of events shaping the world. In the recent days of the National Rifle Association (NRA's) internal chaos, for example, news outlets reported on failing revenue, mounting legal trouble, and discovery of the chief executive's gross misspending. A right-wing liberal anti-gun advocate, who happens to be testifying in a murder case involving the senseless shooting of two sleeping adult-parents by their 16 year old son, might feel the need to pontificate on gun control laws during testimony. This capitalizing on the moment for personal beliefs is profoundly inappropriate for several reasons. First, it distracts the court from the primary jurisprudent duty of procedural due process. Second, it weaken the witnesses' credibility by unmasking a hidden agenda or bias besmirching an earlier or upcoming testimony on facts of some evaluation. Third, if the expert-pundit postures a position antithetical to jurors, all of whom, for example, are loyal lifetime members of the NRA, the expert alienates himself or herself from the jury and nearly hands over a verdict opposite to the goal of prosecution or the defense team who hired the expert. Fourth, on a professional basis, it is purely unethical to exploit a public forum for personal or selfish gain and ignore the principles of forensic psychology, among them to:

1. Respect for the dignity and rights of other people.
2. Show responsibility to clients, society and the profession.
3. Show veracity in being honest and truthful.
4. Show fidelity when entrusted with client's interests.
5. Show beneficence in doing well over selfishly.
6. Protect against maleficence (not doing harm to others).
7. Preserve Justice in being fair and objective.

The tipping point for any forensic testimony that may go sour or slip into non-substantiated, personal ramblings is when answers to questions exceed 15–30 s. A crisp and succinct answer, using scientific or lay language, with proper semantics, and even sound byes, never should exceed 30 s unless the examiner or cross-examiner re-starts the clock for another 30 s for amplification of a response. And even then, each clarification given also respects the 30-s time limitation to assure the audience (judge, jurors) can fully comprehend and digest the complexity of information explained.

## Communication guidelines for effective communication with social and other media

Rule 8, according to *Gibb's rules*, is *never take anything for granted.* Lead investigator Leroy Jethro Gibbs, played by actor Mark Harmon on the detective series *NCIS*, sets bylaws for proper investigative conduct and safety among his crony underlings. His charismatic levity comes when he reminds his staff of rules they violate. The same Gibb's rule applies to mental health professionals asserting expertise across the airwaves and soundwaves of television and radio, or across electronic waves of social media. In the midst of a digital/social media revolution marking the last 10 years, more pundits and experts shifted from appearing on TV and Radio to live streaming over new media outlets. These outlets reliably reach a high percentage of younger and more influential viewers (cf. Geiger & Lampinen, 2014). Educated and intellectually curious listeners, all juggling their I-pod casts and YouTube *Ted Talks,* with updates from Facebook, Snapchat, and Instagram, are today's audience with a voracious appetite for unlimited knowledge. When mental health professionals tap into this vast cauldron of fact-cravers, they take for granted their audience shares similar expertise or is up to date on modern forensic methods. Missing the point entirely, the purpose of expert reporting over a media system is not to feed the insatiable hunger for knowledge; it is to supplement the knowledge an audience already has with new information. In a local embezzlement case, for example, Facebook already is swirling with seamless posts about new stories and commentaries. Viewers already see videos of the crime. What the audience now wants are facts on *why the crime happened.*

Online internet experts who are seasoned in TV and radio broadcasting or who had a history newspaper interviews are savvy followers of the Do's and Don'ts of effective communication about psychological reports. The first fact they know is this: In most pre-trial or post-trial cases, gag orders restrict any unauthorized discussion about the case from being made public. Violations of this court order include strict penalties of contempt from fines to incarceration to complaints filed with one's state or national ethical boards. Even when gag orders are not in effect, suppression of unauthorized commentary is highly advisable since it follows the ethical standards protecting confidentiality. Still, there are post-conviction opportunities where jurors, plaintiff or prosecuting attorneys, and even certain experts are sought after for insight into the courtroom gymnastics of a controversial case. Therapist Susan Forward, for example, was among the first to speak after Jessica's Simpson's death and vindication of accused husband killer O.J. Simpson. Susan Forward spoke about her sessions with then spouse-abused victim Jessica, and subsequently faced license suspension for her breach of confidentiality.

Questioning the mental Fitness of President Trump, in a more recent matter, Yale University psychiatrist Dr. Brandy Lee briefed congress on her doubtfulness of Trump's capacity to serve office. She faced an avalanche of denouncers from the American Psychiatric Association (APA), banning mental health professionals from free-spiritedly diagnosing any person, let alone a public figure, without first personally interviewing (evaluating) the person. Lee's maverick crusade to recruit other psychiatrists and psychologists to speak up, defying the APA's warning, resulted in a book collectively written by prominent mental health experts on the president's abnormal behavior threatening the nation's democracy (Lee, 2017).

Psychiatrist Dr. Lee took exception to *Gibb's rule 8.* She took for granted that a majority of social and traditional media consumers had antipathy toward the president and would welcome her message. Speaking on news shows sympathetic to her cause—like *the Rachel Maddow show or Last Word with Lawrence O'Donnell*—the Yale psychiatrist probably believed she was right. She did attract a homogenous group of liberal thinkers supporting her endeavor to unravel the president's preponderant mental illness. The big mistake Dr. Lee made was less about her message, or her ethical tenacity, or even her enlistment of other tribal conspirators who penned similar opinions. Her errors lied in politicizing her opinions instead of just presenting the facts objectively like a behavioral forensic evaluator. Unlike Dr. Lee or other newcomers to the public forefront, who seek a mouthpiece for social issues, the role of expert in speaking to news media is to succinctly convey evidence-based information without editorial commentary. Here are the Do's and Don'ts when a behavioral (or any) mental health expert submits to public interviews.

## Do's

1. Prepare a set of questions.
2. Know target audience in advance.
3. Stick with facts of the report, and no speculation beyond.
4. Always make the interviewer look good and be grateful.

*Prepare a set of questions.* Interviews may come spontaneously at newsworthy times, catching the expert off-guard or with little time to prepare good answers. The norm, however, is just the opposite. On TV, show producers enlist guests days or months before airtime and even 3–4 h after a breaking story. Ample time usually is available for the expert to formulate a series of 3–5 questions guiding the interviewer during the 5–10 min interview segment. For longer Q & A segments, advanced questions are mandatory for the expert to rehearse or at least cull facts from an evaluation or report supporting some position.

*Know target audience in advance.* Unlike Dr. Lee's gamble of espousing anti-trump slogans across the airwaves to pro-president and anti-president supporters, a sound strategy is to be familiar with the audiences earmarked for the media chosen. Viewers of 9 p.m., 10 p.m. and 11 p.m. shows on *CNN, MSNBC, and FOX* are likely middle age to older adults in middle to upper-middle socioeconomic demographics. Distribution of news across *Facebook and Twitter*, for example, will likely attract older and middle-age down to mid-twenties individuals, widely diverse in their political, religious, and social affiliations. *Snapchat, Instagram, and Reddit*— the most rapid uploaded feeds of breaking news—usually attracts mid-teens (tweens), older adolescents through mid-twenties, from diversely socio economic and usually apolitical backgrounds. Targeting the audience also becomes the guideline on what vocabulary and sound bytes to use, and what examples from real life are more relevant.

*Stick with facts of the report, and no speculation beyond.* Like testifying in court, the single most mortal sin in public interviewing is speculating beyond the facts. For example, a psychologist performing many mental health evaluations of adolescent refugees fleeing Guatemala, Honduras and El Salvador, is called upon to give a clinical impression of their Post-Traumatic Stress Disorder (PTSD) effects. She is not engaging in unethical behavior since she really did meet the refugees one-on-one, and is bundling her opinions together to show trends while maintain confidentiality and anonymity. She describes their grueling ordeal of traveling 1,600 miles, 85 h via train, bus, or walking, waiting at border patrols, waiting in resettlement processing, and losing track of family when released to nonprofit respite centers nationwide. Here is the problem: By advancing these statistics, the psychologist overstepped her boundaries of specialization in elaborating on tangential matters. She can just give the facts of a clinical test finding. Had she stated the overall Verbal Comprehension Index (e.g., WISC-V, Spanish version) was borderline to extremely low, suggesting the possibility of under-schooling of refugees in their indigenous countries, that data and hypothesis would be specific to the test results. As a reminder of a point mentioned earlier in this chapter, the microphone is not a podium for self-righteous pontificating. It is a precious and limited opportunity to display the value of forensic science.

*Always make the interviewer look good, and be grateful.* A secret often overlooked in live, taped, or delayed streaming is that viewers are not tuning in to enjoy the expert who is interviewed. They tune in to enjoy their favorite anchor or interview host. Years ago, when the author (D. Ruben) appeared on the daytime talkfest *Donahue*, accompanied by three groups of parents, all of whom spoke on how their *child hated their lover*, the host Phil Donahue made an outrageously and blasphemously non-scientific comment to the author. "Yes," he said, "Dr. Ruben, author of bestseller *Bratbusters: Say Goodbye to Tantrums and Disobedience*, is here to show you new methods of punishment." He said this to thousands of people in TV-land watching the show, and then the camera turned to the author, sitting in a chair, and the red light above the camera went on: "Yes, Phil," improvised the author, "I agree with your intro, but let's hope we can wait a while for punishment; there are other good ways to handle behavior."

The author did what any interviewer aghast by the negative sound byte would do: Punt. No debate, argument, or disappointment shown. The goal of appearing on Phil Donahue's show was to glorify Phil Donahue. The author was just window dressing. A general rule to follow in any interview media is to compliment and thank the interviewer. When flattery is given to the viewer's favorite host, and the host in turn is laudatory to the interviewee, viewers entrust and like the interviewee as much as the host. Intermingling effects of respondent and operant conditioning serve as powerful marketing agonists in boosting the likability and hence believability of the interviewee expert. To show higher order conditioning effects (or, in operant language, stimulus generalization), the next time this expert is observed by the same viewer on another talk show, he or she will remark positively with, "Hey, look who it is? I really liked this guy when I saw him last night on CNN."

## Don'ts

1. Resist levity.
2. Never post test results or discuss case on social media.
3. Never pitch self for marketing practice.
4. Never give therapy advice during the interview.

*Resist levity.* A legitimate caveat in court testimony is to never break the code of being pleasant and relaxed when presenting forensic facts. The microphone, said earlier, is not a podium for pontificating; it is also not an opportunity to spoof, make jokes about, or be comedic about a case. While all interviews have unpredictable moments, some even outright funny, and deserve unanimous laughter with the anchor, that laughter is prompted by the anchor. Interviewed outside the court-house, the mental health expert is asked if he expects to testify today. Seconds later the clouds part and deluge the streets with a tropical downpour of rain. Both the expert and host get instantly soaked during the live broadcast and cannot help but share a giggle over their non-fortuitous drenching. Humor, in other words, may manifest as an artifact of the broadcast. It should never be sarcasm, cynicism, satire or some whimsical remark at the expense of a serious topic, no matter how uncomfortable the expert feels during the interview.

*Never post test results or discuss cases on social media.* Increasing digital communication, from email to texting to Snapchat to Instagram to Face-Time, has been the modern modem for verbal intimacy. Closeness forms in sharing abbreviated language, emoji symbols, and posting autobiographical events reflecting celebrations or milestone activities in people's lives. Some events or statements posted are less celebratory and more personal such as where a couple spent their honeymoon, or how "wasted" a person got overdrinking at a bar. The explosion of self-posting on internet social media has almost become a norm, promulgated by enthusiastic fans galvanizing the sharer to "dig up" more dirt on himself or herself for public consumption. For forensic evaluators, or mental health providers in general, a good rule to follow contradicts this social latitude for personal-life exhibitionism. Experts should never post anything about themselves. Opening the window into a personal life provides information on ethnicity, religion, socioeconomics, hobbies, rituals, and other sacred attributes easily misconstrued as bad and prejudicial to the expert's opinions, and *prima facie* evidence to discredit the expert.

One expert social worker testified in court as a fact witness being the therapist of the accused. The offender murdered her husband and claimed self-defense against her husband. The expert reported the client was victimized by an abusive alcoholic husband and prone to *Battered Woman Syndrome.* The case went three days, with jurors sworn to secrecy and not to discuss the case with anybody in between trial days. They were asked not to watch the news. *But they did check their Facebook.* On Facebook, one juror spotted the social worker expert celebrating Passover, a Jewish Holiday recognizing the sadness and oppression of the Jews' exodus from Egypt many thousands of years ago. The picture depicted the social worker holding up Elijah's glass of wine and pretending to drink it. Appalled by this picture, the juror immediately uttered an anti-Semitic stereotype of the "Jew" lambasted him for drinking as much as the abusive husband villainized in court earlier in the day. The next day in court, that juror, who should have reported this bias and been excused from the trial, held the bias inside and subsequently dismissed the social worker's smoking-gun testimony of domestic violence.

*Never pitch self for marketing practice.* Advertising mental health services, in most states, is relatively new. States banned marketing for decades based on the antediluvian belief that solicitations were invasive of privacy and thrusted insidiously and unwelcomed changes in a person's life. Fast forward to the last twenty years, championed by advocacy groups (e.g., National Alliance of Mental Illness, Brain and Behavior Foundation, etc.), and witness a robust revolution in promoting mental health awareness and solutions (Funk, Minoletti, Drew, Taylor, & Saraceno, 2006; Morselli, 2000; World Health Organization, 2001). Today many licensed mental health providers freely advertise in the yellow pages, on internet sites, on radio and television, in newspapers and magazines, and during local and national interviews. The parity of mental health and medical health marketing overcame the public stigma of being "seen" with an "illness" and was replaced with a proactive conception of *taking charge of one's life.* As mental health promotion reaches a wider scope of consumers, the question still lingering is *when is the best time to plug one's own business?*

Self-promotion is probably inadvisable during serious media interviews when the mental health provider serves as expert. On any media network, interviews personify the expert to deity status. Reification of the expert occurs from the sound byte or banner fed underneath the expert on Television or during an introduction of the expert. The expert's notoriety spikes from local psychologist to "he's an international consultant on terrorist seizure and negotiation trauma." Rise to fame, in seconds, makes the expert an invincible superhero, guru, and believable prognosticator of behaviors. Emboldening the prophet image further, interviewers may even flash across the screen or in print the latest books authored by the expert. Here, the expert was not the promotor, since it was the host who described the book.

By contrast, when this all-powerful *Wizard of Oz* sneaks in a publicity piece near the end of the interview by stating his or her webpage or phone number, it cheapens the expert's aura of omnipotence. It utterly destroys the mesmerizing vision of the expert as infallible and trustworthy. More destructively, self-promotion deflects attention away from the razor sharp precision of forensic details given during the interview, and leaves the viewer disgusted by feeling betrayed and manipulated by a scam artist. Adding salt to the wounds, behavioral forensic experts are *expected to withhold* self-promotion by their ethical responsibility to society (Guideline 9, cf. Bailey & Burch, 2011; Barlow et al., 1984). While encouraging the culture to make good use of behavioral knowledge (i.e., the principles of behavior), focus of public information should be exclusively upon behavior *per se, as a product of scientific research and therapy, not about the interviewee's clinical practice.* Guideline 9 of the current *Behavior Analyst Certification Board (BACB) Guidelines for Responsible Conduct* (cf. BACB, 2019, pp. 1–24), *specifically* pertains to any public statements including but not limited to paid or unpaid advertising, brochures, printed matter, directory listings, personal resumes or curricula vitae, interviews or comments for use in media, statements in legal proceedings, lectures, and public oral presentations, and presentation materials.

*Never give therapy advice during the interview.* The privilege accorded to a forensic expert is an opportunity to report on and predict outcome effects of measurable data from a psychological report. Estimations, for example, on the probability of recurrence of assaultive behavior at work or in a school require a unique calculus involving principles of behavior, years of assessment and testing experience, knowledge of the court systems, and perceptiveness of the contingencies implicit in the legal case. The advice offered to the prosecution, defense, judge, and jury reflects this carefully calculated analysis that may determine a verdict, sentencing, or series of interventionism for offender rehabilitation. This calculated advice *is not therapy. It neither involves delivery of behavior change methods directly to the offender nor regards the offender as a client.* Offenders are the subjects evaluated independently without the normal conditions of therapy including rapport-building, trust, empathy, and establishment of a vested client interest in treatment. Therapy and its elements of client-bonding are outside the prevue of a forensic evaluation. Externally detached, the investigator-historian is an unbiased observer of functional events between objects (stimuli) and organism (responses). For this reason, interviewed experts restrict their comment to specific (or general) histories of behavior patterns, behavior potentials (of the offender or people in general affecting by similar contingencies) and data culled from the testing or clinical interview supporting conclusions about crime recidivism.

Advice offered outside of these parameters commits as serious mistake. It violates the specialty guidelines for forensic psychologists derived from the "Ethical Principles of Psychologists and Code of Conduct" (APA, 2013, 2017). Guideline 1.03 on avoiding conflicts of interest explicitly states that "forensic practitioners refrain from taking on a professional role when personal, scientific, professional, legal, financial, or other interests or relationships could reasonably be expected to impair their impartiality, competence, or effectiveness, or expose others with whom a professional relationship exists to harm" (p. 9). Meaning, behavioral forensic experts wear only one hat during public media interviews, that of an evaluator. Caring for the welfare of the offender or people in general, afflicted with same behavior problems as the offender, are tangential departures from a scientist role of fact-finding and fact presentation. When interviewers ask the leading question, "So, Doctor Smith, how would you cure the serial rapist? Is chemical castration the best solution?" Barring one's ethical or scientific qualms with this treatment approach, the best answer is, "that topic really falls outside of my role as forensic evaluator."

As digital and social media outlets quadruple over the next 5–10 year, expediting transmission of news by quantum speeds both domestically and globally, the urgency for current information on mind, body, and spirit will also quadruple. Mental health experts become prime sources of populist news feeds, posts, blogs, and columns filling cyber-media with science and pseudo-science about trends in self-help and forensics; yes, even *forensics*. Over 95 television weekday drama series on forensics and crime investigation since 2006 have stimulated an insatiable public appetite for crime and criminals and how forensics allows good to triumph over evil. From *NCIS* to *Law and Order, to Forensic Factors,* TV depictions of the mental health expert can be riveting and compelling, while also take liberties to fictionalize the professional to act beyond their ethical duties. But the largest audience feasting on the forensic buffet is Generation Z (Gen-Z's). Gen-Z's, younger cohorts and offspring of the millennials, grew up with internet, *Net flicks Hulu, and YouTube*, all of which may shape their destiny by going to college and earning degrees in psychology and forensics. Will they become the stereotypical images of a forensic expert seen on TV and imprinted as the golden standard? Or, will they refine their first impressions from TV? Will they evolve into the articulate, word-conscious, and self-respectful scientist who is a neither a showman, nor salesman, nor shaman but rather a humble servant to the court?

That is the hope of this book. Readers can be the voice of objective reason that debunk traditional myths of personality and eliminate misconceptions of criminal behavior. They can become not just a forensic evaluator, but rather a *behavioral forensic evaluator*. The behavioral forensic evaluator can replace obsolete theories and practice with a command for the natural sciences using applied behavior analysis or interbehavioral analysis. In this endeavor, scientific psychology follows in the footsteps of its ancient predecessors (e.g., Plato, Socrates) who foresaw the ethereal value of blending science with law.

## References

Allan, A. (2010). The principles that underlie the 2007 code. In A. Allan, & A. W. Love (Eds.), *Ethical practice in psychology. Reflections from the creators of the APS code of ethics* (pp. 61–76). Chichester, UK: John Wiley & Sons.

American Psychological Association (APA). (2013). Specialty guidelines for forensic psychologists. *The American Psychologist, 68*, 7–19.

American Psychological Association (APA). (2017). *Ethical principles of psychologists and code of conduct*. Washington, DC: American Psychological Association.

BACB. (2019). *Professional ethics compliance code for behavior analysts*. Littleton, CO: Behavior Analyst Certification Board.

Bailey, J., & Burch, M. (2011). *Ethics for behavior analysts*. NY: Taylor & Francis Group.

Barlow, D., Hayes, S. C., & Nelson, R. O. (1984). *The scientist-practitioner: Research and accountability in clinical and educational settings*. NY: Pergamon Press.

Boiven, M. J., Sewell, R. G., & Scott, K. (1986). Attitudes towards behavior modification. *Behavior Modification, 10*, 534-456.

Carey, K. B., Carey, M. P., & Turkat, I. O. (1983). Behavior modification in t media: A five-year follow-up. *American Psychologist, 38*, 498–500.

Cooper, J., Bennett, E., & Sukel, H. (1996). Complex scientific testimony; How do jurors make decisions? *Law and Human Behavior, 20*, 379–394.

Cupon, L. N., & Jahn, W. T. (2002). The testifying expert: Juror's perceptions. *Journal of the American Chiropractic Association, 36*, 46–48.

Dixon, L., & Gill, B. (2002). Changes in the standards for admitting expert evidence in federal civil cases since the Daubert decision. *Psychology, Public Policy, and Law, 8*, 251–308.

Dunault, V., & Dunbar, N. (2017). Nonverbal communication in courtrooms: Scientific assessments or modern trials by ordeal? *The Advocate's Quarterly, 47*, 280-208.

Ebbinghouse, H. (1913). *Uberdas gedachtnis* (H. Ruyer & C. E. Bessenius, Trans.). New York: College Press (Original work published 1885).

Funk, M., Minoletti, A., Drew, N., Taylor, J., & Saraceno, B. (2006). Advocacy for mental health: Roles for consumer and family organizations and governments. *Health Promotion International, 21*, 70–75.

Garfield, S. G. (1983). Some comments on consumer satisfaction in behavior therapy. *Behavior Therapy, 14*, 237–241.

Geiger, R. S., & Lampinen, A. (2014). *Old against new, or a coming of age? Broadcasting in an era of electronic media. 58* pp. 333–341). Journal of Broadcasting & Electronic Media.

Glasgow, R. E., & Rosen, G. M. (1979). Self-help behaviour therapy manuals: Recent developments and clinical usage. *Clinical Behavior Therapy Review, 1*, 1–20.

Greene, E. (1988). Judge's instruction on eyewitness testimony: Evaluation and revision. *Journal of Applied Social Psychology, 18*, 1559–1816.

Groscup, J. L. (2004). Judicial decision-making about expert testimony in the aftermath of Daubert. *Journal of Forensic Psychology Practice, 4*, 57–66.

Holbrook, B., & Howard, J. A. (1999). In P. E. Earl, & S. Kemp (Eds.), *The Elgar companion to consumer research and economic psychology, Cheltenham* (pp. 310–314).

Iwata, B. A., Wong, S. E., Riordan, M. M., Dorsey, M. F., & Lau, M. M. (1982). Assessment and training of clinical interviewing skills: Analogue analysis and field replication. *Journal of Applied Behavior Analysis, 15*, 191–203.

Keane, T. M., Black, J. L., Collins, F. L., Jr., & Vinson, M. C. (1982). A skills training program for teaching the behavioral interview. *Behavioral Assessment, 4*, 53–62.

Kofka, F. (1946). *The trial*. NY: Random House.

Kubrick S. DVD. A clockwork orange. Polaris, Warner Bros., 1971 (1999).

Lee, B. (2017). *The dangerous case of Donald Trump*. NY: Thomas Dunne Books.

Leslie, J. C. (1997). Ethical implications of behavior modification: Historical and current issues. *The Psychological Record, 47*, 637–648.

LeVan, E. A. (1984). Nonverbal communication in the courtroom: Attorney beware. *Law and Psychology Review, 8*, 83–84.

Lillenfeld, S. O., Sauvigne, K. C., Lynn, S. J., Cautin, R. L., Latzmanm, R. D., & Waldman, I. D. (2015). Fifty psychological and psychiatric terms to avoid: A list of inaccurate, misleading, misused, ambiguous, and logically confused words and phrases. *Frontiers in Psychology, 6*, 1–15.

Michael, J. (1974). Statistical inference for individual organism research: Mixed blessing or curse? *Journal of Applied Behavior Analysis, 7*, 647–653.

Morselli, P. L. (2000). Present and future role of mental illness advocacy associations in the management of the mentally ill: Realities, needs and hopes at the edge of the third millennium. *Bipolar Disorders, 2*, 294–300.

Neil, K. S. (2015). Serving as a witness in the court: Trials, testimony, and truth. *Journal of Forensic Nursing, 11*, 121–122.

Newman, R. (1992). The role of the psychologist expert witness: Provider of perspective and input. *Neuropsychology Review, 2*, 241–249.

Otto, R. K. (1989). Bias and expert testimony of mental health professionals in adversarial proceedings: A preliminary investigation. *Behavioral Sciences and the Law, 7*, 267–273.

O'Leary, K. D. (1984). The image of behavior therapy: It is time to take a stand. *Behavior Therapy, 15*, 219–233.

Pantalon, M. V., Lubetkin, B. S., & Fishman, S. T. (1995). Use and effectiveness of self-help books in the practice of cognitive behavioral therapy. *Cognitive and Behavioral Practice, 2*, 213–228.

Pehrsson, D. E., & McMillen, P. (2007). *Bibliotherapy: Overview and implications for counselors*. Professional Counseling Digest (ACAPCD-02). Alexandria, VA: American Counseling Association.

Post, E. (1937). *Etiquette*. NY: Funk & Wagnalls Company.

Pushparajah, D. S., Manning, E., & Michels, E. (2018). Value of developing plain language summaries of scientific and clinical articles: A survey of patients and physicians. *Therapuetic Innovation and Regulatory Science, 52*, 474–481.

Redding, R. E., Herbert, J. D., Foreman, E., & Guadiano, B. (2008). Popular self-help books for anxiety, depression and trauma: How scientifically grounded and useful are they? *Professional Psychology: Research and Practice, 39*, 537–545.

Robertson, D., & Codd, R. T. (2019). Stoic philosophy as a cognitive-behavioral therapy. *The Behavior Therapist, 42*, 42–50.

Ross, D. F., Read, J. D., & Toglia, M. P. (Eds.). (1994). *Adult eyewitness testimony: Current trends and developments* (pp. 223–244). New York: Cambridge University Press.

Ruben, D. H. (1989). Bibliotherapy: Practical considerations when writing for substance abuse readers. *Journal of Alcohol and Drug Education, 34*, 70–78.

Ruben, D. H. (1994). Power skills for lights, camera, action! *Channels of Publication of the Communications, Publishing and Broadcasting Industry of ASTD, 1*, 2–3.

Ruben, D. H. (1995). *Publicity for mental health clinicians: Using TV, radio and print media to enhance your public image*. NY: Haworth Press.

Ruben, D. H. (1997). *Writing for money in mental health*. NY: Haworth Press.

Ruben, D. H. (2002). Do's and Don'ts of using TV and radio for expert commentary on tragedies and homicides. *The Forensic Examiner, 11*, 14–17.

Ruben, D. H. (1986). Alcoholism/drug abuse counselors in industry: Do they need interpersonal skills? *Employee Assistance Quarterly, 1*, 57–62.

Schreibman, L., Koegel, R. L., Mills, J. I., & Burke, J. C. (1981). Social validation of behavior therapy with autistic children. *Behavior Therapy, 12*, 610–624.

Seligman, M. E. P. (1972). Learned helplessness. *Annual Review of Medicine, 23*, 407–412.

Todd, J. T., & Morris, E. K. (1983). Misconception and miseducation: Presentations of radical behaviorism in psychology textbooks. *The Behavior Analyst, 6*, 153–160.

Turkat, I. D., & Feurstein, M. (1978). Behavior modification and the public misconception. *American Psychologist, 33*, 194.

Wells, G. (1995). Scientific study of witness memory: Implications for public and legal policy. *Psychology, Public Policy, and Law, 4*, 726–731.

Wise, R. A., Sartori, G., Magnussen, S., & Safer, M. A. (2014). An examination of the causes and solutions to eyewitness error. *Frontiers in Psychiatry, 5*, 102–110.

World Health Organization. (2001). *World health report 2001. Mental health: New understanding, new hope*. Geneva: World Health Organization.

# Index

'*Note:* Page numbers followed by "f" indicate figures and "t" indicate tables.'

## D



## E



## F

## G



## H



## I

## U



## V



## W

CPI Antony Rowe
Eastbourne, UK
November 20, 2019